THE SEPARATION OF POWERS AND LEGISLATIVE INTERFERENCE IN JUDICIAL PROCESS

This book examines the constitutional principles governing the relationship between legislatures and courts at that critical crossroads of their power where legislatures may seek to intervene in the judicial process, or to interfere with judicial functions, to secure outcomes consistent with their policy objectives or interests. Cases of high political moment are usually involved, where the temptation, indeed political imperative, for legislatures to intervene can be overwhelming. Although the methods of intervention are various, ranging from the direct and egregious to the subtle and imperceptible, unbridled legislative power in this regard has been a continuing concern in all common law jurisdictions. Prominent examples include direct legislative interference in pending cases, usurpation of judicial power by legislatures, limitations on the jurisdiction of courts, strategic amendments to law applicable to cases pending appeal, and attempts directly to overturn court decisions in particular cases.

Because the doctrine of the separation of powers, as an entrenched constitutional rule, is a major source of principle, the book will examine in detail the jurisprudence of the United States and Australia in particular. These jurisdictions have identical constitutional provisions entrenching that doctrine as well as the most developed jurisprudence on this point. The legal position in the United Kingdom, which does not have an entrenched separation of powers doctrine, will be examined as a counterpoint. Other relevant jurisdictions (such as Canada, Ireland and India) are also examined in the context of particular principles, particularly when their respective jurisprudence is rather more developed on discrete points. The book examines how the relevant constitutional principles strive to maintain the primacy of the law-making role of the legislature in a representative democracy and yet afford the decisional independence of the judiciary that degree of protection essential to protect it from the legislature's 'impetuous vortex', to borrow the words of James Madison from *The Federalist (No 48)*.

The Separation of Powers and Legislative Interference in Judicial Process

Constitutional Principles and Limitations

Peter A Gerangelos

·HART·
PUBLISHING

OXFORD AND PORTLAND, OREGON
2009

Published in North America (US and Canada) by
Hart Publishing
c/o International Specialized Book Services
920 NE 58th Avenue, Suite 300
Portland, OR 97213–3786
USA
Tel: +1 503 287 3093 or toll-free: (1) 800 944 6190
Fax: +1 503 280 8832
E-mail: orders@isbs.com
Website: http://www.isbs.com

Hart Publishing Ltd, 16C Worcester Place, Oxford, OX1 2JW
Telephone: +44 (0)1865 517530 Fax: +44 (0)1865 510710
E-mail: mail@hartpub.co.uk
Website: http://www.hartpub.co.uk

British Library Cataloguing in Publication Data

Data Available

ISBN: 978-1-84113-661-5

Typeset by Columns Design Ltd, Reading
Printed and bound in Great Britain by
CPI Antony Rowe, Chippenham, Wiltshire

Contents

Table of Cases

Table of Legislation

NATIONAL LEGISLATION

Australia

Canada

India

Ireland

Sri Lanka (formerly Ceylon)

United Kingdom

United States

EUROPEAN LEGISLATION

INTERNATIONAL LEGISLATION

1

Introduction

THE PURPOSE OF this monograph is to identify those precise constitutional limitations on legislatures, derived specifically from the doctrine of the separation of powers, which protect the *'decisional independence'*, and thus the 'decisional authority', of the judicial branch in common law jurisdictions. Coined by Professor Martin Redish, these terms refer to a very discrete aspect of judicial independence. As defined by Redish, they refer to 'the ability of the ... courts to *interpret* and *apply*, rather than *create*, substantive legal principles *in the specific context of an individual adjudication*, free from control or interference by the purely political branches'[1] (final emphasis added). This is distinct from the 'institutional independence' of the judicial branch, that is, 'the *noncase* specific protections of salary and tenure explicitly provided for' in written constitutions or otherwise in statutes. The latter 'concern the broad independence protections of the ... judiciary as an institution, untied to the adjudication of a specific case, group of cases, or substantive issue'.[2] Although the primary concern will be the protections afforded decisional independence, the maintenance of the integrity of legislative power must also be considered, the concern being to ensure that it is not unduly compromised by the happenstance of pending or concluded litigation which it may affect, especially if only incidentally. Whether it be the decisional independence of the judiciary or the competence of the legislative branch to amend the law affecting particular proceedings, the broader concern is the protection of core, fundamental elements of branch power.[3] Although this issue does not always emerge prominently as a discrete separation of powers issue—and is one which

---

[1] M Redish, 'Federal Judicial Independence: Constitutional and Political Perspectives' (1995) 46 *Mercer Law Review* 697 at 699.

[2] *Ibid*, at 698–9.

[3] It is not possible to define with absolute precision the core functions of each of the branches. Although that is not to deny the possibility of defining, with some confidence, certain commonplace functions of each and identifying them as so fundamental to the identity of the branch that they can be regarded as core. Professor Leslie Zines, for example, when dealing with the identification of fundamental branch functions sought to identify the 'typical', reflecting the fact that even these 'typical' functions, or elements thereof, may in certain circumstances be performed by other branches. See L Zines, *The High Court and the Constitution*, 4th edn (Sydney, Federation Press, 2008).

is often melded to the more dominant concerns of institutional independence and due process—it will be seen that it is both a discrete and certainly not a peripheral separation of powers concern.

In examining this issue, those jurisdictions which have a constitutionally-entrenched separation of powers, such as the United States, Australia and the Republic of Ireland for example, will receive particular attention. By way of counterpoint, attention will also be given to jurisdictions, such as the United Kingdom, where the doctrine remains constitutionally influential, albeit not entrenched. The consequence of the United Kingdom's membership of the European Union will also be considered, together with the impact of European treaties. Although a range of jurisdictions will thus be considered, the aim is to identify constitutional principles and limitations which may be of general application in jurisdictions with an entrenched separation of powers.

The need for such a monograph is underscored by the relative lack of scholarly examination of the specific issue of legislative interference with decisional independence. Although receiving a degree of attention in the United States,[4] this has not quite been the case in Westminster-style jurisdictions. In the Commonwealth of Australia, for example, whose federal constitution in part is modelled on that of the United States, and despite the fact that it was referred to in the writings of Australia's early constitutional scholars, the issue has managed to escape focussed academic scrutiny. Professor George Winterton was the first to explore the issue in 1994 as part of a broader exploration of significant developments relating to the separation of judicial power in Australia which had emerged in the 1990s.[5] Winterton's recognition of the issue as a discrete and important aspect of separation of powers jurisprudence constitutes, in many respects, the point of departure for Australian scholarship on this issue. It is now becoming increasingly common for it to be given discrete treatment in Australian constitutional texts and casebooks, and has been identified by the leading commentator on the separation of judicial power, Professor Fiona Wheeler, as requiring particularised examination.[6] This is also the case in Ireland, as identified in the scholarship particularly of Professor David Gwynn Morgan.[7] It is therefore the

---

[4]   Reference to the extensive American scholarship will be made where relevant; and therefore no attempt will be made at this point to catalogue it.

[5]   G Winterton, 'The Separation of Judicial Power as an Implied Bill of Rights' in GJ Lindell (ed), *Future Directions in Australian Constitutional Law* (Sydney, Federation Press, 1994) 189 at 197–203.

[6]   F Wheeler, 'The rise and rise of judicial power under Chapter III of the Constitution: A decade in overview' (2001) 20 *Australian Bar Review* 283 at 285, fn 18.

[7]   DG Morgan, *The Separation of Powers in the Irish Constitution* (Dublin, Round Hall Sweet and Maxwell, 1997).

aim of this monograph to address this particular problem in far greater detail than has been attempted previously.

I. THE RELEVANT SCENARIOS

The integrity of the decisional independence of the judicial branch is most likely to be compromised in two scenarios. The first, 'the pending case scenario', concerns legislative interference, whether inadvertent or intentional, with the resolution of cases pending within the judicial system, either awaiting first instance hearing or appeal. The second, 'the final judgment scenario', arises where legal controversies have been finally decided within that system and the legislature attempts to interfere with the particular outcome. In both scenarios the particular aspect of judicial power which is being examined is the conclusive adjudication of controversies between parties in litigation, particularly in situations where the government is a party or otherwise has an interest, resulting in an authoritative and binding declaration of their respective rights and duties according to existing law.[8] When examining both pending cases and final judgments, the issue is the extent to which the separation of powers protects both the independent process of adjudicating according to existing law, and the finality of the outcome in the hands of the judicial branch. As will be seen, this constitutes a fundamental or core aspect of judicial power which must be protected by an entrenched separation doctrine. Although 'judicial power' is a concept notoriously resistant to precise definition,[9] and indeed to definition which may render it absolutely distinct from the non-judicial powers,[10] this core element remains

---

[8] These are the elements contained in the oft-quoted classic definition of judicial power in the judgment of Griffith CJ in *Huddart Parker and Co Pty Ltd v Moorehead* (1909) 8 CLR 330 at 357, in the High Court of Australia, who regarded the 'judicial power' in s 71 of the Constitution as 'that power which every sovereign must of necessity have to decide controversies between its subjects, or between itself and its subjects, whether the rights relate to life, liberty or property. The exercise of this power does not begin until some tribunal which has power to give a binding and authoritative decision (whether subject to appeal or not) is called upon to take action'. See also Zines, *The High Court and the Constitution*, n 3 above, 219.

[9] In the words of Windeyer J in *R v Trade Practices Tribunal; Ex parte Tasmanian Breweries Pty Ltd* (1970) 123 CLR 361 at 394, '[t]he concept seems to me to defy, perhaps it were better to say transcend, purely abstract conceptual analysis. It inevitably attracts consideration of predominant characteristics and also invites comparison with the historic functions and processes of courts of law'.

[10] In *Precision Data Holdings Ltd v Wills* (1991) 173 CLR 167 at 188, the High Court of Australia made reference to the 'difficulty, if not impossibility of framing a definition of judicial power that is at once exclusive and exhaustive'.

at the centre of all serious attempts to provide some definitional framework.[11] The extent to which the constitutional limitations derived from the separation of powers provide protection to this fundamental element of judicial power is a measure of its efficacy as a legal rule and of its success in its transition from political theory. The special significance of this particular aspect of judicial power was noted by Kitto J of the High Court of Australia when he stated in *R v Trade Practices Tribunal; Ex Parte Tasmanian Breweries Pty Ltd* that

> judicial power involves as a general rule, a decision settling for the future, as between defined persons or classes of persons, a question as to the existence of a right or obligation, so that an exercise of power creates a new charter by reference to which that question is in future to be decided as between those persons or classes of persons.[12]

It is precisely the protection of this 'new charter' which the relevant constitutional limitations on the legislature must be capable of achieving. Such protection affords citizens the right to enjoy the fruits of litigation free from the vagaries and vicissitudes of political interest and factional influence. There is a particular urgency in this regard in Westminster-style systems, given the obvious advantage afforded it by the power of Parliament to legislate, and potentially to do so strategically, to effect a desired outcome. If the separation of powers is unable to limit the power of the legislature in this context, then a considerable threat is posed to the independent exercise of judicial power vested in the courts.

Thus, the search for separation of powers principles regulating these scenarios invariably involves the identification of constitutional limitations on the legislature. This is an area of quite some considerable complexity in that legislative *interferences* are not always, or indeed often, regarded as a breach of the separation of powers. This is to be contrasted with the more obvious breaches of that doctrine which arise from legislative *usurpations* of judicial power, such as Acts of Attainder,[13] legislatures acting institutionally as courts or reserving to themselves the

---

[11]   See n 3 above. See also *Fencott v Muller* (1983) 152 CLR 570 at 608: 'The unique and essential function of the judicial power is the quelling of such [legal] controversies by ascertainment of the facts, by application of the law and by exercise, where appropriate, of judicial discretion'. (Mason, Brennan, Murphy and Deane JJ); and *R v Trade Practices Tribunal; ex parte Tasmanian Breweries Pty Ltd* (1970) 123 CLR 361 at 374: 'the process to be followed must generally be inquiry concerning the law as it is and the facts as they are, followed by an application of the law as determined to the facts as determined; and the end to be reached must be an act which, so long as it stands, entitles and obliges the persons between whom it intervenes, to observance of the rights and obligations that the application of the law to facts has shown to exist' (Kitto J).

[12]   *R v Trade Practices Tribunal; Ex Parte Tasmanian Breweries Pty Ltd* (1970) 123 CLR 361 at 374.

[13]   See Winterton, 'The Separation of Judicial Power as an Implied Bill of Rights', n 5 above, at 192.

power to review or revise the decisions of the judicial branch. The difficulty also with legislative interferences is that they may not always raise concerns, which the separation of powers may otherwise address, that there has been a denial of due process, that an essential element of the judicial power is being removed from the courts, that the court is being required to exercise judicial power in a manner inconsistent with the essential character of a court or with the nature of judicial power.[14] Thus, a legislature may, without necessarily offending the separation of powers, enact legislation amending the general law which is applicable in a pending case, even if that amendment has consequences for the resolution of the case. Or, it may 'overrule' a final decision of a court by simply amending the law applicable thereafter by statute. It cannot be denied that such legislative action does interfere with the judicial process, but such interference is not necessarily unconstitutional without more. The difficulty which arises, and the central problem which this monograph will seek to address, is the discernment of those qualities in such interfering legislation which render it unconstitutional on separation of powers grounds. When such an interference is effected by otherwise valid legislation, separation of powers concerns are nevertheless engaged when the government is a litigant in the proceedings or has an interest—whether proprietary or policy-related—in the outcome of the litigation, and the purported amendment facilitates an outcome favourable to it. Such concerns are heightened when the legislation is *ad hominem*, restrospective and tailored to address the very issues in a pending case. Prima facie, unrestrained legislative power in this regard potentially undermines a key rationale of the separation of powers, that is, ensuring that legal disputes are protected from the vagaries and vicissitudes of political influence and factional interest and that the litigant, especially if a private party, may enjoy the fruits of victory or the benefits of an independent tribunal unhindered by the legislative or executive power. The difficulty therefore resides in defining principles which may render the more blatant interferences unconstitutional on separation of powers grounds.

Although arising rarely, the issue of legislative interference in judicial process tends to emerge when matters of high political moment and national—sometimes international—significance come before the courts. The temptation, if not political imperative, to legislative intervention can at times be overwhelming. One need only list the facts of some of the main relevant cases here to illustrate the point. In the famous case *Burmah Oil Company (Burma Trading) Ltd v Lord Advocate*[15] the United

---

[14] See, eg, *Chu Kheng Lim v Minister for Immigration* (1992) 176 CLR 1 at 27 (Brennan, Deane and Dawson JJ).
[15] *Burmah Oil Company* [1965] AC 75.

Kingdom Parliament reversed the decision of the House of Lords which established a right to compensation for property damage caused by British forces to prevent vital resources falling into enemy hands in the Second World War, that right being removed from the plaintiff in that particular case.[16] In the pending case scenario, the issue has arisen in various cases involving the criminal prosecution of the perpetrators of an abortive coup,[17] the deregistration of highly controversial industrial unions,[18] the detention of asylum seekers[19] and the admission of evidence in prosecutions for narcotics offences resulting from the illegal conduct of law enforcement officers.[20] In Ireland the leading case relates to the disposition of the assets of the controversial political organisation, Sinn Fein.[21] The United States cases reveal similarly politically sensitive issues: namely, property rights and rights to compensation affected by the Franco-American War[22] and the American Civil War,[23] the effect of presidential pardons,[24] environmental issues relating to logging and endangered species,[25] the protection of claims for securities fraud during the notorious financial excesses of the late 1980s,[26] prison conditions,[27] compensation payable to indigenous people for the taking of tribal land,[28] and the maintenance of life support in cases of permanent and complete incapacity.[29] It has also been an issue in terrorism prosecutions.[30] It is precisely in relation to such matters that legislatures may be tempted to intervene by strategic legislative action, tailored to precise legal proceedings, to facilitate an outcome they favour. And it is precisely in such circumstances that some degree of constitutional limitation becomes critical. As noted by Professor Evan Caminker in the United States context,

> [i]t strikes me as important that federal courts always maintain their proper self understanding of being neutral and final arbiters of what the law is and how it applies to specific cases—even if and when the law applies only to

---

[16] *Burmah Oil Company (Burma Trading) Ltd v Lord Advocate, ibid.*
[17] *Liyanage v R* [1967] 1 AC 259.
[18] *BLF v Minister for Industrial Relations* (1986) 7 NSWLR 372; *BLF v Commonwealth* (1986) 161 CLR 88.
[19] *Chu Kheng Lim v Minister for Immigration, Local Government and Ethnic Affairs* (1992) 176 CLR 1.
[20] *Nicholas v R* (1998) 193 CLR 173.
[21] *Buckley v Attorney-General* [1950] IR 67.
[22] *United States v Schooner Peggy* 5 US (1 Cranch) 103 (1801).
[23] *United States v Klein* 80 US (13 Wall) 128 (1871).
[24] *Ibid.*
[25] *Robertson v Seattle Audubon Society* 503 US 429 (1992).
[26] *Plaut v Spendthrift Farm Inc* 514 US 21 (1995).
[27] *Miller v French* (2000) 530 US 327.
[28] *United States v Sioux Nation of Indians* (1980) 448 US 371.
[29] *Schiavo ex rel Schindler v Schiavo*, 404 F 3d 1233 (11th Cir 2005).
[30] *Lodhi v R* (2006) FLR 303.

single cases. Only this self-understanding can generate sufficient norms of independence and frankly, essentiality, to safeguard long-term fidelity to the rule of law. Widespread public understanding that courts play this independent role is necessary to building long-term public support for it in the face of periodic congressional temptation to cross the line. And linguistic formulations contained in statutes may make a difference to these understandings.[31]

It is therefore imperative that the activity of legislatures in this regard is monitored carefully to ensure that courts' decisional independence is protected and that the separation of powers is not breached. The concern of this monograph is to discern which legislative interferences cross the boundary of constitutional validity.

II. DEFINITIONAL DIFFICULTIES

The issue of identifying precise constitutional limitations on legislative interference can be a vexed one, especially as it arises at a significant crossroads between legislative and judicial power and because not all legislative interferences will offend constitutionally. Absent any express constitutional provisions to the contrary,[32] prima facie the legislature has the undoubted competence to make new law, or amend the law (even retrospectively),[33] which the courts are required to apply in any particular case, even while that case is pending. The position was stated succinctly by Mason J of the High Court of Australia in *R v Humby; Ex parte Rooney*: 'Chapter III [providing for the separation of judicial power in the Australian Constitution] contains no prohibition, express or implied, that rights in issue in legal proceedings shall not be the subject of legislative declaration or action'.[34] This general rule, referred to as the Changed Law Rule subject to the qualifications which will be discussed in more detail in chapters two and three, was also established early in the United States cases.[35] In relation to final judgments, the legislature has the undoubted competence under the separation of powers to legislate to amend the law as declared by the court, so long as it does not reverse the actual decision as between the parties.[36] Although these situations constitute an interference with the judicial process in the broad sense, they are nevertheless tolerated by the doctrine of the separation of powers.

---

[31] E Caminker, '*Schiavo* and *Klein*' (2005) 22 *Constitutional Commentary* 529.

[32] For example the provision in the United States Constitution prohibiting retrospective criminal laws and Bills of Attainder would of course also ensure that such laws do not affect pending criminal trials. See Art 1 s 9 of the US Constitution.

[33] *Polyukhovich v Commonwealth* (1991) 172 CLR 501.

[34] *R v Humby; Ex parte Rooney* (1973) 129 CLR 231 at 250.

[35] See *United States* v *Schooner Peggy* 5 US (1 Cranch) 103 (1801) and *United States v Klein* 80 US (13 Wall) 128 (1871).

[36] This is discussed in detail in ch 4 of this book.

It becomes necessary therefore to seek to identify particular qualities in legislative activity which may render an interference a breach of the separation of powers. In the pending case scenario, the central question is whether there are circumstances when otherwise properly enacted legislation so seriously undermines the court's independent adjudication of a matter that its decisional independence is rendered illusory. In relation to final judgments, the central question is whether there are qualifications, or indeed even exceptions, to the fundamental principle that the legislature may not reverse a final judgment. It is imperative that a resolution to these issues be achieved particularly as it was the precise concern to protect the judiciary from legislative interference in both scenarios that constituted a major catalyst to the doctrine's original legal entrenchment which occurred in the United States Constitution.[37] This concern has rarely found more eloquent expression than in the exposition of the views of those involved in the drafting of that Constitution in their contributions to *The Federalist*.[38]

It is noted by way of introduction that although the concept of judicial decisional independence is located within the 'judicial independence' strand of separation of powers protections, it can also be located within the 'due process' strand of protections afforded by the separation doctrine and in the broader 'rule of law' strand. This, of course, does not change the nature of the concept; it means merely that it can be viewed from a number of perspectives. Thus, if decisional independence is compromised, the parties are being denied a fundamental component of procedural due process. Even if all the other main elements of due process remain intact—notice, a hearing, the opportunity for the parties to present their best case and to cross-examine witnesses, proper legal representation and so on—if the actual final adjudication on the facts and/or the law (whether procedural or substantive) has been compromised by legislative activity, then the parties' access to an independent judgment by impartial judges has also been compromised. These due process and rule of law considerations thus overlap with the concerns to maintain decisional independence, and achieve greater importance in those jurisdictions which do not maintain an entrenched separation of powers.

The extent to which the separation of powers, as a legal rule, is the source of principles successfully defining the limitations protecting core elements of branch power constitutes a significant measure of the efficacy of its legal entrenchment. Indeed, the ability to define such constitutional limitations is fundamental to the question whether entrenchment

---

[37]   See at 10 below.
[38]   The edition of this collection of writings which will be used in this book is that of JE Cooke (ed), *The Federalist* (Middletown CT, Wesleyan University Press, 1961).

responds to the imperatives of the doctrine's underlying rationale: the prevention of the undue concentration of power and the abuses which may thereby arise, the better to secure representative and liberal government and the rule of law. A very significant consideration in this regard, and one which will be examined in more detail below, relates to the most appropriate interpretative methodology which should be applied to the separation of powers. Central to this consideration is whether a formalist or functionalist approach, or any variant thereof, is most reflective of the place of the separation of powers in a written constitution. The precise definition of the relevant constitutional limitations being considered in this monograph is highly dependent on the outcome of this particular enquiry and accordingly it is essential that consideration of this issue occur in detail at the outset. It is also finally noted that the concerns relating to the efficacy of the separation of powers as a legal rule are not limited to the particular constitutional limitations being examined in this monograph. There is a more general concern relating to the translation of a principle whose origins lie in the realms of political and constitutional philosophy and convention, albeit pragmatically based, into the rather more rigid realm of legal rules. Where this occurs there emerges an inexorable imperative toward some definition of the functions of each of the branches in order to maintain their basic division, indeed to make it enforceable. So much was assumed—indeed thought highly desirable—in the very entrenchment of the principle in the United States Constitution,[39] especially with respect to the separation of judicial power. Indeed, it was the Americans who advocated the higher protection afforded the judicial power—particularly from interference by the legislature—by this elevation. Moreover, in the context of the drafting of their Constitution, this was regarded as an issue of the highest priority.[40] And yet, the separation of powers has often not borne well this transition from the sphere of political theory to the more rigidly conceptual sphere of the law. This monograph will examine the extent to which it has been successful in the critical area of protecting the decisional independence of the judicial branch.

---

[39] Although not expressly mentioned, the legal entrenchment of the separation of powers is implied from the exclusive and separate vesting of the executive, legislative and judicial powers in the President, the Congress and the Supreme Court respectively: Art I, s 1; Art II, s 1; Art III, s I of the Constitution of the United States.

[40] In *The Federalist* (Issue No 48) Madison referred to the 'most difficult task ... to provide some practical security for each [of the three main arms of government] or each against the invasion of the others. What this security ought to be, is the great problem to be solved', see n 38 above, 332.

III.   THE ORIGINAL LEGAL ENTRENCHMENT OF THE DOCTRINE AND THE UNDERLYING RATIONALE

It is in the United States where the issue of legislative interference in judicial process has maintained the highest profile as a constitutional issue of the first order. It was precisely to combat the excesses of legislative power that the separation of powers was entrenched in that nation's constitution, elevated by the Framers from the sphere of political and constitutional philosophy into the more rigid realms of constitutional law. This remains their original contribution.[41] Although not expressly mentioned, the legal entrenchment is implied from the exclusive and separate vesting of the legislative, executive, and judicial power in the President, Congress and the Supreme Court respectively.[42] This reflected in particular the influence of Montesquieu's *De L'Esprit Des Lois*,[43] which advocated the separation of the three main branches of government, including the judicial. Such views found expansive articulation in *The Federalist Papers*,[44] a major recurrent theme of which was the precise means by which this outcome was to be achieved. Madison referred to this 'most difficult task . . . to provide some practical security for each [of the three branches of government] or each against the invasion of the others. What this security ought to be is the great problem to be solved'.[45] Of particular concern was the protection of the judicial power from legislative encroachment. Significantly, Madison recognised the potential for legislative encroachments to occur under the guise of otherwise properly enacted legislation.

> The legislative department derives a superiority in our government from other circumstances. Its constitutional powers being at once more extensive, and less

---

[41]   See JE Nowak and RD Rotunda, *Constitutional Law*, 4th edn (St Paul, MN, West, 1991) para 3.5; SG Calabresi and SG Rhodes, 'The Structural Constitution: Unitary Executive, Plural Judiciary' (1992) 105 *Harvard Law Review* 115; GP Miller, 'Rights and Structure in Constitutional Theory' [1991] *Sociology, Philosophy and Policy* 196; MH Redish and E Cisar, '"If Angels Were to Govern": The Need for Pragmatic Formalism in Separation of Powers Theory' (1991) 41 *Duke Law Journal* 449; PR Verkuil, 'Separation of Powers, The Rule of Law and the Idea of Independence' (1989) 30 *William and Mary Law Review* 301. That this is now clearly recognised by the Supreme Court is beyond question, whether a formalist (*Bowsher v Synar*, 478 US 714 (1986); *INS v Chadha* 462 US 919 (1983)) or functionalist (*Morrison v Olson* 487 US 654 (1988); *Mistretta v United States* 488 US 361 (1989)) approach is taken to the separation of powers. In *Springer v Government of the Philippine Islands* 277 US 189 (1928) at 201–2 the Supreme Court stated that, as a matter of constitutional law, 'the legislature cannot exercise either executive or judicial power; the executive cannot exercise either legislative or judicial power; the judiciary cannot exercise either executive or legislative power'. See Zines, *The High Court and the Constitution*, n 3 above, ch 10, in relation to the similar position in Australia.
[42]   See n 39 above.
[43]   Originally published 1748.
[44]   See n 38 above. See eg Issue No 51.
[45]   *The Federalist*, Issue No 48, n 38 above, at 232.

susceptible of precise limits, it can with greater facility, mask, under complicated and indirect measures, the encroachments which it makes on the
co-ordinate departments. *It is not infrequently a question of real nicety in legislative
bodies whether the operation of a particular measure will, or will not, extend beyond
the legislative sphere.* On the other side, the executive power being restrained
within a narrower compass, and being more simple in its nature; and the
judiciary being described by landmarks, still less uncertain, projects of usurpation by either of these departments would immediately betray and defeat
themselves.[46] (emphasis added)

When referring to legislative encroachment which extended 'beyond the
legislative sphere', even though contained within a prima facie valid
statute, Madison was not merely speculating. He, and the other American Framers, had had the experience of colonial and post-revolutionary
legislatures dominating the judicial branch and engaging in egregious
interferences with both pending and finally decided cases. It was not
uncommon for these legislatures to act institutionally as courts, indeed
hearing suits at first instance and commonly functioning as courts of
equity or appellate courts. They made orders, as a court might, declaring
the rights of the parties to disputes under existing law, setting aside
judgments of the courts, or ordering new trials on appeal. Gordon Wood
summarised the practice of these legislatures thus:

[T]he assemblies in the eighteenth century still saw themselves, perhaps even
more so than the House of Commons, as a kind of medieval court making
private judgments as well as public law … [They] constantly heard private
petitions, which often were only the complaints of one individual or group
against another, and made final judgments on these complaints. They continu-
ally tried cases in equity, occasionally extended temporary equity power to
some common law court for a select purpose, and often granted appeals, new
trials, and other kinds of relief in an effort to do what 'is agreeable to Right and
Justice.'

The Revolution scarcely interrupted this development; indeed, it intensified
legislative domination of the other parts of the government…In the judicial
area the constitutions and chaotic conditions of war had the effect of reversing
the growing mid-eighteenth-century distinction between legislative and judicial responsibilities, leading during the 1770's and eighties to a heightened
involvement of the legislatures in controlling the courts and in deciding the
personal affairs of their constituents in private law judgments.[47]

In reviewing the judicial activity of the Massachusetts legislature in the
pre-Constitution period, the editor of the *Harvard Law Review* noted that

---

[46]   *Ibid*, at 334.
[47]   GS Wood, *The Creation of the American Republic 1776–1787* (Williamsburg VA, University of North Carolina Press, 1996) 154–6.

the provincial legislature will often be found acting in a judicial capacity, sometimes trying causes in equity, sometimes granting equity powers to some court of the common law for a particular temporary purpose, and constantly granting appeals, new trials, and other relief from judgments, on equitable grounds.[48]

This was achieved by mandate or orders of the legislature, both in the form of statutes and otherwise.[49]

As noted by Edward Corwin, such practices evoked a strong reaction in the constitutional conventions in the 1780s.[50] The *Pennsylvanian Report* catalogued these as 'abuses' because they were invariably the result of the influence of faction and private interest.[51] Thomas Jefferson referred to the existence of the practice in his state of Virginia, where its Assembly had '*in many* instances *decided rights*' that should have been left to *judiciary controversy*',[52] bemoaning that this practice was 'habitual and familiar'.[53] The Connecticut legislature was also exercising equity jurisdiction, as was the legislature of Vermont, which was in fact interfering in pending cases, reversing judgments and prohibiting actions.[54] Madison remarked in *The Federalist*, referring again to Pennsylvania, that the 'Constitution had been flagrantly violated by the legislature in a variety of important instances ... [including cases] belong to the judiciary department frequently drawn within legislative cognizance and determination'.[55] In this context, Madison made his oft-quoted remark that the '[t]he legislative department is everywhere extending the sphere of its activity, and drawing all power into its impetuous vortex'.[56] Thus, at the precise moment when the Americans were contemplating the terms of their constitution, the specific concerns raised by legislative interference with judicial functions were, inter alia, at the forefront of their deliberations.[57]

---

[48] 'Judicial Action by the Provincial Legislature of Massachusetts' (1901–02) 15 *Harvard Law Review* 208 at 208, fn 1.

[49] MP Clarke, *Parliamentary Privilege in the American Colonies* (New Haven CT, Yale University Press, 1943) 49–51.

[50] ES Corwin, *The Doctrine of Judicial Review* (Princeton NJ, Princeton University Press, 1914) 37.

[51] Cited in *The Federalist*, Issue No 48, n 38 above, at 336–7 and in *INS v Chadha* 462 US 919 (1983) at 963 (Powell J).

[52] T Jefferson, *Notes on the State of Virginia* (London edn, 1787) 196, cited in *The Federalist*, Issue No 48, n 38 above, 335. See also ES Corwin, 'The Progress of Constitutional Theory Between the Declaration of Independence and the Meeting of the Philadelphia Convention' (1925) 30 *American Historical Review* 511 at 514–17.

[53] See also *The Federalist*, Issue Nos 47 and 48, n 38 above.

[54] See D Kairys, 'Legislative Usurpation: the Early Practice and Constitutional Repudiation of Legislative Intervention in Adjudication' (2005) 73 *University of Manchester Kings College Law Review* 945 at 946.

[55] *The Federalist*, Issue No 47, n 38 above, at 333.

[56] *The Federalist*, Issue No 48, n 38 above at 333.

[57] See in particular *The Federalist*, Issue Nos 47, 48, 50, 55, and 78–81 (Alexander Hamilton).

The entrenchment of the separation of powers in the United States Constitution was their solution. Thus, while the legislature would pre-scribe the laws 'by which the duties and the rights of every citizen are to be regulated', the 'interpretation of the laws' would be 'the proper and peculiar province of the courts'.[58] The court was to be the 'least danger-ous' branch in that

> though individual oppression may now and then proceed from the courts of justice, the general liberty of the people can never be endangered from that quarter ... so long as the judiciary remains truly distinct from both the legislature and the executive.[59]

As Powell J commented in *INS v Chadha*,

> [i]t was to prevent the recurrence of such abuses that the Framers vested the executive, legislative, and judicial powers in separate branches. Their concern that a legislature should not be able unilaterally to impose a substantial deprivation on one person was expressed not only in this general allocation of power, but also in more specific provisions, such as the Bill of Attainder Clause, Art I, [par] 9, cl 3 . . .This clause and the separation-of-powers doctrine generally, reflect the Framers' concern that trial by a legislature lacks the safeguards necessary to prevent the abuse of power.[60]

It seems that prevailing British notions of parliamentary supremacy, unrestrained by legally entrenched limitations, had lost the confidence of the Framers,[61] understandably in light of their recent experiences both with the Parliament at Westminster and their own colonial legislatures. The critical decision was thus taken to establish a judicial department independent of the legislature in the constitutional provision that '[t]he judicial Power of the United States, shall be vested in one supreme Court, and in such inferior Courts as the Congress may from time to time ordain and establish',[62] an article which resonates in the terms of section 71 of the Australian Constitution. Referring back to Madison's words above, it would appear that a critical measure of the efficacy of such a measure was the extent to which it was able to prevent legislative prescription of the outcome of pending or finally decided law suits—the extent to which it was capable of identifying and limiting such legislative activity which extended 'beyond the legislative sphere'.

---

[58] A Hamilton, *The Federalist*, Issue No 78, n 38 above, 525.
[59] *Ibid*, at 522–3.
[60] *INS v Chadha* 462 US 919 (1983) at 962.
[61] See Corwin, *The Doctrine of Judicial Review*, n 50 above, 514–17 and MJC Vile, *Constitutionalism and The Separation of Powers*, 2nd edn (Indianapolis, Liberty Fund, 1998) ch 10.
[62] Art III, s 1 of the United States Constitution, 1789.

IV.   THE POSSIBILITY OF GENERAL PRINCIPLES AND
INTERPRETATIONAL METHODOLOGY

To what extent is it possible to define universal constitutional limitations in this context? Of course, the answer to this question must depend on the extent to which the separation of powers is uniformly implemented. As MJC Vile's seminal study has shown, the implementation of the doctrine does vary significantly across jurisdictions and it is not possible to find an implementation of the doctrine in its purest form.[63] However, in jurisdictions with an entrenched separation of powers, which maintain in particular a rigorous separation of the judicial from the non-judicial branches (such as the United States and Australia), the quest for generally applicable principles is more fruitful. This is less the case in those jurisdictions where the doctrine is no more than a non-entrenched underlying constitutional principle or convention. In the latter case, while the same principles and limitations may develop, there is not the same urgency to provide a precise definition thereof. And, if one is attempted, there is not the same certainty that the principle will be capable of enforcement absent restraint from the non-judicial branches.

An additional hurdle is thrown up by the inconsistency in the methodology by which the separation of powers is interpreted. The process of defining precisely the constitutional limitations on branch power derived from the separation of powers is vexed, multifaceted and intricate, even where 'fundamental' or 'core' branch powers and functions are involved. Courts and scholars have recognised—the observation now is almost trite—the immense difficulties involved in attempting to categorize the multifarious functions of government as 'legislative', 'executive' and 'judicial' and to isolate these functions in the hands of one of the respective branches. Such difficulties are revealed, to name some of the more obvious examples, in the phenomena of delegated legislation (executive law-making), administrative tribunals (where some elements of judicial power are exercised by bodies not otherwise constitutionally defined as courts), and in the vesting of judges with non-judicial functions. This has led to sophisticated attempts at resolution, variously involving resort to the use of the qualifier 'quasi' for greater accuracy (bodies such as the Industrial Relations Commission in Australia being referred to as 'quasi-judicial' and 'quasi-legislative'),[64] the concept of 'innominate' powers whose ultimate characterisation is dependent on the

---

[63]   Vile, *Constitutionalism and The Separation of Powers*, n 61 above.
[64]   G Winterton, *Parliament, the Executive and the Governor-General: A Constitutional Analysis* (Melbourne, Melbourne University Press, 1983) 68.

legislature,[65] or 'chameleon powers' which take their character from the body in which they are vested,[66] and the use of the dichotomy between 'core'/'primary' functions and 'incidental'/'secondary' functions.[67] Refined complications are added when consideration is given to the issue of whether this established tripartite division can accommodate the evolution and development of government functions such as the possible recognition of an 'administrative branch' of government.[68] Also, there is the abiding question as to whether it is at all possible to provide mutually-exclusive definitions of branch functions, even at the level of core or primary functions (and even in relation to judicial power).[69] Moreover, the denial of this possibility must somehow be reconciled with the imperative, arising from the very constitutional entrenchment of the separation of powers, toward some form of workable definition of branch functions in order to enable the policing of the boundaries.

Into this mêlée of conflicting imperatives and subtle categorisations enters the rather important question of whether a formalist or function-alist interpretational methodology ought to apply. This issue must be addressed as a consideration preliminary to the examination of the constitutional principles and limitations which are the particular concern of this monograph, and indeed all such principles and limitations derived from the separation of powers. Their precise definition must ultimately depend on which methodology is adopted and on whether a reconciliation of the two methods can be achieved at some level. Prima facie, a strict formalism is singularly unsuited to provide the solution to the definitional problems outlined above given, in particular, the diffi-culty, if not impossibility, of providing mutually exclusive definitions of branch powers. Exponents of formalism have countered by bringing to the fore their concerns that unless some objective universal standard of separation based on conceptual analysis is imposed, at least at some level, a slow but inexorable erosion of the efficacy of the separation of powers will result. It is not the demise of the doctrine per se (as some

---

[65] *Ibid*, at 68–9; S Ratnapala, *Australian Constitutional Law, Foundations and Theory* (Melbourne, Oxford University Press, 2002) 132 ff.

[66] Ratnapala, *Australian Constitutional Law, Foundations and Theory*, n 65 above, 134.

[67] Winterton, *Parliament, the Executive and the Governor-General*, n 64 above, 68–9, including relevant case citations.

[68] *Ibid*, at 67; G Sawer, 'The Separation of Powers in Australian Federalism' (1961) 35 *Australian Law Journal* 177 at 177.

[69] See, for example, the complicated attempts at the resolution of the question whether the power in an administrator to cancel the registration of a trade mark was an exercise of judicial power in *R v Quinn; Ex parte Consolidated Foods Corporation* (1977) 138 CLR 1.

neat form of categorisation) which is the concern, but rather the protections it affords against the erosion of liberal representative government, the rule of law and the values underlying these fundamental tenets of constitutional government.

It is in the United States in particular where the formalism/functionalism debate has come far more to the fore in both judicial exegesis and academic commentary, unlike the position in Australia and elsewhere where separation of powers issues are not often addressed in these terms. However, neither the United States Supreme Court, nor the High Court of Australia, has adopted a uniform approach to this question, although formalism tends to have a greater presence when issues relating to the separation of judicial power arise. This is the case even in the United States where the separation of powers is more fundamental to the whole constitutional settlement.[70] In that jurisdiction, moreover, the legislative/executive separation is not complicated by the existence of responsible government, with its countervailing (to separation) tendencies.

In this section, an attempt will be made to highlight a number of considerations which may assist in determining the most appropriate approach in particular circumstances, and especially in relation to the issue of legislative interference with judicial process. Moreover, it will examine whether, and at what level, a consistent approach can be adopted which reconciles—perhaps even renders otiose—the formalist/functionalist divide. In so doing it will examine the *purposive* elements in formalist thinking which may defend the formalist school, at least partially, from the charge that its strict, conceptualised approach is but meaningless categorisation, artificial, and inadequate in light of the complexities of modern government.

A.   Formalism

The fundamental tenet of the formalist position is that the nature of each branch can be defined with *sufficient* clarity and mutual exclusivity to enable the establishment of a demarcation between the three branches which can be rigorously maintained. This, of course, reinforces the separation of personnel and functions as well as the maintenance of the institutional independence of the branches.[71] More moderate versions acknowledge the difficulty in providing a definition attaining complete

---

[70] Even a cursory glance at *The Federalist* will reveal the reliance being placed on the separation of powers doctrine in this regard. See also Wood, *The Creation of the American Republic 1776–1787*, n 47 above.

[71] See Winterton, *Parliament, the Executive and the Governor-General*, n 64 above, 58–9.

mutual exclusivity, and allowances are made for a degree of fluidity at the edges. Nevertheless, a core of meaning is regarded as existing and capable of being defined conceptually—although history, custom, usage and tradition play a role—and each function so defined is considered capable of being hermetically sealed off from the others. Any act of any of the branches will be declared unconstitutional if it usurps, or even in a minor way trespasses upon, the functions belonging to another branch. However, in those hard cases where the breach is minor, merely technical, and justifiable on public interest grounds, such as the efficient operation of government and good public policy, this can become an issue of some nicety. Nevertheless, the strict formalist will seek to have the separation of powers prevail to declare the breach unconstitutional.

A classic illustration relevant to the central enquiry of this monograph is the case of *Plaut v Spendthrift Farm Inc*,[72] where the United States Supreme Court declared unconstitutional legislation purporting to reinstate meritorious securities fraud suits which had been permanently stayed due to technicalities arising from differences between State and federal statutes of limitations. This was despite the fact that Congress was clearly acting in the public interest in seeking to protect the only remedies available to meritorious litigants. The legislation was nevertheless held to breach the separation of powers because it provided for the re-opening by its own force of suits already finally stayed by federal courts. A legislative direction to re-open a final judgment, which disregarded the federal courts' own discretion derived from inherent jurisdiction, was regarded as a violation of the integrity of final judgments and the decisional independence of the federal courts. The principle emerging from the *Boilermakers* case[73] is another example. In that case it was held that that courts which were vested with federal jurisdiction, and thus protected by the separation of judicial power, could not be vested with non-judicial power unless it was incidental to judicial power. Judicial and academic criticism of the principle as unnecessary, inconvenient and creating inefficiencies in the functioning of government[74] would not, under a formalist approach, ameliorate the strictness with which the doctrine was applied. For the majority in that case,

> [t]he basal reason why such a combination is constitutionally inadmissible is that Chap. III [of the Constitution] does not allow powers which are foreign to

---

[72] *Plaut v Spendthrift Farm Inc* 514 US 211 (1995).

[73] *R v Kirby; Boilermakers' Society of Australia* (1956) 94 CLR 254; *A-G for Australia v R* [1957] AC 288.

[74] Most notably by Barwick CJ in *R v Joske; Ex parte Australian Building Construction Employees and Builders Labourers' Federation* (1974) 130 CLR 87 at 90. See also Zines, *The High Court and the Constitution*, n 3 above, and G Winterton, *Parliament, The Executive and the Governor-General*, n 64 above, 61–4 and 'The Separation of Judicial Power as an Implied Bill of Rights', n 5 above, 192.

the judicial power to be attached to the courts created by or under that chapter for the exercise of the judicial power of the Commonwealth.[75]

The Privy Council stated (famously) in similar vein that 'first and last, the question is one of construction' and it doubted 'whether, had Locke and Montesquieu never lived nor the Constitution of the United States ever been framed, a different interpretation of the Constitution of the Com-monwealth could validly have been reached'.[76] It is clear that it matters not what the practical consequences may be in any particular instance so long as the structural and functional boundaries are maintained. Any balancing of the benefits achieved in the instant case on public policy or efficiency grounds against the seriousness of what is a breach of the doctrine remains anathema to the formalist.

Formalism cannot be dismissed as mere pedantry. In the context of the separation of powers, the method may be grounded in the rationale that only a strictly applied separation can uphold the doctrine's underlying values; that is, the maintenance of liberal, representative government, an independent judiciary, the rule of law and the civil liberties benefits which flow in their train. If the rigours of this approach are ameliorated, even for the best of policy reasons in a particular case, these values will be threatened by the gradual, yet inexorable, erosion of the essential boundaries, even though this may not be apparent in the particular case. Thus, in the hands of its more enlightened exponents, there is recognised a *purposive* element to the rigours of formalism. Scalia J, writing the opinion of the Court in *Plaut*, stated that

> the doctrine of the separation of powers is a *structural safeguard* rather than a remedy to be applied only when specific harm, or risk of specific harm, can be identified. In its major features … it is a prophylactic device, establishing high walls and clear distinctions because low walls and vague distinctions will not be judicially defensible in the heat of interbranch conflict … Separation of powers, a distinctively American political doctrine, profits from the advice authored by a distinctively American poet: Good fences make good neigh-bours.[77]

This notion of the doctrine as a 'safeguard' or 'prophylactic device' adds a purposive element to formalism which redeems its otherwise unyield-ing and artificial rigidity. In addition to *Plaut*, cases often cited as classic examples of the formalist approach in the United States are *Bowsher v Synar*[78] and *INS v Chadha*.[79] In *INS v Chadha* the majority stated: '[T]he fact that a given law or procedure is efficient, convenient, and useful in

---

[75] *Boilermakers'* case (1956) 94 CLR 254 at 288.
[76] *Boilermakers'* case (1957) 95 CLR 529 at 540 (PC).
[77] *Plaut v Spendthrift Farm Inc* 514 US (1995) at 239–40.
[78] *Bowsher v Synar* 478 US 714 (1986).
[79] *INS v Chadha* 462 US 919 (1983).

facilitating functions of government, standing alone, will not save it if it is contrary to the Constitution'.[80] It is a 'death by a thousand cuts' to liberal, representative government which the formalist fears will result. Appeals to efficiency and convenience are rejected as they furnish no reason why the limits apparent in the Constitution should be ignored. While this approach may result in unfortunate results in some cases, the fear of a piecemeal erosion of the efficacy of separation doctrine and its rationale should not be underestimated.

This purposive element comes more to the fore in the United States given the indisputably central place afforded the separation doctrine in the whole constitutional settlement of that nation. In light of the more ambiguous position of the separation doctrine in the Australian Constitution and others like it, this purposive underpinning may stand on less certain ground, as will be discussed below, although it is usually evident when the separation of *judicial* power is in issue. Professor Martin Redish—an exponent of 'pragmatic' formalism[81]—stated that the separation of powers provisions in the United States Constitution

> are tremendously important not merely because the Framers imposed them, but because the fears of creeping tyranny underlying them are at least as justified today as they were at the time the Framers established them. For as the old adage goes, 'Even paranoids have enemies.'[82]

B. Functionalism

Functionalism is not as susceptible to uniform, precise definition as is formalism.[83] All variants of it, however, eschew formalism's maintenance of the rigid division of branches based on precise conceptual definitions, instead taking into account factors external to purely conceptual analysis. Thus, in any particular instance, functionalism may permit what to the formalist would be a technical breach of the separation of powers, if the seriousness thereof is outweighed by public policy factors, efficiency, and the maintenance of good government. The issue for functionalism is the degree of liberality which should be permitted in applying the doctrine. For present purposes it is sufficient to note the two main variants of this

---

[80] *Ibid*, at 944.

[81] This position was originally set out and defended in MH Redish and E Cisar, '"If Angels were to govern": the Need for Pragmatic Formalism in Separation of Powers Theory' (1991) 41 *Duke Law Journal* 449. It was also set out and defended in MH Redish, *The Constitution as Political Structure* (New York, Oxford University Press, 1995) 99–134.

[82] *Ibid*, at 99–100.

[83] For a detailed survey of the various approaches, see MH Redish, 'Federal Judicial Independence: Constitutional and Political Perspectives' (1995) 46 *Mercer Law Review* 697; Redish and Cisar, '"If Angels were to govern"', n 81 above; and Redish, *The Constitution as Political Structure*, n 81 above, 99–134.

school. The 'internal functionalist approach' will not regard as unconstitutional an act of one branch which does not fall within the scope of its own branch power unless 'it is found to reach some unspecified level of intensity' whereby it 'undermine[s] another branch's performance of its essential function' and allows for the accretion of excessive power to the usurping branch.[84] The more liberal 'external functionalist model', which Redish also refers to as the 'ad hoc balancing approach', allows interbranch usurpations to occur if there is a sufficiently compelling social interest to outweigh the deleterious consequence of the usurpation.[85]

While such sophisticated variants of functionalism appear to be limited to the United States, nevertheless, it is certainly possible to identify a general 'unifying philosophy that underlies all of the variants of the functionalist model [which] is a willingness to ignore definitional or conceptual constraints on branch power in light of the needs of the applicable social and political context'.[86] The mainstream position is located more within the internal functionalist approach, whereby the limit for the functionalist appears to be set at that breach which would result in such an accretion of power to one of the branches as would undermine the exercise of the power belonging to another branch, compromising the integrity and efficacy of that particular branch and the separation doctrine in general. The formalist would regard this limiting safeguard as ineffectual because of the lack of objective criteria by which to enforce it with any degree of certainty. Nevertheless it does generally indicate that the functionalist position is sensitive to the need for enforceable limits to protect the integrity of branch power. Significantly, such a limitation would in all likelihood be invoked where an indisputably core function of one of the branches can be identified.

Classic illustrations of functionalism can be found in the majority reasoning in *Morrison v Olson*[87] and *Mistretta v United States*.[88] In *Morrison*, the object of separation of powers scrutiny was legislation which gave to a particular superior federal court the power to terminate the office of independent counsel who investigated ethical violations by executive officers. This power was held to be administrative, not judicial, and as it was vested in a federal court it constituted prima facie a breach of the separation of powers.[89] Nevertheless, it was declared constitutional because, in the reasoning of the majority, '[t]he real question is

[84] Redish, 'Federal Judicial Independence', n 83 above, 711; Redish and Cisar, '"If Angels were to govern"' (n 81 above) 491.

[85] *Ibid*, at 711 and 491 respectively.

[86] Redish, 'Federal Judicial Independence', n 83 above, 711. See also G Lawson, 'Territorial Governments and the Limits of Formalism' (1990) 78 *California Law Review* 853.

[87] *Morrison v Olson* 487 US 654 (1988).

[88] *Mistretta v United States* 488 US 361 (1989).

[89] *Morrison v Olson* 487 US 654 (1988) at 682.

whether the removal restrictions are of such a nature that they impede the President's ability to perform his constitutional duty, and the functions of the officials in question must be analysed in that light'.[90] No such impediment was found to exist and no breach of the separation doctrine was found. In *Mistretta*, the court dealt with a constitutional challenge to the appointment of federal judges as members of the United States Sentencing Commission, a body empowered to make sentencing rules. The court noted that the 'concern of encroachment and aggrandizement … animated our separation-of-powers jurisprudence' while '[b]y the same token, … [the Court has] upheld statutory provisions that to some degree commingle the functions of the Branches, but that pose no danger of either aggrandizement or encroachment'.[91] The fact that Congress had, arguably, delegated certain legislative responsibilities to the judiciary was held permissible and not a breach of the separation of powers doctrine.[92] The court balanced, against the breach (in the formalist sense), the fact that the judicial branch would bring a wealth of sentencing experience to the Commission. The court recognised that the executive and the judicial branches share responsibility for developing sentencing rules without threatening the coordinate status of either branch. In *Victorian Stevedoring & General Contracting Co Pty Ltd v Dignan*[93] the High Court of Australia allowed Parliament to delegate its legislative power in certain circumstances to the Executive on functionalist grounds.[94] The need to accommodate responsible government meant that the separation of legislative and executive power could never be enforced strictly in the antipodean version of the Westminster system.[95]

Given that both formalism and functionalism are prevalent in the jurisprudence of the courts at differing times and in differing cases, the approach of the United States Supreme Court and the High Court of Australia, is flexible and eclectic, combining elements of pragmatism, public policy considerations, tradition and history with the more strictly formalist legal analysis based on the text of the Constitution.[96]

---

[90] *Ibid*, at 691.
[91] *Mistretta v United States* 488 US 361 (1989) at 382.
[92] *Ibid*, at 402.
[93] *Victorian Stevedoring & General Contracting Co Pty Ltd v Dignan* (1931) 46 CLR 73.
[94] Of course, in Australia, the need for the separation of powers doctrine to accommodate responsible government must be taken into account. See Zines, *The High Court and the Constitution*, n 3 above, 198 ff and Winterton, 'The Separation of Judicial Power as an Implied Bill of Rights', n 5 above, 190 ff.
[95] See Winterton, *Parliament, the Executive and the Governor-General*, n 64 above, 64 and Zines, *The High Court and the Constitution*, n 3 above, 198–207.
[96] See generally Zines, *The High Court and the Constitution*, n 3 above, chs 9 and 10.

C. The Preferable Approach

In the United States, the academic commentary appears to be divided
between the (purposive) formalist and functionalist approaches. In Australia, where there is no clear intention in this regard on the part of the
Framers, and where the separation of powers must come to an uneasy
accommodation with responsible government, the leading constitutional
scholars tend to favour a functionalist approach. While the *Boilermakers*
decision exerted a strong jurisprudential influence in the direction of
formalism—at least with respect to judicial power (a tendency which is
still evident)[97]—the degree, some would say excess, of formalism evident
in that case was in many respects innovative.[98] The court had previously
shown functionalist tendencies in such cases as *Dignan*,[99] mentioned
above, in relation to delegated legislation. Even when considering the
separation of judicial power, of which the High Court has always been
more solicitous,[100] there were dicta prior to *Boilermakers* suggesting that
the separation of powers doctrine was not to be applied with formalist
rigour. This was evident in those cases which considered the issue of the
conferral of non-judicial functions on the courts which exercised the
judicial power of the Commonwealth. In *R v Federal Court of Bankruptcy;
Ex parte Lowenstein*,[101] the court exhibited a willingness to allow such
conferral where it was not inconsistent with the proper exercise of
judicial power.[102] Reviewing prior cases, Latham CJ, with whom Rich J
agreed, stated that

> [t]he result of these decisions is that it cannot be said that there is involved in
> the Constitution a strict separation of powers. There are many features of the
> Constitution, either obvious upon the face of the Constitution or elucidated by
> judicial decisions, which show that such a principle cannot be accepted.[103]

Functionalist tendencies were also apparent in the judgment of Starke J:

> The argument that the separation of powers in the Constitution prohibits
> absolutely the performance by one department of the powers of any other
> department of the government is incorrect. The truth is that there is not and

---

[97] For example, *Brandy v Human Rights and Equal Opportunity Commission* (1995) 183
CLR 245; *Re Wakim; Ex parte McNally* (1999) 198 CLR 511.
[98] See Winterton, *Parliament, the Executive and the Governor-General*, n 64 above, 59 for
detailed references in this regard.
[99] *Victorian Stevedoring & General Contracting Co Pty Ltd v Dignan* (1931) 46 CLR 73. See
also *Baxter v Ah Way* (1909) 8 CLR 626; *Roche v Kronheimer* (1921) 29 CLR 329; *Radio
Corporation Pty Ltd v Commonwealth* (1938) 59 CLR 170.
[100] See *New South Wales v Commonwealth* (*Wheat* case) (1915) 20 CLR 54; *Waterside
Workers' Federation of Australia v JW Alexander Ltd* (*Alexander's* case) (1918) 25 CLR 434.
[101] *R v Federal Court of Bankruptcy; Ex parte Lowenstein* (1938) 59 CLR 556.
[102] See Zines, *The High Court and the Constitution*, n 3 above, 211–13.
[103] *R v Federal Court of Bankruptcy; Ex parte Lowenstein* (1938) 59 CLR 556 at 565.

never was any clear line of demarcation between legislative, executive and judicial powers. *Nor can there be if efficient and practical government is to be maintained.*[104] (Emphasis added.)

Even though the majority reasoning in *Boilermakers* went against the grain of such dicta (the compelling dissent of Williams J being a notable exception),[105] concerns persisted in relation to the main *Boilermakers* principle and the degree of formalism on which it was based. This was the gist of the oft-cited criticism expressed by Barwick CJ, which referred to the principle as 'unnecessary ... for the effective working of the Australian Constitution or for the maintenance of the separation of the judicial power of the Commonwealth or for the protection of the independence of the courts exercising that power'.[106] Functionalist concerns were clearly apparent in the appeals to efficiency and good administration:

> The decision leads to excessive subtlety and technicality in the operation of the Constitution without ... any compensating benefit ... [I]t may be thought so unsuited to the working of the Constitution in the circumstances of the nation that there should now be a departure from some or all of its conclusions.[107]

Sir Anthony Mason, formerly Chief Justice of the High Court, generally concurred with the reservations expressed about the formalism of *Boilermakers*[108] and, in his non-judicial writing, expressed a preference that a 'purposive functional' approach be adopted to revisit and qualify the *Boilermakers* principle along the lines suggested in the earlier *Lowenstein* case,[109] 'where ... non-judicial functions could be reposed in a federal court unless they were incompatible with the functions of a court'.[110] Professor Leslie Zines would appear to favour a purposive functional approach—it cannot be put higher than that and it would be inaccurate to locate Zines within any precise 'school'—both in relation to the *Boilermakers* principle and more generally the separation of powers doctrine:

> The factors mentioned by Barwick CJ assume that the basis of the decision in the *Boilermakers'* case is not the text of the Constitution but matters of policy

---

[104] *Ibid*, at 577. It should be observed that Evatt and Dixon JJ dissented in that case, although in the view of Zines, *The High Court and the Constitution*, n 3 above, 213, on the basis that the relevant power being conferred was inconsistent with judicial power.

[105] See *Boilermakers* (1956) 94 CLR 254, especially at 306 ff.

[106] *R v Joske; Ex parte Australian Building Construction Employees and Builders Labourers' Federation* (1974) 130 CLR 87 at 90.

[107] *Ibid*.

[108] *Ibid*.

[109] *R v Federal Court of Bankruptcy; Ex parte Lowenstein* (1938) 59 CLR 556.

[110] A Mason, 'A New Perspective on Separation of Powers' (1996) 82 *Canberra Bulletin of Public Administration* 1 at 5.

related to the exercise of judicial power—the effective working of the Australian Constitution, the separation of the judicial power of the Commonwealth and the protection of the Constitution. It is suggested that this is undoubtedly correct. If the decision was unnecessary to achieve these goals and there are no other compensating benefits, then it is right to look at the text again.[111]

According to Zines, a re-examination of the text in light of these factors permits a number of approaches, challenging the formalist premise that definitional clarity can be achieved with respect to each of the functions:

> The application of the maxim *expressio unius est exclusio alterius* to the distribution of powers is not inevitable in these circumstances … If the application of the maxim seems likely in the circumstances, either in relation to Chapter III or to all three chapters, there is no clear warrant for the view that all functions can be subsumed under categories 'legislative', 'executive' and 'judicial'.[112]

On this basis, the strictly formalist approach to the *Boilermakers* principle can be impugned:

> The conclusion the court arrived at cannot be reached by mere reflection on the distribution of powers in the first three chapters. One is led inevitably to policy or analogy. British and colonial history leads to a different conclusion. The United States analogy was seen, particularly by the High Court, as the appropriate one (but without an extensive examination of the working of that system and its use of legislative courts). Yet in relation to the legislative and executive power, *British history, principles of responsible government and the needs of effective government have been treated as overriding what some of the judges believed to be the proper analytical interpretation of the text.* What is therefore at issue and what is at the root of the judgments in the *Boilermaker's* case is the question, *what desirable arrangements of power in the Commonwealth's sphere are consistent with the text.*[113] (Emphasis added.)

Professor George Winterton similarly has adopted a critical position with respect to the formalism of *Boilermakers*: 'Clearly, any attempt to enforce a rigid separation of governmental functions or powers flies in the face of reality and must fail'.[114] The broader application of a purposive functional approach was supported by Sir Anthony Mason, arguing that 'a purposive functional approach to the separation of powers provided by the Australian Constitution has much to commend it'.[115] In support, he referred to the 'contradictory' treatment of the doctrine in the High Court's jurisprudence, noting in particular the different approach taken with respect to the relationship between Parliament and the Executive

---

[111]   Zines, *The High Court and the Constitution*, n 3 above, 217.
[112]   *Ibid.*
[113]   *Ibid*, at 169–70.
[114]   Winterton, *Parliament, the Executive and the Governor-General* (n 64 above) 60. See also the ensuing discussion at 62–3.
[115]   Mason, 'A New Perspective on Separation of Powers', n 110 above, 52.

and that between the judicial and non-judicial branches of government.[116] He noted also the 'difficulty of precise definition [which] arises
from the impossibility of defining each of the three powers in a way that
reveals them as mutually exclusive concepts'.[117] Moreover, '[t]his problem … has become more acute as the processes of government have
become more complex'.[118]

Even though this debate has been fuelled by the degree of formalism
evident in *Boilermakers*,[119] that is not to deny that it may also have been
part of the broader movement away from formalism in Australian
constitutional interpretation towards the end of the last century. Writing
in 2008, Zines noted:

> Many past decisions have been stigmatised by the High Court judges as
> 'narrow', 'formalistic' or as disregarding 'practical reality'. In many areas of
> constitutional law there can be discerned a rejection of technical formulae or
> criteria, a more open application of policy considerations, more examination of
> historical material, occasional balancing of conflicting social interests and a
> more general denunciation of 'form' as against 'substance'.[120]

The problem is that these developments have not been uniform, and
indeed have at times been unpredictable, with judges disagreeing as to
the weight which should be given to policy issues and social values.
Zines was conscious of this, writing that 'nevertheless, [it is] clear that a
change of attitude and approach is taking place, even if it is not always
clear what will be substituted for old principles and doctrines that have
been weakened or undermined'.[121] To illustrate the unpredictability of
the Australian jurisprudence in this regard, reference need only be made
to the position adopted by Deane J in *Re Tracey; Ex parte Ryan*[122] in
defence of a strict application of the *Boilermakers* principle, given that his
Honour was not otherwise known as a formalist. His rationale was that
to allow the judiciary to undertake non-judicial functions, even for the
very best of policy reasons, would undermine the integrity and independence of judicial power to such an extent that it ran the danger of
being subsumed by the Executive: '[t]he Executive Government cannot
absorb or be amalgamated with the judicature by the conferral of

---

[116]   *Ibid.*
[117]   *Ibid.*
[118]   *Ibid.*
[119]   One clear illustration is the disagreement between Mason (purposive functional
approach) and Walker (formalist approach) in relation to the *persona designata* exception to
the *Boilermakers* principle. See Mason, 'A New Perspective on Separation of Powers', n 110
above; and K Walker, 'Persona Designata, Incompatibility and the Separation of Powers'
(1997) 8 *Public Law Review* 153.
[120]   Zines, *The High Court and the Constitution*, n 3 above, 611 and generally ch 17.
[121]   *Ibid.*
[122]   *Re Tracey; Ex parte Ryan* (1989) 166 CLR 518.

non-ancillary executive functions upon the courts'.[123] The position of Deane J was supported by Kristen Walker, who expressly rejected Mason's advocacy of a functionalist refinement of the *Boilermakers* principle and was highly critical of the application of his 'purposive functional approach'.[124] She made express reference to United States learning to adopt a formalist position with respect to the separation of judicial power. Her rationale was that the separation of judicial power must be strictly adhered to if it is to have any efficacy in achieving its purposes. Thus, the judiciary must not be allowed to exercise non-judicial functions and judicial officers must be kept distinct from the personnel of the non-judicial branches. Relying on the formalist criticism of the lack of objective criteria within functionalism's own limitations on inter-branch usurpation, she stated that 'it will often be difficult to state with certainty that any particular non-judicial function being performed by judges (whether as judges or as individuals) will, viewed in isolation, undermine the independence of the judiciary'.[125] Moreover, she made reference to the danger of 'incremental' erosion of the values protected by the separation doctrine unless a strict formalist approach is taken:

> that is, the separation of powers doctrine only works if it prevents the multitude of small breaches which, taken together, could undermine public confidence in the judiciary; the doctrine cannot work if we must wait for the independence of the judiciary to be undermined before we invoke it, for then it is too late.[126]

On this basis, Walker rejected the application of the incompatibility doctrine, contrary to the views of Mason, as well as the *persona designata* exception (which Mason also rejected) as the important qualification to the *Boilermakers* principle. Her critique of functionalism, however, extended also to functionalism's case-by-case determination of whether a particular branch's action should be held to breach the principle:

> The [separation of powers] doctrine is concerned to ensure that there is no actual or perceived alliance between the judiciary and the other branches of government, particularly the Executive. This can only be effectively achieved if a strict separation of powers and personnel is maintained. For while many non-judicial functions, viewed individually, may not appear to undermine the independence of the judiciary when exercised by judges, taken together they may. So it is not sufficient to focus simply on each non-judicial function in isolation and assess whether it is incompatible with the judicial role; in order for the separation of powers to fulfil its role, it must be strictly adhered to;

---

[123]   *Re Tracey; Ex parte Ryan* (1989) 166 CLR 518 at 580.
[124]   Walker, 'Persona Designata, Incompatibility and the Separation of Powers', n 119 above.
[125]   *Ibid*, at 163.
[126]   *Ibid*.

artificial doctrines, such as the *persona designata* doctrine, which undermine the separation of powers, must be jettisoned. And they must not be replaced by an overarching doctrine of incompatibility, as suggested by Mason, as this would involve an even greater inroad into the separation of powers.[127]

Walker's critique of functionalism reinforces the point that formalists are not merely concerned with some neat but otherwise meaningless allocation of powers. It is based, rather, on the premise that a formalist approach is essential for the maintenance of the integrity of branch power, especially that of the judicial branch. Such *purposive* formalism was also clearly evident in the reasoning of the classically formalist *Plaut* decision referred to above, and in the writings of the more moderate formalists such as Redish.[128] However, the very fact that they are relying on factors beyond the separation apparent in the Constitutional text confirms the point made above by Zines. The purposive nature of this formalism has not come about 'by mere reflection on the distribution of powers in the first three chapters'.[129] Accordingly, it also constitutes a telling, albeit implied, repudiation of that purely textual formalism which takes no account of considerations beyond the text.

The High Court continues to prefer a formalist approach in certain circumstances, albeit not uniformly, as manifested in the strict adherence to *Boilermakers* in *Re Wakim; Ex parte McNally*.[130] In that case, it held that the vesting of State jurisdiction in federal courts was unconstitutional in that it did not constitute the 'judicial power of the Commonwealth', limited to those matters contained in sections 75 and 76 of the Constitution. The result undermined the very important cross-vesting scheme which was based on the significant policy rationale of facilitating the hearing in one court of matters pertaining to both federal and State issues and the development of a national approach to such matters as corporations law and family law. Considerations relating to the important policy issues involved in maintaining the scheme, efficiency and the enhanced operation of legal administration, were regarded as irrelevant in light of the need to maintain a strict separation of the judicial power of the Commonwealth as entrenched in the Constitution.

On the other hand, the court has been capable of functionalist compromises, even with respect to the separation of judicial power, as was evident in those doctrines attacked by Walker above: the *persona designata* exception to *Boilermakers* and the incompatibility principle as a limit on *persona designata*. (Although it is arguable that *persona designata* is merely

---

[127] *Ibid.*
[128] See nn 1, 81 and 83 above.
[129] Zines, *The High Court and the Constitution*, n 3 above, 217.
[130] *Re Wakim; Ex parte McNally* (1999) 198 CLR 511.

an exception to a strict principle, all operating within a formalist frame-work.) This functionalist attitude does enable federal judges to perform a variety of administrative functions which are not incidental to the exercise of judicial power.[131] Similarly thus to the United States, it is clear that there continues to be an eclectic approach to separation of powers jurisprudence, with disagreement persisting in contemporary constitutional writing on these matters. However, it is evident that both approaches are based on policy positions. Formalism, as well as functionalism, can be purposive in its own way, making a determination of which is the most appropriate a vexed one. This recognition of a purposive element to formalism is indicative that absolute reliance on the text alone—that is, an uncompromising *textual* formalism—as a basis for defining separation of powers principles appears to be on the wane.

Thus, given the difficulties in providing mutually-exclusive definitions of branch functions, heightened by the evolving nature of government, the flexible, pragmatic approach to these questions as exhibited by Mason, Winterton and Zines in the Australian context, and Redish in the American, is to be preferred. This is not to say that the writer espouses a functionalist position universally; rather that the formalism/functionalism divide is inadequate alone to resolve such a multi-dimensional issue, particularly in Westminster-inspired jurisdictions which maintain responsible government in the context of an entrenched separation of powers. Each approach contains useful elements which can be used with discrimination across issues. The writer shares the fears of the formalists of a piecemeal and inexorable erosion of the protections afforded by the separation doctrine if a functionalist approach is applied too liberally, at least where core functions (especially judicial) are concerned. To this extent, there may be a very useful role for a *purposive* formalist approach in relation to those branch functions which are indisputably core.[132] Beyond these, however, where precise lines of demarcation remain vague, a more purposive functional approach is certainly warranted and to be preferred. This may be perceived to be too nice a position, but apart from providing some basis for a reasonable accommodation between the two schools, it can also meet the definitional imperatives of an entrenched separation doctrine at a certain level without yielding to artificial rigidity beyond that. It allays the concerns of

---

[131]   The development of the *persona designata* and incompatibility doctrines can be traced in the series of cases: *Hilton v Wells* (1985) 157 CLR 57; *Jones v Commonwealth* (1987) 71 ALR 497; *Grollo v Palmer* (1995) 184 CLR 348; and *Wilson v Minister for Aboriginal and Torres Strait Islander Affairs* (1996) 189 CLR 1.

[132]   The writer is conscious that even such an approach is fraught with difficulties, especially in light of the fact that the determination of which functions are 'core' has itself been the subject of some uncertainty.

each by providing an appropriate starting point for the consideration of the primary sphere of relevance for each approach.

By way of illustration, Mason, generally supportive of a purposive functionalism, did not preclude the adoption of an alternative approach:

> The distillation of entrenched characteristics of judicial power, *by conceptual or purposive interpretation or a combination of both*, will protect the essential integrity of the judicial process from legislative encroachment and distortion. But, if taken too far, the identification of those characteristics may inhibit the potential development of the judicial process in ways that would enhance the resolution of controversies arising for curial determination.[133] (Emphasis added.)

Moreover, he acknowledged the possibility of locating some definitional core to judicial functions, thus meeting to some degree the definitional imperatives arising from entrenchment. 'Some functions are inescapably exercises of judicial power', he conceded.[134] He made reference in this regard to the decision in *Brandy v Human Rights and Equal Opportunity Commission*,[135] where the High Court held that certain sections of the Racial Discrimination Act 1975 (Cth) were invalid as they purportedly vested judicial power in a body which was clearly not judicial, the Human Rights and Equal Opportunity Commission, despite the inconvenience which would result. Significantly, the case turned on that fundamental element of judicial power, the power to make a final, authoritative and enforceable decision on matters of legal dispute. 'To constitutional lawyers', noted Mason, 'the *Brandy* decision came as no surprise'.[136] Some reconciliation may therefore be possible with the formalists at least at the level of core branch functions. This reconciliation must start with an acknowledgment of the purposive elements within the formalist school.

V.   THE PURPOSIVE NATURE OF THE SEPARATION OF POWERS DOCTRINE

Although a trite observation, at the broadest level the separation of powers, in all its myriad forms and variations,[137] is purposive in nature. When legally entrenched in a written constitution this purposive element follows with it and must be factored into any interpretation of it. This, it is submitted, is also the case if the separation doctrine is read into a

---

[133]   *Ibid.*
[134]   *Ibid*, at 6 (citations omitted).
[135]   *Brandy v Human Rights and Equal Opportunity Commission* (1995) 183 CLR 245.
[136]   Mason, 'A New Perspective on Separation of Powers', n 110 above, 6 (citations omitted).
[137]   The classic treatise remains that of MJC Vile, *Constitutionalism and The Separation of Powers*, n 61 above. It sets out in detail the myriad versions of the doctrine.

written constitution as a result of textual analysis. The leading authority, MJC Vile, noted this in his seminal *Constitutionalism and the Separation of Powers*:

> The long discussion of the powers of government has been conducted largely in terms of the legislative, executive, and judicial functions. These abstract concepts emerged after a long period in which men thought mainly in terms of the 'tasks' which government had to perform, such as conducting war and diplomacy, and maintaining order. The emergence of the idea of legislative and executive powers, or functions, had in itself little to do with an analysis of the essential nature of government; it was concerned more with the desire, by delimiting certain functional areas, to be able to restrict the ruler to a particular aspect of government and so to exercise limits on his power. This 'purposive' quality of the traditional classification of government is important, for it makes the discussion of functional analysis much more than simply an attempt at description; *it inevitably carries a normative connotation as well. The very use of these terms assumes a commitment to some form of constitutional government.*[138] (Emphasis added.)

The division of power which the doctrine advocates is thus, at its core, purposive; and this purposive core must inform even the formalist approach to separation of powers jurisprudence. After all, the definition of the 'functions' of the respective branches emerged and evolved from the experience of government, not from an exclusively theoretical, abstract consideration of their essence or nature. Nevertheless, some degree of abstract conceptual analysis becomes unavoidable for constitutional lawyers when the doctrine is entrenched in a written constitution and thus brought into the sphere of legal rules—indeed essential if courts are to be able to adjudicate on questions of inter-branch interference and usurpation.

However, to neglect this purposive element in any attempt at definition of functions would be clearly repugnant to the doctrine's history, development and application in many polities. It developed as part of a pragmatic solution to the perennial problem of preventing the abuse of power by avoiding its undue concentration, the better to secure good government, and preserve those values which are regarded as fundamental thereto. Moreover, the doctrine and its central tenets did not develop in isolation. Vile, in a passage which deserves to be set out in full, put it this way:

> The history of Western political thought portrays the development and elaboration of a set of values—justice, liberty, equality, and the sanctity of property—the implications of which have been examined and debated down through the centuries; but just as important is the history of the debates about

---

[138]   *Ibid*, at 348.

the institutional structures and procedures which are necessary if these values are to be realized in practice, and reconciled with each other. *For the values that characterise Western thought are not self-executing* … Western institutional theorists have concerned themselves with the problem of ensuring that the exercise of governmental power, which is essential to the realization of the values of their societies, should be controlled in order that it should not itself be destructive of the values it was intended to promote. The great theme of the advocates of constitutionalism, in contrast either to theorists of utopianism, or of absolutism, of the right or of the left, has been the frank acknowledgment of the role of government in society, linked with the determination to bring that government under control and to place limits on the exercise of its power. Of the theories of government which have attempted to provide a solution to this dilemma, the doctrine of the separation of powers has, in modern times, been the most significant, both intellectually and in terms of its influence upon institutional structures. It stands alongside that other great pillar of Western political thought—the concept of representative government—as the major support for systems of government which are labelled 'constitutional.[139] (Emphasis added.)

The fact that the doctrine itself is clearly purposive, and normative, relegates the dispute between formalism and functionalism to a narrower sphere of relevance: the determination of those more precise legal principles and constitutional limitations which regulate the inter-branch relationship in light of the purposes which the doctrine—entrenched in a written constitution—is perceived as fostering in any particular polity.

If consistency with purpose is therefore a relevant criterion in the determination of the appropriate interpretative technique, in the context of this monograph, the relevant purpose is that to be served more precisely by the separation of the judicial branch from the non-judicial. Given the relatively pure application of the separation doctrine in the United States, albeit with checks and balances, the determination of the precise purposes to be achieved is a more straightforward exercise than, for example, in Australia, which combines the Westminster model of responsible government with American approaches to federalism and the separation of powers.

In the United States, the records of the various constitutional conventions and *The Federalist* set out the thoughts, purposes and intentions of the Framers with respect to the separation of powers.[140] It is safe to say, as indicated by Vile,[141] that the separation of the main branches of government was a fundamental consideration underlying the creation of

---

[139] *Ibid*, at 1–2.
[140] See, for example, writings of James Madison, in particular in *The Federalist* (Issue nos 48 and 51), n 38 above. See also Wood, *The Creation of the American Republic 1776–1787*, n 47 above, 154–5.
[141] Vile, *Constitutionalism and The Separation of Powers*, n 61 above, ch 6.

constitutional republican government based on representative democracy and the rule of law and its progeny, an independent judiciary and
the maintenance of public confidence in the courts. It was clear that
confidence in the fusion of powers, under Crown and Parliament, was
replaced by confidence rather in a dispersion of power achieved by the
strict adoption of the separation of powers operating pursuant to the
American system of checks and balances. Given the clearer purpose of
the dispersion of power which emerges from the history and whole
context of the United States Constitution, formalists in that jurisdiction
stand on the surer ground that a strict separation was intended to apply
as a safeguard against the abuses of a concentration of power, especially
in the hands of the legislature, irrespective of issues relating to efficiency.

The identification of the purpose underlying the separation of powers
in the Australian context is made difficult by the combination of British
and American precedents influencing its constitutional settlement. It is
worth examining the Australian position as a case study of the contradictions and difficulties which emerge when these two influences, at times
conflicting, are sought to be combined. It will be seen in the chapters
which follow that the question of the precise purposes to be achieved by
the separation of powers in the Australian context is a vexed one. To
begin with, there is no clear evidence of intention, if any at all, on the part
of the Framers to indicate that the doctrine was to be constitutionally
entrenched, despite the obvious influence of the United States Constitution,[142] or to be regarded in the more flexible, pragmatic and understated
way of a constitutional convention pursuant to British precedent. As
noted by Wheeler, the 'question whether the Commonwealth Constitution enshrined a legal doctrine of the separation of powers was not
addressed in the Convention Debates and, by default, was left to the
"Federal Supreme Court" established by s 71'.[143] If there is any prejudice
in this uncertainty, it tells against the formalists to the extent that they
advocate an absolute separation of the three branches.

In fact, constitutional scholars have agonized over whether the separation of powers was in fact incorporated into the Constitution as a legal
principle. Wheeler has succinctly analysed this wavering,[144] as has Winterton,[145] following upon the earlier work of Professor John Finnis in this
regard.[146] For example, it was only in the second edition of W Harrison

[142]   See Winterton, *Parliament, the Executive and the Governor-General*, n 64 above; and F
Wheeler, 'Original Intent and the Doctrine of the Separation of Powers in Australia' (1996) 7
Public Law Review 96.
[143]   *Ibid*, at 104.
[144]   *Ibid*, at 97 ff.
[145]   Winterton, *Parliament, the Executive and the Governor-General*, n 64 above, 54.
[146]   JM Finnis, 'Separation of Powers in the Australian Constitution (1967) 3 *Adelaide Law
Review* 159.

Moore's *The Constitution of the Commonwealth of Australia*[147] that there was unequivocal support from Moore of the views of Quick and Garran (in *The Annotated Constitution of the Australian Commonwealth*)[148] and Quick and Groom (in *The Judicial Power of the Commonwealth*)[149] that there was full legal separation of powers in the Constitution. The earlier edition of Moore's work, published in 1902, exhibited a degree of uncertainty on this point; there being indications, as Wheeler has pointed out, that he in fact denied the relevance of the doctrine as a legal limitation on the distribution of powers.[150] These uncertainties have certainly continued even after *Boilermakers*. While Geoffrey Sawer confidently asserted in 1961 that *Boilermarkers* 'is a way beyond question corresponding to the expectations of the Founders',[151] he re-evaluated his position a few years later, expressing his views on this point with far more equivocation.[152] These are issues which have been seriously examined elsewhere and it is not presently relevant to examine them in detail, except to the extent that they shed light on the issues at hand.[153]

Nevertheless, and despite these uncertainties, if one takes into account the general trends in High Court exegesis on this point, together with the other principles established in the Constitution, one may venture to make the following observations: Clearly, the doctrine must operate in the context of the other constitutional principles which were incorporated in the Constitution, most notably representative and responsible government. Mason put it succinctly when he stated that the role of the separation of powers is

> to maintain and enhance the system of representative and responsible government brought into existence by the Constitution and to ensure the maintenance of the rule of law by an independent judiciary whose responsibility it is to determine justiciable controversies.[154]

[147] W H Moore, *The Constitution of the Commonwealth of Australia*, 2nd edn (Melbourne, Charles S Maxwell, 1910).

[148] J Quick and RR Garran, *The Annotated Constitution of the Australian Commonwealth* (Sydney, 1901, Reprinted Sydney Lexis Nexis Butterworths 2002).

[149] J Quick and LE Groom, *The Judicial Power of the Commonwealth* (Melbourne, Charles F Maxwell 1904).

[150] Wheeler, 'Original Intent and the Doctrine of the Separation of Powers in Australia', n 142 above, 98.

[151] *Ibid*, at 103, quoting from Sawer, 'The Separation of Powers in Australian Federalism', n 68 above, 178.

[152] *Ibid*, referring to the statement by G Sawer in his *Australian Federalism in the Courts* (Melbourne, Melbourne University Press, 1967) 154, that '[t]he historical probabilities are that only a very limited separation of powers was intended'.

[153] In addition to the articles and books mentioned in nn 142–149 above, see also Ratnapala, *Australian Constitutional Law, Foundations and Theory* (n 55 above) chs 5 and 6, and in particular 88; Sawer, 'The Separation of Powers in Australian Federalism', n 68 above; and H Gibbs, 'The Separation of Powers—A Comparison' (1987) 17 *Federal Law Review* 151.

[154] Mason, 'A New Perspective on Separation of Powers', n 110 above, 2.

This is consistent with the view that the implementation of the doctrine must accommodate the countervailing tendencies of responsible government; although in relation to the maintenance of the rule of law, there would be no great countervailing tendency except perhaps that which may arise from issues relating to efficiency and good public policy. Moreover, given the passive role of the judicial branch and its more vulnerable position vis-à-vis the legislature, a stricter separation of the judicial from the non-judicial branches would be consistent with the separation doctrine's purposes as above-stated; and, to that extent, the high formalism of *Boilermakers* is capable of at least some justification. Indeed, if the purpose of the doctrine is to protect judicial independence and the rule of law—which is indisputable—the formalist line is at least respectable that the only sure way to achieve these purposes is by the maintenance of a strict separation.

Such an approach is reinforced by the imperatives of federalism under a written constitution, which adds heightened significance to the place of the highest court on constitutional matters, as borne out in particular by the United States experience, and as observed by Dicey.[155] As the majority stated in *Boilermakers*,

> [t]he position and constitution of the judicature could not be considered accidental to the institution of federalism: for upon the judicature rests the ultimate responsibility for the maintenance and enforcement of the boundaries within which governmental power might be exercised and upon that the whole system was constructed.[156]

In relation to the separation of judicial power in particular, it was 'quite clear from an early date that the judicial power of the Commonwealth was regarded as in a special category'.[157] The purpose to be achieved here, ultimately, was the sure protection of the rule of law.

However, there were other developments, post-dating the framing of the United States Constitution, which affected the separation of powers in such a way as to counter federalism's influence toward a strict application of it. These developments were characterised, in the words of

---

[155] 'Federalism ... means legalism—the predominance of the judiciary in the constitution—the prevalence of a spirit of legality among the people ... That in a confederation like the United States the Courts become the pivot on which the constitutional arrangements of the country turn is obvious ... [N]o legislature throughout the land is more than a subordinate law-making body capable in strictness of enacting nothing but bye-laws; the powers of the executive are again limited by the constitution; the interpreters of the constitution are the judges. The Bench therefore can and must determine the limits to the authority of the government and of the legislature; its decision is without appeal; the consequence follows that the Bench of judges is not only the guardian but also at a given moment the master of the constitution'. AV Dicey, *Introduction to the Study of the Law of the Constitution*, 8th edn (London, Macmillan & Co, 1915) 170–71.

[156] *Boilermakers* (1956) 94 CLR 254, at 276.

[157] Zines, *The High Court and the Constitution*, n 3 above, 208.

Vile, by the 'increasingly insistent search for co-ordinated and efficient government' during the nineteenth century.[158] This was evident in particular in the United Kingdom in the reforms of government which received considerable impetus during and following the premiership of William Pitt, culminating in the Northcote-Trevelyan Report in 1853 and the consequent efficiency-inspired reforms to the civil service.[159] Efficiency and good administration were added to the maintenance of the rule of law and representative government as purposes to be achieved in any liberal polity.[160] However, the separation of powers doctrine, of its nature, tends to obvious inefficiencies in its very impetus to separate the functions and personnel of the respective branches. If, therefore, efficiency concerns were an element of the British constitutional inheritance at the time of the framing of the Australian Constitution, it would be difficult to imagine that the Australian position would be oblivious to its demands in 1901, and more so subsequently, particularly in light of the great increase in the role of government since federation.

The other major factor, and probably the one which has the most significant countervailing tendencies to the separation of powers doctrine, is the principle of responsible government; even though, as noted by Mason, the separation of powers must be interpreted consistently with its maintenance.[161] Clearly adopted from the Westminster tradition into the Constitution, responsible government has meant that the legislative and executive branches cannot be kept separate to the extent that both can be from judicial power.[162] Thus, the countervailing tendencies in the dual influence of British (responsible government and parliamentary supremacy) and American (federalism, separation of powers) constitutional norms, usages and principles on Australian constitutional theory and practice created unresolved tensions. As Winterton noted with respect to the executive power (although his observations are pertinent generally to separation of powers issues), 'much of the uncertainty

---

[158] Vile, *Constitutionalism and The Separation of Powers*, n 61 above, 347.

[159] See K Dowding, *The Civil Service* (London, Routledge, 1995) 9–11. See also P Johnson, *The Offshore Islanders: A History of the English People* (London, Weidenfeld and Nicholson, 1985, revised edn of 1972) 245 ff and 294–7. 'Pitt's main object was to promote efficiency. In pursuing it, he inevitably made government more honest, and the probity of the public service slowly became a feature of British life and (more quickly) was hailed as a British tradition since time immemorial' (at 247).

[160] Vile, *Constitutionalism and The Separation of Powers*, n 61 above, 347.

[161] Mason, 'A New Perspective on Separation of Powers', n 110 above, 2.

[162] See Winterton, 'The Separation of Judicial Power as an Implied Bill of Rights', n 5 above, 190–91. See also Zines, *The High Court and the Constitution*, n 3 above, 198–207 and 220–22; Ratnapala, *Australian Constitutional Law, Foundations and Theory*, n 65 above, ch 5. See also *Victorian Stevedoring and General Contracting Co Pty Ltds v Dignan* (1931) 46 CLR 73.

surrounding federal executive power in Australia stems from the contradictions inherent in the simultaneous operation of the British and American principles'.[163] These observations are clearly consistent with the view that functionalist considerations must play a critical role in separation of powers jurisprudence in the Australian context.

Do these considerations, however, tend against a strict separation of *judicial* power as well? Zines correctly pointed out that despite the views which may have been held in relation to delegated legislation, resulting in a more liberal application of the separation of powers doctrine, this was not the case in relation to the judicial power of the Commonwealth, which was 'regarded as in a special category'. Therefore its separation from the non-judicial branches afforded a stricter application of the separation of powers doctrine.[164]

In the Australian context, therefore, even though the adoption of a strict legal separation of judicial power was a departure from British precedents in this regard, nevertheless, these precedents encouraged the stricter separation of judicial power from the non-judicial branches. As noted by Winterton,

> [i]t is in regard to the separation of judicial power from the other two governmental powers that the judiciary has come closest to enforcing strictly the third component of the separation of powers doctrine; but clearly the necessity for judicial independence, the nature of the judicial function, and the detailed provisions of Chapter III of the Constitution strengthen all three limbs of the doctrine and require the separation of judicial power to be implemented to a greater degree than the separation of the other two powers. The need for judicial independence, asserted as early as 1641 and recognised in the constitutions of Australia, Canada and the United States, especially important under a constitution where the judiciary determines the boundary between the powers of the Commonwealth and the States and the between the branches of the federal government, clearly requires the insulation of the judicial power from the political branches.[165]

Overall, although there is not the same sense in Australia of the separation of powers as an unequivocal foundational constitutional principle as there is in the United States, there has emerged a view that the separation of judicial power deserves special protection. Accordingly, the purposes for such separation do remain consistent with that of the United States, that is, the maintenance of the rule of law and its progeny, an independent judiciary, the maintenance of public confidence in the courts and the accountability of the non-judicial branches to the constitution. While

---

[163] Winterton, 'The Separation of Judicial Power as an Implied Bill of Rights', n 5 above, 1.

[164] Zines, *The High Court and the Constitution*, n 3 above, 208.

[165] Winterton, *Parliament, the Executive and the Governor-General*, n 64 above, 61.

Boilermakers is still authoritative, and its high formalism still influential, the High Court may carve out exceptions without overruling that case, and indeed, without undermining the significant purposes of maintaining the rule of law and an independent judiciary, as it has in fact done.[166] That such purposes are inherent in the Constitution is uncontroversial and clear. This means that the judiciary must be protected from legislative and executive pressure or interference; protected to decide cases and declare the law independently of the interests of faction and government, and in order to maintain its independence generally so as to contribute to public confidence in the administration of justice. It does not mean that the judiciary must be prevented absolutely from exercising non-judicial functions, nor that a strict separation of the judicial power must be maintained in all circumstances. On the other hand, in any interpretation of the separation of powers, there can be no absolute rejection of the notion that there are some elements of judicial power which require total protection from inter-branch interference, which elements can be defined with sufficient precision to enable this to be enforced. The same can also be said of certain aspects of legislative power, although, for reasons to be discussed below, this may be more difficult with respect to executive functions. Before examining these elements more precisely, the preliminary issue which must be addressed is the vexed problem of identifying mutually exclusive definitions of the various branches.

VI.   THE PROBLEM OF DEFINITION AND THE FORMALIST APPROACH

The major weakness in the formalist approach, and the subject of functionalism's most compelling critique thereof, is the difficulty in providing complete and mutually-exclusive definitions of the functions of each of the branches on the basis of conceptual analysis. If this cannot be achieved, at least at some fundamental level, the formalist approach is

---

[166] For example, in *Gould v Brown* (1998) 193 CLR 346, the High Court—albeit evenly divided on the point—upheld that aspect of the cross-vesting scheme whereby State jurisdiction could be vested in federal courts despite the silence of the Constitution on this point and despite the *Boilermakers* principle which insisted that only the judicial power of the Commonwealth and power incidental thereto could be vested in these courts. The decision was overturned subsequently in *Re Wakim; Ex parte McNally* (1999) 198 CLR 511. Other exceptions include the power of Parliament to determine conclusively whether there has been a contempt of Parliament and to punish accordingly (*R v Richards; Ex parte Fitzpatrick and Browne* (1955) 92 CLR 157); the system of military tribunals and courts martial which exist outside the framework of Ch III (*R v Cox; Ex parte Smith* (1945) 71 CLR 1; *Re Tracey: Ex parte Ryan* (1989) 166 CLR 518; *Re Nolan; Ex parte Young* (1991) 172 CLR 460; *Re Tyler; Ex parte Foley* (1994) 181 CLR 18; and *Re Colonel Aird; Ex parte Alpert* (2004) 209 ALR 311); public service disciplinary tribunals (*R v White Ex parte Byrnes* (1963) 109 CLR 665); and the *persona designata* exception.

seriously undermined. Leading commentators, such as Mason, regard this as 'impossible', at least in a comprehensive way.[167] Zines made the point that 'there is no clear warrant for the view that all functions can be subsumed under the categories "legislative", "executive" and "judicial"'.[168] Winterton noted that any attempted enforcement of a rigid separation of the functions or powers of government 'flies in the face of reality and must fail', referring to similar opinions expressed by numerous justices, and indeed quoting even from the majority in *Boilermakers* that it was 'absurd ... to speak as if the division of powers meant that the three organs of government were invested with separate powers which in all respects were mutually exclusive'.[169]

Reference is commonly made to the mix of functions that each of the branches must invariably engage in, cutting across branch divisions. Thus, for example, Mason pointed out that in addition to the legislative branch, judges also 'make law, if only in a minor way,' as does the executive when delegated legislation is enacted.[170] Judges exercise administrative functions and legislators convict and punish for contempt.[171] '[A]dministrators and administrative tribunals determine a range of disputes'.[172] Moreover, '[t]his problem, arising from the inherent absence of mutual exclusivity in the three powers, has become more acute as the processes of government have become more complex'.[173] Vile concurs:

> The pure doctrine of the separation of powers implied that the functions of government could be uniquely divided up between the branches of government in such a way that no branch need ever exercise the function of another. In practice such a division of function has never been achieved, nor indeed is it desirable that it should be, for it would involve a disjuncture in the actions of government which would be intolerable. But the criticism of the threefold conception of government functions can be taken much further than pointing out that it has never been wholly achieved in practice. It can be suggested that 'multifunctionality' of political structures can, and perhaps must, be carried out to the point where any attempt at a division of functions is *quite impossible*.[174]

He continues:

---

[167]   Mason, 'A New Perspective on Separation of Powers', n 110 above, 2.
[168]   Zines, *The High Court and the Constitution*, n 3 above, 217.
[169]   Winterton, *Parliament, the Executive and the Governor-General* (n 64 above) 60, quoting from *Boilermakers* (1956) 94 CLR 254 at 278 (Dixon CJ, McTiernan, Fullagar and Kitto JJ).
[170]   Mason, 'A New Perspective on Separation of Powers', n 110 above, 2.
[171]   *Ibid.*
[172]   *Ibid.*
[173]   *Ibid.* See also Zines, *The High Court and the Constitution*, n 3 above, 216–18 and 295–99.
[174]   Vile, *Constitutionalism and The Separation of Powers*, n 61 above, 349.

The misconception of the functional categories of the separation of powers, therefore, stemmed from the naïve view that there were distinct actions of willing and execution that could be isolated and kept in separate compartments ... [I]f we pursue the analysis to its limits we see that the exclusive allocation of rule-making, rule application, or rule-adjudication to particular organs of government is not only inconvenient, it is probably quite impossible. *Every act of every official*, except perhaps the most routine and trivial operations, *embodies all three types of activity*.[175] (Emphasis added.)

While the accuracy of the above conclusions cannot be denied, it encounters one significant difficulty when the separation of powers doctrine is legally entrenched. This 'impossibility' must somehow be reconciled with the imperative toward some form of workable, mutually-exclusive (at least at some level), definition of branch functions. It is a difficulty which is inevitable in the doctrine's transition from tenet of political philosophy to legal rule. As noted by Mason, '[t]o Montesquieu, the separation of powers was a diffusion or dispersion of powers, rather than a division of functions. However, once the concept came to be translated into constitutional and legal terms, it was transformed into a division of functions'.[176] He noted, further:

To the legal mind, the transformation was a natural one. A division of powers was a logical way of giving effect to a diffusion of powers and a division of powers separating the legislature, the Executive and the judiciary corresponded to the broad separation of powers, as it existed in England in Montesquieu's time.[177]

The critical issue therefore becomes whether any reconciliation can be achieved between this 'impossibility' of comprehensive mutual-exclusivity of definition, on the one hand, with the definitional imperatives which arise from legal entrenchment. Formalist judgements are based on the premise that some enforceable boundary is achievable, at least at some level, and indeed a natural consequence of the entrenchment of the doctrine.[178] As Sawer pointed out, the effect of *Boilermakers* was to give meaning to the tripartite structure of the Constitution such that it 'must in general be regarded not as a convenience of drafting nor

---

[175] *Ibid*, at 351.

[176] Mason, 'A New Perspective on Separation of Powers', n 110 above, 1.

[177] *Ibid*, at 1–2 (citations omitted). See also Gibbs, 'The Separation of Powers—A Comparison', n 153 above, 151.

[178] *Boilermakers* (1956) 94 CLR 254 at 275–6; [1957] AC 288 at 311–12. Support for the existence of a legally entrenched separation of powers and its importance can be found in earlier High Court decisions, such as, for example, *New South Wales v Commonwealth* (the *Wheat* case) (1915) 20 CLR 54. Isaacs J (at 88) in that case referred to the separation of powers as a 'fundamental principle ... marked out in the Australian Constitution'. For a more detailed examination see Sawer, 'The Separation of Powers in Australian Federalism', n 68 above, 179.

as directory, *but as a series of mandatory propositions implying negatives*'[179] (emphasis added). For these 'mandatory propositions' to be enforced, some form of distinguishing definition must be given to each of the branches (at least at some level); even if one were to reject the uncompromising formalism of *Boilermakers*. This of course does not preclude the recognition of exceptions, as has in fact occurred.[180]

In the view of the writer, this imperative may be met if indisputably core functions belonging to each of the branches can be located, precisely defined, and in relation to which no exceptions are to be made for any inter-branch interference or usurpation. This will provide the minimum requirements for the enforcement of the separation of powers, as legal rule, while allowing for due recognition to be given to the 'impossibility' of a comprehensive, mutually-exclusive, definition. This, of course, will mean that a purposive formalist approach will be possible at the level of core functions, while purposive functionalist considerations may (and should) apply beyond this level. The critical question remains: How are these core functions to be identified? To this question, attention will now be given.

VII.   CORE BRANCH FUNCTIONS?

Having examined the weaknesses inherent in each of the formalist and functionalist approaches, and the vexed problem of the precise status of the separation of powers in Westminster-inspired systems, the view of the writer remains that there is no alternative but to concur with the adoption of the more flexible, eclectic approach to these matters which has been advocated above and which is apparent in the jurisprudence of the High Court taken as a whole. This is not to deny, however, the imperative to provide at least some *definitional* core to branch power to allow the separation of powers, as a legal rule, a minimum efficacy consistent with its role as a 'prophylactic' safeguard against the undue concentration of power and in order to protect the fundamental values of constitutionalism underlying a liberal polity. In Australia, however, while this role can be asserted at least in so far as the separation of judicial power is concerned, it is not the same (as it is in the United States) with respect to the separation of executive and legislative powers in light of responsible government and the continuing influence of parliamentary supremacy (subject to the Constitution). Moderate functionalists would concur with this proposition in light of their acknowledgment that there may be some branch functions which are so fundamental that to make

---

[179] *Ibid*, at 178.
[180] See above n 127 and accompanying text and n 166.

allowance for inter-branch intermingling of functions where these are concerned would undermine the integrity of branch power. A strict formalist approach, however, is not entirely consistent with the uncertainties surrounding the intentions (or lack thereof) legally to entrench the doctrine in the Australian Constitution; nor does it sufficiently take into account the difficulties in providing completely mutually-exclusive definitions of branch power. Thus, any approach which is adopted in Westminster-style systems which entrench the doctrine must be sufficiently flexible in order to be consistent with the history, tradition and the (at times countervailing) British constitutional principles with which the doctrine must contend. This may be unsatisfactory to formalists concerned with the piecemeal erosion of the protections which can only be afforded by strict separation. However, if there is an uncertain intention in the first place to entrench the separation of powers, much of the justification for the *purposive* formalist position melts away.

It is clear that the High Court and the United States Supreme Court have already acquiesced to functionalist tendencies in the face of overriding efficiency and public policy concerns. The issue is not that they have done so, but the appropriateness of the *extent* to which they have. On the other hand, the problem with functionalism still remains that of providing sufficiently objective criteria by which to determine the limits to be imposed on the intermingling of functions which it allows. The question of which interpretive technique is preferable depends, to a large extent, on the precise elements of branch power under consideration. It is already the case that functionalist considerations are far more influential in defining the precise relationship between legislative and executive power (even in the United States) as compared with those pertaining to that between judicial and non-judicial power, where a (purposive) formalist position can be more easily accommodated. While formalism can be easily reconciled with attempts to define core branch functions, functionalism can only be so reconciled if it can be established that the alleged usurpation or interference with the core functions so defined will, in all circumstances, constitute so serious a threat to the integrity of branch power that it must not be allowed. To achieve such a reconciliation, two critical issues must be addressed: first, whether it is possible to provide a definition which is sufficiently precise and particular to enable some elements of branch power to be confined exclusively to that branch; and, secondly, whether it is possible at all to isolate certain branch functions as core or fundamental to a particular branch so that their absolute protection without exception is supported whether a formalist or functionalist approach is adopted.

A very useful starting point in this enquiry lies in Zines's observation that the tendency of the High Court of Australia—in order to come to terms with these definitional imperatives—is to proceed by way of identifying what is a 'typical' function of each of the powers, while at the same time acknowledging that these may not necessarily describe all functions exercisable by each branch.[181] This attempt to locate the *typical* constitutes some movement towards establishing at least a minimum degree of mutual exclusivity in definition. For example, in relation to the legislative/judicial relationship, Zines noted the 'contrasts' between a 'typical' judicial function and that 'usually' exercised by the legislature.[182] The definition of the judicial function variously attempted by the High Court 'emphasises' the making of a binding and authoritative determination about rights in a legal controversy between parties, which determination has the 'quality' of 'conclusiveness'.[183] The typical or usual nature of legislative power, by contrast, is that which is concerned with 'the laying down of rules of some degree of generality directing the behaviour of persons for the future'.[184] Also contrasted is the exercise of executive or administrative discretion as it is 'primarily' concerned with future rights and duties.[185] In relation to the executive function to execute and maintain the Constitution and the laws of the Commonwealth, 'it will be necessary to make determinations of existing rights and duties' and 'at times a "controversy" may be involved and administrative proceedings may be provided so that the parties may be heard'.[186] However, such a determination will differ from judicial power to the extent that it lacks that critical element of finality, the 'quality of "conclusiveness"',[187] which belongs exclusively to it.

Zines's approach is expressed in reserved, restrained language, revealing an appropriate reticence in putting too fine a point on those aspects of the functions he describes as 'typical'. It is also marked by a consciousness of the limits of even this approach, making allowance for the impossibility of complete mutual exclusivity in definition. Zines thus stated:

> In the case of courts, for example, they have and do exercise discretions; they make law on a case by case basis, often taking policy considerations into account; in the case of rules of court they make law in the most direct manner; they exercise jurisdiction where no dispute or controversy is involved; they

---

[181]   Zines, *The High Court and the Constitution*, n 3 above, 220 ff.
[182]   *Ibid*, at 221.
[183]   *Ibid*, at 220.
[184]   *Ibid*, at 221. Although of course there is no constitutional bar either to retrospective or *ad hominem* legislation (as long as it is not an Act of Attainder): *Polyuchovich v Commonwealth* (1991) 172 CLR 501.
[185]   Zines, *The High Court and the Constitution*, n 3 above, 221.
[186]   *Ibid*.
[187]   *Ibid*.

make orders that concern the creation of new rights and impose new duties and are not merely the declaration or enforcement of existing rights and duties.[188]

Further, he noted that administrative bodies, typically administrative tribunals, 'exercise functions which seem indistinguishable from those exercisable by a court' in situations where they make 'determinations of law and fact that cannot be challenged in court proceedings' and courts 'have been given the task of applying standards that are so broad that they look like those appropriate to legislative or administrative discretion based on policy; these include such standards as "reasonable", "just", "oppressive"'.[189] Zines's conclusion on the above reflections is compelling:

> [I]n these matters the courts have been guided largely by history, the values involved in the separation of powers and by social policy; as well as by strict analysis. Indeed, in a sense, the concept of judicial power referred to above is itself derived from historical examination, that is, of what courts have done. From this has been distilled *those features that are pre-eminently or exclusively judicial, which have been arrived at by having regard to social values and the reasons for preserving the separateness of judicial power.* The flexibility of the approach of the High Court has therefore to some extent been achieved by distinguishing between the functions which can be conferred only on courts and functions which do not come into that category but which can be exercised by a court.[190] (Emphasis added.)

It thus seems possible at least to attempt a sufficiently precise definition by reliance on the identification of the 'typical' or 'pre-eminent' functions of each branch. Thus, in relation to judicial power, Zines was able to locate and articulate a definition containing the following elements:

> *the adjudication and conclusive settlement of a dispute between parties as to their rights and duties under the law*…The critical elements of the definition of judicial power is the existence of a controversy about rights, and critically, 'a binding and authoritative determination'.[191] (Emphasis added.)

It is precisely these elements in particular litigation that lie at the heart of judicial decisional independence and the particular concerns of this monograph. Zines, no formalist,[192] regards these elements as being 'at the core' of branch power and as 'critical elements' thereof.[193] Such a power,

---

[188] *Ibid* (citations omitted).
[189] *Ibid*, at 221–22 (citations omitted).
[190] *Ibid*, at 222.
[191] *Ibid*, at 220.
[192] Winterton also tends to favour the approach taken by Zines, although it would be quite inaccurate to place Zines and Winterton clearly within any 'school' on this matter. See G Winterton, *Parliament, the Executive and the Governor-General*, n 64 above, 60.
[193] Zines, *The High Court and the Constitution*, n 3 above, 220.

in its fullness, could only be vested in a court. Sawer had previously recognised these same features—'the conclusive decision of a dispute between two or more persons by a third person as to their legal rights, powers, privileges etc, the decision being governed by a legal standard assumed to exist before the decision is given'[194]—as constituting core judicial functions. Moreover, Sawer recognised these elements of judicial power as being, '[o]n a more empirical view ... the *non-transferable* part of judicial activity' (emphasis added).[195] If it is indeed possible to recognise such *'non-transferable'* elements of branch activity, the formalism/ functionalism divide certainly begins to narrow at the level where this becomes possible. Given the importance of such functions, formalism may come into its own with its insistence that no usurpation of such a complete power is permissible under the separation of powers. Although one cannot envisage functionalist compromises on this point in light of the significance of the power to the overall integrity of the branch, formalism's rigour does provide a surer safeguard at these fundamental levels.[196]

It is therefore possible to resolve —at least with respect to the particular issue of decisional independence—two critical interpretational issues. First, it is possible to achieve a sufficient degree of exclusivity in the definition of the core elements of judicial power and the boundaries thereto such as to make possible the consideration of the relevant constitutional limitations on legislative interference with judicial functions. Secondly, given that the elements of judicial power involved in decisional independence can be safely, and, as unequivocally as possible in these matters, be regarded as core—or 'non-transferable' in the words of Sawer—judicial functions, it is possible to define the relevant constitutional limitations with a degree of confidence that, whether a functionalist or formalist approach is taken, the result will be the same. Zines, with his espousal of a search for 'typical' (as opposed to 'exclusive') functions, was nevertheless able to conclude: 'If these three elements are present, that is, the function involves a conclusive

---

[194] Sawer, 'The Separation of Powers in Australian Federalism', n 68 above, 180.

[195] *Ibid*. These are the elements contained in the oft-quoted classic definition of judicial power of Griffith CJ in *Huddart Parker and Co Pty Ltd v Moorehead* (1909) 8 CLR 330 at 357: 'that power which every sovereign must of necessity have to decide controversies between its subjects, or between itself and its subjects, whether the rights relate to life, liberty or property. The exercise of this power does not begin until some tribunal which has power to give a binding and authoritative decision (whether subject to appeal or not) is called upon to take action'.

[196] Such attempts to distinguish core functions from incidental or secondary functions were made in *Federal Commissioner of Taxation v Munro* (1926) CLR 153, 176–9 (Isaacs J); and in *Boilermakers* in the judgments of Williams and Taylor JJ (dissenting) at 314–16 and 333–4, respectively. See also Ratnapala, *Australian Constitutional Law, Foundations and Theory*, n 65 above, 121 ff and his distinction between the 'umbra' and 'penumbra' of judicial power.

determination of a controversy about existing rights, the function belongs *exclusively* to the judiciary'[197] (emphasis added).

However, beyond the question of the separation of *judicial* power, the issue of identifying core branch functions becomes enormously difficult, especially in Westminster-style jurisdictions which maintain responsible government. In relation to legislative and executive power, because of the immense difficulty (if not impossibility) in defining conceptually the latter power in particular,[198] one is invariably reduced to resorting to the most mundane and straightforward aspects of each. For example, one can speak of the enactment of primary legislation, leaving aside the question of delegated legislation, within the institutional and procedural framework of parliament, as a core function of the legislative branch which cannot be usurped either by officers of the executive or by federal judges. In relation to executive power, one may refer to as 'core', 'the capacity to accomplish physical tasks within the limits of the law. For example, the government may … carry out public works on Crown land using funds already appropriated for the purpose by Parliament'.[199] As Professor Suri Ratnapala has pointed out, this 'is purely executive action that does not involve the making of a juristic decision', or indeed any exercise of the core function of the legislative branch.[200]

But are the elements relied upon to identify core branch functions so mundane, and their usurpation so unlikely, that the very exercise of identification becomes rather a sterile one? The centre of strife—where the great separation of powers issues contend, the hard cases of, say, delegated legislation, quasi-judicial/legislative administrative tribunals, arbitral bodies, *persona designata* scenarios—lies elsewhere. Referring to executive power, for example, Winterton pointed out that

> the functions performed by the executive branch clearly involve much more than the mere routine execution of enacted laws—the most obvious executive function—and include the exercise of a vast array of discretionary powers conferred by statute, some clearly legislative in character, some more akin to judicial powers, and generally carrying on the business of the government through the exercise of powers conferred by the Constitution, by statute or by the prerogative.[201]

Added to this is the concern that even the definition of the 'typical' can be an uncertain process, leading to considerable variation in opinion.

---

[197] Zines, *The High Court and the Constitution*, n 3 above, 221.
[198] See nn 219–222 below and accompanying text.
[199] Ratnapala, *Australian Constitutional Law, Foundations and Theory*, n 65 above, 102.
[200] *Ibid.*
[201] Winterton, *Parliament, the Executive and the Governor-General*, n 64 above, 67 (citations omitted).

It is suggested, and this is certainly not precluded by Zines' approach—indeed it is possibly even implied—that greater precision in defining the typical may be achieved by placing explicit reliance on the *procedural* or *institutional* context in which these typical functions are exercised. Thus, by the juxtaposition of the procedural/institutional with the purely functional aspect, a more refined position may be adopted with respect to defining core branch power. The leading American commentator, Redish, was an advocate of just such a juxtaposition, adopting a position very similar in many respects to that of Zines. Although Redish avoided the adoption of too doctrinaire a position, he nevertheless expressly located his separation of powers jurisprudence within the moderate (purposive) formalist school. Certainly, the unequivocal position of the separation of powers in the United States constitutional settlement permits a greater boldness in this regard. Redish accepted the central rationale of the formalist position: fear of a piecemeal destruction of the separation of powers if not strictly enforced, thus eroding the foundation of 'representative and accountable government' which 'has existed in a constant state of vulnerability'.[202] He thus advocated an 'interpretational model that will avoid the diluting impact that recent Supreme Court doctrine has sometimes had on the beneficial protective force of separation of powers'.[203] This 'model' he referred to as a 'type' of 'formalistic approach', 'one grounded on the deceptively simple principle that no branch may be permitted to exercise *any* authority definitionally found to fall outside its constitutionally delimited powers'.[204]

Redish did not discount the major criticism of formalism, that is, the problem of definition. Indeed he was critical of the 'classic' textual formalist method with its 'originalistic and/or rigidly syllogistic approach to the definition of branch power'.[205] He thus drew a distinction between 'epistemological' formalism and his own brand of 'pragmatic' formalism, the former representing 'a commitment to a rigidity and level of abstraction that is quite probably not possible and certainly unwise'.[206] Explaining his own position, he stated:

> 'Pragmatic formalism,' on the other hand, is a 'street-smart' mode of interpretation, growing out of a recognition of the dangers to which a more 'functional' or 'balancing' analysis in the separation-of-powers context may give rise. It recognizes that once a reviewing court begins down those roads in the

---

[202] Redish, *The Constitution as Political Structure*, n 81 above, 100.
[203] *Ibid.*
[204] *Ibid.*
[205] Redish sets out at length the sources of the critiques of formalism. See the text and accompanying notes in Redish, *The Constitution as Political Structure* (n 81 above) 100; and Redish, 'Federal Judicial Independence', n 83 above, 710.
[206] Redish, *The Constitution as Political Structure*, n 81 above, 100.

enforcement of separation of powers, no meaningful limitations on interbranch usurpation of power remain. More importantly, it recognizes that even if functionalism and balancing could be employed with principled limitation, any such interpretational approach inherently guts the prophylactic nature of separation-of-powers protections, so essential a part of that system.[207]

Thus it is a 'pragmatism' based on a 'prophylactic' rationale which brings him into the formalist camp in the first place, there being 'no conceivable alternative which adequately guards against the dangers that the system of separation of powers was adopted to avoid'.[208] Significantly, this pragmatism is brought into the very definition of branch functions so that the 'imposition of rigid, abstract interpretational formulas'[209] based on etymological analysis is eschewed and an approach is adopted that approximates to that favoured by Zines and Winterton. That is, it is an approach based on

> a combination of policy, tradition, precedent, and linguistic analysis. Presumably, within certain linguistic boundaries, the definitions may evolve over time, much as the definitions of other constitutional terms have. The key point, however, is that no matter how the terms are ultimately defined, the *exercise of each branch's power is to be limited to the functions definitionaly brought within those concepts.* In that sense, the powers of each branch would be 'formally' separated from the powers of the other branches.[210] (Emphasis added.)

Redish thus clearly set out to meet the definitional imperatives of the separation of powers doctrine as entrenched constitutional rule, while at the same time addressing both the limitations of a rigid abstract and etymological approach, on the one hand, and that of a purely functionalist approach standing alone, on the other. His approach is well summed up in the following passage:

> It might be argued that the inclusion within the definitional analysis of pragmatic factors effectively allows sufficient manipulability to enable the Supreme Court to employ a form of functional balancing under the guise of a definitional analysis. In a sense, of course, this is correct since purely as a practical matter the Court … may ultimately say anything it wants. But the Court's good-faith adoption of the pragmatic formalist model would go far towards confining the unlimited flexibility inherent in a purely functional or balancing model. Though there will no doubt be close cases, both historical tradition and linguistic common sense will impose restrictions on the Court's use of purely pragmatic factors in its separation-of-powers analysis. To be sure, a Court *not* acting in good faith could manipulate the suggested standard into

---

[207] *Ibid.*
[208] *Ibid*, at 101.
[209] *Ibid.*
[210] *Ibid*, at 101. For a detailed statement of the pragmatic formalist approach, see Redish and Cisar, '"If Angels were to govern", n 81 above.

meaninglessness. But that is just as true of any conceivable doctrinal standard, for the interpretation of any constitutional provision.[211]

Redish appears to have achieved reconciliation between formalism and functionalism by achieving definitional clarity at a certain fundamental level, heavy reliance being placed on judicial attempts at definition. However, as with the Zines approach above, the factors which Redish relies upon to determine meaning, as well as the pragmatic aspect to definition, are still susceptible to considerable uncertainty, especially in that area between the branches where a blurring of the distinctions necessarily occurs.[212] In hard cases, even pursuant to Redish's pragmatic formalism, it would be preferable if additional factors were expressly identified to assist in the definition of those elements which are core, or essential elements, and which under no circumstances can be allowed to be usurped or intermingled with the powers exercised by another branch.

It is for this reason that the writer returns to the point made above that use can and should be made of the relevant procedural and institutional context in which branch functions are commonly, or usually, exercised as part of the attempt to locate what is essential and exclusive to each branch. Thus, for example, while is can be said that judges do 'make law' in the process of declaring it or interpreting it, their role in this regard is passive, limited by the fact that they do so within the procedural parameters of litigation, limited by the legal issues raised by the parties, by precedent and guided by other legal authority. Their law-making role is thus incidental to the declaration of rights and obligations pursuant to existing law in the resolution of a particular legal dispute in legal proceedings. Similarly, while parliament may delegate in certain circumstances some part of its law-making function to the executive, the making of delegated legislation would be ancillary to the executive's primary, essential role of executing the laws. It is inconceivable that parliament could abrogate its legislative functions entirely, or that civil servants (or judges) could replace members of parliament to enact primary legislation pursuant to normal parliamentary procedure—surely a core legislative function which, in its procedural and institutional context, cannot be abrogated or usurped. In relation to the typical judicial function of deciding legal controversies finally and conclusively, the legislature may, for example, overrule a decision by enacting legislation which changes the law. However, it cannot itself review, in the manner of an appeal court, the outcome of a decision as between the parties or order a retrial

---

[211] Redish, *The Constitution as Political Structure*, n 81 above, 101–2.
[212] See n 69 above, referring to the difficulties emerging in *R v Quinn: Ex parte Consolidated Foods Corporation* (1977) 138 CLR 1.

or revision of a final judgment.[213] This would be an indisputable usurpation of a core judicial function, which would constitute a breach of the separation of powers under both a formalist or functionalist approach, although the protection of the position is more certain in the hands of the formalists.

This juxtaposition of the conceptual with the procedural and institutional received the very considerable support of Vile who noted that while on the one hand 'it is not possible to allocate particular functions exclusively to each branch of government', on the other,

> it is possible to say that there is a function which is more appropriate to a particular procedure, to attempt to restrict each branch to particular *procedures*, and therefore to make one function the dominant concern of the branch. In a sense this is the aim of those who espoused the 'functionalist' tendency on the Supreme Court in recent years, but they have attempted to achieve it without setting out a clear basis for their decisions.

> Thus we can accept that the rule-making function is exercised in some degree by all branches of government but nevertheless assert that the legislature should be concerned only with rule-making of a general kind and that the rules it makes should be binding on both the policy branch and the administration and subject to being over-ruled by the judiciary only on the grounds of their having offended against certain basic constitutional principles.[214]

Redish also supported this juxtaposition and posited a similar solution, noting that

> legislative power includes only the authority to promulgate generalised standards and requirements of citizen behaviour or to dispense benefits, for the purpose of achieving, maintaining, or avoiding particular social policy results. So broadly phrased, of course, such a standard could conceivably be employed to describe the functions performed by the judicial and executive branches as well. However, *the difference is the structural 'baggage'* that the exercise of the judicial and executive powers are required to carry—baggage which does not affix itself to the legislative power. The judicial branch may establish such rules of behavior only in the context of the performance of the 'traditional' judicial function of the adjudication of live cases or controversies. Indeed, that it is, at least to a large extent, the procedural and structural context in which a policy

---

[213]   This is a fundamental proposition, even though no legislation has been held invalid by the High Court precisely on this basis. Quick and Garran put it succinctly: 'the legislature may overrule a decision, though it may not reverse it' (*The Annotated Constitution of the Australian Commonwealth*, n 148 above, 722). Nevertheless, it is a proposition which emerges clearly from the classic definitions of judicial power above-mentioned (above nn 8, 191–194 and accompanying text)). Moreover, the US Supreme Court in *Plaut v Spendthrift Farm Inc* 514 US 211 (1995), invalidated legislation on this point. See Winterton, 'The Separation of Judicial Power as an Implied Bill of Rights', n 5 above, 199 and see also for elaboration on this issue from a comparative perspective chs 4 and 5 of this book.

[214]   Vile, *Constitutionalism and The Separation of Powers*, n 61 above, 415–16.

choice is made—rather than the substance of that choice—that distinguishes the legislative and judicial functions is demonstrated by the fact that, on non-constitutional issues, Congress may overrule judicially created substantive rules that have been fashioned in the context of the case adjudication.[215] (Emphasis added.)

Similarly with respect to the executive:

> The executive branch, on the other hand (with exceptions specified by the Constitution), is confined to the function of 'executing' the law. Such a function inherently presupposes a pre-existing 'law' to be executed. Thus, the executive branch is, in the exercise of its 'executive' power, confined to the development of means for enforcing legislation already in existence. Hence, every exercise of executive power not grounded in another of the executive's enumerated powers must be properly characterized as enforcement of existing legislation. It should be emphasised that this requirement in no way implies that the executive branch's power should somehow be confined to the performance of 'ministerial' functions, bereft of any room for the exercise of creativity, judgment or discretion. All it means is that, unless some other specifically delegated executive branch power applies, the executive branch must be exercising that creativity, judgment, or discretion in an 'implementational' context. In other words, the executive branch must be interpreting and/or enforcing a legislative choice or judgment; its actions cannot amount to the exercise of free-standing legislative power.[216]

The examples provided by Vile and Redish above do furnish a very significant basis for establishing core functions even for the legislative and executive powers within these institutional procedural parameters. This is particular significant for the principal concern of this monograph, viz, the decisional independence of the judicial branch as defined above. Applying the juxtaposition of the conceptual definition with the procedural/institutional context, the judicial functions which are sought to be protected by the maintenance of decisional independence, given that they relate precisely to adjudicative role of the courts in particular litigation, must be regarded as core functions. So put, the major critique of the functionalist opposed to the formalist position—the impossibility of mutually exclusive definition—begins to melt away.

But not entirely. In the Australian context, for example, this approach can only be taken with any degree of confidence with respect to the separation of judicial power and legislative power. The leading authority on executive power, Winterton, is not so confident when it comes to that power, and indeed the separation of the non-judicial powers from each other. In his seminal work, Winterton noted that, on the one hand, '"[c]ore"/"incidents" analysis is useful in resolving issues relating to the

---

[215]   Redish, *The Constitution as Political Structure*, n 81 above, 117.
[216]   *Ibid.*

judicial power of the Commonwealth because courts have recognised that certain functions are inherently "judicial" in nature'.[217] 'This is true', he continued, 'in the Anglo-American context because Australian and American courts … perform the functions traditionally exercised by the Royal Courts of Justice at Westminster'.[218] The same could be said in relation to the exercise of legislative power by Westminster-style parliaments. However, when it comes to the executive power, Winterton's observations make any attempt at even a core definition very difficult if not impossible:

> [E]ven in a purely Anglo-American context there are no functions *inherently* 'executive' in nature. Besides referring to powers expressly or impliedly granted by the constitution, 'executive power' in abstract is meaningless; *its content depends entirely upon the frame of reference employed to determine the scope of executive power*….The futility of attempting to define the ambit of federal executive power by allusion to abstract notions of 'executive power' and not by reference merely to expressly conferred powers and the prerogative is demonstrated by the poor result of endeavours to do so; the conclusion reached is the apparently tautologous one that 'executive' functions are those governmental functions which are neither 'legislative' nor 'judicial'. This 'definition' is not only unhelpful but also unsatisfactory because it ignores 'secondary' or 'incidental' functions which may be exercised by more than one branch. Moreover, a generalisation from this formulation of executive power can lead to the dangerous notion that the executive may do whatever it is not forbidden to do. This conceit cannot be maintained in Australia, where the scope of 'the executive power of the Commonwealth' conferred by s 61 of the Constitution is determined by reference to the prerogative, which cannot mark the boundary between legislative and executive powers because it is inherently subject to legislation.[219] (Emphasis added.)

Winterton has further pointed out, compellingly, that any attempt, even by such an eminent figure as Sir Owen Dixon, to enforce a strict legal separation of executive and legislative power has foundered on the shores of responsible government, the implications of which cannot be limited purely to the political sphere.[220] If nothing else, the fact that responsible government is itself constitutionally established prevents its relegation to the purely political sphere.[221] Be that as it may, both American and Australian courts have not maintained a strict separation of the power from legislative power as witnessed by the accommodations

---

[217] Winterton, *Parliament, the Executive and the Governor-General*, n 64 above, 69.
[218] *Ibid*.
[219] *Ibid*, at 70 (citations omitted).
[220] *Ibid*, at 65; G Winterton, 'The Relationship Between Commonwealth Legislative and Executive Power' (2004) 25 *Adelaide Law Review* 21 at 37.
[221] *Ibid*, at 37; Winterton, *Parliament, the Executive and the Governor-General*, n 64 above, 66.

relating to delegated legislation and the vesting of executive power in bodies other than the executive.[222] 'Indeed', as Winterton has pointed out, 'in not a single case has the High Court invalidated legislation for contravening the separation between legislative and executive power'.[223]

Leaving aside the complex issue of executive power, what fundamental principles therefore can be established with respect to the primary concerns here, judicial and legislative power? Before examining the cases in detail in the chapters which follow, the following introductory remarks can be made.

As for legislative power, its definition is relatively straightforward. As SA de Smith pointed out, '[t]he term "legislative" does not give rise to a great deal of difficulty in practice, for most of us can recognise legislation when we see it'.[224] Thus, it was described by him variously as the power which consisted of 'making rules of general application with prospective effect [without precluding *ad hominen* and/or retrospective rules]'[225] or 'the creation and promulgation of a general rule of conduct without reference to particular cases'.[226] Ratnapala noted that the 'most unambiguous feature of legislative power is its capacity to change existing legal relations'.[227] But it is clear from the various examples mentioned above, that, so defined, this power cannot be hermetically sealed off in the hands of Parliament given the licence granted to the Executive with respect to delegated legislation, the making by judges of 'rules of court,' the fact that judges sometimes 'make law'[228] when deciding cases (even when ostensibly they are declaring it or interpreting it),[229] and the fact that, as de Smith pointed out, 'the boundary line between a not very "general" legislative rule and particular administrative decisions affecting many people can become so blurred as to be imperceptible'.[230] However, if reliance is placed on the institutional and procedural factors accompanying the 'typical' exercise of legislative power—that is, the

---

[222] *Ibid*, at 101–10; Winterton, 'The Relationship Between Commonwealth Legislative and Executive Power', n 220 above, 38.

[223] *Ibid*, at 38.

[224] SA de Smith and R Brazier, *Constitutional and Administrative Law*, 7th edn (London, Penguin Books 1994) 582.

[225] *Ibid*.

[226] Quoted in Ratnapala, *Australian Constitutional Law, Foundations and Theory*, n 65 above, in SA de Smith, *Judicial Review of Administrative Action*, 4th edn (London, Stevens and Sons, 1980) 71 at 90.

[227] Ratnapala, *Australian Constitutional Law, Foundations and Theory*, n 65 above, 90.

[228] Above n 170, at 2.

[229] Although see Ratnapala, *Australian Constitutional Law, Foundations and Theory*, n 65 above, 91 for a discussion of the differences between judicial 'law-making' and the making of law by legislatures.

[230] De Smith and Brazier, *Constitutional and Administrative Law*, n 224 above, 582. In the Australian context, decisions of the Industrial Relations Commission, to take a prominent example, and like quasi-judicial/quasi legislative bodies, would fit into this category.

enactment of primary legislation by Parliament pursuant to proper parliamentary procedure—this power can be regarded as such a core and fundamental exercise of legislative power that its absolute protection in the hands of the legislative branch can be supported by the adoption of a purposive formalist approach. That is not to deny that pursuant to functionalism the inter-branch violation of such a power would almost inevitably lead to separation of powers censure.

Turning to judicial power, and applying the same juxtaposition of the conceptual with the procedural/institutional context, the following principles can be derived from the separation of powers. The most fundamental principle is that judicial power and power incidental thereto (defined pursuant to the core definition above-recognised by courts and leading scholars)[231] may only be vested in the judicial branch.[232] This principle remains undisputed and uncontroversial as a principle to be derived from the separation of powers. However, it does not necessarily follow that the courts can only be vested with judicial power (for the above-mentioned reasons)[233] and the extent to which this principle applies will depend on how the pure the separation doctrine is in any particular jurisdiction. However, the fears of the formalists[234] of a piecemeal erosion of the independence of the judicial branch from the influence of the political branches should not be discounted. An Act of Attainder, on the other hand, as a clear usurpation of judicial power, would clearly breach the separation of powers doctrine; so would any attempt by the non-judicial branches directly to intervene in legal proceedings before a court to direct an outcome[235] or to review a final decision in the manner of an appeal court, amending final orders, ordering retrials, or hearing legal disputes at first instance (beyond the narrow exceptions outlined above based on usage).[236]

These principles are the point of departure for this monograph and only provide assistance to a limited degree to the more precise issue of the decisional independence of the judicial branch. The relegation of the formalist approach to core aspects of branch power, and then only to judicial and legislative power, however, leaves very little room for its operation. The most difficult separation of powers problems do not normally arise when branch power is being exercised in its traditional institutional setting. It is when there is a degree of dislocation of the

---

[231] See nn 8, 191–194 above and accompanying text.
[232] Above nn 100, 178.
[233] See nn 110–127 above and accompanying text.
[234] See nn 77–81 above and accompanying text.
[235] See chs 2 and 3 of this book where this issue is treated in more detail.
[236] This was a rather frequent occurrence in pre-Constitution America and a major catalyst for constitutional entrenchment of the separation of powers doctrine. See above, at 10ff.

relevant function—such as delegated legislation and administrative tribunals—from such a setting that problems arise. Therefore, to say that at the *limited* level of core functions a (purposive) formalist approach should be adopted is of little assistance in the resolution of this larger problem. However, formalism will provide a surer protection to those branch functions which, within their institutional setting, are so fundamental as to be deserving of it. While this role may be regarded as minor, that is so because it is unlikely that egregious interferences with branch power will occur. On the other hand, if a broader historical view is taken, it could be said that this very unlikelihood is all the more reason to insist upon formalist rigour, to ensure that it remains an unlikelihood. It is worth recalling that just such interventions and usurpations of core branch power are historical realities, not mere hypotheticals. Indeed such egregious interferences with judicial power did not occur in the distant past only, as evidenced by the *Burmah Oil* case and in the *Plaut* case, decided in 1965 and in 1995 respectively. Moreover, it is worth noting that while the interference in the former case could not be invalidated, that in the latter could be held unconstitutional because it occurred in a jurisdiction which entrenched the separation of powers and the majority judges adopted a purposive formalist approach to the doctrine in relation to this core aspect of judicial power.

In conclusion therefore, leaving aside the vexed question of executive power (where it seems that there is no alternative than to adopt a purposive functionalist approach assuming its legal separation is entrenched), it is possible to reach the following conclusions. First, the proper level of operation of the purposive formalist approach is the level of core legislative and judicial powers, the main instances of which were mentioned above. It is at this level that formalism's concern for piecemeal erosion of the values upheld by the doctrine must be taken seriously and therefore applied with rigour. In this context, it cannot be denied that formalism does constitute a surer safeguard. Secondly, it may be stated that at such a fundamental level, it is inconceivable that even pursuant to a purposive functional approach any allowances would be made for inter-branch intrusions. This is because the negative effect on the integrity of branch power would certainly reach the requisite level of intensity to trigger functionalism's rejection of it. To the extent that that is the case, one might posit the disappearance of the formalist/functionalist divide at this level. That is, it seems a reasonable proposition that whichever approach is taken, the result would be the same. However, this latter conclusion breaks down because, as has been shown in the United States cases, it is not possible to have complete confidence in functionalism in this regard. To name but the most glaring example, in *Plaut v Spendthrift*

Farm Inc,[237] legislative *direction* to federal courts to reinstate (on the plaintiff's motion) individual civil actions for securities fraud (under federal legislation) which had previously been dismissed by these courts as statute-barred—a clear breach of core judicial power, given that the legislation simply mandated this re-opening in disregard of the courts' inherent discretion in such instances[238]—was nevertheless held by two dissenting judges, adopting functionalist reasoning, not to be a breach of the separation of powers doctrine.[239] Only one judge, who adopted a functionalist approach, concurred with the majority who, adopting a purposive formalist approach, found this to be a breach of the inviolability of the final judgment of federal courts and thus a clear and fundamental violation of the separation of judicial power. Given the undeniably core nature of the judicial functions involved in the making by the federal courts of final decisions, which surely must be rendered inviolable from inter-branch interference under the separation of powers doctrine,[240] this dissent undermined the confidence expressed above that a functionalist approach will also protect these core and fundamental branch functions. The (formalist) majority reasoning in that case, even if one may not concur entirely with the strength of the language used by Scalia J in expressing it, certainly inspires greater confidence that core branch functions will be protected and, as a result, so will the values underlying the separation of powers. If such a core aspect of judicial power cannot be guaranteed pursuant to a functionalist approach, then there can only be resort to formalist reasoning, for purposive reasons. This is the approach which will be tested in the chapters which follow dealing with the precise issue of the decisional independence of the judicial branch.

---

[237] *Plaut v Spendthrift Farm Inc* 514 US 211 (1995).

[238] See K Mason, 'The Inherent Jurisdiction of the Court' (1983) 57 *Australian Law Journal* 449; P de Jersey, 'The Inherent Jurisdiction of the Supreme Court' (1985) 15 *Queensland Law Society Journal* 325 at 351; W Lacey, 'Inherent Jurisdiction, Judicial Power and Implied Guarantees Under Chapter III of the Constitution' (2003) 31 *Federal Law Review* 57 at 63.

[239] Stevens J, with whom Ginsburg J joined: *Plaut v Spendthrift Farm Inc* 514 US 211 (1995) at 246.

[240] This is not to deny the inherent jurisdiction of courts to consider the re-opening of final judgments at their own discretion: above n 238.

2

Legislative Interference in the Pending Case Scenario: The Foundation of Principle and the Australian Position

I. INTRODUCTION

THIS CHAPTER AND the following will focus on those jurisdictions which have an entrenched separation of powers doctrine in a written constitution. Particular emphasis will be placed on the constitutions of the Commonwealth of Australia and the United States of America. It will examine the intentions of the respective framers of those constitutions and the views of their early constitutional scholars as to the significance of this entrenchment for the *decisional* independence of the judicial branch. It will commence by establishing the primary importance of this issue to separation of powers jurisprudence. Reference will be made to the fact that a key catalyst for the original entrenchment of the separation of powers in the United States Constitution was precisely the concern to prevent legislative interference with pending and decided cases. It will then focus on the development of jurisprudence on the issue in Australia to provide a basis for establishing the key principles and the main issues which have arisen. The following chapter will continue with an analysis of the United States jurisprudence and that of other relevant jurisdictions with an entrenched separation of powers

II. THE AUSTRALIAN CONSTITUTIONAL POSITION AND THE EARLY AUSTRALIAN CONSTITUTIONAL SCHOLARS

Although the separation of powers first emerged as an influential constitutional principle in the writings of John Locke,[1] an explicit recognition of

---

[1] In his *Second Treatise on Government* (1689). Cf E Barendt, 'Separation of Powers and Constitutional Government' [1995] *Public Law* 599 at 601, referring to the views of Shackleton that Locke did not regard the separation of powers as fundamental. R Shackleton, 'Montesquieu, Bolingbroke, and the Separation of Powers' (1949) *French Studies* 25.

the need *legally* to entrench that doctrine cannot be found in the broader tradition of British constitutionalism. This was the case even after the judiciary achieved the status of a co-equal branch of government in the writings of Blackstone.[2] Following Blackstone's *Commentaries* and Dicey's *Law of the Constitution*, the primary principles of parliamentary supremacy and responsible government have constituted the pillars of the prevailing constitutional ethos, and it is with these that the separation of powers has had to come to an uneasy accommodation. This has been especially the case with respect to the issue of limitations on legislative power inherent in judicial review of legislative action, the independence of the judiciary and protections of the integrity of the judicial process.[3] Consequently, the separation doctrine continues to remain influential as a convention, or underlying (non-entrenched) constitutional principle, whose precise influence remains uncertain.[4] The main concern in the United Kingdom, and other Westminster-style jurisdictions, remains the maintenance of an independent judiciary in terms of its 'institutional independence' (security of tenure and remuneration), as opposed to 'decisional independence' and its discrete requirements.[5] The creation of the new Supreme Court to replace the Judicial Committee of the House of Lords by the Constitutional Reform Act 2005 (UK), and its separation from Parliament, continued in this tradition. That Act eschewed the adoption of a United States Supreme Court model and a strict legal separation of judicial power. Indeed, the proposals leading to its enactment expressly rejected the doctrine of judicial review of legislation. The Consultation Paper produced by the Department for Constitutional Affairs stated that '[i]n our democracy, Parliament is supreme. There is no separate body of constitutional law which takes precedence over all other law'.[6]

The constitutional position in Australia at the federal level constitutes a departure from this Westminster tradition in relation to its treatment of the separation of powers. Although that doctrine sits uneasily with the principle of responsible government, the High Court of Australia has

---

[2] MJC Vile, *Constitutionalism and the Separation of Powers*, 2nd edn (Indianapolis, Liberty Fund, 1998) 59–60, 67, 86–8, 96, 103–5.

[3] W Blackstone, *Commentaries on the Laws of the England* (1765, London, reprinted by Dawsons of Pall Mall, 1966); AV Dicey, *Law of the Constitution*, 8th edn (London, Macmillan & Co, 1915). See G Winterton, 'The British Grundnorm: Parliamentary Supremacy Reexamined' (1976) 92 *Law Quarterly Review* 591.

[4] See ch 6 at 272.

[5] As in, for example, the Act of Settlement 1701 (UK) and the Constitutional Reform Act 2005 (UK).

[6] Department for Constitutional Affairs, *Constitutional Reform: A Supreme Court for the United Kingdom* (July 2003). For a complete collection of consultation papers, proposal and reports, see the website of the UK Department of Constitutional Affairs, www.dca.gov.uk/constitution/holref/holrefindex.htm.

nevertheless held that it has been constitutionally entrenched by implication from the structure of the Constitution, which separately vests the legislative, executive and judicial power.[7] Unlike the relationship between legislative and executive power,[8] the High Court has adopted a more formal approach to the separation of judicial power, an approach confirmed by the Privy Council.[9] This is despite the fact that it is very doubtful that the Framers of the Constitution, unlike their American counterparts, intended such an outcome.[10] There is certainly no explicit particular concern with the maintenance of the decisional independence of the Chapter III courts. Nevertheless, that the separation of powers was legally entrenched in the Constitution, that it had particular importance in limiting the power of the legislature vis-à-vis the judiciary and that this resulted in the strict separation of the judicial power are beyond doubt following the *Boilermakers* decision.[11]

This view of an entrenched separation of powers was supported by the early constitutional commentators. Harrison Moore stated that 'between legislative and executive power on the one hand, and judicial power on the other, there is a great cleavage',[12] a sentiment echoed in the early decisions of the High Court which held that the judicial power of the

---

[7]   *R v Kirby; Ex Parte Boilermakers' Society of Australia* (1956) 94 CLR 254 (*Boilermakers*). The Australian courts have followed the lead of the United States in this regard, where this legal entrenchment was inferred from the structure of its Constitution which expressly and separately vests the executive, legislative and judicial power in the President, Congress and the Supreme Court (and other federal courts) respectively (Art I, s 1; Art II, s 1; Art III, s 1). This structure is mirrored in ss 1 (legislative power), 61 (executive power) and 71 (judicial power) of the Australian Constitution. See L Zines, *The High Court and the Constitution*, 5th edn (Sydney, Federation Press, 2008) ch 10; G Sawer, 'The Separation of Powers in Australian Federalism' (1961) *Australian Law Journal* 177; F Wheeler, 'Original Intent and the Doctrine of the Separation of Powers in Australia' (1996) 7 *Public Law Review* 96 at 97, who cites the following as examples of this tendency to draw out the full implications of the doctrine: *R v Davison* (1954) 90 CLR 353 at 380–81 (Kitto J); *R v Trade Practices Tribunal; Ex parte Tasmanian Breweries Pty Ltd* (1970) 123 CLR 361 at 392 (Windeyer J); *Polyukhovich v Commonwealth* (1991) 172 CLR 501 at 618 and 623 (Deane J).

[8]   See generally Zines, *The High Court and the Constitution*, n 7 above, ch 10.

[9]   *Boilermakers* (1956) 94 CLR 254; affirmed *sub nom Attorney-General for Australia v R* (1957) 95 CLR 529.

[10]   This has been carefully explored in Wheeler, 'Original Intent and the Doctrine of the Separation of Powers in Australia', n 7 above. See also Sawer, 'The Separation of Powers in Australian Federalism', n 7 above.

[11]   See *Boilermakers* (1956) 94 CLR 254, especially at 275–6 and 297 (Dixon CJ, McTiernan, Fullagar and Kitto JJ). This was merely a consolidation and confirmation of earlier authority: See *Huddart, Parker & Co Pty Ltd v Moorehead* (1909) 8 CLR 330 at 335 (Griffith CJ): '[T]he parliament has no power to entrust the exercise of the judicial power to any other hands'. Cf G Sawer, 'The Separation of Powers in Australian Federalism', n 7 above, 178. For a thorough analysis of developments in this regard preceding the milestone *Boilermakers* case see Zines, *The High Court and the Constitution'*, n 7 above, 208.

[12]   WH Moore, *The Constitution of the Commonwealth of Australia*, 2nd edn (Melbourne, Maxwell, 1910) 101.

Commonwealth was the exclusive preserve of the Chapter III courts.[13] Moore emphasised the establishment of the institution of judicial review as a powerful check on legislative activity, which check arose directly from the legal separation of judicial power.[14] The novelty of this development was not lost on Moore. The normal state of affairs within the British sphere at that time rendered the separation of powers 'no more than a rule of expediency subject to political sanctions'.[15] 'Whereas, in Australia', he continued, 'the doctrine had the sanction of law and could be used to check legislative power'.[16] Accordingly, there was a heightened appreciation of the constitutional limitations which had thus arisen:

> The rule which assigns the judicial power of the Commonwealth to Courts is thus a safeguard against arbitrary power more important than at first appears and imposing restrictions upon the power of Parliament more extensive than is at first realised.[17]

Moore noted that these constitutional limitations extended beyond the more obvious institutional usurpations of judicial power by Parliament to include limitations on its powers in relation to otherwise properly enacted legislation:

> It is not merely that the Legislature may not constitute itself or any other body unauthorised by the Constitution, a Court of justice with functions which might be validly performed by a Court regularly constituted, i.e. the determination, after hearing, of rights according to law. *If this were all that is imported by the separation of powers, it would be of small importance legally, for a power of this nature is very rarely usurped by a Legislature.* The temptation to which Legislatures are liable, to which American Legislatures have succumbed, and which American Courts have met by the allegation of an invasion of judicial power, is to apply a new rule to past acts or events, or to deal with a specific matter of injury or wrong independently of all rule. However mischievous and dangerous may be *ex post facto* laws and *privilegia*, their very mischief lies in the fact that *they are something other than judicial acts*; that what should have been done in a judicial way and according to law has been done by the assumption of arbitrary power.[18] (Emphasis added.)

---

[13] *New South Wales v Commonwealth* (*Wheat* case) (1915) 20 CLR 54; *Waterside Workers' Federation of Australia v JW Alexander Ltd* (1918) 25 CLR 434 (*Alexander's* case) confirmed in *Boilermakers* and in *Re Wakim; Ex parte McNally* (1999) 198 CLR 511. This is based on the requirement in s 71 of the Constitution that '[t]he judicial power of the Commonwealth shall be vested in ... the High Court of Australia and in such other federal courts as the Parliament creates'.

[14] He wrote, '[the] duty of passing upon the validity of Acts whether of the Commonwealth or of the State Parliament exists purely as an incident of judicial power': Moore, *The Constitution of the Commonwealth of Australia*, n 12 above, 361.

[15] *Ibid*, at 93.

[16] *Ibid*, at 96.

[17] *Ibid*, at 322.

[18] *Ibid*.

The significance of this early recognition that Parliament may usurp judicial power under the guise of otherwise properly enacted legislation, and that there was a need to examine the substantive nature of legislation, should not be underestimated. He did not, however, elaborate on the nature of the limitations on Parliament or on what he meant by dealing with 'a specific matter independently of all rule'. He stated merely that

> [t]he grant of judicial power to a special organ means that if the matter be done which from its nature is proper for judicial determination alone, the Legislature cannot deal with it otherwise, or authorise anyone, even a Court properly constituted, to deal with it except in the way of adjudication.[19]

Moore's awareness of the novel implications of a legal entrenchment of the separation doctrine was echoed in the writings of Inglis Clark who noted that

> the provisions of the Constitution ... which distributively and categorically vest the legislative, the executive, and the judicial powers in three separate organs of government, impose upon the legislative authority of the Parliament of the Commonwealth a legal limitation which does not exist in regard to the Parliament of any other portion of the British Empire.[20]

He opined that legal entrenchment had particular significance for the power of Parliament, compromising the supremacy it enjoyed within the Westminster tradition at a time when the influence of Dicey was at its peak:

> [I]f this explicit distribution of distinct governmental powers is to have any legal and substantial results in the exercise of them, the Parliament of the Commonwealth is clearly prohibited from assuming either executive or judicial functions.[21]

The doctrine thus became the source of constitutional limitations on the power of Parliament,[22] establishing judicial review of both legislative and executive action, which could be thus invalidated. The High Court became 'the final arbiter within the Commonwealth of the limits of its

---

[19] *Ibid*, at 322–3.
[20] A Inglis Clark, *Studies in Australian Constitutional Law* (1901, reprinted St Leonards, NSW, Legal Books, 1997) 30–31. He went on to emphasise that 'within the limits of the British Empire it is only in the Constitution of the Commonwealth of Australia that such a distribution of governmental functions is made by a written organic law' (at 28). As noted in ch 1 of this book, the position of the constitutional scholars on this point has not been unequivocal. The Canadian Constitution (British North America Act, 1867, 30 & 31 Vict c 3 (Imp) (renamed the Constitution Act, 1867)) has not been interpreted as incorporating the principle of the separation of powers. See *Attorney-General for Ontario v Attorney-General for Canada* [1912] AC 571.
[21] *Ibid*, at 33.
[22] *Ibid*, at 36.

own functions and of the question of whether any encroachment upon its jurisdiction has been made or attempted by the Parliament or the Crown'.[23] He maintained, like Moore, the need for a rigorous examination of legislative action to ensure that it did not extend beyond its boundaries, especially when it was entering the proper realms of judicial power.[24] He emphasised the passive nature of the latter to reinforce the need for its special protection.[25]

The following particular limitations on the legislature were emphasised by Inglis Clark: First, 'after a law has been made and promulgated the Parliament cannot control its operation otherwise than by altering it'.[26] This was an early recognition of the fundamental premise underlying the Changed Law Rule. Secondly,

> [t]he Parliament can at any time alter or repeal any law which it has made; but the alteration or repeal *must be effected by an exercise of the legislative power*, because that is the only power possessed by the Parliament, and any attempt on the part of the Parliament to do *anything which would not be an exercise of legislative power* would not be a law, and therefore would not be binding on the Judiciary or on any person in the Commonwealth.[27] (Emphasis added.)

This second observation is particularly germane for present purposes. Clark perceived that there would be a breach of the separation of powers if Parliament acted in a way which was other than 'an exercise of legislative power', whether or not that action could properly be defined as belonging precisely to one of the non-legislative branches. While it is trite to observe that the legislature is limited to exercising a power that is properly 'legislative'—that is, a change in the law by properly enacted legislation—Clark made the very significant and often overlooked observation that the opposite might in fact be a possibility. That is, Parliament might seek to control a law's operation by means other than by altering it; by means that are other than legislative. This failure to act in a substantively legislative manner may result in a breach of the separation of powers. The concern is not necessarily the fact that Parliament was abrogating in any particular instance all, or indeed any, of the hallmarks of judicial power; merely that it was not exercising a power or function which was *legislative*.

This critical realisation constitutes the foundation for any limitation on legislative interference with judicial functions in the pending case. Clark gave the following example pertinent to the pending case scenario:

---

[23]   *Ibid*, at 33.
[24]   *Ibid*, at 37–8.
[25]   This power 'cannot operate until a law is in existence for enforcement or exposition' (*ibid*, at 38).
[26]   *Ibid*.
[27]   *Ibid*.

A new rule of conduct may be prescribed by the Parliament by the repeal or the alteration of an existing law, but any exposition of the purport of the language of an existing law, or any declaration of the existence of any rights or liabilities as the result of its enactment, *is not an exercise of legislative power*; and if any such exposition or declaration is made by the Parliament *in the shape of apparent legislation*, it is an attempted encroachment on the provinces of the Judiciary and is therefore invalid, if the explicit distribution of the legislative, the executive and the judicial powers made by the Constitution is to be enforced as part of the supreme law of the Commonwealth.[28] (Emphasis added.)

This statement of principle was not limited to the pending case scenario. It extended to any situation where the Parliament attempted to define, other than by an exercise of substantively legislative power, the interpretation to be given to a statute. The constitutional offence lay in the element of legislative *prescription* aimed at the courts. This element thus emerged as the primary element in identifying that quality of the legislation which rendered it other than substantively legislative.

Legislative prescription, or direction, was also considered by Clark as constituting a basis, although not the only basis, for invalidating legislation which compromised the integrity of *final* judgments.[29] Exhibiting his keen interest and detailed study of the United States experience and its relevance to the Australian situation, he stated that

the depository and organ of the legislative power cannot be permitted, as it has been forcibly expressed by an eminent American jurist, 'to retroact upon past controversies and to reverse decisions which the courts, in the exercise of their undoubted authority, have made; for this would… be the exercise of it in the most objectionable and offensive form, since the legislature would in effect sit as a court of review to which the parties might appeal when dissatisfied with the rulings of the courts'.[30]

Sir John Quick and Robert Garran made similar observations, albeit limited more to the integrity of final judgments and their conclusiveness:

It cannot be doubted that any attempt by Parliament, under cover of a declaratory law or otherwise, to set aside or reverse the judgment of a court of federal jurisdiction, would be void as an invasion of the judicial power.[31]

---

[28] *Ibid*, at 39.

[29] Judgments from which there has been no appeal, or judgments of the highest appellate court in a jurisdiction.

[30] Clark, *Studies in Australian Constitutional Law*, n 20 above, 41, quoting from Cooley's *A Treatise on the Constitutional Limitations Which Rest Upon the States of the American Union*, 6th edn (Boston MA, Little, Brown & Co, 1890) 112.

[31] J Quick and RR Garran, *The Annotated Constitution of the Australian Commonwealth* (1901 reprint, St Leonards, NSW, Legal Books, 1976) 721. And elsewhere: 'The simple rule would seem to be that, just as the legislature cannot directly reverse the judgment of the court, so it cannot, by a declaratory law, affect the rights of the parties in whose case the

Like Clark, they recognised that the cover of properly enacted legislation will not suffice to shield the purported exercise of legislative power from separation of powers scrutiny. Moreover, the constitutional offence did not lie in the fact that the legislation was *exercising* judicial power, that is usurping it, but rather that it was *interfering* with its independent operation by the courts by prescribing the outcome of cases.

These early Australian constitutional scholars thus recognised that breaches of the separation of powers may occur under the guise of otherwise properly enacted legislation purporting to be an amendment to the law yet in substance being an attempt to interfere with the judicial process. The efficacy of the separation of powers in maintaining the integrity of the judicial process is in large part dependent on the extent to which heed is given to the injunction to discern the substance of the legislation in order to determine its true nature. The Supreme Court of the United States had already adopted such an attitude in the seminal decision of *United States v Klein*, decided in 1871.[32] By so doing, it held unconstitutional, as a breach of the separation of powers, legislation which sought to direct the outcome of a pending case. Despite reliance on United States constitutional precedents, however, the early commentators did not refer to this case. Indeed, this lack of awareness of *Klein* and its significance persists currently in Australia. Moore did refer to the case, but without appreciating its significance in this context.[33] Nevertheless, this case did indicate, as will be shown in the following chapter, that the United States Supreme Court had already appreciated that the element which rendered legislation an unconstitutional interference with judicial functions was legislative prescription or direction. This provided independent reinforcement of the observations of these early Australian scholars. As separation of powers jurisprudence of the High Court of Australia developed, these prescient observations of the early commentators eventually, though without express reference or reliance, informed the Court's slow development of principle in this area.

---

judgment was given ... That is to say, the legislature may *overrule* a decision, though it may not *reverse* it; it may declare the rule of law to be different from what the courts have adjudged it to be, and may give a retrospective operation to its declaration, except so far as the rights of parties to a judicial decision are concerned ... In other words, the sound rule of legislation, that the fruits of victory ought not to be snatched from a successful litigant, is elevated into a constitutional requirement' (*ibid*, at 722).

[32]   *United States v Klein* 80 US (13 Wall) 128 (1871). This is the seminal US case on legislative interference in pending cases, and will be examined in detail in the next chapter.

[33]   Moore, *The Constitution of the Commonwealth of Australia*, n 12 above, 323. However, the same can be said of the American commentators who did not draw out the full implications of *Klein* until one hundred years later. See the seminal article by HM Hart, 'The Power of Congress to Limit the Jurisdiction of Federal Courts: an Exercise in Dialectic' (1953) 66 *Harvard Law Review* 1362; and GC Young, 'Congressional Regulation of Federal Courts Jurisdiction and Processes: *United States v Klein* Revisited' [1981] *Wisconsin Law Review* 1189.

III.   EARLY DEVELOPMENT OF PRINCIPLE BY THE HIGH COURT

The earliest High Court authority directly relevant to the pending case scenario is *Nelungaloo Pty Ltd v Commonwealth*.[34] In that case, the plaintiff claimed it had been inadequately compensated for the compulsory acquisition of wheat six years earlier, pursuant to a Ministerial order under subordinate legislation.[35] It argued that the Ministerial order was not authorised by the regulations. While the matter was pending at first instance, Parliament enacted legislation which provided that the ministerial order

> shall be deemed to be, and at all times to have been, fully authorized by that regulation [pursuant to which it was purportedly made], and shall have, and be deemed to have had, full force and effect according to its tenor in respect of wheat harvested in any wheat season up to and including the 1946–1947 season.[36]

The plaintiff submitted that this provision was unconstitutional because it was not in substance an amendment to the law but rather a legislative prescription as to the construction of an existing law, which the court was required to adopt, the plaintiff highlighting the section's retrospectivity in this regard.

Prima facie, this (retrospective) validation of the ministerial order was achieved by force of the enactment and thus not necessarily problematic to separation of powers concerns. However, the deeming provision, without more, might have been. In the later case of *Building Construction Employees and Builders Labourers' Federation of New South Wales v Minister of Industrial Relations* ('*BLF NSW*'), the New South Wales Court of Appeal held that similar retrospective legislative validation of administrative action, relying on a deeming provision, constituted a direction to the court, and not an amendment to the law.[37] It would have attracted a declaration of invalidity if that separation of powers had been entrenched in that State. In *Nelungaloo*, however, despite the consequences for the pending proceedings, the deeming provision was not as prescriptive—vis-à-vis the judicial branch—as was the provision in *BLF*

---

[34]   *Nelungaloo Pty Ltd v Commonwealth* (1948) 75 CLR 495.
[35]   Reg 14 of the National Security (Wheat Acquisition) Regulations 1939.
[36]   S 11 of the Wheat Industry Stabilisation Act (No 2) 1946 (Cth).
[37]   *Building Construction Employees and Builders Labourers' Federation of New South Wales v Minister of Industrial Relations* ('*BLF NSW*') (1986) 7 NSWLR 372. However, it was held that the legislation could not be invalidated, as the separation of powers was not constitutionally entrenched in New South Wales. Cf *Australian Building Construction Employees' and Builders Labourers' Federation v Commonwealth* (1986) 161 CLR 88. See now also *Kable v Director of Public Prosecutions (NSW)* (1996) 189 CLR 51 in relation to the implications of Chapter III of the Constitution for State courts, discussed in more detail at n 77 below.

NSW, discussed in detail below.[38] In addition to the deeming element were the words 'shall have ... full force and effect', suggesting that the legislature achieved the validation of the order by reliance on legislative power as opposed to legislative direction to the courts. Moreover, the legislation was general in application and it was not entirely clear that it was targeting the particular pending proceedings. Williams J, at first instance, thus held that any invalidity in the ministerial order was cured by force of the statute and not by any prescription to the judicial branch in the pending case.[39] The court was therefore required to apply the new provision to the pending case, thus acknowledging and applying the Changed Law Rule.

No reference, however, was made to the possible constitutional outcome if the deeming provision in the section stood alone and if the legislation was more obviously targeted at the pending case. Nor was there any express recognition that the central element to any unconstitutional interference with judicial functions was a legislative prescription, although perhaps it may be inferred. The plaintiff submitted that the section's retrospectivity was one aspect of the legislation that supported its major submission impugning the section's substantively legislative nature. While Williams J appeared to have been sensitive to the possibility that this may have been indicative of unconstitutional interference, he did not state so expressly. Given the absence of the relevant element of prescription, retrospectivity could not stand alone as a ground for invalidating the provision.[40]

In the appeal to the Full Bench, Dixon J alone referred to the plaintiff's submission in this regard, only to dismiss it as 'an erroneous complexion to place upon the enactment'.[41] Did this mean that had it been the correct complexion, the statement of principle on which it was based was correct? The question was left unanswered. Nevertheless it appears that, while countenancing a *constitutional* interference with judicial functions only within the boundaries of the Changed Law Rule, the High Court acknowledged the possibility of an unconstitutional one, even though it did not elaborate on its identifying features. The possibility which arose immediately, in the absence of further refinement of principle, was the relegation of the rule against legislative interference to a mere hurdle for deft legislative drafting, as opposed to a clearly enforceable limitation to curb the excesses of an overzealous legislature.

---

[38]   Below at n 87 and accompanying text.
[39]   *Nelungaloo Pty Ltd v Commonwealth* (1948) 75 CLR 495 at 503–4.
[40]   *Nelungaloo Pty Ltd v Commonwealth* (1948) 75 CLR 495 at 503.
[41]   *Ibid*, at 579.

This reticence was also apparent in the next case to consider the issue: *R v Humby; Ex parte Rooney*.[42] In that case, Mason J, applying *Nelungaloo*, observed briefly that 'Chapter III contains no prohibition, express or implied, that rights in issue in legal proceedings shall not be the subject of legislative declaration or action'.[43] While thus clearly endorsing the Changed Law Rule, there was no elaboration on what might constitute unconstitutional legislative interference in the pending case. This was despite the fact that the decision post-dated the seminal decision in Commonwealth jurisdictions in this regard, *Liyanage v R*,[44] a decision of the Privy Council, to which detailed reference will now be made before returning to *Rooney*.

IV. THE FOUNDATION OF A DISCRETE SET OF PRINCIPLES GOVERNING THE PENDING CASE SCENARIO: *LIYANAGE V R*

The facts of *Liyanage* provide a classic example of unconstitutional legislative interference with judicial functions in a pending case. At issue was the enactment by the Parliament of Ceylon of the Criminal Law (Special Provisions) Act (No 1) 1962 which purported to amend the Criminal Procedure Code in its application to some 60 persons accused of offences against the State for their part in an abortive coup in 1962. Although these persons and their trial were not expressly mentioned, the legislation left no doubt as to against whom it was directed. The Act purported to:

(a) operate retrospectively from a date just prior to the coup and until 'after the conclusion of all legal proceedings connected with or incidental to any offence against the State committed on or about 27 January 1962, or from one year after the commencement of this Act, whichever is later';

(b) limit its application 'to any offence against the State alleged to have been committed on or about January 27, 1962, or any matter, act or thing connected therewith or incidental thereto';

(c) legalise ex post facto the detention of any persons suspected of having committed an offence against the state;

(d) allow arrest without warrant for 'waging war against the Queen' and for trying to overawe the government by criminal force and to widen the scope of that offence;

---

[42] *R v Humby; Ex parte Rooney* (1973) 129 CLR 231.
[43] *Ibid*, at 250.
[44] *Liyanage v R* [1967] 1 AC 259.

(e)   widen the class of offences for which trial without jury could be ordered including those with which the accused were charged;[45]

(f)   add a new offence ex post facto to meet the circumstances of the coup;

(g)   make admissible in evidence in any proceedings for breach of the Act certain statements and admissions made to the Police which were otherwise inadmissible under the Evidence Code; and

(h)   alter ex post facto the punishment which could be imposed.[46]

It was argued that 'the pith and substance of [the impugned statute] was that there was a legislative plan designed *ex post facto* to facilitate, if not ensure, the conviction and punishment of the appellants'.[47] Further, in jurisdictions with an entrenched separation of powers, 'in the exercise of what is merely a legislative power parliament cannot under the guise of what is called legislation either usurp the judicial function of the judges or interfere with them'.[48]

The Privy Council accepted that the legislation interfered with the mode of trial, the nature of the offences, the admissibility of evidence and the sentencing in the particular case. However, although these circumstances provided the Privy Council with the opportunity to define a precise set of constitutional limitations in this context, it stated that it was

---

[45]   The Act originally contained a provision that the Minister for Justice would nominate the judges to hear the matter. This was held to be unconstitutional in preliminary proceedings, as a legislative interference with the judicial process. The nomination of the judges was left to the Supreme Court.

[46]   As a preliminary step, the Privy Council dealt at some length with the issue of whether the separation of powers was legally incorporated in the Constitution of Ceylon. This it regarded as a prerequisite to its jurisdiction to invalidate the legislation on separation of powers grounds: *Liyanage v R* [1967] 1 AC 259 at 283 ff, especially from 287. The Privy Council found that the judicial power had already been invested exclusively in courts by the Charter of Justice in 1833, cl 4, where the 'entire administration of justice shall be vested exclusively in the courts erected and constituted by this Our Charter'. Therefore, the Council was able to come to terms with the fact that there was no explicit exclusive vesting of the judicial power in the Constitution which was in force in 1962. 'There was no compelling need therefore [in the Constitution] to make any specific reference to the judicial power of the courts when the legislative and executive powers changed hands'. On the basis of the prior vesting of judicial power in the 1833 Charter of Justice, the Privy Council was able to find that a legal separation of powers in Ceylon had already been established. This confirmed the necessity of legal entrenchment of the separation of powers for it to be enforceable against the legislature by legal sanction and not the vagaries of politics. Cf TRS Allan, *Law, Liberty, and Justice; The Legal Foundations of British Constitutionalism* (Oxford, Clarendon Press, 1993) 69ff, where it is argued that the decision could stand without the need to establish as a prerequisite the legal incorporation of the separation principle. He stated this in support of his broader thesis that the United Kingdom Parliament is bound by the separation of powers to limit judicial interference even though it has an unwritten constitution. Such alternate basis for the doctrine's legal force is discussed in *Liyanage*, [1967] 1 AC 259 at 283ff.

[47]   *Liyanage v R* [1967] 1 AC 259 at 275.

[48]   *Ibid*, at 276.

not 'necessary to attempt the almost impossible task of tracing where the line is to be drawn between what will and what will not constitute such an interference'.[49] Although eschewing an all-encompassing definition of limitations, the decision did go some way in laying some foundations by settling for the identification of indicia of unconstitutional interference. These did not constitute a closed set, but rather were to be determined by the 'facts and circumstances of each case',[50] which included:

> the true purpose of the legislation, the situation to which it was directed, the existence (where several enactments are impugned) of a common design, and the extent to which the legislation affects, by way of direction or restriction, the discretion or judgment of the judiciary in specific proceedings.[51]

Thus espousing a substance over form approach, the critical element became the existence of prescription. This prescription was not limited to the ultimate outcome of the case but apparently included the judicial discretion or judgement in the case relating to particular legal or evidentiary issues which arise therein and which may facilitate the ultimate outcome desired by the legislature. Clearly, the greater the facilitation of a particular outcome, the greater was the likelihood that a court would invalidate the statute as being merely prescriptive and not substantively legislative. In the present case, the impugned Act 'altered the fundamental law of evidence so as to facilitate conviction'.[52]

A number of indicia of direction were indentified. First, the Privy Council examined the *ad hominem* nature of the legislation.[53] While of course the Ceylonese Parliament could enact statutes relating to criminal conduct, relevant penalties and the law of evidence, in this case the legislation was clearly aimed at 'particular individuals who had been named in a White Paper and were in prison awaiting their fate'.[54] The amendments

> were not intended for the generality of the citizens or designed as any improvement of the general law [as] shown by the fact that the effect of those alterations was to be limited to the participants in the … coup and that, after these had been dealt with by the judges, the law should revert to its normal state.[55]

Secondly, the legislation was *ad hominem* not only in its specificity with regard to persons, but also with regard to precise proceedings and the

---

[49] *Ibid*, at 289–90.
[50] *Ibid*, at 290.
[51] *Ibid*.
[52] *Ibid*.
[53] *Ibid*, at 289.
[54] *Ibid*.
[55] *Ibid*.

issues raised therein. Thirdly, the retrospectivity in the legislation was designed to operate precisely around the dates of the alleged offences and any prosecutions arising, returning the law to its previous state thereafter.[56] The judiciary was therefore required to apply a different law to these particular accused than it would have applied to the generality of the citizenry in other circumstances. This reinforced the argument that there had been a targeting of these individuals and their prosecutions.

Although the conjunction of these indicia in the context of pending proceedings suggested to the Privy Council that the legislation was other than a substantive change in the law, it was careful to stress that these factors were not per se determinative of the issue.[57] It also had regard to the fact that the legislation sought to interfere with matters traditionally reserved for judicial discretion. It was pertinent that the legislation made provision for a trial without jury, legalised arrest without warrant, made admissible evidence which was otherwise inadmissible under the general law of evidence, and increased the sentence to be imposed on the particular accused.

The Board was thus able to conclude that the 'the pith and substance of [the legislation] was a legislative plan *ex post facto* to secure the conviction and enhance the punishment of those particular individuals'.[58] Moreover, it held that

> [t]he *true* nature and purpose of these enactments was revealed by their *conjoint* impact on the specific proceedings in respect of which they were designed, and they *take their colour*, in particular, from the alterations they purported to make as to their ultimate objective, the punishment of those convicted. These alterations constituted a grave and deliberate incursion into the judicial sphere.[59] (Emphasis added.)

The core of the offence was that the legislation could not be regarded as a change in the law but rather a 'grave and deliberate incursion into the judicial sphere', which impugned the substantively legislative nature of the provisions.[60] The difficulty with the Board's decision lies in determining whether it was necessary for the prescription to be geared toward a particular outcome of the case, or whether it was sufficient if it simply interfered with fact-finding, the resolution of particular legal issues in the

---

[56] *Ibid.*

[57] '[S]uch a lack of generality in criminal legislation need not, of itself, involve the judicial function, and their Lordships are not prepared to hold that every enactment in this field which can be described as *ad hominem* and ex post facto must inevitably usurp or infringe the judicial power'. *Ibid.*

[58] *Ibid.*

[59] *Ibid*, at 290.

[60] *Ibid*, at 291.

pending proceedings or the exercise of judicial discretion therein. Certainly the Board on these facts regarded the legislation as engineering a result.[61] However, it appeared to leave open as a matter for judgement in each case the extent to which it was necessary to show that the legislation facilitated the ultimate outcome and whether unconstitutional direction could still be found when the interference was limited to particular legal issues in the case regardless of ultimate outcome.

Take the example of the admissibility of statements to the police, an issue relevant in *Liyanage,* in the following hypothetical situation: The legislature desires to liberalise the law of evidence so as to facilitate the admission of such statements, including those that had already been obtained and to be used in pending prosecutions. In purporting to amend the law of evidence, legislation provided that particular police conduct in the obtaining of statements which had hitherto been prohibited would now be permissible and thus not a ground of inadmissibility. The law purported also to apply retrospectively, but in its retrospective element, instead of amending the law so that it not longer prohibited such police conduct, it simply directed the courts in pending proceedings not to have regard to such conduct when exercising their discretion whether to admit these statements as evidence. In this scenario the aim of the legislature is not necessarily to secure or facilitate the conviction of known accused in pending proceedings, but rather to amend the law of evidence. Would this render the directive aspect of the retrospective provisions valid? Clearly, the court in pending proceedings would still be free to determine guilt or innocence. However, can it not be argued that in achieving this outcome the retrospective provision has done so not by amending the law, as it has done prospectively, but by directing the courts how to exercise a particular discretion and thus impermissibly interfering with judicial functions in breach of the separation of powers? *Liyanage* does not necessarily preclude such an outcome. Of course the legislature may amend the applicable law retrospectively and make it expressly applicable to pending proceedings (subject to the degree to which it may be targeting particular individuals and proceedings) to achieve the same outcome as the legislative direction. However, this fact alone, as will be discussed below, does not per se validate the measure in fact adopted.

Following *Liyanage*, the foundations for a discrete set of principles applicable to the pending case scenario began to emerge and can be summarised as follows. Unconstitutional legislative interference is defined primarily by the existence of the element of direction or prescription aimed at the exercise of judicial functions in the pending case. It

---

[61]   *Ibid*, at 290.

must have that quality which negates the substantively legislative nature of the legislation. It is not necessarily essential that the direction expressly or directly effect a particular final outcome, so long as it does affect the court's independent adjudication of the matter. The existence of the requisite direction is to be determined by reference to the consequences of the legislation for the actual pending proceedings, for the legal issues which the court must address and the application of the law to the facts. There needs to be some indication that the legislation is targeting particular proceedings, or a group of proceedings.

This principle shall be referred to as the 'direction principle'. It is a principle which accords with those statements of the early Australian commentators referred to above, recognising that Parliament may be acting in a non-legislative manner under the guise of otherwise properly enacted legislation. This is not to suggest that the enquiry is unconcerned with the effect of the legislation on the exercise of *judicial* power, or indeed that the legislature is usurping core aspects of that power. It is concerned with the extent to which the legislature is reaching into the exercise of that power, restricting its independent operation and directing how it is to be exercised. This concern reflects a core purpose of the separation doctrine: preventing the more powerful political branches from treating the more passive judicial branch as a mere appendage, requiring the latter to decide issues in a way predetermined by it. Such legislative activity 'takes its colour', to use the language of *Liyanage*,[62] from its impact on the pending proceedings.

The difficulties faced by the Privy Council in *Liyanage* highlight the fact that the *indicia* of direction are by no means a closed set and that no one individual factor is determinative of the issue. Consideration must be given to the interplay of these factors and their cumulative effect in the particular instance of the pending case. The *degree* of relevance of each is equally dependent on the facts of each case. The Privy Council also recognised that the direction principle was critically interrelated with the Changed Law Rule, the former acting as a threshold test for the application of the latter. *Liyanage* was also valuable in its identification of a number of relevant indicia of direction, which can almost be regarded as a canon given that the list has not been significantly expanded upon in subsequent cases and remains a very useful guide:

- the *ad hominem* nature of the legislation;
- its retrospectivity, involving the delineation of a precise time period and types of offences to which it is directed;
- an express or clearly implied and ascertainable application in

---

[62] *Liyanage v R* [1967] 1 AC 259 at 290.

particular proceedings and in relation to particular legal issues in those proceedings, even if it does not expressly direct the final outcome thereof;

- the very existence of pending proceedings and the extent to which the legislation appears to be tailored to those proceedings or targeting them.
- an attempt to affect the exercise of traditional judicial discretions such as those relating to sentencing or the admissibility of evidence, the weight given to and conclusions to be drawn from evidence, the legality of warrants and arrest procedures, and the true purpose of the legislation where this can be discerned.

A clarification is needed before proceeding. It was suggested above that the enquiry as to whether the legislation is preventing the court from exercising an element of judicial power, or requiring it to act inconsistently with that power or its nature as a court, is relegated to subsidiary importance in the present enquiry.[63] This is not to deny, however, that unconstitutional direction in substance does prevent the court from exercising a core element of judicial power, that is, the independent and conclusive adjudication of a legal dispute pursuant to the statement and application of existing law to facts. As the High Court stated in the oft-quoted passage from *Fencott v Muller*, an 'essential function of the judicial power is the quelling of … controversies by ascertainment of facts, by application of the law, and by exercise … of judicial discretion'.[64] Legislation may also offend against the integrity of judicial power in other ways. But the focus of attention here remains the extent to which an exercise of legislative power becomes unconstitutional if it offends in no other way than in seeking to influence the outcome of pending proceedings, given its power to amend the law which the courts must apply. True it is that the removal of independent adjudication may constitute a denial of (procedural) due process, also protected by the separation of powers.[65] Again, in the present context, the question whether this particular aspect of due process has been denied is determined by the existence of legislative direction.

---

[63] See F Wheeler, 'Due Process, Judicial Power and Chapter III in the New High Court' (2004) 32 *Federal Law Review* 205.

[64] *Fencott v Muller* (1983) 152 CLR 507 at 608.

[65] See Wheeler, 'Due Process, Judicial Power and Chapter III in the New High Court', n 63 above.

V.   CONSOLIDATION OF PRINCIPLE POST-*LIYANAGE*

The problematic nature of the application of the direction principle does not become fully apparent until it is considered in factual scenarios less egregious than that in *Liyanage*. The *Liyanage* imperative to look to substance over form poses considerable challenges, especially in the hard case.[66] And yet the efficacy of the direction principle as a constitutional limitation depends to a significant degree on the extent to which the courts are willing to heed this imperative. The concern to secure the development of principle emerging from *Liyanage* was not, however, immediately apparent in High Court jurisprudence. In the *Rooney* case the High Court considered retrospective legislation—the Matrimonial Causes Act 1971 (Cth) —that purported, 'by force of this Act',[67] to validate orders made by Masters of State Supreme Courts exercising federal jurisdiction in matrimonial causes that defined rights, liabilities

---

[66] It should be mentioned for the sake of completeness that there are aspects of the opinion in *Liyanage* which leave ambiguous the precise nature of the constitutional offence being described here. This is revealed in those statements in which the Board juxtaposed the question of usurpation of judicial power and interference with judicial functions without seeming to appreciate the subtle differences. For example, when referring to the indicia of direction in the legislation, its *ad hominem* and retrospective nature, they denied that these indicia 'must inevitably usurp or infringe the judicial power' ([1967] 1 AC 259 at 289). Elsewhere, the Board held that the legislation, in addition to being an unconstitutional interference, was also a 'legislative judgment; and an exercise of judicial power' ([1967] 1 AC 259 at 290). In the writer's view, there should be a more careful and precise use of the terms 'exercise (or usurpation) of judicial power' and 'interference with judicial process'. The writer is not advocating an absolute dichotomy between the two concepts, as, in one sense, the latter may be regarded as an instance of the former, though in more specialised circumstances. Thus, an Act of Attainder would clearly constitute an exercise of judicial power and a usurpation thereof, as would the situation where Parliament were institutionally to act as a court. These would not be *interferences* with judicial functions in that the judicial branch is being bypassed entirely. However, the situation is different where the legislation does not expressly direct the court to come to a particular conclusion, but rather amends the law which the court must apply in pending proceedings in such a way as to facilitate a particular outcome. The appearance is thus maintained that it is the judicial branch which reaches the ultimate conclusion in the case, and does so by merely applying the (amended) law. This is the situation which pertained in *Liyanage* and it should be referred to as an *interference* with judicial process, as opposed to an *exercise* of judicial power. By using the term 'interference' a more accurate description of the constitutional offence is given, in turn encouraging a more accurate appreciation of it. This is not merely a nice point. The failure to appreciate it, as will be seen, has led to a degree of confusion as to the application of the separation of powers in this scenario. The reason lies in the fact that in cases of interference one is not primarily trying to locate elements of the judicial power in the legislation, rather one is looking for elements of direction. Accordingly, precise definitions of what constitutes judicial power are not as important as they are in determining situations of usurpation or exercise of judicial power. Nevertheless, the Council in *Liyanage* was highly sensitive to the possibilities of legislative interference tending to an eventual usurpation of the judicial role by legislatures if left unchecked: 'If such Acts as these were valid the judicial power could be wholly absorbed by the legislature and taken out of the hands of the judges' ([1967] 1 AC 259 at 291).
[67]   Matrimonial Causes Act 1971 (Cth) s 5.

and obligations.[68] The High Court had previously ruled that orders made by Masters were not valid.[69] The applicant sought to invalidate the legislation on the ground that it was in some way an unconstitutional interference with judicial power, or usurpation thereof; 'in some way' because his submissions were rather curious, indeed confused, as they appeared to be based on an assumption that the section was a valid exercise of legislative power.[70] When the legislation was enacted, the applicant was a party to pending proceedings in relation to which the validity or otherwise of the orders made by Masters was a critical factor.

The court, with little elaboration, held that there was no unconstitutional interference. Mason J made reference to *Liyanage* as an example of legislative interference that 'circumscribed the judicial function and the discretions incidental to it'.[71] He confirmed the centrality of the element of direction in unconstitutional interferences. This element did not exist in the present case because the legislation, like that in *Nelungaloo*,[72] operated by its own force to achieve its purposes. There was little, if anything, to suggest that the interference in the particular proceedings was anything other than incidental. The approach was consistent with the position that the Changed Law Rule can apply only if the direction principle itself is not breached:

> It is plain enough that the circumstance that a statute affects rights in issue in pending litigation has not been thought to involve any invasion of the judicial power ... Chapter III contains no prohibition, express or implied, that rights in issue in legal proceedings shall not be the subject of legislative declaration or action.[73]

Even though indicia of direction existed, such as retrospectivity and clear consequences for the outcome of pending proceedings, in all the circumstances of the case these did not work together to establish that the legislation was other than substantively legislative. In particular, it cannot be said that the legislation was intended to apply specifically to any particular person, or identifiable group thereof, or that particular pending proceedings were being targeted. The main object of the legislation was to secure the validity of orders of Masters. The other justices made little reference to the issue, though Gibbs J agreed with the reasons of Mason J. Stephen J, with whom Gibbs J also agreed, as did Menzies J,

---

[68]   Pursuant to s 23 of the Matrimonial Causes Act 1959 (Cth).
[69]   *Knight v Knight* (1971) 122 CLR 114.
[70]   *R v Humby; Ex parte Rooney* (1973) 129 CLR 231 at 250.
[71]   *Ibid.*
[72]   See nn 34 and 35 above and accompanying text.
[73]   *R v Humby; Ex parte Rooney* (1973) 129 CLR 231 at 250.

went no further than confirming that the legislation merely attached to the orders of Masters consequences which it declared them always to have had 'as acts in the law'.[74]

The Privy Council's approach in *Liyanage*, which *Rooney* appeared to endorse, was subsequently confirmed by the High Court in *Australian Building Construction Employees' and Builders Labourers' Federation v Commonwealth ('BLF (Cth)')*.[75] Again the Court did not embark upon an expansive treatment of the issue but the case achieved a greater significance as a counterpoint to the decision of the New South Wales Court of Appeal in *BLF (NSW)*,[76] dealing with analogous State legislation which sought to effect the deregistration of the State branch of the Builders Labourers' Federation ('BLF'), although adopting a significantly different strategy. Although there is no entrenched separation of powers at the State level, it was the latter court which examined the present concerns in more detail than any federal court had at that time.[77] Its reasoning will be considered in more detail below.

---

[74]   *Ibid*, at 243: '[the legislation] declares the rights, liabilities, obligations and status of individuals to be and always to have been the same as if purported decrees had in fact been made by a single judge of a Supreme Court. It does not deem those decrees to have been made by a judge nor does it confer validity upon them; it leaves them, so far as their inherent quality is concerned, as they were before the passing of *this Act*. They retain the character of having been made without jurisdiction, as was decided in *Knight v Knight*; as attempts at the exercise of judicial power they remain ineffective. Instead, the sub-section operates by attaching to them, as acts in the law, consequences which it declares them to have always had and it describes those consequences by reference to the consequences flowing from the making of decrees by a single judge of the Supreme Court of the relevant State'.

[75]   *Australian Building Construction Employees' and Builders Labourers' Federation v Commonwealth* (1986) 161 CLR 88.

[76]   *Building Construction Employees and Builders Labourers' Federation of New South Wales v Minister of Industrial Relations (BLF (NSW))* (1986) 7 NSWLR 372. See F Wheeler, '*BLF v Minister for Industrial Relations*: The Limits of State Legislative and Judicial Power' in G Winterton (ed) *State Constitutional Landmarks* (Sydney, Federation Press, 2006) 362.

[77]   See now, however, *Kable v Director of Public Prosecutions (NSW)* (1996) 189 CLR 51 where the separation of judicial power in Chapter III of the Constitution was held to be a source of limitations on State parliaments vis-a-vis State courts vested with federal jurisdiction. This was based on the finding of the majority (Toohey, Gaudron, McHugh and Gummow JJ, Brennan CJ and Dawson J dissenting) that State courts are part of an integrated system of State and federal courts for the exercise of federal judicial power, as well as State judicial power. Accordingly those State courts vested with federal jurisdiction are afforded some of the protections of Chapter III and the constitutional limitations flowing from an entrenched separation of judicial power. Beyond the fact that the limitation applies only to State parliaments vis-à-vis State courts vested with federal jurisdiction, the precise extent of these limitations was not set out and remains uncertain. The position of the majority is best summed up by McHugh J who stated (at 119) that a 'State may invest a State court with non-judicial functions and its judges with duties that, in the federal sphere, would be incompatible with the holding of judicial office. But under the Constitution, the boundary of State legislative power is crossed when the vesting of those functions or duties might lead ordinary reasonable members of the public to conclude that the State court as an institution was not free of government influence in administering the judicial functions invested in the court'. This incorporation of an 'incompatibility' limitation does not

The catalyst for the federal proceedings was a declaration by the Australian Conciliation and Arbitration Commission[78] that the BLF had engaged in the type of improper conduct which thus permitted the relevant Minister to order its deregistration.[79] The BLF applied to the High Court to have the Commission's declaration quashed and to prohibit the Minister from ordering the Registrar of the Commission to proceed with the deregistration. While these proceedings were pending, the Commonwealth Parliament enacted the Builders Labourers' Federation (Cancellation of Registration) Act 1986 (Cth), which, pursuant to section 3, cancelled the BLF's registration 'by force of this section'. The BLF challenged the validity of the legislation on the grounds that, inter alia, it was either an exercise of the judicial power of the Commonwealth, or an interference with judicial functions, in breach of the separation of powers.[80] The Act, it was submitted, abrogated the function that would otherwise have been performed by the High Court in the pending proceedings because Parliament itself had already prescribed the outcome.[81] The Court[82] unanimously rejected this submission, relying on *Rooney* and *Nelungaloo*, on the basis that 'Parliament may legislate so as to affect and alter rights in issue in pending litigation without interfering with the exercise of judicial power in a way that is inconsistent with the Constitution'.[83] Confirming the High Court's previous acceptance of the direction principle, and its essential role in testing the substantively

---

expressly extend to preventing absolutely the vesting of non-judicial functions on State courts, unless of course the incompatibility principle is breached. Whether the *Kable* principle extends to apply the direction principle to State parliaments is not expressly addressed. However, it could be argued that if the legislative direction is sufficiently egregious, especially if the situation is created where it appears that the court is acting at the behest of Parliament, then the *Kable* incompatibility principle is also breached. If a State parliament is not amending the law which a State court must apply, but rather directing the outcome of a pending case, or directing the resolution of a legal issue therein, then the independence of the Court from the Parliament may be put in doubt. The words of Gaudron J in relation to the impugned Act in *Kable* might be applicable: 'They are proceedings which the Act attempts to dress up as proceedings involving the judicial process. In so doing, the Act makes a mockery of that process and, inevitably, weakens public confidence in it. And, because the judicial process is a defining feature of the judicial power of the Commonwealth, the Act weakens confidence in the institutions which comprise the judicial system brought into existence by Ch III of the Constitution' (at 108).

   [78]   Upon application by the relevant minister pursuant to s 4(1) of the Building Industry Act 1985 (Cth) that it was satisfied that the BLF had engaged in conduct that constituted a contravention of certain undertakings it had made and agreements to which it was a party.

   [79]   The BLF had previously sought relief by way of prohibition in relation to this ministerial application, which relief was refused: *Re Ludeke; Ex parte Australian Building Construction Employees' and Builders Labourers' Federation (No 2)* (1985) 159 CLR 636.

   [80]   *Australian Building Construction Employees' and Builders Labourers' Federation v Commonwealth* (1986) 161 CLR 88 at 93.

   [81]   *Ibid*, at 94.

   [82]   Gibbs CJ, Mason, Brennan, Deane, Dawson JJ.

   [83]   *Australian Building Construction Employees' and Builders Labourers' Federation v Commonwealth* (1986) 161 CLR 88 at 96.

legislative nature of the legislation, it further held that '[i]t is otherwise when the legislation in question interferes with the judicial process itself, rather than with the substantive rights which are at issue in the proceedings'.[84] The distinction between a valid legislative act that is a change in the law, on the one hand, and an unconstitutional one which interferes with judicial process, was maintained.

The Court did not, however, elaborate on what it precisely meant by 'interference with judicial process', although it is possible to discern in its reasoning the critical element of direction to facilitate a desired outcome. In characterising the legislation here as indeed substantively legislative, the Court emphasised the provision's express statement that deregistration was achieved by the force of the statute, that is, by a change in the law. The Court did have regard to the *ad hominem* nature of the legislation and the fact that it addressed an issue, the registration of the BLF, which was the key issue in the pending proceedings. However, it did not attempt to address, or indeed fashion itself, to the particular legal issues that the Court had to consider in those proceedings. It merely by-passed them.

The Court stated that in this type of enquiry legislative purpose was irrelevant.[85] It is unclear whether this was an entirely irrelevant consideration, whether it was irrelevant on the present facts, or whether the critical question was not what Parliament actually intended, but the effect of what it actually enacted. It is not necessary to resolve the issue here, for, whatever view the Court took, it was consistent both with the direction principle and its use of indicia of direction, as well as the Court's adopted position of scrutinising the means adopted by the legislature as the major determinative factor.[86] Thus, legislative purpose is only relevant in so far as it may assist in determining, together with other factors, the existence or otherwise of direction. This probably explains why it was able to discount the clear targeting of the BLF by the legislation.

Would the Court's position have altered if the legislation did not contain the words 'by force of this section'? As in the *Rooney* case, it was clearly held that these words should not be taken at face value to indicate

---

[84]   *Ibid.*

[85]   *Ibid*: 'It matters not that the motive or purpose of the Minister, the Government and the Parliament in enacting the statute was to circumvent the proceedings and forestall any decision which might be given in those proceedings' (at 96–7).

[86]   This issue of legislative purpose is taken up again in future cases. The safest conclusion which can be drawn is that legislative purpose can be determined by the legislation it enacted and the facts of the case. Where the facts reveal indicia of direction, it may be possible to refer to the parliamentary speeches and the explanatory memorandum to assist in the final determination of the issue as to whether unconstitutional direction exists.

a change in the law. They were no more than a relevant consideration. The telling factor in this case was that the legislation did not seek directly and precisely to address the legal issues which were before the Court in the pending proceedings. Parliament merely resolved the ultimate issue by sidestepping the judicial process entirely. The procedure for deregistering the BLF under the previous law had been followed. All that was left to be done was for the Minister to make the relevant order; and it was at this point that the BLF commenced its proceedings. The legislation had the effect of pre-empting the decision, essentially making the proceedings redundant.

The High Court's reticence in setting out a comprehensive definition of principle was thrown into sharp relief by the judgments of Street CJ and Kirby P in the analogous decision of the New South Wales Court of Appeal in *BLF (NSW)*.[87] The Court found that the impugned legislation, because of its prescriptive nature, was in breach of the separation of powers as an interference with judicial functions, and would have declared it invalid if the doctrine had been legally entrenched in the State.[88] The relevant minister had cancelled, by declaration, the registration of the State branch of the BLF pursuant to his statutory powers.[89] The BLF unsuccessfully challenged the decision in the Supreme Court of New South Wales on natural justice grounds, whereupon the BLF appealed. In the week prior to the hearing of the appeal, Parliament enacted the Builders Labourers' Federation (Special Provisions) Act 1986. Section 3(1) thereof provided that the BLF's registration 'shall, *for all purposes*, be taken to have been cancelled' by the ministerial declaration (emphasis added). Section 3(2) provided that the Minister's certificate, as the prerequisite in the deregistration process, 'shall be treated, *for all purposes*, as having been validly given from the time it was given or purportedly given' (emphasis added). Section 3(3) provided that this shall be so notwithstanding any decision in any court proceedings relating to the certificate or to the executive declaration. In addition, section 3(4) provided that the costs in any such proceedings should be borne by the party 'and shall not be the subject of any contrary order of any court'. The difference between the wording used in the State Act— 'for all purposes'—and the analogous Commonwealth provision—'by

---

[87] *Building Construction Employees and Builders Labourers' Federation of New South Wales v Minister of Industrial Relations* (1986) 7 NSWLR 372.

[88] Following *Clyne v East* (1967) 68 SR (NSW) 385; see also in other states: *Gilbertson v South Australia* (1976) 15 SASR 66 at 101 (Zelling J) and *Nicholas v Western Australia* [1972] WAR 168 at 175. A great deal of consideration was given to the possibility of establishing in the court a power to invalidate legislation based on fundamental common law principles, which were ultimately rejected by the Court. See Allan, *Law, Liberty, and Justice*, n 46 above. See also n 77 above in relation to the *Kable* principle.

[89] Industrial Arbitration (Special Provisions) Act 1984 (NSW).

force of this section'—should be noted as the significant factor which led to the opposite conclusion of those justices of the State court which considered the issue.

Street CJ and Kirby P[90] made approving reference to the High Court *BLF* decision and the distinction drawn there between unconstitutional interference with judicial functions, and constitutional legislation, which merely altered the substantive rights of parties in pending proceedings. The direction principle and the Changed Law Rule were clearly accepted. Both justices expressly recognised the vital constitutional issue at stake and the need for discrete principles to deal with it. Street CJ opined:

> For Parliament, uncontrolled as it is by any of the safeguards that are enshrined in the concept of due process of law, to trespass into this field of judging between parties by interfering with the judicial process is an affront to a society that prides itself on the quality of its justice. Under the Commonwealth Constitution it would . . . attract a declaration of invalidity.[91]

In holding that there was a breach of the direction principle, Street CJ noted in particular that part of the first two subsections which prescribed the effect that the relevant executive actions 'shall for all purposes' have. The phrase did not exempt, and was therefore held to be applicable to, the court's adjudication in the pending proceedings.[92] The impugned provisions were 'cast in terms' that 'amount[ed] to commands to this Court as to the conclusion that it is to reach in the issues about to be argued before it'.[93] The corollary of course is that had the legislation been cast in other terms it may have achieved the same ends without breaching the direction principle. However,

> [r]ather than substantively validating the cancellation of the registration and the Ministerial certificate, Parliament chose to achieve its purpose in terms that can be more accurately described as *directive rather than substantive*.[94] (Emphasis added.)

He contrasted this legislation with the corresponding federal legislation that, validly, achieved its purpose by its own force and was therefore a substantive change in the law that the court upheld. In short, his Honour

---

[90] Commencing (1986) 7 NSWLR 372 at 375 and 387 respectively.

[91] *Building Construction Employees and Builders Labourers' Federation of New South Wales v Minister of Industrial Relations* (1986) 7 NSWLR 372 at 375–6 (Street CJ). Earlier he stated: 'Fundamental to the rule of law and the administration of justice in our society is the convention that the judiciary is the arm of government charged with the responsibility of interpreting and applying the law as between litigants in individual cases. The built in protections of natural justice, absence of bias, appellate control, and the other concomitants that are the ordinary daily province of the courts, are fundamental safeguards of the democratic rights of individuals' (*ibid*).

[92] *Ibid*, at 376.

[93] *Ibid*, at 378.

[94] *Ibid*.

clearly endorsed the direction principle, the fact that it operated as a test of the substantively legislative nature of the legislation and that it operated as a threshold test for the operation of the Changed Law Rule. The existence of a discrete set of principles applicable in the pending case scenario was clearly recognised. Beyond the wording of the provisions, Street CJ examined all the facts and circumstances of the case to locate indicia of direction; in particular, the fact that the legislation appeared to be fashioned to the precise issues in the pending case.[95] He contrasted the analogous federal legislation which did not deal with any of the individual legal issues in the federal case. The *ad homimen* nature of the State legislation was also indicative, though not per se determinative, of direction. He also noted in particular sub-section (4), dealing with costs, which strongly reinforced the other indicia of direction, and the fact that it was indicative of a targeting not merely of the BLF but of the actual pending legal proceedings.

In agreement, Kirby P recognised the foundational distinction between a change in the law and mere direction[96] and he accepted that the enquiry was about means and not ends. He approved the position taken by the High Court in *BLF Cth* notwithstanding the 'motive [behind] enacting the legislation, even if it were to circumvent and frustrate the proceedings in the Court'.[97] Improper motive was not relevant when Parliament acted within the proper bounds of legislative power. In relation to the State legislation, however, both the *ad hominem* nature of the legislation and 'the terms in which it was cast' indicated that it was 'more apparently a direct intrusion into the judicial process than was the case with the Federal Acts'.[98] Highly indicative of direction was the precise tailoring of the legislation to the matters in issue in the pending appeal, including the question of costs. 'The 1986 State Act … deal[t] specifically with matters which were then within the judicial domain'.[99] By contrast, 'in the federal sphere, there was no equivalent matter under appeal which the Federal legislation of 1986 terminated'.[100] It was 'in perfectly general terms' which did no more than cancel 'by legislative act, the registration of the Federal BLF'.[101] Even though it was *ad hominem*, it did not reach into the judicial process in such a way as to amount to a direction to the court or to restrict the court's independent adjudication of a matter. As indicated, it merely bypassed the judicial process entirely.

---

[95] *Ibid.*
[96] *Ibid*, at 392.
[97] *Ibid.*
[98] *Ibid*, at 394.
[99] *Ibid.*
[100] *Ibid.*
[101] *Ibid.*

Kirby P reinforced his position by reference to the *Rooney* decision. The critical point in relation to that legislation[102] was the fact that, as Stephen J in those proceedings had stated, 'it did not effect a "validation" of the earlier purported orders. Instead, it attached to those orders, as acts in the law, consequences which it declared them always to have had'.[103] The Minister in the present case had argued that that was all that the legislation did: apply legal consequences to events in 1985, if those consequences did not already flow from the 1984 Act: '[f]ar from being an interference in the performance by the judiciary of its functions this was simply a clarification by the legislature of the matters upon which the judicial function was to operate'.[104] In addressing this submission, Kirby P noted that

> whereas the *Matrimonial Causes Act 1971* (Cth) [in the *Rooney* case] was addressed in terms of generality to all cases in respect of which the purported decrees had been made by a court officer, the 1986 Act has a much narrower focus. It is addressed to a particular legal person, namely the BLF. It deals, with specificity, with incidents of particular litigation involving the BLF. Thus, particular provision is made in respect of the costs incidental to the proceedings already on foot in the Court. Doubtless this provision was included to obviate argument, for the purpose of resolving costs, of the validity of the BLF's cancellation. But the result is that the legislature has passed *ad hominem* legislation. Its disclosed purpose is to remove doubts that had arisen in the argument of the cases before Lee J. *Its plain object was to remove any risk of an adverse determination of the appeal from Lee J.* It amounts, in effect, although not in its terms, to a legislative judgment.[105] (Emphasis added.)

The significance of the phrase 'in effect, although not in its terms' is clearly indicative that Kirby P was squarely within the *Liyanage* method of looking to substance over form. Both he and Street CJ were able to take the step of declaring the legislation to be a direction to the judiciary of sufficient extent as to make it an unconstitutional interference with judicial functions which they would enforce were the separation of powers legally entrenched in the State.[106]

The different outcome of the State and federal cases does raise questions about the efficacy of the legal entrenchment of the separation of powers. The avoidance of constitutional offence would appear to be a question of Parliament choosing its words very carefully. As Street CJ recognised,

---

[102]   *Ibid*, at 395.
[103]   See *R v Humby; Ex Parte Rooney* (1973) 129 CLR 231 at 243.
[104]   *Building Construction Employees and Builders Labourers' Federation of New South Wales v Minister of Industrial Relations* (1986) 7 NSWLR 372 at 395.
[105]   *Ibid*.
[106]   Although see now *Kable v Director of Public Prosecutions (NSW)*, n 77 above.

it was plainly open to the … Parliament without criticism—indeed probably with widespread acclaim—to cancel the Federation's registration by an express Act to that effect, as did the Commonwealth Parliament. But the method chosen … was a legislative interference with the judicial process of this Court by directing the outcome of particular litigation.[107]

Does this then reduce the constitutional principle here to a mere guide for deft legislative drafting? Up to a point this is the case. However, the wording of the legislation is not itself the sole determinant of direction. If there are sufficient independent indicia of direction, legislation which expressly states that it operates by its own force may not survive constitutional scrutiny. In such circumstances, the *Liyanage* imperative to look to substance over form becomes particularly pertinent. It ought also to be noted that the development of principle here does not neglect the need also to protect the integrity of *legislative* power; hence the Changed Law Rule. If Parliament, for example, has the constitutional competence to de-register a trade union by force of legislation, it will not be prevented from doing so by the happenstance of pending litigation involving that union, even if the litigation concerns the very issue of that union's registration.[108]

One issue that remained somewhat uncertain was the question of legislative purpose as an indication of direction. Street CJ referred to a passage in *BLF (Cth)* relegating the issue of legislative purpose to irrelevance,[109] and regarded himself bound by this.[110] The point being made, however, is that in considering whether the direction principle is being breached, a court is not attempting to determine the intention of Parliament as an independent step. Rather it is seeking to identify the existence of unconstitutional prescription by a close scrutiny of the terms of the legislation, the issues with which it deals and the nature of the pending proceedings as part of the examination of all the circumstances for evidence that the legislature is directing the court, not changing the law. Thus, when Street CJ examined section 3(4) relating to costs in prior

---

[107] *Building Construction Employees and Builders Labourers' Federation of New South Wales v Minister of Industrial Relations* (1986) 7 NSWLR 372 at 379.

[108] Kirby P also dismissed as irrelevant a whole host of legislation cited by the Minister which interfered with the judicial process, but remained on the statute books , saying that '[t]he fact that error has been oft repeated does not make it less an error. The failure of other litigants, perhaps with less at stake, to challenge the intrusion of the Parliament into matters before the courts does not relieve the Court of evaluating the challenge once made'. *Building Construction Employees and Builders Labourers' Federation of New South Wales v Minister of Industrial Relations* (1986) 7 NSWLR 372 at 392.

[109] '[i]t matters not that the motive or purpose of the Minister, the Government and the Parliament in enacting the statute was to circumvent the proceedings and forestall any decision which might be given in those proceedings'. (1986) 161 CLR 88 at 97.

[110] *Building Construction Employees and Builders Labourers' Federation of New South Wales v Minister of Industrial Relations* (1986) 7 NSWLR 372 at 377.

proceedings he could not 'see any nexus at all in a legislative sense between the cancellation of the Federation's registration and the disposition of costs in the pending court proceedings'.[111] He then proceeded to characterise that section as a 'direct interference with the ordinary operation of the judicial process' that 'can be described *as directive to the Court rather than as substantively legislative*'[112] (emphasis added). Kirby P, while acknowledging the High Court authority in this regard, also made a determination of legislative purpose in the same way. He held that the 'disclosed purpose is to remove doubts which had arisen in the argument' in the first instance decision and '[i]ts plain object was to remove any risk of an adverse determination of the appeal'.[113] The legislation, he stated, was 'enacted specifically for the purpose of terminating proceedings which had been brought in the court, ostensibly for the vindication of legal rights'.[114]

Both *BLF* decisions thus appear to confirm the acceptance in Australian jurisprudence of the discrete set of principles emanating from tentative beginnings in *Nelungaloo, Rooney* and particularly *Liyanage.*

This development was reinforced by the decision of the High Court in *Lim v Minister for Immigration, Local Government and Ethnic Affairs*[115] in which a number of amendments to the Migration Act 1958 (Cth) were challenged. Prior to their enactment, the plaintiffs—Lim and 35 other Cambodian nationals who had arrived illegally in Australia—were being held in custody pending the reconsideration of their failed applications for refugee status. They applied to the Federal Court for orders that they be released. Two days prior to hearing, Parliament amended the Act by the addition of section 54R, which provided that '[a] court is not to order the release from custody of a designated person'. That section 54R was directed at the plaintiffs was made clear by the definition of 'designated person' in section 54K as referring to illegal immigrants arriving by boat on Australian shores. Sections 54L and 54N were also added, requiring, respectively, that a designated person in custody must be kept in custody until either removed from the country or given an entry permit; and that a designated person not in custody may be arrested without warrant, detained and kept in custody for the purposes of section 54L.

In challenging these provisions, the plaintiffs argued,[116] relying on *BLF (Cth), Rooney* and *Nelungaloo,* that although Parliament may legislate to alter rights in issue in pending litigation (the Changed Law Rule), these

---

[111]   *Ibid*, at 378.
[112]   *Ibid.*
[113]   *Ibid*, at 395.
[114]   *Ibid*, at 387.
[115]   *Lim v Minister for Immigration, Local Government and Ethnic Affairs* (1992) 176 CLR 1.
[116]   *Ibid*, at 4ff.

provisions breached the separation of powers by interfering with the 'very judicial process involved in the release proceedings'.[117] They likened the legislation to the State legislation in *BLF (NSW)*. 'The present Act', it was submitted, 'is specifically directed to courts and their processes'.[118] Heavy reliance was placed not only on the existence of the pending proceedings as an indication of direction, but also the *ad hominem* nature of the legislation:

> The legislation selects particular persons and, without otherwise affecting their legal rights, provides for them what is in effect imprisonment … Sections 54K, 54L and 54R are a legislative prejudgment in substitution of a deliberation and determination of the Federal Court that the plaintiffs had sought to invoke. The judicial process of the application of law to fact is thwarted.[119]

In the alternative, it was submitted that the Act was unconstitutional as an Act of Attainder.[120] In reply, the Minister sought to discount the significance of these elements as indicia of direction, in order to establish that the legislation was a substantive change in the law.[121] He submitted, consistently with the authorities, that the specificity and the *ad hominem* nature of the legislation were not unconstitutional. Neither was it unconstitutional per se for the legislature to enact legislation for the purpose of circumventing or forestalling any decision in a pending case, so long as it constituted a substantive change in the law.[122] As the Act did 'not direct or restrict the discretion or judgment of the judiciary to decide matters according to law'[123] it was therefore constitutional.

The Court unanimously upheld the validity of sections 54L and 54N, but by a majority struck down section 54R as unconstitutional.[124] Brennan, Deane and Dawson JJ, in the majority, first examined these provisions from the point of view of the integrity of the 'judicial power of the Commonwealth', stating that this power could not be conferred upon any organ of the executive, nor was the legislature permitted to enact a law which

---

[117]   *Ibid*, at 5.
[118]   *Ibid*.
[119]   *Ibid*, at 5–6.
[120]   *Ibid*, at 5.
[121]   *Ibid*, at 6ff.
[122]   Relying on the authority of *BLF (Cth)), Rooney* and *Nelungaloo.*
[123]   *Lim v Minister for Immigration, Local Government and Ethnic Affairs* (1992) 176 CLR 1 at 6.
[124]   The majority in relation to the s 54R issue consisted of Brennan, Deane, Dawson JJ (in a joint judgment) and Gaudron J in a separate judgment.

requires or authorises the courts in which the judicial power of the Commonwealth is exclusively vested to exercise judicial power in a manner which is
inconsistent with the essential character of a court or with the nature of judicial
power.[125]

The determination and punishment of criminal guilt under a Commonwealth law was one of those functions which 'by reason of their nature or
because of historical considerations, have become established as essentially and exclusively judicial in character'.[126] Thus, there were limitations on Parliament enacting laws vesting the Executive with power to
detain citizens in custody 'notwithstanding that the power was conferred
in terms which sought to divorce such detention in custody from both
punishment and criminal guilt' as it sought to do in the impugned
legislation.[127] Such power to detain 'exists only as an incident of the
exclusively judicial function of adjudging and punishing criminal
guilt',[128] excepting those situations of non-punitive executive detention
such as arrest and detention pursuant to a warrant pending trial and
detention on the basis of mental illness or infectious disease for the
protection of the community.[129] Thus, the separation of judicial power
created a 'constitutional immunity from being imprisoned by the Commonwealth except pursuant to an order by a court in the exercise of the
judicial power of the Commonwealth'.[130] Gaudron J, agreed generally,
although she was not 'presently persuaded that legislation authorizing
detention in circumstances involving no breach of the criminal law and
travelling beyond presently accepted categories is necessarily and inevitably offensive to Ch III'.[131] Sections 54L and 54N, given their exclusive
application to non-citizens, were held to be valid by the court as examples of valid non-punitive executive detention, pursuant to 51(xix) of the
Constitution, the 'aliens' power. It did not involve the exercise of judicial
power as '[w]hen conferred upon the Executive, it takes its character
from the executive powers to exclude, admit and deport of which it is an
incident'.[132] The existence of the plaintiff's pending action was not a

---

[125]   *Lim v Minister for Immigration, Local Government and Ethnic Affairs* (1992) 176 CLR 1 at
26–7.
[126]   *Ibid*, at 27.
[127]   *Ibid*.
[128]   *Ibid*.
[129]   *Ibid*, at 29.
[130]   *Ibid*.
[131]   *Ibid*, at 55.
[132]   *Ibid*, at 32.

relevant consideration in this regard.[133] This reasoning was thus independent of considerations relating to legislative interference in the pending case, which were, in any event, subject to a discrete submission by the plaintiff and considered separately by the Court.

On the question of legislative interference the majority reasoned that constitutionality was determined by reference to 'known or prospective legal proceedings'[134] and whether the legislature was predetermining the outcome of legal disputes under the guise of properly enacted legislation. This issue was not determined primarily by reference to any particular or precise power that the legislature was granting to itself, or to the executive, in order to determine whether it was judicial in nature. Nor was it determined primarily by reference to a particular power that it was requiring the courts to exercise which itself was not judicial or inconsistent with judicial power. Rather, the enquiry was exclusively concerned with whether the legislature had predetermined the outcome of pending proceedings, or the legal or factual issues therein, by directing the court to make certain findings, and in so doing acting in a way which was other than substantively legislative. It could also be said that the judicial nature of the power the court was required to exercise was compromised because its independent adjudication on certain critical matters was compromised. It was these considerations in particular which were the basis for the declaration of invalidity of section 54R.

Sections 54L and 54N were not regarded by the Court as unconstitutional legislative interferences because they were held to be laws generally relating to executive powers of detention of non-citizens, and they did not address the precise legal issues that were to be addressed in the pending litigation. The plaintiffs relied heavily on section 54N(2), which provided that a person must be taken into custody, or maintained in

---

[133] This is a different issue to that relating to the determination of whether the legislature was requiring the court to exercise a power which was consistent with the essential character of a court or with the nature of judicial power. It too merely examines the nature of the power that is given to the courts by reference to the power itself, and not its effect on actual or future judicial proceedings.

[134] *Ibid*, at 34. In addition to pending proceedings, their Honours were also referring to proceedings which had not yet been commenced but which *might* be commenced and which involved a class of persons which was so precisely defined by the impugned legislation that it was possible to identify them precisely. When they used this phrase, their Honours were responding to a submission by the plaintiffs that the impugned sections were invalid as a 'usurpation' of the judicial power of the Commonwealth because they applied only to a class of persons which was 'so limited by definition as to amount in substance to a specification of individuals' and 'were enacted in order to affect the outcome of known or prospective legal proceedings by those individuals'. The difference, however, is not of consequence for present purposes in discovering their attitude on the precise issue of pending cases. It is indicative, however, that the propositions which emanate from the judgment are applicable also to prospective proceedings of the type which would precisely arise relating to issues of release from custody of 'designated persons'.

custody, even where their release was ordered by a court prior to the section's enactment. The new circumstances created by the amendments meant that the overriding of previous release orders was not a legislative revision of final judgments. Moreover, this section did not purport 'to authorize an executive overriding of an order made by a court' pursuant to these amendments.[135] Hence, the Changed Law Rule applied.

> The fact that the proceedings seeking an order for release of the plaintiffs were pending in the Federal Court did not have the effect that the conferral by [these provisions], or the subsequent exercise, of a new executive power of detention constituted a usurpation of, or an impermissible interference with, the exercise of the judicial power of the Commonwealth.[136]

Section 54R, on the other hand, was held to be expressly addressed to the judiciary, directing it not to order the release of a designated person from custody. The majority concluded that it purported 'to direct the courts, including this Court, not to order [a designated person's] release from custody regardless of the circumstances'.[137] That it was possible that there might be circumstances where such imprisonment may be unlawful was critical to the ultimate conclusion: '[O]nce it appears that a designated person may be unlawfully held in custody in purported pursuance of Div 4B, it necessarily follows that the provision of s 54R is invalid'.[138] Brennan, Dawson and Deane JJ, with whom Gaudron J agreed, stated:

> In terms, s 54R is a direction by the Parliament to the courts as to the manner in which they are to exercise their jurisdiction. It is one thing for the Parliament, within the limits of the legislative power conferred upon it by the Constitution, to grant or withhold jurisdiction. *It is quite a different thing for the Parliament to purport to direct the courts as to the manner and outcome of the exercise of jurisdiction.* The former falls within the legislative power that the Constitution, including Chapter III itself, entrusts to the Parliament. The latter constitutes an impermissible intrusion into the judicial power which Ch III vests exclusively in the courts which it designates.[139] (Emphasis added.)

The majority thus confirmed the critical distinction between a substantive amendment to the law—which in this context would have been a statute that limited the jurisdiction of the courts in accordance with the Constitution[140]—and a prescriptive act. The fact that the majority did not

---

[135]   *Ibid*, at 34.

[136]   *Ibid*, at 35.

[137]   *Ibid*.

[138]   *Ibid*, at 36. The other ground for holding the section invalid was that it contravened the direct vesting of jurisdiction pursuant to s 75(v) of the Constitution.

[139]   *Ibid*, at 36–7.

[140]   Parliament may legislate to limit the jurisdiction of the federal courts in relation to all matters, excepting of course the original jurisdiction of the High Court in s 75 of the Constitution.

examine in any detail the usual indicia of direction reflected the clear indication of direction on the face of the statute, as in the *BLF (NSW)* legislation. The majority made passing reference to *BLF (NSW)*, *Liyanage* and *Polyukhovich* only to dispose, correctly, of a submission that section 54R, together with other related sections, was of specific application to the plaintiffs and the pending proceedings, and that this, per se, was sufficient to make a finding of unconstitutional legislative interference.[141] Gaudron J was in general agreement with this aspect of the judgment.[142]

The minority[143] can also be said to have been in general agreement on principle because they upheld the validity of section 54R only by reading it down to mean that a court might not release from custody a designated person *lawfully* detained.[144] Otherwise, Toohey J would have regarded it as 'clearly an interference with the judicial power [which] cannot be sustained'.[145] McHugh J stated that in as much as 'it directs a court not to give effect to substantive rights while exercising federal judicial power, it would usurp the judicial power of the Commonwealth and be invalid'.[146]

The minority judgments also referred specifically and precisely to the previous line of authority. Toohey J relied on it to establish that it was constitutional for a legislature to enact legislation that affected substantive rights in pending proceedings, but not the judicial adjudication in those proceedings.[147] McHugh J also referred to the exact same passage from *BLF (Cth)*[148] relied on by Toohey J, adding that 'there is no automatic interference with the judicial process even when the motive or purpose of the Parliament in enacting the legislation is to circumvent or forestall the relevant proceedings'.[149] Nevertheless, section 54R was not such a provision that could be characterised as a change in the law in the situation where it was ordering a court not to order the release from custody of persons *unlawfully* detained.[150]

---

[141] *Lim v Minister for Immigration, Local Government and Ethnic Affairs* (1992) 176 CLR 1 at 34.

[142] *Ibid*, at 53.

[143] Mason CJ, Toohey and McHugh JJ.

[144] *Lim v Minister for Immigration, Local Government and Ethnic Affairs* (1992) 176 CLR 1 at 11–14, 50–51, and 68 respectively.

[145] *Ibid*, at 50.

[146] *Ibid*, at 68.

[147] *Ibid*, at 49.

[148] *Lim v Minister for Immigration, Local Government and Ethnic Affairs* (1992) 176 CLR 1 at 73.

[149] This passage is from (1986) 161 CLR 88 at 96.

[150] Subsequent to *Lim*, the High Court in *Leeth v Commonwealth* also confirmed in obiter that the developments in relation to the issue of legislative interference were recognised by the court. It regarded it as a particular type of usurpation of judicial power by Mason CJ, Dawson and McHugh JJ: '[L]egislation may amount to a usurpation of judicial power, particularly in a criminal case, if it prejudges an issue with respect to a particular individual and requires a court to exercise its function accordingly (see *Liyanage v The Queen*). It is upon this principle that bills of attainder may offend against the separation of judicial

Accordingly, both majority and minority judgments confirmed the development of principle centred on the Changed Law Rule, the direction principle and related principles. Following *Lim*, these principles appear to have been firmly established in the jurisprudence of the High Court as a discrete set of principles applicable in the pending case scenario.

VI.   THE DIRECTION RULE AT THE CROSSROADS: *NICHOLAS V THE QUEEN*

In *Nicholas v The Queen*,[151] however, the High Court appeared to retreat from this position to the extent that a majority of the judges either did not apply these discrete principles to a factual scenario that clearly warranted their application or downplayed the significance of the direction principle and set a very high threshold for its application. They held that there was no breach of the separation of powers.[152] While both Kirby and McHugh JJ in the minority did accept the principles, only Kirby J regarded them as a basis for invalidating the impugned legislation on the facts. The problematic aspect of the majority judgments was not that they upheld the validity of the legislation, but rather that they appeared impliedly to reject the subtle interplay between the Changed Law Rule and the direction principle or set too high a threshold for their application.

Nicholas was presented in the County Court of Victoria on an indictment for possession of a prohibited import (heroin) pursuant to section 233B of the Customs Act 1901 (Cth) and on two other counts of criminal breaches of Victorian statutes. The heroin had been deliberately imported by law enforcement officers as part of a 'controlled operation', although such conduct was itself in contravention of section 233B, and thus illegal. While Nicholas's trial was pending, the High Court in *Ridgeway v R*[153] rendered inadmissible as evidence the fact of illegal importation of any prohibited substance even if it was part of a 'controlled operation' by law enforcement agencies. The *Ridgeway* prosecution was permanently

---

power. (see *Polyukhovich v Commonwealth* (1991) 172 CLR 501). But a law of general application which seeks in some respect to govern the exercise of a jurisdiction which it confers does not trespass upon the judicial function' (*Leeth v Commonwealth* 174 CLR 455 at 469–70).

[151]   *Nicholas v The Queen* (1998) 193 CLR 173.

[152]   By a majority of five (Brennan CJ, Toohey, Gaudron, Gummow and Hayne JJ), to two (McHugh and Kirby JJ).

[153]   *Ridgeway v R* (1995) 184 CLR 19. This was an appeal from a conviction for criminal breaches of the Customs Act 1901 (Cth) in the Supreme Court of South Australia.

stayed.[154] The stated rationale was the need for the maintenance, by the court, of the integrity of the administration of justice and the protection of its own processes.[155] Relying on *Ridgeway*, Nicholas applied success-fully to the County Court to have the evidence of the importation of the heroin excluded at his trial and for orders permanently staying his trial in relation to the Customs Act offences. He was to be tried for the other offences and his trial remained pending in this regard.

In response, Parliament amended the Crimes Act 1914 (Cth) by insert-ing Part 1AB to secure the viability, post-*Ridgeway*, of 'controlled opera-tions' and any resulting prosecutions.[156] It is significant that it provided differently for future and past operations. Division 2 declared *future* 'controlled operations', precisely defined, to be legal. Of direct relevance to Nicholas's case, however, was Division 3 dealing with *past* 'controlled operations', whether completed or commenced. Rather than remove the taint of illegality from such operations, the Division expressly addressed the exercise of the relevant judicial discretion as to the admissibility of evidence obtained from such operations.[157] The intention of Parliament was to reverse, retrospectively, the effect of *Ridgeway* on such evidence, although maintaining the illegality of the conduct which brought it about.[158] Thus, the pivotal section 15X provided expressly for prosecu-tions for offences pursuant to section 233B of the Customs Act 1901 (Cth) as follows:

> In determining ... whether evidence that narcotic goods were imported into Australia in contravention of the *Customs Act 1901* should be admitted, the fact that a law enforcement officer committed an offence in importing the narcotic goods, or in aiding, abetting, counselling, procuring, or being in any way knowingly concerned in, their importation *is to be disregarded*. (Emphasis added.)

However section 15G(2) provided that the new Part 1AB was 'not intended to limit a discretion that a court has ... a) to exclude evidence in criminal proceedings; or b) to stay criminal proceedings in the interests of justice', this was made, very significantly 'subject to section 15X'. Given the key significance of such evidence in the Nicholas prosecution, and

---

[154] Two of the judges, Brennan and Toohey JJ held that Ridgeway was entitled to acquittal.

[155] *Ridgeway v R* (1995) 184 CLR 19 at 31–2 in the joint judgment of Mason CJ, Deane and Dawson JJ, with whom Gaudron J agreed.

[156] See the Explanatory Memorandum to the Crimes Amendment (Controlled Opera-tions) Bill 1996, Second Reading Speech to the Crimes Amendment (Controlled Operations) Bill 1996, House of Representatives, *Parliamentary Debates*, (Hansard), 20 June 1996, MC 2510ff. See also in relation to an earlier Bill to the same effect, Senate Legal and Constitu-tional Legislation Committee, Crimes Amendment (Controlled Operations) Bill 1995.

[157] Section 15G.

[158] This was clearly stated in the Explanatory Memorandum to the amending Act.

indeed any other pending prosecutions, the apparent direction in section 15X prima facie gave rise to an issue of legislative interference in a pending case. It stated expressly that the provisions of the section were 'for the purposes of a prosecution' for the very offence for which Nicholas had been charged. Indeed, the legislation appeared tailor-made for such a pending prosecution based on past 'controlled operations'. Although limited to that particular discrete aspect of judicial discretion relating to the admissibility of evidence, this was a critical determinant as to whether the stay would be lifted and as to whether Nicholas would be found guilty in the resulting prosecution.

The Crown thus subsequently applied to vacate the orders permanently staying that aspect of the prosecution based on the Customs Act offences. In response, Nicholas challenged the constitutional validity of the amendments relying on two main submissions. First, that by Division 3, Parliament infringed or usurped the exercise of the judicial power of the Commonwealth. Relying on *Ridgeway*, it was submitted that the section undermined the integrity of the judicial process, and public confidence in the administration of justice, by directing the court to disregard the illegal conduct. Because the protection of the integrity of its processes was an essential aspect of the 'judicial power of the Commonwealth' exclusively to be exercised by the Chapter III courts, Parliament was purporting to require such a court to exercise its discretionary power in a manner, or to produce an outcome, which was inconsistent with the essential character of a court and/or with the nature of judicial power. Secondly, as a separate argument, Parliament impermissibly interfered with judicial functions in relation to Nicholas's case and other pending and prospective prosecutions based on past controlled operations. Section 15X applied to identifiable cases and was directed specifically to the accused in those cases. The matter was removed to the High Court,[159] which, by a majority of five to two,[160] found section 15X to be valid. While the majority judgments focussed primarily on the first of the above arguments, the minority judgments of Kirby and McHugh JJ considered the direction principle in greater detail.

A. The Judgment of Kirby J

It was in the reasoning of Kirby J that the existence of the pending proceedings was a vital factor in the determination of constitutional

---

[159] The issue of whether the stay should be lifted did not here give rise to the issue of whether a final judgment of the court was being specifically overruled by the legislature. The court itself was left to decide whether to lift the stay.

[160] Brennan CJ, Toohey, Gaudron, Gummow and Hayne JJ; Kirby and McHugh JJ dissenting.

validity.[161] 'Parliament may not *enter into* the activities properly belonging to the judicial power in a way inconsistent with its exercise by the courts'[162] (emphasis added). It is not a case of the legislature requiring the courts to exercise non-judicial functions, or requiring them to act inconsistently with the exercise of judicial power or their nature as a court, except to the extent that it is hindering their 'decisional independence'. He emphasised the *non-legislative* nature of an exercise of power by the legislature *entering into* activities properly belonging to the courts.

The clearest example was an institutional usurpation whereby the legislature purported 'to constitute itself or some other non-court body, a tribunal to perform functions reserved by the Constitution to the courts'.[163] Given the strict application of the separation of judicial power in the Australian constitutional context, it was almost inconceivable that such egregious forms of legislative interference would occur.[164] More likely they would occur under the guise of otherwise properly enacted legislation such as purported 'to prejudge an issue which is before a court affecting a particular individual and which required that court to exercise its functions in accordance with such pre-judgment'.[165] The nature of such legislation may range from, on the one extreme, a Bill of Attainder 'which amounts to a parliamentary finding of guilt and is thus offensive to the separation of powers'[166] to, at the other extreme, 'a law of general application', that is, properly enacted legislation of general and prospective application.[167] Without more, the latter does not offend constitutionally even if it does have consequences for the determination of a particular issue in a pending case, if not the final outcome thereof.[168] Thus, Kirby J confirmed the dichotomy central to the established position between a valid change in the law and an unconstitutional direction that does not amend the law. In these most obvious situations, the application of the direction principle did not pose great difficulties. Between the two extremes, however, 'lie a myriad of instances which fall on one side of the

---

[161]   *Nicholas v The Queen* (1998) 193 CLR 173 at 254.
[162]   *Ibid*, at 254.
[163]   *Ibid*.
[164]   See above, at 57ff.
[165]   *Nicholas v The Queen* (1998) 193 CLR 173 at 254.
[166]   *Ibid*, at 256 (Kirby J). See *ibid* at 221–2 (McHugh J).
[167]   *Ibid*, at 256 (Kirby J).
[168]   *Ibid*. That is, the pending case may be affected if that law alters the law which is applicable in the case, though the affect does not constitute an unconstitutional interference as the amendment is an exercise of power by the legislature which is substantively legislative.

line of constitutional validity or the other'[169] and in relation to which 'minds will reasonably differ'.[170] Kirby J recognised that section 15X had to be judged in this context.

The determination of a precise definition of the 'judicial power of the Commonwealth', the elusiveness of which concept both minority judgments referred to,[171] was not therefore fundamental to this enquiry.[172] Kirby J in particular queried the value which can be derived from it in the present context given that the critical factor here was unconstitutional *direction* and *its* definition.[173] In any event, he was seeking to protect that core, undisputed element of judicial power represented by the independent adjudication of a legal controversy pursuant to existing law. Thus, Kirby J referred to legislation that 'impermissibly seeks to dictate how the [judicial] power or discretion will operate in a particular case'.[174] He determined whether the direction principle had been breached not by reference to a predetermined exclusive definition of the elements of direction but rather by a careful scrutiny of the particular legislation *in the context of the pending proceedings* to locate the existence of relevant indicia of direction.[175]

Four of these were evident on the facts: the legislation's *ad hominem* nature, its retrospectivity, its 'high particularity', and the fact that it affected matters which were traditionally regarded as within the province of judicial discretion. In relation to the *ad hominem* issue, it was not necessary that individuals be named[176]; although, if they were, its force as an indicator was magnified.[177] It sufficed if the legislation was 'highly selective and clearly directed at a particular individual or individuals

---

[169] *Ibid.*

[170] *Ibid.*

[171] *Ibid*, at 219 (McHugh J) and 256 (Kirby J). See also *R v Davidson* (1954) 90 CLR 353 at 366 (Dixon CJ and McTiernan J.)

[172] They nevertheless confirm that the central attributes relevant to the present enquiry to be that the judicial power consists of the exercise of that power required for the resolution of controversies between citizens or between citizens and the Crown, which resolution is a binding and authoritative decision based on the determination of existing rights and duties according to law. See the oft-quoted standard definitions in *Huddart, Parker and Co Pty Ltd v Moorehead* (1909) 8 CLR 330 at 357 (Griffith CJ) and in *Fencott v Muller* (1983) 152 CLR 570 at 608.

[173] Kirby J, in particular, queries whether any valuable assistance can be derived from a precise definition, in the present enquiry. '[S]uch generalities give scant guidance when, as here, a particular statutory provision is challenged and is said to be an impermissible legislative intrusion upon, or derogation from, the judicial power'. *Nicholas v The Queen* (1998) 193 CLR 173 at 256.

[174] *Ibid*, at 257.

[175] *Ibid*, at 256 ff.

[176] See *Lim v Minister for Immigration, Local Government and Ethnic Affairs* (1992) 176 CLR 1 at 26–9.

[177] See the United States decision *Robertson v Seattle Audubon Society* 503 US 429 (1992) discussed in detail at p 135.

[whereupon] it is much more likely that it will amount to an impermissible intrusion upon, or usurpation of, the judicial power'.[178] Nowhere did he treat the existence of *ad hominem* legislation, or indeed any of the other indicia he identified, as per se determinative.[179] In relation to retrospectivity,[180] while there was no constitutional bar to the enactment of retrospective legislation,[181] Kirby J nevertheless regarded it as potentially indicative of legislative direction. The third factor, the 'high particularity' of the legislation, concerned the extent to which the legislation was fashioned to address those precise issues which the pending case would have to resolve.[182] Finally, his Honour made specific reference to the legislation affecting the laws of evidence. As Parliament had an 'undoubted' power to make and amend laws relating to the laws of evidence,[183] to the extent, therefore, that section 15X could be characterised as an amendment to such laws, the constitutional challenge would not prevail. Nevertheless, it may heighten judicial sensitivity to the possibility of unconstitutional interference, as rules of evidence can be critical to the outcome.

Before examining these indicia and their interplay, Kirby J examined carefully the interplay between the intention of Parliament and the circumstances of the pending proceedings.[184] The records of the parliamentary debates revealed that Parliament was concerned that, following *Ridgeway,* a number of prosecutions would have to be abandoned with the consequent community disapproval that this would entail. However, 'the motivation of the parliament or the fact that it might have gone about the legislation in Div 3 in a different way was irrelevant. The only duty of the court is to measure Div 3, and specifically s 15X, against the requirements of the Constitution'.[185] In *Ridgeway*, the High Court invited Parliament to remove the taint of illegality from controlled operations, to

---

[178] *Nicholas v The Queen* (1998) 193 CLR 173 at 257; See also *Liyanage v R* [1967] 1 AC 259 at 267; *Leeth v Commonwealth,* (1992) 174 CLR 455 at 460–70; *Polyukhovich v Commonwealth* (1991) 172 CLR 501 at 650; and cf *Plaut v Spendthrift Farm* 514 US 211 (1995).

[179] *Nicholas v The Queen* (1998) 193 CLR 173 at 257. See also *Lim v Minister for Immigration, Local Government and Ethnic Affairs* (1992) 176 CLR 1 at 27 and *Liyanage v R* [1967] 1 AC 259 at 280–90.

[180] *Nicholas v The Queen* (1998) 193 CLR 173 at 259.

[181] *Polyukhovich v Commonwealth* (1991) 172 CLR 501 at 533; *Nelungaloo Pty Ltd v Commonwealth* (1948) 75 CLR 495 at 503; *R v Humby; Ex parte Rooney* (1973) 129 CLR 231 at 250.

[182] *Nicholas v The Queen* (1998) 193 CLR 173 at 260ff.

[183] *Ibid*, at 260. See *Williamson v Ah On* (1926) 39 CLR 95 at 108–9, *Milicevic v Campbell* (1975) 132 CLR 307 at 316 and *Sorby v Commonwealth* (1983) 152 CLR 281 at 298–9.

[184] *Ibid*, at 244ff. He examined very carefully in this regard the parliamentary debates, statements of the relevant minister, the explanatory memorandum to the bill, and other background materials relating to it.

[185] *Ibid*, at 249.

legitimise them.[186] But although that invitation was heeded for future operations, it was significant for Kirby J that this was not attempted for past operations.[187] Instead, section 15X was prescriptive with respect to the admission of evidence relevant to the public policy discretion that the court was to exercise, even though the court had previously turned its face against the admission of evidence procured by illegal conduct:

> Given the history, language and obvious purpose of the Act, I do not consider that s 15X, if valid, could be interpreted to preserve any residual discretion based upon the *fact* that narcotic goods were illegally imported as distinct from the *offence* thereby committed. Such a construction would also contradict the materials placed before the court relevant to the purposes of the parliament in enacting the provision.[188]

Kirby J proceeded to find that the legislation directed the court, when exercising its discretion to admit illegally obtained evidence, to disregard the offence committed by law enforcement officials in controlled operations, notwithstanding that the High Court in *Ridgeway* had found that condoning and rewarding such unlawful conduct was incompatible with the integrity of the judicial power and the maintenance of public confidence in the judicial process.[189] The *ad homimen* nature of the legislation, and its selective application to prosecutions based on past 'controlled operations', reinforced the fact that this was not a change in the law of evidence, but instead an unconstitutional direction.

In so finding, Kirby J rejected the Crown's submission that although section 15X did affect a relatively small number of people, it was of general application.[190] The Crown also submitted that although the legislation did affect pending prosecutions, there was no legislative direction, as parliament had simply provided statutory guidance for the exercise of a general judicial discretion, long regarded as a legitimate and indeed proper legislative function.[191] It had simply clarified the relevant public policy with the intention of repairing the technical default of the law enforcement officers who had acted in good faith under the ministerial agreement before *Ridgeway*. In rejecting this constitutionally innocuous view of the legislation, Kirby J, relying on *Liyanage*,[192] noted that although the impugned legislation in that case did not expressly refer to any particular party, it was nevertheless *ad hominem* as it was clear to

---

[186]   *Ridgeway v The Queen* (1995) 184 CLR 19 at 44 (Mason CJ, Deane and Dawson JJ).
[187]   *Nicholas v The Queen* (1998) 193 CLR 173 at 249.
[188]   *Ibid*, at 251. Relevant materials being the Explanatory Memorandum, Crimes Amendment (Controlled Operations) Bill 1996.
[189]   *Ibid*, at 264.
[190]   *Ibid*, at 260 ff.
[191]   Reliance was placed on the authority of *BLF v Commonwealth* (1986) 161 CLR 88.
[192]   *R v Liyanage* [1967] 1 AC 259.

whom the legislation referred. Significant also in *Liyanage* was the fact that the legislation clearly dealt with the very issues that were the subject of the pending hearing. Although he acknowledged that the present case did not match it in this regard, Kirby J found that 'in material respects' there were 'close parallels'.[193] Section 15X was addressed to particular offences on particular and identifiable occasions in the past and was designed to make admissible evidence which, at the time it was gathered, and until the Act came into effect, was likely to be held inadmissible as illegally obtained.[194] Also,

> it was designed to direct the court [to] disregard illegality ... [by] law enforcement officers although no defence, immunity or excuse was provided by the Act to such officers to exempt them from the illegality which, in the case of the applicant, *Ridgeway* holds otherwise to require orders for a permanent stay.[195]

The retrospectivity of the legislation became relevant to the extent that, '[i]t requires courts to disregard past illegality on the part of law enforcement officers *although such illegality is admitted and, indeed, is a pre-condition to the operation of the section*'[196] (emphasis added). Kirby J thus recognised and endorsed the rigour with which the Privy Council in *Liyanage* examined the legislation for indications of unconstitutional direction, echoing the position he took in *BLF (NSW)*: 'In *Liyanage*, the Privy Council looked to substance not form. So should we'.[197]

He also emphasised the need to look to substance when he dealt with the issue of the 'high particularity' of the legislation.[198] It clearly dealt with the precise legal issues in Nicholas's case, upon which the future conduct of the prosecution depended, and all those against whom prosecutions would be brought as a result of past 'controlled operations':

> In their cases, and theirs alone, the law governing their pending trials has been changed in a way that seriously affects them. There could be few more significant changes of substance to the law affecting a person awaiting trial on

---

[193]   *Nicholas v The Queen* (1998) 193 CLR 173 at 263.
[194]   *Ibid*. He also stated that: '[t]he number of persons who would be affected by s 15X can be no mystery. It is not as if "controlled operations" pursuant to the Ministerial Agreement were a daily affair. By this time, the number would be conclusively ascertained. Almost certainly, only five individuals are involved. The fact must therefore be faced that this is very special legislation addressed to the courts directly affecting five or so particular persons already charged and awaiting trial in those courts. In their cases, and theirs alone, the law governing their pending trials has been changed in a way that seriously affects them' (at 261).
[195]   *Ibid*, at 263.
[196]   *Ibid*.
[197]   *Ibid*.
[198]   *Ibid*, at 261.

criminal charges than the passage of particular provisions which, in effect, deprive that person of a permanent stay of proceedings.[199]

Kirby J recognised that if the form of the legislation alone was considered, it would not allow for a proper discernment of the existence of *indicia* of unconstitutional legislative direction to the judiciary. Kirby J recognised that '"[v]alue judgments" are inescapably involved in such questions',[200] the complexities involved and that the line between legislative and judicial powers was complicated by the fact that '"[t]he boundary of judicial power defies, or transcends, purely abstract conceptual analysis"'.[201] Nevertheless, he urged that these difficulties not deter attempts to discern the true nature of the legislation. It is interesting to note, therefore, that although adopting an important aspect of the functionalist critique of the formalist approach to separation of powers, the result is a strict application of the direction principle. This reinforces the point that was made above that when dealing with uncontroversially core branch functions, the functionalist analysis of an alleged breach of the separation of powers will almost always produce the same outcome as a formalist one.[202] Thus, the above indicia ought at the very least to have put the court on notice that there was a serious possibility of constitutional invalidity on this basis. This was reinforced by the fact that the legislation distinguished and treated differently past and future 'controlled operations'.

Kirby J, however, fell short of declaring invalidity on the basis of the direction principle alone, although such a conclusion was open to him on the facts. The additional factor emerged from the separate, though related, set of principles concerning the integrity of the exercise of 'judicial power' by Chapter III courts.[203] His Honour was troubled by the direction to disregard unexcused illegality or criminality on the part of law enforcement officers. A critical aspect of the 'judicial power of the Commonwealth' was the power, exercisable exclusively by the courts pursuant to the separation of powers, to protect the integrity of their own processes and to prevent the administration of justice from falling into disrepute. This he regarded to be the essence of the *Ridgeway* discretion: 'a principle of public policy bound up in the self-regard of the courts constituted or invested with the judicial power of the Commonwealth'.[204] Section 15X was that type of interference that purported to prevent the

---

[199]   *Ibid.*
[200]   *Ibid*, at 263.
[201]   *Ibid*, quoting from *R v Trade Practices Tribunal; Ex Parte Tasmanian Breweries Pty Ltd* (1970) 123 CLR 361 at 394.
[202]   See ch 1 at 40ff.
[203]   *Ibid*, at 264ff.
[204]   *Ibid*, at 259.

judiciary from exercising this exclusive power of protecting the integrity of its processes and was therefore invalid on *Ridgeway* grounds. Nevertheless, this should not overshadow the fact that Kirby J clearly endorsed the direction principle and related principles as they had been developing to date.

B. The Judgment of McHugh J

McHugh J likewise acknowledged the directive nature of section 15X.[205] He too emphasised that element of the legislation preventing the courts from exercising the discretion defined by *Ridgeway* as exclusive to Chapter III courts.[206] *Ridgeway* 'did more … than extend the *Bunning v Cross* discretion to cases where the illegal or improper conduct of law enforcement officers has created one of the elements of an offence' because the majority judgments made 'it clear that this discretion depends on the necessity to preserve the integrity of the administration of justice and to protect the processes of the courts of justice'.[207] Accordingly, 'it is "an incident of the judicial powers vested in the courts in relation to criminal matters"'.[208] Parliament therefore did not have the competence to remove it, or any element of it, from the exclusively judicial domain. Section 15X, while not changing the law to legalise the importation of narcotics inherent in past 'controlled operations', to the extent that it purported to remove the discretion of the courts to reject the admission of evidence based on such events, was invalid.

His Honour acknowledged that the separation of powers doctrine, 'to be fully effective', must protect the judicial branch from legislative interference.[209] He drew the important distinction between an interference with judicial power—'legislative interference with the exercise of judicial power by the courts'—and usurpation—'when the legislature has exercised judicial power on its own behalf'.[210] The legislation invalidated in *Lim* he regarded as an example of the latter because it provided for detention of certain persons and directing the courts not to order their release. Similarly, he regarded the legislation impugned in *Liyanage* as a 'grave and deliberate incursion into the judicial sphere'.[211] He invoked Patrick Lane's definition of impermissible interference with judicial functions, which did not limit unconstitutionality to legislation

---

[205] *Ibid*, at 215.
[206] *Ibid*, at 216.
[207] *Ibid*.
[208] *Ibid*, at 217–18.
[209] *Ibid*, at 220.
[210] *Ibid*.
[211] *Ibid*.

which directed the ultimate outcome of the pending suit.[212] Lane had written that a breach of the *Liyanage* principle would occur when there was:

> legislative interference 'in *specific* proceedings'; (b) the interference 'affect[s] … *pending* litigation'…(c) the interference affects the judicial process itself, that is, 'the discretion or judgment of the judiciary', or 'the rights, authority or jurisdiction of [the] court'.[213]

Lane had also stated that legislation 'altering evidentiary rules' may be invalid if 'specifically directed against particular individuals and intended to make their conviction easy'.[214] McHugh J referred to *Polyukhovich* to note that there would be a usurpation of judicial power if a law inflicted punishment on specified persons without a judicial trial.

While distinguishing the present facts from the cases mentioned in the previous paragraph, his Honour nevertheless did locate the existence of an impermissible direction because section 15X

> does … direct courts exercising federal jurisdiction to disregard a fact that is critical in exercising a discretion that is necessary to protect the integrity of Ch III courts and to maintain public confidence in the administration of criminal justice. That being so, s 15X infringes the judicial power of the Commonwealth just as effectively as if it purported to change the direction or outcome of *pending* proceedings.[215]

It is clear from his Honour's reasoning that he did not regard section 15X as a substantive amendment to the law at all but rather an unconstitutional legislative prescription, which purported to direct the court not to take into account a factor—the criminality of the conduct of law enforcement officers—which it had already held was 'at the core of a Ch III court's power to protect the integrity of its processes'.[216] His Honour reasoned as follows:

> Section 15X operates on the hypothesis that law enforcement officers have committed an offence against s 233B and that it is their criminal conduct that has brought into existence an essential element of the charge against the accused. Yet the section then directs courts exercising the judicial power of the Commonwealth to disregard the critical fact that the offence by the accused exists as a result of the criminal conduct of a law enforcement officer. That is to say, s 15X directs those courts to disregard a fact that, according to *Ridgeway*, is crucial in determining whether the integrity of the processes of the courts are

---

[212]   *Ibid*, at 221.
[213]   PH Lane, *Lane's Commentary on The Australian Constitution*, 2nd edn (North Ryde NSW, Law Book Co 1997) 483.
[214]   *Ibid*, at 484.
[215]   *Nicholas v The Queen* (1998) 193 CLR 173 at 222.
[216]   *Ibid*, at 224.

being demeaned … I cannot accept the claim that such a direction does not infringe the judicial power of the Commonwealth.[217]

He distinguished section 15X from substantive amendments to the law, such as those regulating judicial discretions by requiring certain matters to be taken into account and which can, therefore, be categorised as *legislative* definitions of the elements to be taken into account when the discretion is exercised.

> It is true that under *Ridgeway* the ultimate issue is whether evidence establishing an element of a criminal charge should be rejected. But if that evidence is rejected, it is partly, perhaps wholly, because the processes of the court would be demeaned if the evidence was admitted. What s 15X does is to prevent a court exercising federal jurisdiction from considering a fact which is a relevant step in determining whether its process is being demeaned. Its effect is to hamper, and in some cases to prevent, such a court from protecting its processes and thereby maintaining public confidence in courts exercising the judicial power of the Commonwealth.[218]

Moreover, section 15X was not comparable to those enactments which regulate the admission of evidence or which govern the practice and procedures of courts exercising federal jurisdiction. It was not an amendment to the rules of evidence.[219] Nor was it a provision 'which merely reverses the conclusion of a federal court as to what the public interest requires'.[220] Rather,

> s 15X … strikes at the capacity of a court, exercising federal jurisdiction, to protect its processes. True it is that the section does not take that power away from such a court. But it does direct that court to disregard a fact that in *Ridgeway* was, and in other cases might be, critical to the exercise of the power.[221]

In short, a legislative direction to exercise a particular discretion that is at the core of a court's capacity to protect its processes, and therefore exclusive to it, will constitute an unconstitutional interference in breach of the separation of powers. Of course, it was open to the legislature to remove the taint of illegality from past controlled operations, as had been done with future operations. Albeit that the practical result would have been the same, both minority justices reasoned that merely because the same result could have been achieved by constitutional means did not excuse the choice of unconstitutional ones. By not changing the law

---

[217] *Ibid*, at 224.
[218] *Ibid*, at 225.
[219] *Ibid*, at 225.
[220] *Ibid*, at 226.
[221] *Ibid*, at 225–6.

relating to the legal status of past controlled operations and simply directing the courts to disregard the illegality, the legislature had over-stepped the constitutional mark.

C.   The Direction Rule Diminished: The Majority Reasoning

The judgments of Gummow and Gaudron JJ did not consider the application of the direction principle, at least not as a discrete constitutional limitation. Brennan, Toohey and Hayne JJ did consider *Liyanage*, but interpreted it unnecessarily restrictively. They appeared simply to reject the application here of the *Liyanage* principles on the basis that the legislation did not direct the court in relation to the ultimate outcome of the case—that is, the guilt or innocence of the accused. Their primary concern was with the arguments based on *Ridgeway*, and the more established concerns relating to the institutional integrity of the exercise of the judicial power of the Commonwealth by the Chapter III courts. Brennan CJ held that the discretion that the court was required to exercise pursuant to section 15X was not inconsistent with the essential character of a court or with the nature of judicial power, it being merely an evidentiary provision; and Parliament had the power to make or amend the rules governing the discretionary exclusion of evidence.[222] The impugned legislation did not affect the judicial function of fact-finding. It did not affect the judicial power to be exercised in determining guilt or innocence,[223] nor did it undermine public confidence in the administration of justice.[224] Toohey J agreed. He repeated his critical statement in *Polyukhovich*[225] that '[i]t is *only* if a law purports to operate in such a way as to require a court to act contrary to accepted notions of judicial power that a contravention of Ch III may be involved'[226] (emphasis added). Section 15X was no more than an 'evidentiary provision'.[227] It was analogous with 'a statutory provision removing a requirement of cor-roboration'.[228] It is apparent that Toohey J was addressing a separate issue entirely to that of pure legislative direction in the pending case scenario. Of course, this is not per se problematic as the facts of the case certainly did warrant such an approach. Similarly, this was the approach of Hayne J. He held that as the legislature may make or change the rules

---

222   *Ibid*, at 185 ff.
223   *Ibid*, at 188–91.
224   *Ibid*, at 193 ff.
225   *Polyukhovich v Commonwealth* (1991) 172 CLR 501 at 689.
226   *Nicholas v The Queen* (1998) 193 CLR 173 at 202.
227   *Ibid*.
228   *Ibid*.

of evidence, it might also change or make rules governing the discretionary exclusion of evidence. This was held to be the effect of section 15X, which was, on that account, valid.[229]

However, it was the easy dismissal of the direction principle which warrants consideration, particularly as these judgments seriously limited the applicability of *Liyanage*. For Brennan CJ, because section 15X did not seek directly to prescribe the final outcome relating to guilt or innocence, the impugned provisions bore 'no resemblance' to those in *Liyanage*, which therefore had no present applicability.[230] But it was undeniable that section 15X did seek to address the major legal hurdle faced by the prosecution in the pending trial. It certainly did facilitate a successful prosecution and was enacted with that in mind. Moreover, it was not the directing of the ultimate result which was regarded as the constitutional offence in *Liyanage*. It was rather the direction to the court in its consideration of legal and factual issues in the pending case which had an impact on the outcome. It just so happened that in *Liyanage* the purpose of the legislature was more transparent in its aims to secure a conviction and in its targeting of a specific prosecution. Brennan CJ also sought to distinguish section 15X from the legislation considered in *Liyanage* on the basis that it was not directed exclusively to the trial of persons whose prosecutions were pending (although clearly it had enormous significance for Nicholas's pending trial) but rather to 'any prosecution which thereafter required proof of illegal importation in an authorised controlled operation started before Div 2 commenced'.[231] This is a rather fine distinction. The principles enunciated in *Liyanage* were broad enough to encompass legislation which appeared to be of general application on its face, but was clearly applicable to known litigants or an identifiable group thereof, as was the case in the present circumstances.

To distinguish *Liyanage* further, Brennan CJ stated that the impugned *Nicholas* legislation was merely concerned 'with the effect of illegality on the part of law enforcement officers … It remains for the court … to determine whether the elements of the offence … have been proved'.[232] This is also, with respect, too narrow a reading of *Liyanage*, as there were elements in the legislation in that case which were relevant not so much to the conviction of the accused as to the conduct of the law enforcement officers and the conduct of the legal proceedings. In addition to time limits being set for the operation of the amendment, in *Liyanage* the detention of the accused was legalised ex post facto, and arrest was allowed without warrant in the particular circumstances. Moreover, it

---

[229] *Ibid*, at 274.
[230] *Ibid*, at 193.
[231] *Ibid*.
[232] *Ibid*.

dealt with aspects of the court proceedings by broadening the class of offences for which trial by jury could be ordered, including those with which the accused were charged. And, most significantly, the legislation made particular provision for the admissibility of certain statements and admissions made to law enforcement officials, which were otherwise inadmissible. Thus, there were indeed significant similarities between the two cases, which made *Liyanage* less obviously distinguishable. Was not section 15X enacted to overcome the critical evidentiary hurdle to a successful prosecution, albeit less obviously?

Finally, even if one were to accept such a very narrow reading of *Liyanage*, that is, that the legislative direction must require the conviction of a particular accused in a pending criminal case, cannot this be said to be the consequence of Division 3 in any event? It clearly had a limited temporal application because it was limited to past 'controlled operations' and any resulting prosecutions. It clearly interfered with the very viability of a particular prosecution and a small number of prospective prosecutions which were easily identifiable, by directing that the courts disregard the illegal conduct of law enforcement officers. It was this very issue that led to the prosecution of Customs Act offences being stayed in the first place. It went to the very success or otherwise of the prosecution. Accordingly, *Liyanage* cannot be so easily distinguished. Be that as it may, this is not a ground of distinction which emerges from *Liyanage* in any event.

Toohey J decided the case by reference to the more established separation of powers concerns as opposed to the principles emanating from *Liyanage*. The emphasis was placed on the proposition contained in his earlier judgment in *Polyukhovich*[233] that '[i]t is *only* if a law purports to operate in such a way as to require a court to act contrary to accepted notions of judicial power that a contravention of Ch III may be involved'[234] (emphasis added). He held that this was not the effect of section 15X. It was an 'evidentiary provision' which was within the competence of Parliament to enact.[235] It was not an Act of Attainder. It was, rather, analogous with 'a statutory provision removing a requirement of corroboration'.[236] That Toohey J addressed the issue in this way is not, of course, problematic. However, his Honour appeared too readily to assume that the impugned legislation was a change in the law when, at the very least, it should have raised some concerns about legislative direction. *Liyanage* was distinguished on the basis that the legislation in that case 'went a great deal further by purporting to legislate ex post

---

[233]   *Polyukhovich v Commonwealth* (1991) 172 CLR 501 at 689.
[234]   *Nicholas v The Queen* (1998) 193 CLR 173 at 202.
[235]   *Ibid.*
[236]   *Ibid.*

facto the detention of particular persons charged with offences on a particular occasion'.[237] Too much emphasis was placed on the significance of the *ad hominem* element, almost to the point of suggesting that the *ad hominem* element alone was enough to establish an unconstitutional interference. He held that although section 15X did not single out individuals, the class of persons to whom it was applicable 'may be ascertainable', even though 'identifying the persons affected by a controlled operation is another matter'.[238] The problem with this approach, according to both *Liyanage* and *BLF (Cth)* in particular, was that the *ad hominem* nature of the legislation was not the determinative, or even major, test of invalidity. It was but one indicator of direction. Indeed, the legislation in *BLF (Cth)* was clearly specific and *ad hominem*, yet held to be valid. Toohey J, however, did not examine the *ad hominem* nature of the legislation in this light. For him,

> [t]he proposition is that the legislature cannot direct a court exercising the judicial power of the Commonwealth as to the manner in which the power is exercised. If necessary, this is further refined to say, at least not in such a way as is inconsistent with the essential powers of a court or with the nature of judicial process.[239]

This narrow approach was also taken by Hayne J. This emerged from the outset in the way he referred to the main submission on behalf of Nicholas: 'Div 3 … deals only with a small and identifiable group of persons and is, *on that account*, an impermissible interference with the exercise of judicial power'[240] (emphasis added). The main thrust of his judgment lay elsewhere, however. He held that as the legislature may amend the rules of evidence, it might also amend rules governing the discretionary exclusion of evidence. This was the effect of section 15X, which was accordingly valid.[241] In so finding, there was no mention of the element of legislative prescription that arises in these circumstances. Instead, like Toohey J, he focused on the question of the *ad hominem* nature of the legislation as if it were the only major consideration. Although he unreservedly acknowledged that the legislation was in fact *ad hominem* in nature—given the existence of pending proceedings and the ability to identify all pending prosecutions that had not commenced—he did not regard the issue as a test of the substantively legislative quality of section 15X, that is as one of the indicia of direction. On the contrary, his treatment of the issue appeared to be based on the assumption that the legislation constituted a substantive change in the

---

[237] *Ibid*, at 203.
[238] *Ibid*.
[239] *Ibid*, at 200.
[240] *Ibid*, at 272.
[241] *Ibid*, at 274.

law, without testing this pursuant to the direction principle.[242] He referred to the *ad hominen* element, and indeed the retrospectivity of the legislation, merely to confirm that it was possible to identify all persons who may be affected by Division 3 and that this in itself was not fatal to the constitutional validity of the legislation.[243]

Also, he regarded the major issue to be whether the legislation dealt with the ultimate issue to be decided by the court:

> For present purposes it is enough to say that because the legislation in issue does not deal directly with ultimate issues of guilt or innocence but only with whether evidence of only one of several elements of an offence can be received and deals not with a single identified, or identifiable, prosecution but with several prosecutions…it does not have the character of a bill of attainder or like impermissible interference with the judicial process.[244]

Yet, as indicated above, according to *Liyanage* and the line of authority emerging from that case, unconstitutional legislative interference was not determined solely with respect to the ultimate issue of a pending case, but rather as to whether there was some prescriptive interference with the court's independent adjudication of particular questions of law or fact, facilitating a result desired by the legislature. The point is that the direction may not necessarily 'deal directly with ultimate issues of guilt or innocence', but it may have profound indirect consequences for these ultimate questions, as indeed happened in *Liyanage*. To confuse matters, Hayne J appeared to support this last made point when he postulated that there might be changes to the law of evidence or procedure which

> would be so radical and so pointed in their application to identified or identifiable cases then pending in the courts that they could be seen, in substance, to deal with ultimate issues of guilt or innocence. The legislation dealt with by the Privy Council in *Liyanage v The Queen* might be seen to have been of that kind'.[245]

In the present case, section 15X certainly removed an insurmountable hurdle to the progression of the prosecution and its ultimate success and therefore the possibility of direction should not be precluded. His Honour, however, did not think it went this far and the threshold he set for a breach of the *Liyanage* principle was set high.

In the judgment of Gaudron J the emphasis also lay in determining whether section 15X affected directly the ultimate outcome of the case. In a criminal trial, this would involve a legislative determination of guilt or innocence, and in all cases, 'making binding determinations as to rights,

---

[242]   *Ibid*, at 277.
[243]   *Ibid*.
[244]   *Ibid*.
[245]   *Ibid*, at 278.

liabilities, powers, duties or status put in issue in justiciable controversies, and, in making binding adjustments of rights and interests in accordance with legal standards'.[246] As section 15X affected the 'ancillary [to judicial] power to exclude evidence in the exercise of a discretion which permits that course',[247] it was not therefore an exercise by the Parliament of judicial power. These ancillary powers 'are not properly identified as judicial power for the purpose of Ch III of the Constitution'.[248] The emphasis was, therefore, not on legislative prescription in relation to the court's independent adjudication, but rather on whether any aspect of the legislation constituted an exercise of judicial power, pursuant to a previously defined notion thereof. This is to be contrasted with the approach taken by Kirby J, who, consistently with the direction principle, regarded that very element of legislative direction to the courts—regardless of whether it usurped an element of the 'judicial power' or an 'ancillary power'—as being a sufficient determinant of unconstitutional interference. That Gaudron J was not adopting the direction principle was clearly apparent in the way she interpreted the plaintiff's submission:

> The argument that s 15X infringes Ch III of the Constitution because it directs the manner in which the *Ridgeway* discretion is to be exercised and because it is specific and not general in its operation is, in effect, an argument that s 15X transforms the power to determine guilt or innocence in any case in which that section applies *with the result that that power is not then properly characterised as judicial power.* To understand that argument, it is necessary to say something as to the nature of judicial power.[249] (Emphasis added.)

The balance of the judgment proceeded on the unchallenged assumption that the impugned legislation was a substantive change in the law. There followed an examination as to whether section 15X 'transforms the power to be exercised in determining guilt or innocence'[250] in a way which is *inconsistent with the nature of judicial power* as opposed to whether it constituted a direction to the court without amending the law. Thus, section 15X was regarded as doing

> no more than exclud[ing] the bare fact of illegality on the part of law enforcement officers from consideration when determining whether the *Ridgeway* discretion should be exercised in favour of an accused person. So construed, it is clear that it does not prevent independent determination of the question whether the evidence should be excluded, *or, more to the point, independent determination of guilt or innocence.* And so construed, it is also clear

---

[246] *Ibid*, at 207.
[247] *Ibid*.
[248] *Ibid*, at 208.
[249] *Ibid*.
[250] *Ibid*, at 209.

that it neither authorises nor requires a court to proceed in circumstances which bring or tend to bring the administration of justice into disrepute.[251] (Emphasis added.)

Gaudron J emphasised one aspect of the direction principle which overlapped with her particular approach: the independent adjudication of a legal controversy which is an essential element of judicial power. *Liyanage* supported the proposition that

[i]f legislation which is specific rather than general is such that, nevertheless, it neither infringes the requirements of equal justice nor prevents the independent determination of the matter in issue [that is, the ultimate issue to be decided by the court], it is not in my view, invalid.[252]

Because her Honour held that section 15X offended in neither respect, it was valid. The mere question of 'the independent determination of the matter', without more, may, however, be misleading. It is clear from the context in which she used this phrase that her Honour was referring to the independent determination of the ultimate issue to be decided in the case; such as for example, guilt or innocence in a criminal trial, or the determination of rights or liabilities in a civil case. Clearly, legislation which had this effect would both constitute a breach of the direction principle and also offend against the integrity of the judicial process in that it would prevent the court from determining the legal controversy pursuant to law, instead requiring the court to make orders pre-ordained by the legislature. However, as has been argued previously, these two issues, although related, are separate and discrete. Pursuant to the direction principle, Parliament, can 'interfere' with the outcome of a pending case by substantively amending the law as indicated in the *BLF* cases, *Rooney*, and indeed *Liyanage* itself. Thus, in *BLF (Cth)* the pending proceedings were rendered redundant, as Parliament intervened by deregistering the union by force of its own legislative competence. It would be unconstitutional, as suggested in *BLF (NSW)*, if the means it had adopted constituted a direction to the court to deregister the union, or directed precise findings to be made in relation to specific issues in the case. Guadron J overlooked this particular approach in her attempt to discover whether the legislation constituted an *exercise* of judicial power, or somehow compromised the integrity of judicial process.[253] The emphasis was on the principle enunciated in *Lim* that Parliament cannot require the exercise of judicial power in 'a manner which is inconsistent with the essential character of a court or with the nature of judicial

---

[251]   *Ibid*, at 210–11.
[252]   *Ibid*, at 212.
[253]   *Ibid*, at 207.

power'.[254] In interpreting this requirement, she affirmed the position she took in *Leeth v Commonwealth*[255] in which she posited the existence of a guarantee of some degree of substantive as well as procedural due process against the Commonwealth. Thus, a court

> cannot be required or authorised to proceed in a manner that does not ensure equality before the law, impartiality and the appearance of impartiality, the right of party to meet the case made against him or her, the independent determination of the matter in controversy by application of the law to facts determined in accordance with rules and procedures which truly permit the facts to be ascertained and, in the case of criminal proceedings, the determination of guilt or innocence by means of a fair trial according to law.[256]

It is in accordance with these concerns that she proceeded to determine the constitutional validity of section 15X.

For Gummow J the constitutionally relevant consideration was whether the court was being required to exercise a power which was either not 'judicial' or was incompatible with that power. It was assumed throughout that section 15X was a substantive change in the law:

> [the] dispute does not turn upon the alteration or abrogation by statute of antecedent private substantive rights or status which are at stake in, or which provide the foundation for, particular pending civil litigation. Indeed the validity of such a law has been upheld.[257]

While relying on the *BLF (Cth)* case, his Honour did not mention the relevant aspects of *BLF (NSW)*, which suggested qualifications to the position so stated, and the reasoning proceeded along these more established separation of power lines. The determination of guilt for a criminal offence was a matter pertaining exclusively to the judicial power.[258] The question was therefore whether the impugned legislation abrogated the exclusive judicial function of adjudging criminal guilt. It was this issue his Honour addressed, not the direction principle, when he stated that 'the heart of the complaint by the accused is legislative prescription as to the manner of the exercise of the judicial power at his trial'.[259] The relevant issue was stated thus:

> Is this such an interference with the governance of the trial and a distortion of its predominant characteristics as to involve the trial court in the determination

---

[254] *Ibid*, at 208, citing *Lim v Minister for Immigration* (1992) 176 CLR 1 at 27.
[255] *Leeth v Commonwealth* (1992) 174 CLR 455 at 502–3.
[256] *Nicholas v The Queen* (1998) 193 CLR 173 at 208–9.
[257] *Ibid*, at 231.
[258] *Ibid*, at 231ff.
[259] *Ibid*, at 232.

of the criminal guilt of the accused otherwise than by the exercise of the judicial power of the Commonwealth.[260]

This was because '[t]he legislative powers of the Commonwealth do not extend to the making of a law which authorises or requires a court exercising the judicial power to do so in a manner which is inconsistent with its nature'.[261] The 'governance of the trial for the determination of criminal guilt' is a '"classic example" of one element of judicial power that is reserved exclusively for exercise by the Chapter III courts in the Australian constitutional system'.[262] *Liyanage* was considered essentially on this basis. The laws were held invalid in that case because they required the court to exercise a power inconsistent with the nature of judicial power to the extent that issues which were central to the exercise of judicial power, such as guilt or innocence and length of sentence, were purportedly to be decided pursuant to statutory provisions as opposed to judicial discretion.[263]

The difference between his Honour's approach and the direction principle is a subtle one, which needs careful explanation. Both approaches overlap in that they are concerned with the protection of a core element of the judicial power, the independent, exclusive and conclusive adjudication of a legal dispute. His Honour approaches this question not by impugning the substantively legislative nature of the legislation, but by asking simply whether it seeks to determine the guilt or innocence of the accused, thereby preventing the court from exercising this exclusive aspect of judicial power. The legislation is assumed to be a change in the law. The direction principle, on the other hand, conducts its analysis one step prior to this. The question is first whether the purported legislation is in substance a change in the law and thus the indicia of direction are examined at this point. If there is legislative direction without a change in the law, the interference with the exclusively judicial function of final adjudication of legal disputes is thereby rendered unconstitutional because the legislature is acting in a non-legislative manner such as to interfere with this judicial function.

His Honour noted the conceptual difficulties which arise in examining questions of this kind, and noted the importance of considerations of 'predominant characteristics'.[264] Like the other majority justices, he approached the issue as one of determining whether the 'courts are left with the determination of the facts in light of the law which created the

---

[260]   *Ibid.*
[261]   *Ibid.*
[262]   *Ibid,* at 231, citing *R v Quinn; Ex parte Consolidated Food Corporation* (1977) 138 CLR 1.
[263]   *Ibid,* at 232.
[264]   *Ibid,* at 233.

offence, as a matter of form and substance'.[265] But he, like Hayne J,[266] placed great store by the distinction between legislation dealing with procedural or evidentiary matters and legislation which dealt with substantive issues which arose in the pending case. It is the very fact that he created this dichotomy that is indicative of an approach which is separate to that of the direction principle:

> The section [15X] in its operation, if not necessarily on its face, deals not with proof but with a discretion to exclude evidence of facts. It operated to facilitate the proof by the prosecution of its case by the admission of evidence that otherwise was liable to exclusion. The case for the accused is made that much more difficult than it would have been if s 15X had not been enacted. However, the section does not deem any ultimate fact to exist, or to have been proved. It leaves untouched the elements of the crimes for which the accused is to be tried. Nor does section 15X change the amount or degree of proof essential to convict him from that required when the alleged offences were committed.[267]

He further stated that section 15X

> does not operate so to prescribe the manner of exercise of the judicial power upon trials of offences against s 233B...*as to deny the basic rights referred to by Jacobs J in Quinn* [exclusive governance of a trial by the courts in the determination of criminal guilt]. The courts are left with the determination of facts in the light of the law which created the offence, as a matter of form and substance.[268] (Emphasis added.)

Thus, the legislation is impugned only because it interferes with key and inviolable elements of the judicial power. Thus, for example, if all the legislation did in *Liyanage* was to change the law of evidence on the eve of the trial, applicable only to the trial of the accused persons, but left the determination of innocence or guilt to the court based on these new laws, then query whether the Privy Council, if it had followed his Honour's approach, would have found a breach of the separation of powers given that it did not affect one of those elements critical to the 'judicial power' or its integrity. His Honour's treatment of *Lim* was similarly limited to the proposition that '[t]he legislative powers of the Commonwealth do not extend to the making of a law which authorises or requires a court exercising the judicial power to do so in a manner which is inconsistent with its nature'.[269] His analysis of the issue of retrospectivity was also along these lines.[270] Significantly also, his analysis of the United States authorities related only to the issue of the significance of the procedural

---

[265]   *Ibid*, at 239.
[266]   *Ibid*, at 277–8.
[267]   *Ibid*, at 238.
[268]   *Ibid*, at 239.
[269]   *Ibid*.
[270]   *Ibid*, at 234.

nature of particular laws.[271] He did not mention the critically important *United States v Klein*, now regarded as the leading case on the issue of legislative interference with judicial functions and as the first expression of the direction principle in that jurisdiction[272]; another indication that the direction principle was not a consideration in his Honour's assessment of the constitutional validity of section 15X.

In conclusion, *Nicholas* reveals the difficulties faced by the direction principle in establishing itself as a discrete separation of powers principle, especially given its obvious relevance on the facts. The tendency to limit its application, to distinguish *Liyanage*, or to set a very high threshold for its application, does not augur well for its future consolidation as a discrete constitutional limitation in Australia. The focus thus would remain on those principles centred on the more established concerns relating to institutional independence and the more recently identified principles emanating from the separation of judicial power which deal with due process guarantees, and the principle of incompatibility between judicial and non-judicial functions.[273] To test the constitutionality of legislation which did have substantial consequences in a pending case and was enacted while the case was pending, it would be necessary to show that, for example, the legislature was itself deciding the outcome of a case and thus exercising judicial power, that the legislature was removing an essential element of judicial power from the court, or was requiring it to exercise a power inconsistent with judicial power. Given that a critical aspect of the judicial power is the independent adjudication of legal disputes, it could be argued that this approach is not problematic, given that legislation which directed the courts to a conclusion without changing the law could still be invalidated on this ground. However—and herein lies the crux of the issue—by what test will this be determined if not something akin to the direction principle in the absence of any other constitutional offence? What if the direction is carefully hidden within an otherwise apparently innocuous statute? The import of the direction principle, and its efficacy if applied rigorously, is that it articulates indicia of direction which can be used to impugn the

---

[271]   *Ibid*, at 237.

[272]   See n 32 above.

[273]   See F Wheeler, 'The rise and rise of judicial power under Chapter III of the Constitution: A decade in overview' (2001) 20 *Australian Bar Review* 283; 'The Doctrine of Separation of Powers and Constitutionally Entrenched Due Process in Australia' (1997) 23 *Monash University Law Review* 248 and 'Due Process, Judicial Power and Chapter III in the New High Court', n 63 above; G Winterton, 'The Separation of Judicial Power as an Implied Bill of Rights' in G J Lindell (ed), *Future Directions in Australian Constitutional Law* (Sydney, Federation Press, 1994); L Zines, 'A Judicially Created Bill of Rights?' (1994) 16 *Sydney Law Review* 166; and C Parker 'Protection of Judicial Process as an Implied Constitutional Principle' (1994) 16 *Adelaide Law Review* 341.

substantively legislative nature of the statute, thus rendering it unconstitutional at an earlier stage in the enquiry.

VII.   THE UNCERTAIN STATUS OF THE DIRECTION PRINCIPLE IN AUSTRALIA

Following *Nicholas*, beyond egregious scenarios such as those in *Liyanage*, the continuing relevance of the direction principle as a source of significant constitutional limitations remains uncertain. Except for the judgments of Kirby and McHugh JJ in *Nicholas*, the High Court has not consolidated earlier attempts to provide a solid foundation for future development, although it has not rejected the existence of a direction principle. The High Court's interpretation of that principle, and its uneasy reception, however, remains only part of the problem. Imprecision exists in the very nature of the principles identified. The direction principle suffers from uncertainty not only in definition, but also as to method of its application. The inadequacies identified are problematic in light of the significant emphasis placed on the need to limit interference by the legislature in pending cases by those who originally advocated the legal entrenchment of the separation of powers, particularly in the United States.[274] The foundations for a more precise and efficacious application of the principle may be achieved if the reasons for the current uncertainties and weaknesses are addressed. Clearly, the survival of the principle in the form which has been described will depend a great deal on the extent to which position adopted by the minority judgments in *Nicholas* will prevail to reinforce the development of principle to date.

Signs that the principle has not been entirely undermined can be found in the most recent case to consider the issue in any detail, *HA Bachrach Pty Ltd v Queensland*.[275] An appeal was pending from a decision of the Supreme Court of Queensland upholding a decision of a local authority not to approve a major commercial building development. The Queensland Parliament enacted legislation expressly relating to the area of the development, the effect of which was to permit the development to proceed. Even though the legislation would have had an affect on the outcome of the pending appeal, the High Court, in a joint judgment,[276] held the legislation to be constitutionally valid and not an impermissible interference with judicial functions. In its reasoning, the court did not

---

[274] See chapter 1 at 10ff.

[275] *HA Bachrach Pty Ltd v Queensland* (1998) 195 CLR 547. It should be noted that this case involved a State parliament enacting State legislation that affected proceedings of a State court. The reason Chapter III of the Constitution arose at all was as a result of *Kable's* case. See n 77 above.

[276] Gleeson CJ, Gaudron, Gummow, Kirby and Hayne JJ.

examine the issue of legislative interference in any detail, although it appears to have recognised the continuing importance and status of the critical principles involved. Thus, having examined all the circumstances surrounding the enactment, the court examined the nature of the legislation to conclude that

> both in form and in substance, the Act is legislation with respect to the use that may lawfully be made of the ... land. Its provisions are of general effect, for the future, and they bind the Council, Keylim, the plaintiff, and any other person who may have interest in, or claim to exercise rights in relation to, the use of the subject land.[277]

This was the court's response to the submission by the plaintiff that the enactment was 'designed' to affect the outcome of the pending appeal, demonstrating that the Queensland Parliament did not respect the authority of the courts in its willingness to interfere in pending litigation. The High Court did acknowledge that '[a]n adequate appreciation of the operation of the Act, and its proper characterisation, as a matter of substance and not merely of form, may require consideration of the history of the plaintiff's pursuits of its legal rights'.[278] It found that the facts of this case were analogous to those in *BLF (Cth)* in that Parliament changed the law, which, because the court had to apply it, made the pending proceedings redundant.[279] It distinguished *BLF (NSW)* because the legislation here did not 'specifically address current litigation, prescribe ... that for the purposes of determining the issues in the litigation certain facts were taken as established, and dealt with the costs of the litigation'. In other words, there were insufficient indicia of direction to warrant a declaration of invalidity. This was despite the fact that the legislation had a clear impact on the pending proceedings and that it mentioned expressly the land that was subject to the development application. That impact, significantly, was not by way of addressing the very legal issues which were at issue in those proceedings. Rather, the legislation amended the law by the creation of a new legislative regime governing the land such that the legal issues were simply by-passed.

Again, the High Court did not set out a clear and comprehensive set of principles to govern the issues, which was particularly needful after *Nicholas*. Very general principles were mentioned without any precise examination of their status and their relationship with other principles protecting the judicial power of the Commonwealth. There is no comprehensive analysis of indicia of direction. There is no explicit examination of the relationship between the direction principle and Changed Law

---

[277]   *HA Bachrach Pty Ltd v Queensland* (1998) 195 CLR 547 at 560.
[278]   *Ibid*, at 561.
[279]   *Ibid*, at 564.

Rule. However, despite its reticence to explore these matters in any great detail, it can be stated with some confidence that the court did still recognise that there is a prohibition on legislative direction in pending proceedings with respect to the legal and factual issue therein, or the final outcome. The High Court thus did still give some recognition of the importance, in a very broad way, of the central principles underlying the direction principle.

It was indicated above that the reason for this uncertain reception of the direction principle may lie within the very principles upon which it is based, particularly the reliance on indicia of direction in any particular case. Also, even if the rule is accepted, its efficacy does depend on the extent to which the courts are willing to apply it rigorously, particularly its imperative to look to substance over form. Clearly, there needs to be some attempt to formalise the indicia of direction to support the efficacy of the rule itself, rather than making it so dependent on the facts of each case. What is precisely required in such a formalisation will be examined following a consideration of the United States jurisprudence in the next chapter, which examination will shed considerable light on the issue of legislative interference in the context of separation of powers jurisprudence.

3

Legislative Interference with Judicial Functions:

The Jurisprudence of the United States, Evaluation of Principle, and Towards Resolution

I. INTRODUCTION

IN LIGHT OF the difficulties, highlighted in the previous chapter, in identifying a discrete set of principles prohibiting legislative intervention with judicial functions, is it the case that the formulation of the direction principle itself contains inherent critical weaknesses? This question underlies the analysis which follows in this chapter, the primary aim being to articulate a refined version of the relevant principles to ameliorate any inherent weaknesses which presently exist. Because of the advanced nature of the United States jurisprudence in this area, it will be central to the analysis which follows.

The first striking aspect of the American debate is the unambiguous and clear appreciation, by both academy and court, of the central significance of the constitutional issues which are at stake. To choose one example from amongst many, J Richard Doigt wrote:

> The Supreme Court has long held that retroactive changes in law are to be applied to adjudicated cases pending appeal ... The Changed Law Rule inevitably creates conflict between the legislative and judicial branches, since, if applied without limitation, the Changed Law Rule allows Congress to alter judgements prior to the conclusion of the appeals process. Given that one of the purposes of the separation of powers doctrine is to insulate the litigation of private disputes from the vagaries of political power, there should seemingly be some limit on Congress's ability to employ this power.[1]

---

[1] JR Doigt, 'Is Purely Retroactive Legislation Limited by the Separation of Powers? Rethinking *United States v Klein*' (1994) 79 *Cornell Law Review* 911 at 942.

He added that 'the legislature's ability to manipulate the results of pending litigation undermines the ideal of ordered liberty and the protections against tyranny for which divided government strives'.[2] Professor Amy Ronner went further to suggest that principles based on the direction principle and the Changed Law Rule do not go far enough as constitutional limitations:

> A separation of powers test, which allows a Congressional Act to intrude on judicial power as long as it can be construed as amending or repealing the law is not merely a nullity, but an invitation to Congress to aggrandize itself as the Last Court of Resort.[3]

Ronner's concern, even with the Changed Law Rule, is indicative of the heightened American sensitivities to these questions, sensitivities which place at the forefront the need for constitutional limitations safeguarding the judiciary's decisional independence. Professor Evan Caminker expressly referred to the importance of not eroding separation of powers restraints on legislative direction, even if the direction principle 'is reducible in operation to a rule of drafting etiquette'.[4] He added that

> it remains a rule that can matter. It strikes me as important that federal courts always maintain their proper self-understanding of being neutral and final arbiters of what the law is and how it applies in specific cases—even if and when the law applies only to single cases. Only this self-understanding can generate sufficient norms of independence and, frankly, essentiality, to safeguard long-term fidelity to the rule of law. Widespread public understanding that courts play this independent role is necessary to building long-term public support for it in the face of periodic congressional temptation to cross the line. And linguistic formulations contained in statutes may make a difference to these understandings. For these reasons, it is perfectly sensible for courts to continue enforcing the *Klein* [direction] principle, even if Congress can usually or perhaps always achieve its desired ends by actually changing the law.[5]

The United States constitutional provision on the separation of judicial power, is virtually identical to that in the Australian Constitution:

> The judicial power of the United States shall be vested in one Supreme Court, and in such inferior courts as the Congress may from time to time ordain and establish.[6]

---

[2] *Ibid*, at 941.
[3] AD Ronner, 'Judicial Self-Demise: The Test of When Congress Impermissibly Intrudes on Judicial Power After *Robertson v Seattle Audubon Society*' (1993) 35 *Arizona Law Review* 1037 at 1070.
[4] '*Schiavo* and *Klein*' (2005) 22 *Constitutional Commentary* 529 at 542.
[5] *Ibid*, at 542–3.
[6] Art III, s 1 of the Constitution of the United States.

The extensive American coverage also confronts the very same issues which have been problematic in Australia: the difficulty in providing mutually-exclusive definitions of the functions of the branches of government, and thus in establishing precise lines of demarcation between the branches; the uncertainty as to whether a functionalist or formalist approach ought to be applied; and the uncertainties surrounding the very concept of 'interference' and 'direction'. Of course, when comparing the United States' position to that pertaining in Westminster-style systems, caution must be exercised in light of the adoption of a purer form of the separation of powers in that jurisdiction—without responsible government, yet with 'checks and balances'—and its clearly conscious adoption by the Framers to protect the decisional independence of the federal courts.[7]

This view of the separation of powers as a continuing safeguard of decisional independence in particular remains at the forefront of United States constitutional jurisprudence to a far greater extent than elsewhere. In Australia, for example, even with an entrenched separation of powers, the articulation of such fundamental concerns is rather the exception than the rule. Be that as it may, the United States jurisprudence remains highly significant because it independently reinforces the development of principle in Australia and, as will be discussed below, in Ireland. It is powerful testimony to the status of the direction principle as a discrete separation of powers limitation that an almost identical set of principles emerged in each of these three jurisdictions, quite independently, centred around a form of the direction principle and the Changed Law Rule. It is also significant that this development in the United States seems to be diminishing for the same reasons that it is in Australia. The most recent decisions of the Supreme Court[8] reveal interesting parallels to the High Court's decision in *Nicholas*: a failure to apply the direction principle rigorously, to appreciate its nature fully, and a tendency to qualify it so as to impair seriously its efficacy as a constitutional limitation. This has resulted in almost unanimous criticism in the United States by the constitutional scholars and by a significant body of judicial opinion in the federal courts in which these cases were originally decided. Whether the Supreme Court will reverse the course upon which it has embarked, and heed the dissenting judicial and academic commentary, remains uncertain. Whatever the final outcome, this ongoing debate furnishes ample material upon which to reflect upon the weaknesses which may be inherent in the principle and to provide a way forward.

---

[7] See above, ch 1, at 10.

[8] *Robertson v Seattle Audubon Society* 503 US 429 (1992); *Plaut v Spendthrift Farm* 514 US 211 (1995); *Miller v French* 530 US 327 (2000). All these cases will be examined in detail in this chapter.

Despite these set backs, the application of the direction principle by the Supreme Court as a limitation to the Changed Law Rule has not been entirely overruled and its central core appears to remain secure. Moreover, the fundamental distinction which lies at the heart of the principle—between a change in the law and an unconstitutional direction to the judiciary—has not been compromised. Thus, the main issue for consideration is not whether the direction principle should or should not exist as a discrete separation of powers principle, but whether its current formulation and interpretation will ensure its continuing efficacy as a constitutional limitation of the highest order.

The survival of these fundamentals of the principle is an indication of the ascendancy, where this particular separation of powers issue is concerned, of a moderate formalist approach; an approach which even moderate functionalists regard as appropriate in these circumstances, although for different reasons. Formalism remains apparent in the conceptual analysis of the functions of the legislature and the judiciary, which continues to postulate the existence of core judicial functions with which the legislature is prohibited from interfering. The imperative to recognise at least a definitional core to the functions of government arising from the entrenchment of the separation of powers is thus met. However, as in Australia, it will be seen that, over this formalist underlay, the United States' version of the direction principle incorporates significant functionalist elements, there being no precisely defined set of criteria by which to determine in each case the existence or otherwise of direction. As in Australia, reliance is therefore placed on indicia of direction which can be located in the circumstances of the enactment of impugned legislation and the nature of the pending proceedings with which it interferes. Thus, despite this functionalist overlay upon a formalist base, the precise definition of relevant constitutional limitations has in many respects moved beyond the formalist/functionalist divide, particularly in the pending case scenario, as will be seen.

This chapter will commence by tracing the tentative development of the direction principle in the United States, the seminal decision being *United States v Klein*[9] in 1871. In that case, the Supreme Court held that it was a breach of the separation of powers to allow 'the legislature [to] prescribe rules of decision to the Judicial Department of the government in cases pending before it',[10] where 'no new circumstances are created by legislation',[11] that is, where there was no substantive change to the law. However, a number of uncertainties surround the precise holding of this case and it will therefore be necessary to explore the various possible

---

[9]   *United States v Klein* 80 US (13 Wall) 128 (1871).
[10] *Ibid*, at 146.
[11] *Ibid*, at 147.

interpretations. This will be centred around an examination of the significant work of Henry Hart in an important article published in 1953 which rehabilitated *Klein* from relative obscurity, doing much in the process to identify the precise constitutional principles for which it remains authority.[12]

There will follow a detailed consideration of the highly significant developments which occurred in the 1990s in the trio of Supreme Court cases alluded to above. In *Robertson v Seattle Audubon Society*[13] and *Miller v French*,[14] the Supreme Court applied the central finding of *Klein*, as interpreted by Hart, that the legislature had power to interfere with decisions in pending cases only by means of an amendment to the underlying law which the court then had to apply; that is, by a proper exercise of *legislative* power. However, the outcome of these cases and their method of application of the direction principle was highly problematic and in fact seriously undermined its efficacy. The qualifications to the direction principle expressed in *Miller v French* were particularly corrosive of an accurate and precise definition of the principle consistent with the separation of powers. *Plaut v Spendthrift Farm*,[15] a case of most relevance for the final judgment scenario, nevertheless contained significant dicta which had the effect of reinforcing the weakening of the direction principle. In light of the apparent weakening of the direction rule, it is questionable whether the Supreme Court has maintained the proper balance between the proper exercise of legislative power and the decisional independence of the courts in that jurisdiction.[16] These developments will now be explored in detail.

II. THE EMERGENCE OF THE CHANGED LAW RULE AND THE DIRECTION PRINCIPLE IN THE UNITED STATES

Although the concern to maintain the judicial branch's decisional independence was a primary catalyst in the legal entrenchment of the separation of powers,[17] it is remarkable that it was not until 1871 in *Klein* that the issue achieved any degree of prominence as an established constitutional limitation on the legislature. Prior to *Klein*, Thomas Cooley,

---

[12]   HM Hart, 'The Power of Congress to Limit the Jurisdiction of the Federal Courts: an Exercise in Dialectic' (1953) 66 *Harvard Law Review* 1362.

[13]   *Robertson v Seattle Audubon Society* 503 US 429 (1992).

[14]   *Miller v French* 530 US 327 (2000).

[15]   *Plaut v Spendthrift Farm* 514 US 211 (1995).

[16]   See LC Anderson, 'Congressional Control over the Jurisdiction of the Federal Courts: A New Threat to James Madison's Compromise' (2000) 39 *Brandeis Law Journal* 417 at 420.

[17]   See LS Branham, 'Keeping the "Wolf out of the Fold": Separation of Powers and Congressional Termination of Equitable Relief' (2000) 26 *Journal of Legislation* 185.

in his influential treatise *Constitutional Limitations*,[18] recognised that the legislature could not, pursuant to the separation of powers, 'set aside the construction of the law already applied by the courts to actual cases, neither can it compel the courts for the future to adopt a particular construction of a law which the legislature permits to remain in force'.[19] Expanding on this proposition, Cooley clearly gave expression to a form of the Changed Law Rule, and the direction principle as a threshold test for its application:

> If the legislature would prescribe a different rule for the future from that which the courts enforce, it must be done by statute, and *cannot be done by a mandate to the courts, which leaves the law unchanged*, but seeks *to compel* the courts to construe and apply it, not according to the legislative judgement.[20] (Emphasis added.)

He expanded this principle so that it constituted a protection of final judgments also:

> If the legislature cannot thus indirectly control the action of the courts, by requiring of them a construction of the law according to its own views, it is very plain it cannot do so directly, by setting aside their judgements, compelling them to grant new trials, ordering the discharge of offenders, or directing what particular steps shall be taken in the progress of a judicial enquiry.[21]

Cooley derived these notions from first principles based on the entrenchment of the separation of powers, *Klein* not being mentioned even in those editions of Cooley's work which post-dated the case. The early development and statement of these principles assumed a formalist methodology in its reliance upon a definitional core to the respective functions of the relevant branches, from which the others were to be excluded.

The Changed Law Rule had been well established prior to Cooley's writings and judicially expressed as early as 1801 in *United States v Schooner Peggy*.[22] The rule has been stated succinctly thus: 'the courts are obligated to apply law (otherwise valid) as they find it at the time of their decision, including, when a case is on review, the time of the appellate

---

[18]   Originally published in 1868 and influential in Australia also.

[19]   TM Cooley, *A Treatise on the Constitutional Limitations Which Rest Upon the States of the American Union*, 7th edn (Boston, Little, Brown, 1903) at 137.

[20]   *Ibid*.

[21]   *Ibid*, at 137–8.

[22]   *United States v Schooner Peggy* 5 US (1 Cranch) 103 (1801). The term was originally used by GC Young, 'Congressional Regulation of Federal Courts Jurisdiction and Processes: *United States v Klein* Revisited' [1981] *Wisconsin Law Review* 1189 at 1240. See also Doigt, 'Is Purely Retroactive Legislation Limited by the Separation of Powers?', n 1 above, 918.

judgment'.[23] The case concerned the seizure, condemnation and forfei-
ture to the United States of a French trading vessel pursuant to a federal
court order. While the matter was pending appeal, the United States
entered into a treaty with France by which all vessels which were not yet
'definitively' condemned were to be returned to their respective nations
and were not be made the subject of condemnation orders. The agreement achieved the status of law, and, as this was held to be a change in
the law, it had to be applied by the appellate court. Thus, as the vessel
was not yet *definitively* condemned, the matter being on appeal, the
Supreme Court applied the new law and ordered the return of the vessel
to France:

> [A]s such [a change in the law it] affects the rights of the parties litigating in
> court … It is in general true that the province of an appellate court is only to
> enquire whether a judgment when rendered was erroneous or not. But if
> subsequent to the judgment and before the decision of the appellate court, a
> law intervenes and *positively changes the rule which governs*, the law must be
> obeyed, or its obligation denied … I know of no court which can contest its
> obligation.[24] (Emphasis added.)

The decision laid the foundations for the direction principle by stating
the fundamental condition necessary for the application of the statute to
the pending case, that is, that it be 'a law' that '*positively changes the rule
which governs*'. The reasoning of Marshall CJ, delivering the opinion of
the court, revealed a strong appreciation of the need to maintain the
integrity and independence of the exercise of judicial functions, especially in the face of legislative power. The mere fact that a suit was
pending which may be affected by the changed law did not diminish the
paramount power of the legislature to enact new law, and indeed the
obligation of the courts to apply it. He was concerned, however, not to
allow for completely unbridled legislative power in this context, expressing some disquiet about the retroactive application of new law to
pending cases and commenting that a court will 'struggle against a
construction' which will by retroactive operation affect the rights of the
parties.[25] Moreover, he exhibited a concern for the potential of the
legislature to manipulate the outcome of pending suits when he drew a
distinction between suits involving entirely private parties and those

---

[23] RH Fallon, DJ Meltzer, and DL Shapiro, *Hart and Wechsler's The Federal Courts and the Federal System*, 4th edn (New York, Foundation Press 1996) 368. For other examples of the application of the rule see *Carpenter v Wabash Railway Co* 309 US 23 (1940); *Vandenbark v Owens-Illinois Glass Co* 311 US 538 (1941); *Cort v Ash* 422 US 66 (1975).

[24] 5 US (1 Cranch) 103 (1801) at 110.

[25] *Ibid*.

involving the government as litigant.[26] In the latter situation, he tentatively suggested the possibility of a higher threshold for the validity of retroactive application of statutes in cases involving private rights.[27] Nevertheless, this concern was not manifested in any legal principle beyond the mere expression of disquiet. It was not until *Klein* was decided in 1871, some 70 years later, that the issue received a more elaborate consideration.

III.   *KLEIN* AND ITS UNCERTAIN MEANING

At issue in *Klein* was a federal statute enacted in 1863 which provided a right to those whose property had been confiscated during the American Civil War to seek compensation in the Court of Claims, an Article III court, by presenting proof of ownership and proof that they had never given 'any aid or comfort' to the Confederate cause.[28] The President subsequently granted a full pardon to those who had assisted that cause, granting them amnesty and the restoration of all property rights on condition that they took, and kept, an oath of allegiance.[29] Klein, the administrator of a deceased estate, had succeeded in a suit in the Court of Claims relating to the seizure and sale of the deceased's cotton, relying on a pardon granted to the deceased and the fact that the deceased had kept the prerequisite oath of loyalty.[30] The government appealed. While the appeal was pending, the Supreme Court decided in *United States v Padelford*[31] that presidential pardons had the effect of erasing disbarment to compensation by those who had aided the cause against the Union.[32]

Concerned about the outcome of *Padelford*, Congress sought to change the law with effect on pending and future cases, including the *Klein* suit, culminating in legislation referred to as 'the 1870 proviso'.[33] It provided that

---

[26]   *Ibid.*

[27]   For subsequent applications of the Changed Law Rule, see *United States v Preston* 28 US (3 Peters) 57 (1830) at 66–7, and *Fairfax's Devisee v Hunter's Lessee* 11 US (7 Cranch) 603 (1813) at 612.

[28]   Abandoned Property Collection Act (US), ch 120 para 3, 12 Stat 820 (1863). See *United States v Klein* 80 US (13 Wall) 128 (1871) at 131.

[29]   Proclamation No 11 of Dec 8, 1863, 13 Stat 737 at 737–8. See *United States v Klein* 80 US (13 Wall) 128 (1871) at 131.

[30]   For a very detailed account of the facts of the case set in the political context, see Young, 'Congressional Regulation of Federal Courts Jurisdiction and Processes, n 22 above.

[31]   *United States v Padelford* 76 US (9 Wall) 531 (1870).

[32]   *Ibid*, at 543.

[33]   Act of July 12 1870, ch 251 12 Stat 230 at 235. For a comprehensive account of congressional efforts to have *Padelford* overruled, and Congress' purpose in defeating its consequences in pending litigation, see Young, 'Congressional Regulation of Federal Courts Jurisdiction and Processes', n 22 above, 1201–13.

(a)   proof of presidential pardon was inadmissible in the Court of Claims (or in any appellate court) in support of suits for the return of property, or to establish that a litigant had the right to bring or maintain the suit;

(b)   where such pardon had been given, reciting a person's involvement in aid of the rebel cause, and accepted with no protestation as to involvement, such pardon would be deemed conclusive evidence that the recipient did take part in and give aid and comfort to the Confederate cause; and

(c)   on proof that such pardon had been granted, the 'jurisdiction of the court in the case shall cease, and the court shall forthwith dismiss the suit of such claimant'.[34]

Klein challenged the constitutional validity of 'the 1870 proviso'. The Supreme Court held that any legislation which 'prescribes rules of decision to the Judicial Department of the government in cases pending before it' is constitutionally invalid on separation of powers grounds.[35] Congress had done just that in enacting the impugned statute and had

> inadvertently passed the limit which separates the legislative from the judicial power … It is of vital importance that these powers be kept distinct. The Constitution provides that the judicial power of the United States shall be vested in one Supreme Court and such inferior courts as the Congress shall from time to time ordain and establish.[36]

Chase CJ, delivering the opinion of the court and foreshadowing *Liyanage* in Commonwealth jurisdictions by almost a century, emphasised substance over form. Prima facie, the legislation purported to regulate the jurisdiction of the Court of Claims and appeals from it to the Supreme Court. Because, pursuant to the Constitution, Congress had 'complete control', in a jurisdictional sense, over the Court of Claims, if the 1870 proviso did no more than regulate federal court jurisdiction then 'there could be no doubt that it must be regarded as an exercise of the power of Congress to make "such exceptions from the appellate jurisdiction" as should seem to it expedient'.[37] However, in substance—and this was clear from the very language itself—the legislation did

> not intend to withhold appellate jurisdiction *except as a means to an end*. Its great and controlling purpose is to deny to pardons granted by the President the effect which this court had adjudged them to have. The proviso declares that pardons shall not be considered by this court on appeal. We had already

---

[34]   *United States v Klein* 80 US (13 Wall) 128 (1871) at 129.
[35]   *Ibid*, at 147.
[36]   *Ibid*, at 146.
[37]   *Ibid*, at 145.

decided that it was our duty to consider them and give them effect, in cases like the present, as equivalent of proof of loyalty.[38] (Emphasis added.)

The court thus held that the effect of the legislation was to direct the outcome of decisions in which the issue of the legal effect of presidential pardons in this context was a critical issue:

> [T]he denial of jurisdiction to this court … is founded solely on the application of a rule of decision, in causes pending, prescribed by Congress. The court has jurisdiction of the cause to a given point; but when it ascertains that a certain state of things exists, its jurisdiction is to cease.[39]

It is at this point that Chase CJ gave expression to the direction principle, the central rationale of which was the testing of the substantively legislative nature of the conduct of Congress in enacting the legislation:

> It seems to us that this is not an exercise of the acknowledged power of Congress to make exceptions and prescribe regulations of the appellate power … The court is required to ascertain the existence of certain facts and thereupon to declare that its jurisdiction on appeal has ceased, by dismissing the bill. What is this but *to prescribe a rule for the decision of a cause in a particular way?*[40] (Emphasis added.)

The court was sensitive to the fact that the proviso was enacted while the government's appeal was pending and that Congress, by enacting intervening legislation which the Changed Law Rule required the court to apply, was in a position to influence the outcome in its own favour. Special vigilance therefore was required in such situations, and this was to be manifested in a rigorous scrutiny of the substantively legislative nature of any statute. If it was purely prescriptive, the separation doctrine would be breached because, first, it was not a proper exercise of legislative power per se; and secondly, it prevented the judiciary from exercising a core element of the judicial power—the independent adjudication of a legal issue. In the present context,

> [t]he Court of Claims has rendered judgment for the claimant and an appeal has been taken to this court. We are directed to dismiss the appeal, if we find that the judgment must be affirmed, because of the pardon granted to the intestate of the claimants. Can we do so without allowing one party to the controversy to decide it in its own favor? Can we do so without allowing that the legislature may prescribe rules of decision to the Judicial Department of government in cases pending before it? We think not.[41]

---

[38]   *Ibid.*
[39]   *Ibid.*
[40]   *Ibid*, at 146.
[41]   *Ibid.*

However, the reasoning of Chase CJ was framed in terms which were sufficiently imprecise as to make the ratio problematic and eventually to spawn an extensive literature. One commentator described the judgment as combining 'the clear with the Delphic' and capable of being 'viewed as nearly all things to all men'.[42] The seminal work on *Klein* was the above-mentioned article by Henry Hart,[43] which explored the various possible interpretations of the case, resuscitated it from relative obscurity and cemented its position as the leading case on legislative interference. A critical issue was whether in fact *Klein* constituted authority for any proposition beyond the purely jurisdictional question, that is, the extent of congressional power to limit the jurisdiction of the federal courts. As Professor Redish noted, '[w]hether *Klein* can be understood as establishing an independent [from the purely jurisdictional question] separation-of-powers restraint which limits Congress' power, is uncertain'.[44] Hart had suggested that the narrowest possible ratio of the case was that Congress may not condition the court's jurisdiction to hear a matter on the court's abstaining from declaring certain acts as unconstitutional—in this case the interference by the legislature in the Executive's power of pardon.[45] A broader interpretation was required to establish the case as authority to support propositions relating to Congressional control over the Supreme Court's appellate jurisdiction arising under Article III of the Constitution, or indeed for the direction principle. Hart articulated such an interpretation.

For present purposes, the purely jurisdictional issue is not of immediate relevance[46] except to note its importance and the fact that Hart and

[42]   Young, 'Congressional Regulation of Federal Courts Jurisdiction and Processes', n 22 above 1195. 'Hardly a model of clarity' opine the authors of *Hart and Wechsler's The Federal Courts and the Federal System*, n 23 above, 368.

[43]   Hart, 'The Power of Congress to Limit the Jurisdiction of the Federal Courts', n 12 above, especially at 1373. In the writer's view, the most comprehensive and detailed examination of *Klein* following Hart is the article by Young, 'Congressional Regulation of Federal Courts Jurisdiction and Processes', n 22 above. For an excellent review of the various interpretations of *Klein*, see Anderson, 'Congressional Control over the Jurisdiction of the Federal Courts', n 16 above. For a comprehensive pre-1981 review of the literature see Young, 'Congressional Regulation of Federal Courts Jurisdiction and Processes', n 22 above, 1194, nn 26–37 and accompanying text. For a review of the more recent literature on *Klein* see Ronner, 'Judicial Self-Demise', n 3 above.

[44]   MH Redish, *Federal Jurisdiction: Tensions in the Allocation of Judicial Power* (Indianapolis, Michie Co, 1980) 31.

[45]   Hart, 'The Power of Congress to Limit the Jurisdiction of the Federal Courts', n 12 above, 1373.

[46]   The precise scope of the decision in *Klein* in relation to purely jurisdictional issues has been the subject of some uncertainty, and quite some degree of both judicial and academic scrutiny. For an excellent review thereof see Anderson, 'Congressional Control over the Jurisdiction of the Federal Courts', n 16 above. As this issue is beyond the scope of this monograph, it can only be given a cursory mention. It should be noted, however, that the issue of congressional control over the Supreme Court's appellate jurisdiction arising from Article III of the Constitution ranks as an issue of the highest order in the constitutional

other leading academic commentators recognised that the significance of *Klein* extended beyond it. Hart's main concern was the issue of the control by Congress over the jurisdiction of the federal courts and the extent to which this control was consistent with the principle of the rule of law and the type of representative government set up under the United States Constitution. His thesis was that while Congress, pursuant to Article III,[47] was granted plenary power to remove jurisdiction from the lower federal courts, legislative exceptions to the Supreme Court's appellate jurisdiction 'must not be such as will destroy the essential role of the Supreme Court in the constitutional plan'.[48] More important for present purposes were the two subsidiary limbs: First, Congress could not direct a result in any case which was contrary to judicial interpretation of the Constitution.[49] Secondly, and more precisely relevant, Hart interpreted *Klein* as authority for the proposition that once a federal court has jurisdiction, Article III of the Constitution is 'a limitation on the power of Congress to tell the court how to decide it'.[50] Other leading commentators agreed. Of the most prominent, Young saw *Klein* as 'establish[ing] some protection from interbranch intrusion for the federal judiciary' based on the principle of direction.[51] As the authors of *Hart and Wechsler* put it,

jurisprudence of the United States. It is also a recurring issue of real concern, as witnessed by Congressional attempts over the years to limit the jurisdiction of the federal courts in bussing, housing and school prayer cases. (See Young, 'Congressional Regulation of Federal Courts Jurisdiction and Processes', n 22 above, 1190–91: 'On many occasions Congress has been asked to use its regulatory powers over the jurisdiction of federal courts to avoid the effects of decisions of those courts'.) The considerable debate which has arisen in relation to the issue is divided between those who would advocate broad Congressional power in this regard (eg PM Bator, 'Congressional Power Over the Jurisdiction of the Federal Courts' (1982) 27 *Villanova Law Review* 1030; G Gunther, 'Congressional Power to Curtail Federal Court Jurisdiction: An Opinionated Guide to the Ongoing Debate' (1984) 36 *Stanford Law Review* 895 and those who would advocate a more circumscribed congressional power in this regard (see eg LG Sager, 'The Supreme Court 1980 Term Forward: Constitutional Limitations on Congress' Authority to Regulate the Jurisdiction of the Federal Courts' (1981) 95 *Harvard Law Review* 17; AR Amar, 'The Two-Tiered Structure of the Judiciary Act of 1789' (1990) 138 *University of Pennsylvania Law Review* 1499).

[47]   Art III, s 2 confers appellate jurisdiction on the Supreme Court with such exceptions as Congress shall make, which exceptions do not of course apply to the Supreme Court's original jurisdiction.

[48]   Hart, 'The Power of Congress to Limit the Jurisdiction of the Federal Courts', n 12 above, 1364–5. See also MH Redish and CR Pudelski, 'Legislative Deception, Separation of Powers, and the Democratic Process: Harnessing the Political Theory of United States v Klein' (2006) 100 *Northwestern University Law Review* 437.

[49]   *Ibid*, at 1370–73.

[50]   *Ibid*, at 1373.

[51]   Young, 'Congressional Regulation of Federal Courts Jurisdiction and Processes', n 22 above, 1196.

[w]hatever else the Court may have had in mind, it is surely right, isn't it, that invocation of the language of 'jurisdiction' is not a talisman, and that not every congressional attempt to influence the outcome of cases can be justified as the exercise of a power over jurisdiction.[52]

That *Klein* is authority for the broader proposition of the direction principle is now, on the whole, undisputed in both academic commentary and judicial exegesis at the highest level.[53]

That the Supreme Court was espousing the direction principle was confirmed when it expressly contrasted the '1870 proviso' with the legislation unsuccessfully challenged in its earlier decision in *Pennsylvania v Wheeling and Belmont Bridge Co.*[54] That legislation[55] amended the criteria by which a structure was to be declared an obstruction to the public right of navigation on a river, thus rendering lawful a bridge which had previously been declared by a court to be an unlawful structure. This was despite the fact that the owners of the bridge were the subject of a previous injunction either to raise the bridge so that it met the previous legislative requirements, or demolish it. Referring to *Wheeling Bridge*, Chase CJ stated:

No arbitrary rule of decision was prescribed in that case ... [T]he court was left to apply its ordinary rules to the new circumstances created by the act. In the case before us, *no new circumstances* are created by the legislation. But the court is forbidden to give effect to evidence which, in its own judgement, such evidence should have, and is directed to give it an effect precisely contrary.[56] (Emphasis added.)

It was precisely because the court saw in the '1870 proviso' a direction to the court without a change to the underlying law that it was able to hold

[52] Fallon, Meltzer and Shapiro, *Hart and Wechsler's The Federal Courts and the Federal System*, n 23 above.

[53] This is apparent in the three significant Supreme Court cases which will be examined in detail below: *Robertson v Seattle Audubon Society*, *Miller v French* and *Plaut v Spendthrift Farm* (see nn 13–15 above and accompanying text). As for the academic commentary, see also, for example, Young, 'Congressional Regulation of Federal Courts Jurisdiction and Processes, n 22 above, 1233–44; Redish and CR Pudelski, 'Legislative Deception, Separation of Powers, and the Democratic Process', n 48 above; Ronner, 'Judicial Self-Demise', n 3 above, 1046; AR Amar, 'Of Sovereignty and Federalism' (1987) 96 *Yale Law Journal* 1425 at 1474; SL Carter, 'The Morgan "Power" and the Forced Reconsideration of Constitutional Decision' (1986) 53 *University of Chicago Law Review* 819 at 857; T Eisenberg, 'Congressional Authority to Restrict Lower Federal Court Jurisdiction' (1974) 83 *Yale Law Journal* 498 at 526–7; A Parnell, 'Congressional Interference in Agency Enforcement: The IRS Experience' (1980) 89 *Yale Law Journal* 1360 at 1379 n 116; LJ Ratner, 'Congressional Power Over the Appellate Jurisdiction of the Supreme Court (1960) 109 *University of Pennsylvania Law Review* 157 at 158.

[54] *Pennsylvania v Wheeling and Belmont Bridge Co* 59 US (18 How) 421 (1855).

[55] This case was decided on the issue of whether the legislation unconstitutionally amended a previous court order as between the parties. It is a very significant case for the final judgment scenario and discussed in detail in the next chapter at p 222.

[56] *United States v Klein* 80 US (13 Wall) 128 (1871) at 146–7.

'that Congress has inadvertently passed the limit which separates the legislative from the judicial power'.[57]

Klein also acknowledged the status of the direction principle as a threshold test for the application of the Changed Law Rule, as had occurred in the Australian cases. Indeed, how can it be conceived otherwise? The direction principle itself was fashioned out of an attempt to identify legislation which does not in fact amount to a change in the underlying law. While this may be stating the obvious, it will be seen that in subsequent United States decisions this fundamental proposition has not always been appreciated.[58] In establishing this position, the Supreme Court in *Klein* exhibited a concern to preserve the integrity of judicial functions in the pending case by regarding decisional independence as a key element in the exercise of judicial power. It thus also maintained the integrity of the *legislative* power in recognising that Congress was competent to amend the law, requiring the courts to apply such amendment in any pending case.[59]

The third important factor to emerge from *Klein* was its adoption of the same method as in *Liyanage* in locating indicia of direction, eschewing a precise and definitive set thereof. Thus, the court examined first the 'language of the proviso' itself,[60] particularly the following wording:

> [S]uch [presidential] pardon ... *shall be taken and deemed in such suit ...* conclusive evidence that such person did take part in and give aid and comfort to the late rebellion ... and on proof of such pardon and acceptance the jurisdiction of the court in the case *shall cease*, and *the court shall forthwith* dismiss the suit.[61] (Emphasis added.)

Furthermore, the legislation appeared to be designed precisely to address the key issue: whether a person was disbarred from compensation where such person had been granted and accepted a presidential pardon.[62] Moreover, the legislation clearly favoured the government as a party:

---

[57] *Ibid*, at 147.

[58] See L Weinberg, *Federal Courts, Case and Comments on Judicial Federalism and Judicial Power* (St Paul, MN, West Pub Co, 1994) 380: 'This reading of *Klein* ... states that *Klein* held that Congress had overstepped the line separating the legislative from the judicial power because its true intention was not to change the jurisdictional law but to change the result in pending cases without changing the substantive law. This reading of *Klein's* case acknowledges that Congress has power to change federal law and make the change applicable in pending cases'.

[59] Fallon, Meltzer and Shapiro, *Hart and Wechsler's The Federal Courts and the Federal System*, n 23 above, 368, n 21, referring to the relevant passages above from *Klein*, note: 'Given the context [they] surely do not cast ... general doubt on the principle, clear since ... *Schooner Peggy* ... that the courts are obligated to apply law (otherwise valid) as they find it at the time of their decision, including, when a case is on review, the time of the appellate judgement'.

[60] *United States v Klein* 80 US (13 Wall) 128 (1871) at 145.

[61] *Ibid*, at 129.

[62] *Ibid*, at 145–6.

Congress has already provided that the Supreme Court shall have jurisdiction of the judgments of the Court of Claims on appeal. Can it prescribe a rule in conformity with which the court must deny to itself the jurisdiction thus conferred, because and only because its decision, in accordance with settled law, must be adverse to the government and favorable to the suitor? This question seems to us to answer itself.[63]

Despite the absence of a precise *ad hominem* element in the legislation, unconstitutional direction was nevertheless found to exist, reinforcing the point that it is only one factor. Nevertheless, the '1870 proviso' was clearly aimed at an identifiable set of cases, one of which was pending.

Although, following *Klein* and the observations of Cooley, a form of the direction principle appears to have been established, the indicia of direction were not sufficiently explored or clarified. In fact, the United States jurisprudence on this issue was for a time overtaken by developments in Commonwealth jurisdictions, particularly following the opinion of the Privy Council in *Liyanage*[64] and the Australian decisions which followed soon after. In the United States, prior to Hart's article in 1953, there was only one significant decision which dealt with *Klein*—*Pope v United States*[65] in the Court of Claims—and then only in dicta relating to the final case scenario and its different, though related, concerns. The Court of Claims merely noted that Congress could not direct the rehearing of a case already decided in favour of the government.[66] Although the Supreme Court reversed the decision on the basis that no such rehearing was required by the act in that case, it nevertheless did not conclusively deal with the proposition expressed in the dicta of the lower court.

Given the uncertainties surrounding the precise meaning of *Klein*, and given the significance of Hart's thesis in resuscitating *Klein*, a more detailed analysis of Hart's more critical propositions will be attempted as a prelude to the examination of the trio of Supreme Court cases which so affected the status of the direction principle.

IV. HART'S THESIS AND THE UNITED STATES FOUNDATION OF THE DIRECTION PRINCIPLE

While Hart recognised Congress's sweeping constitutional power over the jurisdiction of the federal courts, his thesis was based squarely on the

---

[63] *Ibid*, at 147.

[64] *Liyanage v R* [1967] 1 AC 259.

[65] *Pope v United States* 100 Ct Cl 375 (1944) at 375–6; reversed by the Supreme Court, 323 US 1 (1944).

[66] In relation to the final judgment scenario where the government is a party, and as to whether the government as a party can waive the benefits of a judgment in its favour, see chs 4 and 5 of this book which deal with this in some detail.

premise that such power is limited by other constitutional principles, principally the separation of powers. To allow unqualified congressional control over the Supreme Court's jurisdiction would clearly violate that doctrine with respect to the establishment of an independent judiciary with power to check constitutional violations. At the very least, while Congress could severely limit the appellate jurisdiction of the Supreme Court, it could not remove from the court its basic jurisdiction to review constitutional issues. As Lloyd Anderson stated it, '[t]he way to reconcile the competing values of judicial independence and political control, in Hart's view, is that Congress should be free to do as it sees fit, as long as it leaves some room for the exercise of judicial power'.[67]

In his attempt to give some definition to this 'room', Hart turned to the maintenance of the decisional independence of the courts, thus rehabilitating the issue of legislative interference in pending cases to its central position in separation of powers jurisprudence and befitting its role as a key catalyst for the very entrenchment of the separation doctrine in the United States Constitution. Hart emphasised the discrete nature of the constitutional principles which applied. 'When *the way of exercising jurisdiction* is in question, rather than its denial, the constitutional tests are different' (emphasis added).[68] Herein lay the significance of his thesis. Citing *Klein* as authority, he was thus able to conclude that 'if Congress directs an Article III court to decide a case, I can easily read into Article III a limitation on the power of Congress to tell the Court how to decide it'.[69] This thesis represented a moderately expansive view of *Klein*. That is, it acknowledged the limitation on Congress not to direct the outcome of pending cases. It also allowed Congress a degree of control over pending cases on condition that it acted legislatively by altering the law, even if with retrospective affect.[70] This position is very similar to that established by *Liyanage* and the Australian cases which followed in its immediate train.

To underline the balanced and moderate nature of Hart's view of *Klein*, and indeed to put it in perspective, it should be noted that a broader reading of *Klein* has been postulated. That reading is that Congress cannot indirectly dictate decisions in pending cases even when it *does* amend the relevant substantive law, at least where the government is a

    [67] Anderson, 'Congressional Control over the Jurisdiction of the Federal Courts', n 16 above, 425–6.
    [68] Hart, 'The Power of Congress to Limit the Jurisdiction of the Federal Courts', n 12 above, 1372.
    [69] *Ibid.*
    [70] Anderson, 'Congressional Control over the Jurisdiction of the Federal Courts', n 16 above, 438. See also L Mullenix et al, *Understanding Federal Courts and Jurisdiction* (New York, Matthew Bender, 1998) 30; E Chemerinsky, *Federal Jurisdiction*, 3rd edn (Gathesburg, Aspen Law and Business, 1999) 1813–85.

party.[71] This view would constitute a clear exception, or indeed abrogation, of the Changed Law Rule in certain circumstances and it is a
proposition which has not garnered any mainstream support in the
United States, and none at all in other common law jurisdictions. In the
view of the writer, it is inconsistent with the separation of powers. The
principal difficulty is that it is in effect establishing an *exception* to the
Changed Law Rule but it is not accompanied by the articulation of clear
criteria for carving out an exception to such a fundamental rule, and it is
questionable whether the mere fact that the government is a party is
sufficient. Moreover, such a view clearly challenges the primary legislative function of the legislature under the separation of powers. This
broader interpretation is not available from the reasoning in *Klein* in light
of the court's distinguishing of the *Wheeling Bridge* legislation on the basis
that it created 'new circumstances', that is, that it changed the law. If this
were the ratio of *Klein*, it would amount to an *overruling* of the Changed
Law Rule, and indeed run contrary to the separation of powers, which
naturally defends the power of the legislature to amend the law.[72] This
very expansive view of *Klein* is therefore not only not supported by the
reasoning in the judgment, but also runs counter to the Constitution and
its protection of legislative functions. It cannot be sustained.

Nevertheless, *Klein* itself remains problematic, particularly with
respect to its construction of the '1870 proviso'. For example, Redish,
who, following Hart, adopted the broader, yet still conservative reading
of the case, nevertheless was conscious of these uncertainties. He noted,
for example that

> [w]hether the legislation struck down in *Klein* actually constituted the resolu-
> tion of a particular litigation, rather than the adoption of a generally applicable
> rule of decision, is debatable. One might reasonably view the challenged
> legislation in that case as merely a generally phrased enactment having an
> impact in individual litigation, even though when enacted the legislation was
> quite obviously directed to the resolution of that litigation. However, that
> congressional proviso was also problematic because, to the extent it actually
> represented adoption of a generally applicable rule, that rule did not alter the
> applicable substantive rule of decision. Rather, the rule imposed on the Court
> an obligation to treat probative evidence differently from the way the Court
> would otherwise have chosen to treat it, with the goal of effectively altering the
> substantive rule of decision without legally doing so.[73]

---

[71] These broader interpretations of *Klein* have been identified and examined in the
important article of Young, 'Congressional Regulation of Federal Courts Jurisdiction and
Processes', n 22 above.

[72] Anderson, 'Congressional Control over the Jurisdiction of the Federal Courts', n 16
above 438.

[73] M Redish, 'Federal Judicial Independence: Constitutional and Political Perspectives'
(1995) 46 *Mercer Law Review* 697 at 720–21.

The most comprehensive and detailed academic review of *Klein* since Hart in 1953 was that of Professor Gordon Young.[74] While exploring in detail the various possible interpretations of *Klein*, he too followed Hart's *via media*, agreeing that the case was authoritative for a position beyond the narrowest possible ratio limited to the jurisdictional question. The two main threads of authority from *Klein* he identified thus:

> The first is what will be called a flat withdrawal or withholding of jurisdiction over defined classes of cases or appeals. The result of such a withholding, where effective, is that the trial or appellate court renders no judgment except the narrow one that the trial or appeal is dismissed on jurisdictional grounds. The second sort of regulation permits the court to entertain the suit or hear the appeal but requires it to decide the case in a certain way. This sort of regulation, which will be called 'regulating the decision', involves an attempt to use *jurisdictional* powers to limit how a court may decide a case over which it generally has jurisdiction.[75]

Young agreed with Hart that one clear constitutional limitation with respect to this second type of legislative regulation was that the legislature is prohibited from such regulation if 'the effect of … legislation is to require a decision which would otherwise be unconstitutional'.[76] However, Young expressly concurred with Hart that the constitutional limitation also extended to limit Congress from directing a court how to decide a case both in relation to final outcome, but also with respect to the issues which might arise therein even though not dealing directly with outcome.[77] 'What is prohibited', stated Young, 'is regulating the decision'.[78] He did not, however, espouse any broader interpretation of *Klein* even though he examined it in detail. The outer limits of *Klein* were clearly set up by the Changed Law Rule to which no exceptions were permissible consistent with the separation of powers. The direction principle thus could not be allowed to intrude upon Congress's legislative function to amend the law. Expressing himself cautiously on this point, he stated that '[d]espite some language in *Klein* which suggests a general repudiation of the Changed Law Rule, that Rule was well established at the time *Klein* was decided. Consequently it is unlikely that the Changed Law Rule was rejected in *Klein*'.[79] Hart and Young thus reinforced the prior observations of Cooley and, while acknowledging the uncertainties of the judgment, it is a position on *Klein* with which the writer concurs. However, as will be

[74] Young, 'Congressional Regulation of Federal Courts Jurisdiction and Processes', n 22 above.
[75] *Ibid*, at 1217.
[76] *Ibid*, at 1219.
[77] *Ibid*, at 1223.
[78] *Ibid*, at 1219.
[79] *Ibid*, at 1240.

discussed, the efficacy of the *Klein* rule is challenged more by the modern cases than by the uncertainties in the judgment of Chase CJ.

V.   THE DECLINE OF THE DIRECTION RULE: THE *ROBERTSON* CASE

When the Court of Appeals for the Ninth Circuit in 1990 decided *Seattle Audubon Society v Robertson*,[80] it appeared that the direction principle, pursuant to Hart's interpretation, was well established. In a strong endorsement, the Ninth Circuit applied it rigorously to invalidate the impugned legislation against the backdrop of the Changed Law Rule and its protection of the proper exercise of legislative power: 'Congress exists to write and change our laws, and the courts are bound to apply the law extant at the time of decision … Congress can *amend* or *repeal* any law, even for the purpose of ending pending litigation'.[81] Manifest in this statement, however, was the underlying tension between the Changed Law Rule and the direction principle; yet the delicate balance in the operation of the two rules was struck appropriately by the Ninth Circuit. The significance of the case, however, lay rather in the fact that the Supreme Court on appeal[82] not only overruled the Ninth Circuit, but did so in such a way as to seriously undermine this balance. While the Supreme Court applied the Changed Law Rule rigorously, it adopted a very dismissive attitude toward the direction principle. Its method reduced the principle to a mere formality, which any deft legislature, intent on directing the outcome of a pending case, might avoid.

A.   The Facts of *Robertson*: a Classic Pending Case Scenario

The *Robertson* litigation arose from a dispute between environmental advocates, government land management authorities, and the timber industry. In two separate proceedings in the lower federal courts, the environmental interests challenged the land management plans of the relevant government authorities on the basis that they breached a battery of environmental statutes. The key factual issue was whether the implementation of these plans would result in the prohibited killing of an endangered bird species. While these suits were awaiting appeal, Congress purported to amend the law applicable to the relevant land areas in

---

[80]   *Seattle Audubon Society v Robertson* 914 F 2d 1311 (9th Cir 1990); on appeal from the District Court which had found that there was no unconstitutional interference in breach of the direction principle.
[81]   *Seattle Audubon Society v Robertson* 914 F 2d 1311 (9th Cir 1990) at 1315.
[82]   *Robertson v Seattle Audubon Society* 503 US 429 (1992).

such a way as to render immune the relevant plans from the legal challenge and *without* repealing or amending the pre-existing regime of environmental statutes.

The legislation—'the Northwest Timber Compromise' ('NTC')[83]— sought to facilitate the sale of timber from the relevant forests, yet also maintain the protection of the endangered birds. The central provision, section 318(b)(6)(A) of the NTC provided:

> Congress hereby determines and directs that management of areas according to subsections (b)(3) and (b)(5) of this section on the thirteen national forests [which are named individually] . . . is adequate consideration for the purpose of meeting the statutory requirements that are the basis for the consolidated cases captioned Seattle Audubon Society et al., v F. Dale Robertson . . . and the case Portland Audubon Society et al.

The critical sub-sections, (b)(3) and (b)(5), prohibited the sale of timber from specifically designated areas known to be the habitat of the relevant endangered bird. Moreover, unlike previous cases considered, the legislation expressly named the pending proceedings to which it was to apply. Congress thus sought to achieve what it hoped might be a compromise solution by preventing the invalidation of the plans, and yet providing some protection for the birds. It did so not by repealing the prohibition on the killing of the endangered species, but by requiring the federal courts *to deem* that there would be no breach of existing environmental statutes if the requirements of (b)(3) and (b)(5) were met. This deemed compliance operated irrespective of whether killing had occurred, or might occur—still prohibited under the pre-existing legislation—if there were no sales of timber from the designated areas. This materially altered the legal position in the pending cases without actually repealing or amending the relevant law. These facts set up a classic pending case scenario, which clearly warranted a serious consideration of the direction principle

B.   The Ninth Circuit Decision: The Direction Rule Applied

The Ninth Circuit immediately recognised a *Klein* issue and applied the direction principle to invalidate the legislation because it directed a result without amending the law. Obvious indicia of direction were present.[84] The NTC was very specific. It named the precise pending proceedings as well as the land affected, leaving the pre-existing legislative regime intact. Congress did not attempt, by force of the statute alone, to exempt

[83] The Interior and Related Agencies Appropriation Act 1990.
[84] *Seattle Audubon Society v Robertson* 914 F 2d 1311 (9th Cir 1990) at 1315.

the public bodies in those cases from the relevant environmental statutes. Rather, it deemed compliance with the statutory regime if certain conditions were met, *which conditions were unrelated to the precise requirements of those earlier statutes.* In all the circumstances, the legislation appeared to be designed to produce the outcome desired by Congress[85] in the pending case, clearly deviating from the typical pattern of a general law of prospective operation.

The method of the application of the direction principle followed *Klein* precisely:

> [T]he critical distinction, for the purpose of deciding the limits of Congress's authority to affect pending litigation through statute, is between the actual repeal or amendment of the law . . ., which is permissible, and the actual direction of a particular decision in a case, without repealing or amending the law underlying the litigation, which is not permissible.[86]

Section 318 did not 'by its plain language repeal or amend the environmental laws underlying this litigation'.[87] Rather, because the effect of sub-section (b)(6)(A) was 'to direct that' if the government authorities follow the plan set out in sub-sections (b)(3) and (b)(5) then the government will be deemed to have complied with the environmental statutes, even if otherwise it would be in breach of them[88]:

> Subsection (b)(6)(A) here at issue does not establish new law, but directs the court to reach a specific result and make certain factual findings under existing law in connection with two cases pending in federal court. This is what *Klein* and subsequent cases argue is constitutionally proscribed[89] . . . The language of section 318 is clear: *Congress not only legislated a forest management plan . . .but also directed the courts to find that that plan satisfied the environmental laws underlying the ongoing litigation* . . . In doing so, Congress did not amend or repeal laws, as it unquestionably could do, but rather prescribed a rule for a

---

[85]   See *ibid* at 1312 for detailed background to the enactment.

[86]   *Ibid.* In this regard see also the Supreme Court decision of *United States v Sioux Nation of Indians* 448 US 371 (1980) at 405. The Ninth Circuit followed one of its earlier decisions, *Konizeski v Livermore Labs (In re Consolidated United States Atmospheric Testing Litigation)* 820 F 2d 982 (9th Cir 1987) at 992 where it stated that '[c]ongressional attempts to alter the rule of decision in pending cases in favor of the government have been condemned as a violation of Article III'. It should be noted that in that latter case, it was held that for such a violation of Article III to occur, it was necessary that there be legislation which *both* constituted a dictation to the court as to how it was to decide an issue of fact *and* purported to bind the Court to decide a case in accordance with a rule of law independently unconstitutional on other grounds. (See *also United States v Brainer* 691 F 2d 738 (4th Cir 1982). This was not a correct statement of the legal position. The Ninth Circuit, however, corrected itself in *Grimsey v Huff* 876 F 2d 738 (9th Cir 1989) by holding these requirements to be disjunctive, not conjunctive.

[87]   *Ibid*, at 1316.

[88]   *Ibid.*

[89]   *Ibid.*

decision in a particular way, without changing the underlying law, as it unquestionably cannot do.[90] (Emphasis added.)

For the Ninth Circuit, the connection between the legislation and the pending proceedings was too close and obvious to allow the legislation to stand as a mere change in the law and to which the imperatives of the Changed Law Rule had to be applied. While none of the indicia considered were themselves finally determinative of the issue, in combination their overall effect led the court to this characterisation. The Ninth Circuit paid careful consideration to *Wheeling Bridge*, in relation to which it stated: '[n]o arbitrary rule of decision was prescribed in [*Wheeling Bridge*], but the court was left to apply its ordinary rules to the new circumstances created by the act. In [*Klein*], no new circumstances ha[d] been created by the legislation'.[91] It then aligned the NTC with the '1870 proviso' at issue in *Klein*. Its sole purpose was to prescribe, under certain precise circumstances, how to determine rights under pre-existing laws, which laws had not been amended. As the Ninth Circuit stated by direct reference to *Klein*, 'Congress can amend or repeal any law, even for the purpose of ending pending litigation, but it cannot "prescribe a rule for a decision of a cause in a certain way' where 'no new circumstances have been created by legislation"'.[92] Thus, the Ninth Circuit created a degree of confidence, albeit short-lived as it turned out, that the direction principle remained a potent constitutional limitation.

C.   *Robertson* in the Supreme Court: the Direction Principle Diminished

The reasoning of the Supreme Court[93] was remarkable in that, unanimously, the opposite conclusion was reached; remarkable because it did so with very little elaboration and explanation, and indeed with very little consideration of the obvious separation of powers issues which arose in the litigation.[94] The *Klein* direction principle, although acknowledged, was mentioned almost as if in passing.[95] The court too easily accepted the legislation at face value as a change in the law, and accepted too easily, and with little explanation, the argument of the government authorities that sub-section (b)(6)(A) 'replaced the legal standards underlying the two original challenges with those set forth in subsections (b)(3) and (b)(5), without directing particular applications under either the old

[90]   *Ibid*, at 1317.
[91]   *Ibid*, at 1315.
[92]   *Ibid*.
[93]   *Robertson v Seattle Audubon Society* 503 US 429 (1992).
[94]   The opinion was delivered by Thomas J.
[95]   *Robertson v Seattle Audubon Society* 503 US 429 (1992) at 436.

law or new standards'.[96] The Act was held valid because it only 'compelled changes in law, [and] not findings or results under old law'.[97]

The court remained faithful to *Klein* only to the extent that it acknowledged that there would be no breach of the separation doctrine if there was a change in the law. Beyond that, *Klein*, its principles, its rigorous examination of indicia of direction and their subtle interplay—the *Klein* method—were remarkably ignored in a case which so clearly warranted their serious consideration. By emphasising the imperative of the Changed Law Rule, the Supreme Court lost the necessary balance provided by a serious application of the direction principle. It is an appreciation of this balance which is essential for the maintenance of the decisional independence of the federal courts at this critical crossroads with legislative power.

The Supreme Court appeared to be fixated on one aspect of the legislation which counted against even the 'three textual features of the Compromise' which to the Ninth Circuit were strong indicators of unconstitutional direction[98]: The impugned statute maintained the judiciary's independence to determine compliance.

> Before the Compromise was enacted, the courts adjudicating these claims were obliged to determine [pursuant to the previously existing environmental statutes] whether the challenged harvesting would 'kill' or 'take' any [of the protected birds]. Subsection (b)(6)(A), however, raised the question whether the harvesting would violate different prohibitions – those described in subsections (b)(3) and (b)(5). If not, then the harvesting would constitute management ... according to subsections (b)(3) and (b)(5), and would therefore be deemed to 'meet' [the environmental statutes] regardless of whether or not it would cause an otherwise prohibited killing or taking. Thus, under subsection (b)(6)(A), the agencies could satisfy their [obligations under the pre-existing environmental statutes] in either of one of two ways: by managing their lands so as neither to 'kill' nor 'take' any of the [endangered] birds or by managing their lands so as not to violate the prohibitions of subsections (b)(3) and (b)(5).[99]

Thus, according to the Supreme Court, new statutory criteria for compliance of particular provisions were introduced, 'amending' the previous law despite the fact that the previous law had not actually been repealed. There was no unconstitutional direction, as the section did not 'direct any particular findings of fact or application of law, old or new, to fact'.[100]

---

[96] *Ibid*, at 437.
[97] *Ibid*, at 438.
[98] *Ibid*, at 437–8.
[99] *Ibid*.
[100] *Ibid*, at 438.

Moreover, '[t]o the extent that [the statute] affected the adjudication of . . . cases, it did so by effectively modifying the provisions at issue in those cases'.[101]

This approach exhibited a degree of formalism too great for the facts to bear. The point was that by these deeming provisions the legislature removed from judicial consideration an issue which was of critical significance to the outcome of the pending cases expressly mentioned. Indeed it was that very issue which most threatened the success in the pending litigation of the government authorities and logging interests. Of course, it could have done so without breaching the direction principle by simply removing the prohibition on killing. This, however, it did not do. The illegality of land management which resulted in the killing of endangered birds was maintained.[102] Thus, a federal court, already seized of the matter when the legislation intervened, was now directed to treat, as being in compliance with the law, any such killing *which may in fact result from the land management plan* if the *unrelated* condition could be met that no sales of timber from designated areas would occur. Such a court was in fact required to disregard the pre-existing law and adjudge the issue according to criteria which were completely irrelevant to the issue of the killing of endangered species. Congress was in substance engineering a result in the pending proceedings in circumstances where it was highly questionable that substantive amendment to the law had occurred. Such considerations do not seem even to have engaged the Supreme Court as they did so compellingly the Ninth Circuit.

At best, the Supreme Court's treatment of the indicia of direction is indicative of a 'soft' application of *Klein*. Thus the words in sub-section (b)(6)(A)—'Congress hereby determines and directs' that compliance with the two new provisions would constitute compliance with five old ones—did not appear to have caused the court any concern. It was correct, as the court held, that these words per se did not amount to unconstitutional direction. Nor did it deny, again correctly, that in certain circumstances, they may constitute indicia thereof. What was problematic, however, was its outright dismissal of the suggestion, without explanation, that these words were relevant as indicative of direction in the present case: 'what Congress directed—to agencies and courts alike— was a change in the law, not specific results under old law'.[103] It is very difficult to reconcile this statement with the fact that the pre-existing

---

[101]   *Ibid*, at 440.
[102]   An analogy can be drawn here with the legislation considered in the *Nicholas* case, mentioned in the previous chapter, which maintained the illegality of the importation of heroin, and directed the courts to disregard the illegality when conducted by law enforcement agencies in exercising its discretion whether to admit evidence of importation of the illegal substance.
[103]   *Robertson v Seattle Audubon Society* 503 US 429 (1992) at 438–9.

laws, and indeed the pre-existing illegalities, were left operative. Surely the very point of the application of the direction principle, at least in the *Klein* tradition, was to encourage a rigorous scrutiny of legislation so worded. The court's easy dismissal of this issue remains unconvincing.

A similarly dismissive attitude is evident with respect to the other indicia considered highly relevant by the Ninth Circuit. Even their cumulative effect, in all the circumstances, did not seem to engage the Supreme Court. The naming of the pending cases, it reasoned, was not for the purpose of directing an outcome, but 'served only to identify' the five 'statutory requirements that are the basis for' adjudication in those cases.[104] But why did the legislature not simply name those statutory provisions rather than mention the pending cases by name? This must have raised, at the very least, some suspicion that Congress was seeking to direct an outcome. Indeed, the legislation was more extreme in its specificity than the legislation considered in *Liyanage*, the most egregious of the factual scenarios already considered.

The Ninth Circuit had emphasised that merely because Congress could have achieved a similar outcome by simply repealing or amending the pre-existing environmental statutes, this should not be taken as discounting in any way the element of direction apparent in the legislation in fact enacted.[105] However, the Supreme Court not only disagreed with this argument, it did so without acknowledging any merit in it whatsoever. 'We fail to appreciate the significance of this observation'.[106] The court reasoned that there were available to Congress other less constitutionally controversial means of amending the statute and this fact should be taken as diminishing significantly any indication of direction. This stance alone inclines one at least to sympathy with the harsh words of one commentator that the court's explicit refusal 'to address any broad question of Article III jurisprudence proclaims vacuity'.[107] A true appreciation of the direction principle would have relegated this consideration to irrelevance. The court, in applying the direction principle, must decide on the constitutionality of the impugned legislation, not the legislation which might have been enacted. In this very sensitive area of the legislative and judicial relationship, especially in the heat of inter-branch conflict, the question of means is at least as important as outcome. And it is at this point that the Supreme Court came very close to overruling *Klein*. As Ronner pointed out,

> in rejecting the environmental groups' contention that certain textual features of the Compromise showed that Congress had improperly intruded upon the

---

[104]   *Ibid*, at 440.
[105]   *Ibid*, at 439–40.
[106]   *Ibid*, at 439.
[107]   Ronner, 'Judicial Self-Demise', n 3 above, 1054.

judicial domain, the Supreme Court focused not on what Congress actually did, but on what Congress might have done. Stated otherwise, because Congress might have issued a directive without the explicit imperative preface or might have identified the five statutory requirements instead of naming the pending cases, then all is kosher. Thus, at least from this portion of the reasoning in *Robertson*, emerges the notion that how Congress actually does what it did is virtually meaningless. Consequently, to the extent that *Klein* required courts to scrutinize 'the statute that Congress in fact enacted' then *Robertson* invalidates the *Klein* approach.[108]

Academic commentary on the Supreme Court's reasoning has been highly adverse.[109] In the view of the writer, it is not entirely unwarranted. If nothing more, the Supreme Court by-passed an ideal opportunity to address and settle the difficult issues arising from *Klein*. At worst, it appears the court may have failed to appreciate the critical constitutional issues which arose on these facts. This harsh conclusion appears to have been borne out by the court's own words in the following extraordinary passage:

> *We have no occasion to address any broad question of Article III jurisprudence.* The Court of Appeals held that subsection (b)(6)(A) was unconstitutional under *Klein* because it directed decisions in pending cases without amending any law. Because we conclude that subsection (b)(6)(A) did amend applicable law, we need not consider whether this reading of *Klein* is correct.[110] (Emphasis added.)

In addition to the apparent failure to appreciate the significance of the issue, the above statement is quite inconsistent with *Klein* itself because it suggested that the *Klein* test need not even be considered when determining whether impugned legislation is an amendment to the law. Yet, the point of *Klein* is that the direction principle is a threshold test in determining the very question whether the legislation is amending the law. The above statement appears to suggest that, because the court has already determined that an amendment to the law has taken place, there is no need to consider *Klein* at all. This is a clear example of the failure to appreciate that the direction principle is the threshold test, and suggests an implied repudiation of the rule in *Klein*.

Be that as it may, the influence of *Klein* remained in at least one critical area: the maintenance of the central dichotomy of a substantive amendment as opposed to unconstitutional direction. Ronner noted that the Supreme Court confronted

---

[108]   *Ibid*, at 1054–5.

[109]   See particular Ronner, 'Judicial Self-Demise', n 3 above, and Anderson, 'Congressional Control over the Jurisdiction of the Federal Courts', n 16 above.

[110]   *Robertson v Seattle Audubon Society* 503 US 429 (1992) at 439–40, 441.

the very question it purports to avoid. The Supreme Court acknowledged that the Ninth Circuit read *Klein* to hold that a statute is unconstitutional when 'it direct[s] decisions in pending cases without amending any law' but declined to consider whether this reading was correct for the express reason that the Compromise 'did amend the applicable law'. The Court's description of the challenged provision as one that 'affected the adjudication of the cases', when combined with the Court's validation of the provision for the reason that it amended the law, amounts to the Court putting its imprimatur on the Ninth Circuit's interpretation of the *Klein* test. If we view it this way, *Robertson* boils down to the proposition that there can be no separation of powers infirmity as long as Congress can be said to have amended or repealed the law.[111]

It therefore becomes very difficult to state precisely what the legal position on this constitutional point was following *Robertson.* The position adopted by the Ninth Circuit is clearly preferable in its statement of the law, its fidelity to established authority, its appreciation of the constitutional significance of the direction principle and the separation of powers values it seeks to maintain, and its application to the facts. It is a position more clearly consistent with the detailed scholarly analysis of Hart and Young. Did the Supreme Court overrule *Klein*, as Ronner suggests? The writer thinks not, given that it did accept, albeit superficially and without appearing to appreciate it fully, the central distinction on which the direction principle is based. Its principal failing was its lack of appreciation of the subtleties, the role of the indicia of direction, and its apparent repudiation of the method of its application. The baleful influence of the *Robertson* decision has nevertheless remained, seriously undermining the efficacy of the direction principle.

Promising signs that the case may not be followed emerged from the very negative academic reaction to the decision, and the lack of enthusiasm with which the decision was received by other federal courts. The Ninth Circuit gave expression from time to time to its disapproval. In *Gray v First Winthrop Corp*[112] it remarked—the hint of criticism is obvious—that *Robertson* indicated a 'high degree of judicial tolerance for an Act of Congress that is intended to affect litigation so long as it changes the underlying substantive law *in any detectable way*'[113] (emphasis added). It stated that the

> statute at issue in *Robertson* was extremely narrow in scope, directing the courts to deem statutory requirements satisfied in two named and numbered

---

[111] Ronner, 'Judicial Self-Demise', n 3 above, 1054.
[112] *Gray v First Winthrop Corp* 989 F 2d 1564 (9th Cir 1990).
[113] *Ibid*, at 1569–70.

environmental cases. The Court nevertheless held that the challenged statute had modified the underlying substantive law rather than directed results under old law.[114]

It followed the Supreme Court's lead only because it was binding upon it, doing so with almost palpable reluctance and its disapproval barely disguised. Given that the impugned provision it was considering was not so obviously a legislative direction as that in *Robertson*, it concluded that it *'amply* passes *whatever is left* of the *Klein* test' (emphasis added).[115]

'[W]hatever is left of the *Klein* test'. The words of the Ninth Circuit accurately reflect the quandary that the Supreme Court had left in its wake following *Robertson*. Redish remarked of this case:

> There are two troubling features of the Supreme Court's decision in *Robertson*. First, it is difficult to understand how a statute that expressly directed a result in two specifically mentioned pending litigations can be deemed not to resolve specific litigation. Second, whether or not the Court was correct in its assessment of the specific situation involved in *Roberston* itself, it is surprising that the Court would suggest that the constitutionality of a congressional attempt to alter the outcome of litigation without simultaneously altering pre-existing, general substantive law is an open question. As to the former question, it is at least arguable that the Robertson Court was correct in concluding that the congressional action had, in fact, altered pre-existing law; the statute did, after all, provide that specified behaviour would now be deemed to satisfy certain statutory requirements that it had not previously satisfied. Any legislation, however, that directs findings in specifically referenced litigation should categorically be deemed to violate *Klein*, if only as a prophylactic effort to avoid confusion. If Congress is truly changing substantive law, it can do so without express reference to specific pending cases, and any case-specific reference in legislation is certainly suspect.[116]

Despite the concern that Robertson left very little scope for the operation of the direction principle, *Klein* was not overruled. In the words of one of the harshest critics of *Robertson*, '[a]lthough I interpret the *Robertson* decision as the implicit overruling of *Klein*, I do not believe that *Robertson* means that there is and can no longer be a point at which legislation impermissibly impinges upon the exercise of judicial power'.[117] The future of the direction principle nevertheless remained uncertain.

---

[114]   *Ibid*, at 1569.

[115]   *Ibid*, at 1570.

[116]   Redish and Pudelski, 'Legislative Deception, Separation of Powers, and the Democratic Process', n 48 above, at 457.

[117]   Ronner, 'Judicial Self-Demise', n 3 above, 1041.

VI.   *ROBERTSON'S* UNCERTAIN LEGACY: *PLAUT V SPENDTHRIFT FARM INC*

Robertson's uncertain legacy and baleful influence continue to weigh upon United States jurisprudence. The fact that a very high threshold was set for the application of the direction principle was borne out in the other two major relevant Supreme Court decisions in the decade of the 1990s, *Plaut v Spendthrift Farm Inc*[118] and *Miller v French*.[119] This was despite the fact that the Supreme Court, under the influence of Scalia J in particular, was adopting an increasingly formalist approach to separation of powers analysis and was seemingly less tolerant of even innocuous breaches of the separation doctrine.

Plaut was a case primarily concerned with the inviolability of final judgments, although relevant also to present concerns. At issue was the constitutionality of section 27A of the Securities Exchange Act 1934.[120] It was enacted in the wake of two Supreme Court decisions which resulted in a large number of meritorious civil actions for securities fraud becoming statute-barred, creating a degree of public consternation. On 19 June 1991, in *Lampf et al v Gilbertson*[121] the Supreme Court prohibited the hitherto accepted practice of relying on the forum State's statute of limitations in civil actions which were commenced pursuant to the implied right of action under federal law in section 10(b) of the Securities Exchange Act 1934 (US).

It held that the exclusively applicable limitation period for such actions was the relevant federal period which was of less duration than the relevant State periods upon which a great number of suits had relied when commenced, including the *Plaut* claim. The suit in *Lampf*, which was such a case, along with many others, was therefore dismissed as statute-barred under the more stringent, and now exclusively applicable, federal limitation period. On the same day that *Lampf* was decided, the court decided *James B Beam Distilling Co v Georgia*,[122] in which it disallowed the judicial practice known as 'selective prospectivity', that is, deciding a case by applying a new rule that does not necessarily accord with precedent and limiting the application of the new rule to the parties before the court. This excluded its application to other parties in pending actions which had been filed prior to the decision in question. Thus, by a

---

[118] *Plaut v Spendthrift Farm Inc* 514 US 211 (1995).
[119] *Charles B Miller, Superintendent, Pendleton Correctional Facility, v Richard A French*, 530 US 327 (2000) ('*Miller v French*').
[120] Now codified at 15 USC s78aa-1. It came into force on 19 December 1991.
[121] *Lampf v Gilbertson* 501 US 350 (1991).
[122] *James B Beam Distilling Co v Georgia* 501 US 529 (1990).

combination of *Beam* and *Lampf*, in all pending and future section 10(b) litigation, the shorter federal limitations period became exclusively applicable.

This proved to be a considerable boon to defendants in pending suits, many of whom successfully moved to dismiss claims that had been filed in reliance on the more generous State limitation periods.[123] At a time when the financial excesses of the 1980s were beginning spectacularly and publicly to unravel before the courts—many of which involved high profile figures and securities firms and were the subject of very significant public reflection and anger—the spectre of legitimate and meritorious claims failing on a 'technicality' aroused Congress to intervention. There were often related criminal proceedings involved. The issue would not tolerate an indifferent Congress.[124]

Section 27A of the Securities Exchange Act was Congress's response. A successful constitutional challenge was mounted against that aspect of the provision, contained in section 27A(b), which provided for the re-opening of cases dismissed purely as a result of *Beam* and *Lampf*. In a highly formalist judgment, delivered by Scalia J for the majority,[125] this was held to be a legislative re-opening of a finally decided case and thus a breach of the separation of powers.[126] However, when it came to that aspect of the section applicable to pending cases the court exhibited a different attitude. Section 27A(a) provided:

> *Effect on pending causes of action.* The limitation period for any private civil action implied under section [10(b) of the Securities Exchange Act 1934] that was commenced on or before June 19, 1991, [the date that *Lampf* and *Beam* were handed down] shall be the limitation period provided by the laws applicable in the jurisdiction, including principles of retroactivity, as such laws existed on June 19, 1991.

In other words, for this specific class of pending cases, courts were directed to disregard the current law, and allow for the application of the longer State limitations periods. Because it was questionable whether the legislature was in fact making a substantive amendment to the law, the issue of the direction principle arose.

---

[123]   See Doigt, 'Is Purely Retroactive Legislation Limited by the Separation of Powers?', n 1 above, 914–15. See also CH Sturdy, 'Section 27A Confronts *Lampf* and the Constitution' (1994) 74 *Boston University Law Review* 645. At n 7, at 646 of the Sturdy article, the many federal court decisions which examined s 27A are catalogued. The congressional response to *Lampf* has spawned a wide literature.

[124]   The pressure on Congress to intervene and the Congressional debates are amply set out in the various articles cited in the previous footnote.

[125]   The majority consisted of Rehnquist CJ, O'Connor, Kennedy, Souter and Thomas JJ; Breyer J concurring in the result with Stevens, and Ginsburg JJ dissenting.

[126]   See p 224ff below.

With little elaboration, as in *Robertson*, the court regarded section 27A(a) as a change in the law and, by implication, not a breach of the direction principle.[127] It was referred to as the 'new statute of limitations' which the courts 'could and would' apply.[128] Revealing its ambivalent attitude to *Klein*, although indicating its acceptance of its fundamental rationale, the Supreme Court remarked that '[w]hatever the precise scope of *Klein*, however, later decisions have made clear that its prohibition does not take hold when Congress "amend[s] applicable law"'.[129] It also easily regarded section 27A(b) as a change in the law: 'Section 27A(b) indisputably does set out substantive legal standards for the Judiciary to apply, and in that sense changes the law (even if solely retroactively)'.[130] Reminiscent of *Robertson*, the court dismissed the application of *Klein* to the present facts almost out of hand: 'When a new law makes clear that it is retroactive, an appellate court must apply that law in reviewing judgments still on appeal that were rendered before the law was enacted, and must alter the outcome accordingly'.[131] In other words, the Changed Law Rule was applied almost as if the *Klein* direction principle was an insignificant hurdle, and without attempting any *Klein* analysis. The status of the direction principle as a threshold test for the application of the Changed Law Rule continued to suffer a serious reversal.

Perhaps this aspect of the judgment ought to be discounted given that section 27A(a), relating to pending cases, was not in issue and the court therefore declined to give it due attention for this reason. Nevertheless, the spectre of *Robertson* was evident. It was also evident in many of the other federal court decisions which had considered section 27A(a) and found it to be a change in the law. To take but one example, the Court of Appeals for the Fifth Circuit in *Pacific Mutual Life Insurance Co v First Republicbank Corp*[132] addressed a submission that section 27A(a) 'affects the outcome of cases without changing the law in violation of the rule announced in *United States v Klein*'.[133] Its response was simply that it adopted the analysis of the Eleventh Circuit in *Henderson v Scientific-Atlanta*[134] that section 27A respected *Klein* by 'changing the law'. It is significant to note that in *Henderson*, the influence of *Robertson* was particularly marked.[135] In the words of the Ninth Circuit, *Robertson*

---

[127] *Plaut v Spendthrift Farm* 514 US 211 (1995) at 217. This view was shared by the minority judgment of Stevens J, in which Ginsburg J joined (at 247).

[128] *Ibid.*

[129] *Ibid*, at 218.

[130] *Ibid.*

[131] *Ibid*, at 226.

[132] *Pacific Mutual Life Insurance Co v First Republicbank Corp* 997 F 2d 39 (5th Cir 1993).

[133] *Ibid*, at 53.

[134] *Henderson v Scientific-Atlanta* 971 F 2d 1567 (11th Cir 1992) at 1572.

[135] *Ibid*, at 1572–3. Other significant Court of Appeals decisions which found that s 27A changed the law were: *Anixter v Home-Stake Production Co* 977 F 2d 1533 (10th

established a 'high degree of judicial tolerance' for acts of Congress that sought to affect the outcome of pending cases.[136] Pending cases were thus saved from *Lampf* and *Beam*.[137]

As a sign that the direction principle was still relevant, the common thread in all of these decisions remained that fundamental distinction between a change in the law and a direction to the judiciary. However, it is possible to identify the following common reasoning which discounted the principle's efficacy: As a result of the *Lampf* decision, two limitation periods were set up. The pre-*Lampf* rule allowed for a choice between the federal and forum State statute of limitation. The post-*Lampf* rule made the shorter federal statute of limitations exclusively applicable. It was accepted, nevertheless, that section 27A did not expressly provide for a new statutory limitation period. Rather, it gave legislative instruction as to which limitation period was applicable in specific circumstances. Revealing that 'high degree of judicial tolerance' referred to above,[138] this instruction was regarded as having the effect of 'changing' the statute of limitation[139] and regarded as a legitimate exercise of legislative power. It was stated that the question of the length of limitations periods 'traditionally reside[d] in the legislative branch'.[140] In other words, the fundamental indicator of direction, the absence of a clear amendment to the law, was disregarded. Congress merely exercised its legitimate power to legislate so as to 'overrule' the Supreme Court in *Lampf*.[141] The Tenth

Cir 1992) at 154–6; *Gray v First Winthrop Corp* 989 F 2d 1564 (9th Cir 1993) at 168–79; *Berning v AG Edwards & Sons* 990 F 2d (7th Cir 1993) at 278–9; and *Cooke v Manufactured Homes, Inc* 998 F 2d 1256 (4th Cir 1993) at 1264–5.

[136]   *Gray v First Winthrop Corp*, 989 F 2d 1564 (9th Cir 1993) at 1569–70. See Sturdy, 'Section 27A Confronts *Lampf* and the Constitution', n 123 above, for academic comment to the same effect.

[137]   For an elaborate catalogue and description of the split in the federal courts on the issue of s27A, see Sturdy, 'Section 27A Confronts *Lampf* and the Constitution', n 123 above, 648–50, and in particular the elaborate footnotes on those pages; and MA Lazarus, 'Life After *Lampf*: The Constitutionality of New Section 27A of the Securities and Exchange Act of 1934' (1994) 68 *Tulane Law Review* 975 at 981 with the extensive catalogue of cases in fn 36. For an elaborate treatment of the numerous cases dealing with the issue, see also: JO Himstreet, 'Section 27A and the Statute of Limitations in 10b-5 Claims: Section 27A is Necessary, It's Proper, but it's Probably Unconstitutional' (1994) 30 *Williametter Law Review* 151; CW Palm, 'The Constitutionality of Section 27A of the Securities Exchange Act: Is Congress Rubbing *Lampf* the Wrong Way?' (1992) 37 *Villanova Law Review* 1213; Doigt, 'Is Purely Retroactive Legislation Limited by the Separation of Powers?', n 1 above, 1; HJ Goldstein, 'When the Supreme Court Shuts its Doors, May Congress Re-Open Them?: Separation of Powers Challenges to S 27A of the Securities Exchange Act' (1994) 34 *Boston College Law Review* 853 at 875–9.

[138]   This is also a significant theme in the articles referred to in n 137.

[139]   See *Rabin v Fivzar Associates* 801 F Supp 1045 (SDNY 1992) at 1054.

[140]   *Anixter v Home-Stake Productions Co* 977 F 2d 1533 (10th Cir 1992) at 1546.

[141]   A clear example of this is in the reasoning of the Court of Appeals in *Co-operative de Ahorro v Kidder, Peabody and Co* 993 F 2d 269(1st Cir 1992) at 273.

Circuit in *Anixter v Home-Stake Productions Co*,[142] the First Circuit in *Co-operative de Ahorro v Kidder, Peabody and Co*,[143] adopting the reasoning of the former court, and the Eleventh Circuit in *Henderson v Scientific-Atlanta Inc*[144] clearly revealed the influence of the *Robertson* decision in that they all likened section 27A to the legislation held to be constitutional in *Robertson*. Indeed, it would have been a defiant lower federal court which would have declared section 27A(a) to be unconstitutional.[145]

Yet such defiance was not entirely absent. A significant minority of the federal courts avoided the soft *Robertson* approach, without explicitly saying so, and applied rather the *Klein* rule rigorously to the section 27A issue. The Sixth Circuit in *Plaut* itself,[146] in addition to quite a number of federal district courts,[147] found that section 27A was not in substance a change in the law, but rather legislation directed toward a particular result in a small number of cases in breach of the direction principle. These courts were sensitive to the background to the legislation. They noted that section 27A was drafted in that way because two bills which sought to effect a change in the statute of limitations so as to adopt a two-year/five-year period did not pass through Congress.[148] Therefore, it appears that it was amended to its final form in order to achieve Congress's purpose in maintaining meritorious claims, and yet, at the same time, not alter the position with respect to the statute of limitations. For these courts, therefore, section 27A was a congressional direction as to which statute of limitation was applicable, 'even though [Congress] did not enact a substantive or procedural law'.[149] They squarely aligned themselves with the position taken by the Ninth Circuit in *Robertson*.[150] The general reasoning in these cases is compelling. Nothing had changed with respect to the actual period of limitations, excepting the legislative direction to the courts as to which was to apply in a pending case. A rigorous application of the direction principle should at least have strongly engaged the court that this may have been the case and that therefore there was a breach of the separation of powers.

On the other hand, those courts which, with the Supreme Court, maintained that section 27A changed the law emphasised the fact that the

---

[142] *Anixter v Home-Stake Productions Co* 977 F 2d 1533 (10th Cir 1992) at 1546.
[143] *Co-operative de Ahorro v Kidder, Peabody and Co* 993 F 2d 269(1st Cir 1992) at 273.
[144] *Henderson v Scientific-Atlanta Inc* 971 F 2d 1567 (11th Cir 1962).
[145] See Lazarus, 'Life After *Lampf'*, n 137 above, 984–5.
[146] *Plaut v Spendthrift Farm Inc* 1 F 3d 1487 (6th Cir 1993).
[147] All these district court cases have been catalogued in Himstreet, 'Section 27A and the Statute of Limitations in 10b-5 Claims', n 137 above, 177 nn 172–3.
[148] See *In re Brichard* 788 F Supp 1098 (ND Cal 1992) at 1104.
[149] *Ibid.*
[150] *Seattle Audubon Society v Robertson* 914 F 2d 1311 (9th Cir 1990).

section did not direct factual findings on the merits of a particular case. Thus the Tenth Circuit found that the provision 'merely turns back the legal clock to the period just prior to *Lampf* and then permits the courts independently to adjudicate any reopened actions on the basis of the law'.[151] By contrast, the courts which resisted *Robertson's* influence placed great express reliance on *Klein* itself. Indeed, the extent to which detailed reference was made to *Klein* was indicative of a more general willingness to apply *Klein* rigorously. Like the '1870 proviso', section 27A did not compel a specific final judgment, but did provide instructions for courts to employ when evaluating a particular rule of decision. As the court in *Bank of Denver v Southeastern Capitol Group*[152] noted, Congress cannot, as it did here, direct federal courts to ignore Supreme Court precedent in a discrete category of pending cases without violating the separation of powers doctrine.

These cases also challenged the identification of section 27A with the 'NTC' in *Robertson*, upon which so much reliance was placed by those courts maintaining that the section changed the law. Even if one were to accept the Supreme Court's view that the NTC did change the law, section 27A differed from it markedly. Taking the most innocuous view of the former, it deemed compliance with particular statutes if certain requirements were met which were unrelated to the conduct prohibited by those statutes. By contrast, section 27A(a) directed specific applications of law to particular parties. As one commentator, JO Himstreet, noted,

> [c]ourts in one universe were to apply one law, i.e., those hearing cases filed prior to *Lampf*, and courts in another universe were to apply another, i.e., those hearing cases filed after *Lampf*. Had Section 27A expressly overruled or amended *Lampf's* limitations period, the statute would be constitutional…Unfortunately, reality dictates that Section 27A does not have the 'effect' of changing the statute of limitations. It simply changes the retroactive application of *Lampf* and *Beam*. Thus despite the Tenth Circuit and Eleventh Circuits clinging to *Robertson* to authenticate Section 27A's constitutionality, *Robertson* is inapplicable.[153]

Himstreet suggested[154] that the amending provision, to be constitutional, should have expressly provided for a new statutory limitation period and abolished the distinction between pre-*Lampf* and post-*Lampf* situations; and have made the new section retroactive. Of course his suggested amendments would have exactly the same effect as section 27A in

---

[151] *Anixter v Home-Stake Productions Co* 977 F 2d 1533 (10th Cir 1992) at 1545.
[152] *Bank of Denver v Southeastern Capitol Group* 789 F Supp 1092 (D Colo 1992) at 1097.
[153] Himstreet, 'Section 27A and the Statute of Limitations in 10b-5 Claims', n 137 above, 185–6.
[154] *Ibid.*

terms of outcome. This is not unimportant. However, the issue here, it should be stressed, is not what Congress might have done, but what it actually did. Process is equally important in this scenario. To dismiss the changes wrought by section 27A as purely cosmetic is to miss the significant underlying point: Congress may indeed affect the outcome of pending cases, but only by changing the law; not by directing the courts as to how they are to decide factual or legal issues or indeed the final outcome in any particular case or set of cases. Transparency is critical to the workings of any legislature within a system of representative government, and hence the means by which it achieves its desired outcome can often be as important as the outcome itself. Given the way the Supreme Court in *Plaut* decided the issue on the question of final judgments, and the way it uncompromisingly punished even minor technical breaches of the separation of powers (as will be discussed in detail in the next chapter[155]), it is surprising that it did not yet adopt the same approach with respect to the direction principle and the pending case scenario. It would appear that the soft approach in *Robertson* was still exercising its influence.

The position adopted by those courts that section 27A was unconstitutional on *Klein* principles was strongly supported by the academic commentators. Himstreet stated '[t]he legislation's effect is to direct the result in those cases filed before *Lampf* without changing the underlying statute of limitations itself'.[156] JD McNally noted that '[r]eading parts (a) and (b) of section 27A together ... reveals the clear congressional intent to address the outcome of a limited group of cases rather than provide a general statute of limitations for section 10(b) actions'.[157] This targeting of specific cases was not of itself fatal, but was a very significant factor to be taken into consideration in determining the true nature of Congress's action. By examining the background to the case and the congressional consideration of what should be done about *Lampf* and *Beam*, he concluded as follows:

> Congress had no intention of changing the statute of limitations through section 27A except in the cases of particular litigants. In effect, Congress sought to reach into the proceedings involving those particular litigants and change the outcome of their cases, without changing the underlying law ... [S]ection 27A simply reversed cases which had been dismissed and allowed a more liberal statute of limitations in pending cases. The *Lampf* rule, establishing a stringent and uniform section 10(b) statute of limitations, remains intact. The

---

[155] See 244ff below.
[156] Himstreet, 'Section 27A and the Statute of Limitations in 10b-5 Claims', n 137 above, 185–6.
[157] JD McNally, 'Constitutional Law: Did Congress Overreach in its Reaction to Lampf?' (1994) 16 *Western New England Law Review* 397 at 420.

statute of limitations applying to all other litigants remains as it was prior to the passage of section 27A. There is no practical difference between the congressional action in *Klein* and the congressional action in passing section 27A ... Section 27A only changed the judicial treatment to be given to certain factual circumstances, i.e., the filing dates of claims made under section 10(b).[158]

PJ McCarthy, in agreement, was also quite emphatic:

> No language in Section 27A changes the law; the statute merely prohibits the retroactive application of the *Lampf* decision ... [t]here is still no express statute of limitations within Section 10 (b). Congress did not enact a uniform statute of limitations, instead, it passed Section 27A(a) which allows plaintiffs to renew claims that would otherwise be dismissed on statute of limitations grounds had *Lampf* been applied retroactively.[159]

There is sufficient indication in both judicial exegesis and academic commentary that the *Klein* direction principle, as interpreted by Hart, may still yet survive the influence of *Roberston*. Whether *Robertson* is overruled, or limited to its facts, will greatly depend on the attitude of the Supreme Court in the future. There is sufficiently strong authority and legal opinion to support a restoration of the pre-*Robertson* approach. However, the Supreme Court, in the third of the seminal cases to be considered, created additional hurdles.

VII.   *KLEIN* QUALIFIED, OVERRULED OR MISINTERPRETED? *MILLER V FRENCH*

Miller v French,[160] of all the cases mentioned, had the greatest impact on the orthodox adoption of the direction principle in the United States. The decision itself would not appear to have been possible were it not for the precedent set by *Robertson*. It was a curious decision in that, while allowing for the survival of the *Klein* direction principle, it introduced curious and novel qualifications and refinements which, if accepted in future cases, would constitute a further significant dilution of the protection afforded the judicial branch in pending cases. As the *Miller v French* litigation progressed through the courts, the pattern set by the judicial consideration of section 27A of the Securities Exchange Act repeated itself: The lower federal courts, including the Court of Appeals, together

---

[158]   *Ibid*, at 421.
[159]   PJ McCarthy, 'The Constitutionality of Section 27A of the Securities and Exchange Act of 1934: Congressional Response to the Upheaval of the Lampf Decision' (1994) 20 *Journal of Legislation* 236 at 247.
[160]   *Miller v French* 530 US 327 (2000).

with the academic commentary, almost unanimously regarded the impugned legislation to be a breach of the direction principle. The Supreme Court disagreed.

The legislation at issue was the Prison Litigation Reform Act 1995 ('PLRA'),[161] and in particular that aspect thereof which provided for the imposition and termination of injunctions regulating conditions in prisons. It provided that a federal court shall not grant injunctive relief relating to prison conditions, or approve the continuation of existing injunctive relief, unless such relief was 'narrowly drawn', extended 'no further than necessary to correct the violation of a Federal right', and was 'the least intrusive means necessary to correct the violation of the Federal right'.[162] Provision was made for an 'automatic stay' of a prior injunction in circumstances where a motion (usually by a prison authority) was brought before a federal court seeking its removal or modification on the basis that it did not now meet the requirements of the new Act.[163] Once such a motion was brought, the relevant court was directed to stay the pre-existing injunction on the expiration of 30 days following the filing of the motion, the stay ending on the date of the court's eventual ruling on the matter.[164] This automatic stay was triggered by the mere expiration of the relevant time period and was to come into effect independently of any ruling by the court.[165]

The Pendleton Correctional Facility, of which Miller was the superintendent, was the subject of an existing injunction to remedy violations of the Eighth Amendment of the Constitution regarding conditions of confinement.[166] Miller filed a motion pursuant to the PLRA to terminate this injunction on the basis that it no longer met the new standards prescribed by the Act. The respondent inmates moved to prohibit the application of the automatic stay provision[167] on the basis that it was unconstitutional as an impermissible direction to the judiciary in pending cases and that it constituted a legislative revision of a prior final

---

[161] Prison Litigation Reform Act 1995 110 Stat 1321–66 to 1321–77 which is codified at 18 USC § 3626. References to the relevant sections hereafter shall be from the United States Code.

[162] United States Code, 18 USC § 3626 (a)(1)(A) (1994 edn) Supp IV.

[163] *Ibid*, § 3626 (b)(2).

[164] *Ibid*, § 3626(e)(2). Sub-s (e)(3) provided that the 30-day period was extendable to 90 days by the court for 'good cause'.

[165] *Ibid*, § 3626(e)(2): 'Any motion to modify or terminate prospective relief made under subsection (b) shall operate as a stay during the period—
(A)(i) beginning on the 30th day after such motion is filed, in the case of a motion made under paragraph (1) or (2) of subsection (b); … and
(B) ending on the date the court enters a final order ruling on the motion'.

[166] This injunction had been granted as result of prior suit by prisoners of the facility in the federal District Court, *Miller v French* 777 F Supp 910 (SD Ind 1982) and was upheld in the Court of Appeals (7th Circuit) 777 F 2d 1250 (7th Cir 1985).

[167] 18 USC § 3626(e)(2).

judgment of the judicial branch. The prisoners were originally successful in the lower courts, including the Court of Appeals (Seventh Circuit)[168] before Miller appealed to the Supreme Court. For the purposes of this chapter, it is that aspect of the submissions relating to legislative direction in the pending case which will be examined.

The Seventh Circuit was very responsive to the prisoners' submission and affirmed the position taken by the District Court that the provision did not permit the federal courts to exercise an independent discretion as to whether an injunction in a pending case should be stayed, and, to that extent, it violated separation of powers principles. Indeed the automatic stay provision was drafted in unequivocal terms, clearly providing that a motion to terminate prior relief '*shall* operate' as a stay during a specified time period (emphasis added).[169] The Seventh Circuit, noting that it did not come lightly to the conclusion that Congress meant to restrict the equitable powers of the federal courts, nevertheless found it 'impossible to read this language as doing anything less than that'.[170] The provision was 'a self-executing legislative determination that a specific decree of a federal court . . . must be set aside at least for a period of time'.[171] As such, it breached both the principle confirmed in *Plaut* prohibiting the legislative suspension of a final judgment and the principle established in *Klein* in that it mandated a particular rule of decision.[172]

On the *Klein* point, the Seventh Circuit followed the Sixth Circuit's consideration of the automatic stay provision in *Hadix v Johnson*,[173] which held that the provision was clearly and unambiguously 'a legislative command that a stay of prospective relief occurs as a matter of law no later than 90 days after the state's petition is filed, and that this legislative stay continues in effect until the findings required by (b)(3) have been made'.[174] However, the Sixth Circuit, alone of all the various courts which had considered it, avoided a finding of unconstitutionality by reading down the provision as one which allowed the courts to retain the power to suspend the automatic stay in accordance with general equitable principles.[175] The Seventh Circuit, however, expressly rejected this interpretation, finding the wording to be too unequivocal for such a conclusion:[176]

---

[168]   *French v Duckworth* 178 F 3d 437 (7th Cir 1999).
[169]   *Ibid*, at 443.
[170]   *Ibid*.
[171]   *Ibid*, at 446.
[172]   *Ibid*.
[173]   *Hadix v Johnson* 144 F 3d 925 (6th Cir 1998).
[174]   *Ibid*, at 937.
[175]   *United States v Michigan*, 989 F Supp 853 (WD Mich 1996); *Glover v Johnson*, 957 F Supp 110 (ED Mich (1997); *Hadix v Johnson* 933 F Supp 1362 (WD Mich 1996); *Hadix v Johnson* 933 F Supp 1360 (ED Mich 1996).
[176]   *French v Duckworth* 178 F 3d 437 (7th Cir 1999) at 443.

The automatic stay ... operates directly on the internal adjudication of a case in federal court. It strips from the court the authority to decide whether the status quo (defined by the earlier decree the court entered that required prospective relief) should be continued or modified pending the court's decision on the immediate termination petition.[177]

And further,

[i]t addresses what should happen during the pendency of the case. For that time period, the statute does mandate a particular rule of decision: the prospective relief must be terminated. In our view, *this falls comfortably within the rule of Klein,* and as such, it exceeds the power of the legislative branch.[178] (Emphasis added.)

Thus, despite the *Robertson* influence, the Seventh Circuit and a number of other federal courts confirmed and applied the *Klein* direction principle to invalidate the impugned provisions.

The Supreme Court, however, again without rejecting *Klein* outright, held that the provision did not breach the direction principle. This was despite the fact that it agreed with the Seventh Circuit that its meaning was unequivocal and that Congress had clearly intended to make the operation of the PLRA's automatic stay provision mandatory, precluding the federal courts from exercising their equitable jurisdiction to enjoin the stay.[179] This makes all the more curious its finding that the direction principle was not breached. The majority commenced by dismissing the other separation of powers challenges to the automatic stay provision. First, this legislative supervision of judicial decrees did not violate the principle that Congress cannot confer power on the executive branch to review judicial decisions, based on the principle in *Hayburn's case,*[180] as the automatic stay provision 'does not involve the direct review of judicial decisions by officials of the Legislative or Executive Branches'.[181] Secondly, the majority disposed of the argument that the automatic stay provision revised or suspended a final judgment, which was unconstitutional as the court had recently found in *Plaut,*[182] which principle it nevertheless reaffirmed. The court distinguished *Plaut* on the basis that that case involved a legislative attempt to re-open a final judgment which

---

[177] *Ibid*, at 444.
[178] *Ibid*, at 446.
[179] *Miller v French* 530 US 327 (2000) at 336. The majority opinion was delivered by O'Connor J and the majority consisted of Rehnquist CJ, Scalia, Kennedy and Thomas JJ. Souter J filed an opinion concurring in part, and dissenting in part, in which Ginsburg J joined. They dissented on the basis of their holding that the direction principle had been breached. The points of concurrence and dissent will be discussed in the text which follows. Breyer J filed a dissenting opinion in which Stevens J joined.
[180] *Hayburn's case* 2 US 408 (2 Dall 409) (1792).
[181] *Miller v French* 530 US 327 (2000) at 340.
[182] *Plaut v Spendthrift Farm Inc* 514 US 211 (1995).

had made an award of damages, whereas the present case involved the prospective effect of injunctions. 'Prospective relief under a continuing, executory decree remains subject to alteration due to changes in the underlying law'.[183] Congress here had altered the law by providing that federal courts must make required findings before injunctive relief could be granted in prison conditions cases and, 'when Congress changes the law underlying a judgment awarding prospective relief, that relief is no longer enforceable to the extent it is inconsistent with the new law'.[184] As will be discussed in the next chapter, it made this finding despite the fact that the automatic stay took effect *without regard* to a change in the law. In coming to these conclusions, the majority introduced what, in the opinion of the writer and many commentators, were novel and questionable qualifications: Because the automatic stay 'merely reflect[ed]', 'assist[ed] in the enforcement', or 'helped to implement' the change in the law, and because the prospective relief that did not meet the new requirement and was 'no longer enforceable',[185] the rule in *Plaut* was not breached.[186]

It is highly problematic that these novel qualifications were made applicable also to the direction principle, even though the court explicitly recognised the central tenet thereof,[187] and by relying on these it found that it had not been breached. It came to terms with its acknowledgment of the unequivocally directive nature of the automatic stay provision by stating that it 'must be read not in isolation, but in the context of § 3626 as a whole'.[188] When so read, the section 'helps to implement the change in the law caused' by the other sub-sections in that provision.[189] Accordingly, it 'merely reflects the changed legal circumstances—that prospective relief under the existing decree is no longer enforceable, and remains unenforceable unless and until the court makes findings required by § 3626(b)(3)'.[190] Because the stay 'operates in conjunction with the new standards'[191] it was somehow incorporated into the change in the underlying law, thus losing its status as a legislative direction. The court thus came to the tortuous conclusion that even though, when read alone, the provision did not change the underlying law, it nevertheless did not breach the direction principle. The ratio of the case therefore appeared to

---

[183]   *Miller v French* 530 US 327 (2000) at 344, referring to the distinction drawn in *Pennsylvania v Wheeling Bridge* 54 US 13 (How) 518 (1851) and *Pennsylvania v Wheeling Bridge and Belmont Bridge Co* 59 US (18 How) 421 (1855). This aspect of the case will be discussed in more detail in the next chapter.

[184]   *Ibid*, at 347.

[185]   *Ibid*, at 348.

[186]   *Ibid*, at 346–8.

[187]   *Ibid*, at 349.

[188]   *Ibid*.

[189]   *Ibid*, at 348.

[190]   *Ibid*.

[191]   *Ibid*, at 349.

be that a provision which is an unconstitutional direction when examined in isolation can nevertheless be valid when read in light of the Act as a whole if it merely facilitates a change in the law, or, even 'merely reflects' the changed legal circumstances which are implemented by other legislative provisions.

One might be tempted to regard this approach as exhibiting functionalist tendencies, standing in stark contrast to the high formalism of the *Plaut* judgment written by Scalia J. This would not be an accurate assessment, however. The judgment maintains a formalist approach by accepting the definitional core of the direction principle and its fundamental tenet that legislation is either a substantive amendment to the law or an unconstitutional direction. It is not suggesting, in the way of the functionalist, that such strict definitional dichotomies be rejected, or that countervailing public policy considerations be taken into account in determining whether there has been an impermissible inter-branch intrusion. Rather, *exceptions* to the application of the direction principle are being carved out; and, being exceptions, they are based on the maintenance of the critical dichotomy above-mentioned. They operate by somehow transforming—the basis of such transformation remaining unconvincing—that which would otherwise be a clear legislative direction into a substantive amendment to the law. It is difficult to find any reasoned justification for such a position in separation of powers jurisprudence. For one thing, given the imperatives of the Changed Law Rule, the ready way in which it is implemented by the court, and the high threshold set already set for the application of the direction principle, that is facilitation enough to ensure that impugned legislation will be construed as an amendment to the law. The *Miller* qualifications simply make it easier still to bypass the direction principle. Furthermore, as indicated, the direction principle sought to protect what to both formalists and functionalists was such a core function of the judicial branch, viz, the independent adjudication of legal disputes. To accept such an exception seriously undermined this protection. The Supreme Court's unwillingness to adopt a rigorously applied direction principle, whether deliberate or based on a misunderstanding of it, nevertheless presented considerable dangers to the decisional independence of the judicial branch. In the respectful view of the writer, the decision should not be followed either in the United States or elsewhere. At most, the *Miller* qualifications should be limited to the facts of the case.

This point is reinforced by the fact that even if one were to accept the *Miller v French* qualifications, it is difficult to see how the automatic stay provision could be salvaged. First, the stay did not assist in the implementation of the new provisions except in the most perfunctory procedural way by suspending the injunction while a motion was being considered as to whether or not the prior injunction met the new standards. This is something that could have been well left to judicial discretion without hindering the operation of the PLRA. Indeed, it is on this very issue that the court is being moved. As Lloyd Anderson pointed out,[192]

> [i]t is crucial to understand that the automatic stay provision suspends injunctions for prospective relief against official conduct that courts have found to violate the Constitution *solely upon the passage of a specified time period after the filing of a motion.* The Court's assertion, that the stay operates only if such injunctions are no longer enforceable because they do not meet the new standards for injunctive relief, is simply not true. *The unambiguous words of the statute state that it is the motion to terminate prospective relief that operates as a stay, not any ruling by a court that the new standards are not satisfied* … Thus, the automatic stay provision will have taken effect even though the required findings were previously made and it has not been shown that the prerequisites for injunctive relief no longer exist.[193] (Emphasis added.)

By allowing such a provision to survive the rigours of the direction principle, despite very strong federal court decisions to the contrary, the Supreme Court was in effect establishing an extraordinary principle. It provided for the existence of certain circumstances in a pending case scenario where the legislature could provide for the suspension of injunctive relief, albeit temporarily, without recourse to any independent exercise of judicial discretion. Congress was being given licence to enter directly into the heart of pending proceedings, to influence them pursuant to its direction despite any exercise of judicial power to the contrary.

> The *Miller* majority thus conferred upon Congress a new power to control the way in which the judicial branch exercises existing jurisdiction: a power to suspend prospective injunctive relief whether or not such relief satisfies new legal standards, *so long as the suspension can be said to 'merely reflect', or 'assist in the enforcement' of, or 'help to implement' the new legal standards.* That this is a new power is demonstrated by the fact that the very case cited to support the holding actually stands for the proposition that prospective relief must be modified or vacated if it does not comply with new legal standards enacted by Congress.[194]

---

[192]   Anderson, 'Congressional Control over the Jurisdiction of the Federal Courts', n 16 above, 442–3.

[193]   *Ibid*, at 443–4. Anderson noted (*ibid* at 443, fn 136) that the complex and protracted nature of prison conditions litigation made it very likely that judges would, in particular cases, have inadequate time in which to allow discovery, conduct evidentiary hearings and make the findings of fact and conclusions of law required by Fed R Civ P 52. (See eg *Madrid v Gomez* 889 F Supp 1146 (ND Cal 1995) at 1156, a case tried over a two and a half month period, and *Canterino v Wilson*, 546 F Supp 174, (WD Ky 1982) at 179 in which the pre-trial proceedings lasted for 18 months and the trial four months).

[194]   *Ibid*, at 443.

The case which was erroneously applied, and to which Anderson made reference, was *Wheeling Bridge*.[195] That case did not support the proposition that, whether or not prospective relief complies with new legal standards, Congress can suspend it by establishing an automatic stay. Rather, it stands for the proposition that prospective, or equitable injunctive, relief can be modified only if the legislature changes the underlying law upon which the relief was based, thus rendering the injunction otiose. This occurs not by legislative fiat but by the court itself exercising its discretion to declare that a previous injunction has been so rendered. It is not for the legislature to direct the court to do so. So much *Wheeling Bridge* stood for, not the qualifications the *Miller* court was making to the *Klein* rule.

Given that the automatic stay provision was merely procedural, of limited duration, and only triggered when a motion was made to the court, it is arguable that the decision does not pose such a serious threat to decisional independence and separation of powers values. It might also be argued that a declaration of this relatively innocuous provision as a breach of the separation of powers would be excessively formalistic. The point remains, however, that the provision was an unambiguous legislative direction to the judiciary. The reasoning of the *Miller* majority does not adequately explain why this is not so. Its qualifications to the direction principle, by which alone it salvaged the provision, were vague, easily capable of manipulation and of such broad interpretation as to allow for more serious threats to decisional independence. Thus, at least in this context, the fears of the formalists that such qualifications may result in the gradual erosion of fundamental separation of powers protections appear to be justified. The Supreme Court's validation of this seemingly innocuous automatic stay provision touched on issues fundamental and profound. If there is insistence upon the requirement that the legislature must substantively amend the law before the court is required to apply it in the pending case, the core aspect of judicial power to interpret the law and decide whether on the facts it has been complied with is maintained. It is this core authority of the courts which *Miller* put at risk. In the words of Anderson,

[i]f the judiciary were to decide that Congress has such power, the Madisonian Compromise would be gutted because judicial independence would be at the

---

[195] *Pennsylvania v The Wheeling and Belmont Bridge Co* 59 US (18 How) 421 (1855). In the earlier *Wheeling Bridge* case, the court had held that a bridge was an unlawful obstruction to navigation and must be raised or removed. (*Pennsylvania v The Wheeling and Belmont Bridge Co* 54 US (13 How) 518 (1851). Congress then passed legislation declaring the bridge a lawful structure. In the second *Wheeling Bridge* case, the court held that the decree from the earlier case could no longer be enforced because the bridge was no longer an unlawful structure (at 431–2). In the hypothetical situation mentioned and in *Miller* itself by contrast, it had not yet been determined that the new prerequisites for injunctive relief did not exist.

mercy of Congress. It would mean that the legislative branch could direct a particular result in pending cases even if the courts' independent evaluation of the existing law would require a different decision. A core function of the judiciary is to apply the law in existence at the time of decision, and Congress would have the ability to deprive the courts of that function. Unthinkable? *Miller v French* represents a step in that very direction.[196]

This argument is compelling because the automatic stay applied whether or not the standards for injunctive relief were being met and indeed without reference to any change in the law. This point was perceived by the two dissentients on the *Klein* point, Souter and Ginsburg JJ. Both held that the *Klein* rule had in fact been breached. However, to add to the confusion, they based their decision on a functionalist analysis. That is, it was not simply because the automatic stay was triggered by the expiration of a period of time that constituted a breach of the direction principle, but rather because it was unclear whether the amount of time allowed for a consideration of the existing injunction pursuant to the new standards was sufficient:

> [I]f determining whether a new rule applies requires time (say, for new factfinding) and if the statute provides insufficient time for a court to make that determination before the statute invalidates an extant remedial order, the application of the statute raises a serious question whether Congress has in practical terms assumed the judicial function. In such a case, the prospective order suddenly turns unenforceable not because a court has made a judgment to terminate it due to changed law or fact, but because no one can tell in the time allowed whether the new rule requires modification of the old order. *One way to view this result is to see the Congress as mandating modification of an order that may turn out to be perfectly enforceable under the new rule, depending on judicial factfinding.* If the facts are taken this way, the new statute might well be treated as usurping the judicial function of determining the applicability of a general rule in particular factual circumstances. Cf. *United States* v. *Klein*.[197] (Emphasis added.)

This approach, however, was certainly not consistent with the direction principle's strict application based on direction. Any comfort which may be derived for advocates of the direction principle from this minority judgment is limited. Souter and Ginsburg JJ would have found the automatic stay provision constitutional if it could be shown that there was sufficient time for the court to examine the appropriateness of the existing injunction to the new standards.[198]

---

[196]   Anderson, 'Congressional Control over the Jurisdiction of the Federal Courts', n 16 above, 447.

[197]   *Miller v French* 530 US 327 (2000) at 351–2.

[198]   The dissent of Breyer J, in which Stevens J concurred, is not relevant for present purposes in that that they construed the stay provision not to be mandatory, thus avoiding the issue of whether Congress was directing the courts.

In conclusion, therefore, the *Miller v French* decision eroded further the protections afforded by the direction principle to the decisional independence of the judicial branch commenced in *Robertson*. Its qualifications were both novel and unjustifiable in light of the existing authority of *Klein* and the imperatives of the separation of powers to protect the judicial branch from incursions by the legislature. The position adopted by the other federal courts were far more consistent with *Klein*. Unless the Supreme Court reverses the trend, the weakening of the protections to decisional independence will remain. This will not be a result of the failure of the separation of powers as entrenched constitutional principle, but rather the failure of the judicial branch itself, at least its highest court, to appreciate the precise principles which emerge from such entrenchment that are protective of its decisional independence.

This, however, begs the question: Why did the Supreme Court adopt such a dismissive position to the direction principle, yet without actually repudiating it? To the writer's knowledge, this is an issue which has not received any detailed consideration. Two apparent possible explanations are these: First, the Supreme Court simply failed to appreciate *Klein*, with all its attendant subtleties, and failed to appreciate the relationship between the direction principle and the Changed Law Rule. With respect, it simply misunderstood the case. The 'delphic' judgment of Chase CJ in *Klein* may have contributed to this. On the basis of the above analysis of the case, this appears to be the most reasonable explanation. However, this proposition fails to come to terms with the fact that the Supreme Court had available to it the reasoning of, for example, the Ninth Circuit in *Robertson* and the Seventh Circuit in *Miller v French*, which, as indicated, set out the 'orthodox' position quite clearly. Moreover, by the time these cases were decided, Hart and Young had clearly expounded the position which had emerged from *Klein*. This does not explain the failure of the Supreme Court in *Miller* to strike down a provision which was clearly in breach, by resorting to the introduction of quite novel qualifications. This leads to the second possible explanation. Could it be that the Supreme Court was reluctant to apply the direction principle too rigorously out of an excessive deference to Congress, possibly to avoid the impression of self-aggrandisement at the expense of congressional power? Could it be that the Supreme Court was reluctant to add such an unpredictable weapon to the armoury of judicial review; at least not until the direction principle had been tamed somewhat by a more precise formulation? Perhaps the court was concerned that the direction principle constituted too powerful, and yet too unpredictable, a limitation to the legislative competence of Congress. Or perhaps the court did not want to appear to formulate, and then place in its own hands, such a powerful check on the legislative competence of Congress. This second explanation must remain mere speculation. There is no apparent explanation in any of the judgments based on such policy considerations. Nevertheless, from the standpoint of legal analysis, constitutional scholars are presently limited to the reasoning in the judgments. These would suggest that the first explanation outlined above is the only one which can be proffered with any degree of confidence.

In light of the significant opinion in the federal courts supporting a rigorous, unqualified application of the direction principle, and the overwhelming concurrence of constitutional scholarship in this regard, it is arguable that the existence of the direction principle as an efficacious separation of powers doctrine will survive. Should such views begin to influence the Supreme Court it is possible that the approach adopted by the Supreme Court in the cases above-mentioned will be limited to their facts and not used as the basis for future development.

VIII.   THE *SCHIAVO* LITIGATION

That the direction principle continues to suffer from a lack of appreciation is borne out by the facts of one very high-profile case which clearly warranted a careful consideration of the principle and yet it remained largely ignored. *Schiavo ex rel Schindler v Schiavo*[199] was the final decision in protracted litigation which had moved its way to the Court of Appeals from the Florida State courts. Theresa Marie Schiavo had been severely brain damaged as a result of previous medical complications and was kept alive in a vegetative state by artificial nutrition and hydration. The dispute had arisen because Schiavo's husband favoured the removal of life support, claiming that his wife had expressed such a wish to him before she deteriorated, whereas her parents wanted her kept alive. The matter had moved its way through the Florida State courts over a number of years, apparently concluding when the Supreme Court of Florida declined to review a decision of a lower court, already affirmed on appeal,[200] which had authorised the removal of artificial life support.[201]

The case achieved considerable notoriety at both national and international levels, attracting the keen interest of State and federal governments, right-to-life advocates, euthanasia advocates, and religious and ethics institutions and agencies. Pope John Paul II in fact expressed his

---

[199]   404 F 3d 1270 (11th Cir 2005); *application for stay of enforcement denied*, 544 US 957 (2005).
[200]   *Schindler v Schiavo*, 851 So 2d 182 (Fla Dist Ct App 2003).
[201]   *In re Guardianship of Schiavo*, 855 So 2d 621 (Fla 2003).

views on the case.[202] The Governor of Florida and a majority of the
Florida legislature set their faces against this final judicial outcome and
enacted emergency legislation, passed within 24 hours, to reverse it. The
legislation[203] authorised the Governor

> to issue a one-time stay to prevent the withholding of nutrition and hydration
> from a patient if, as of October 15, 2003 [the patient] has no written advance
> directive ... the court has found that patient to be in a persistent vegetative
> state ... that patient has had nutrition and hydration withheld, [and] a member
> of that patient's family has challenged the withholding of nutrition and
> hydration.

The legislation was to be operative for a period of 15 days. Although no
express reference was made to the *Schiavo* case, it was beyond doubt that
the legislation was targeting the Supreme Court's final decision. The
Governor immediately signed the Act into law and issued an executive
order to 'stay' the withholding of nutrition and hydration from Schiavo.
In *Bush v Schiavo*[204] the Supreme Court of Florida held the legislation to
be unconstitutional because it authorised executive reversal of a finally
decided case contrary to explicit provisions in the Florida Constitution
which provided for a separation of powers.[205] The Supreme Court had no
difficulty in finding that, as in *Plaut*, this legislation was an unconstitutional reversal of a final judgment.

Although the matter had thus reached finality within the State judicial
system, the federal government sought to intervene in the matter. Following intense and impassioned debate, Congress enacted in 2005 An Act
for the Relief of the Parents of Theresa Marie Schiavo (the 'Relief Act'),[206]
enabling Shiavo's parent to bring the matter to the federal courts. Section
2 of the Act provided, expressly, that any parent of Schiavo had standing
to bring a suit under the Act against

> any other person who was a party to State court proceedings relating to the
> withholding or withdrawal of food, fluids, or medical treatment necessary to
> sustain the life of Theresa Marie Schiavo, or who may act pursuant to a State

---

[202] See William Thompson, 'Terri's Law: The Limit of the Florida Legislature to Decide
an Individual's Right to Die" (2005) 31 *New England Journal on Criminal and Civil Confinement* 485; Arian Campo-Flores et al, 'The Legacy of Terri Schiavo: One Woman's Journey
from Marital Bliss to Medical Darkness—and the Forces that Made her Story a Political and
Ethical Watershed' *Newsweek*, Apr. 4, 2005; Miriam Rosenblatt-Hoffman, 'The Schiavo
Odyssey: A Tale of Two Legislative Reprieves' 2006 7 *Marquette Elder's Adviser* 357.
[203] Ch 2003–418, Laws of Florida.
[204] *Bush v Schiavo* 885 So 2d 321 (Fla 2004).
[205] Art II, s 3. See BA Noah, 'Politicizing the End of Life: Lessons from the Schiavo
Controversy' (2004) 59 *University of Miami Law Review* 107, at fn 36 and accompanying text.
[206] An Act for the Relief of the Parents of Theresa Marie Schiavo, Pub L No 109–3, 119
Stat 15 (21 March 2005).

court order authorizing or directing the withholding or withdrawal of food, fluids, or medical treatment necessary to sustain her life;

the (federal) District Court

> shall determine *de novo* any claim of a violation of any right of Theresa Marie Schiavo within the scope of this Act, notwithstanding any prior State court determination and regardless of whether such a claim has previously been raised, considered, or decided in State court proceedings;

and the District Court

> shall entertain and determine the suit without any delay or abstention in favor of State court proceedings, and regardless of whether remedies available in the State courts have been exhausted.

Irrespective of the merits of the case, the federal intervention was extraordinary, especially as the matter had reached finality in the State judicial system after so many years of protracted and bitter litigation. It illustrates well the determination of government to intervene in legal proceedings in order to achieve an outcome consistent with its own policy agenda. If the issues are important enough and if the circumstances are compelling, governments may be tempted to cast aside the constitutional niceties. And, as previously discussed, it was precisely to prevent the executive and legislative branches overreaching themselves in such circumstances that the Framers of the United States Constitution sought to entrench the separation of powers. The circumstances of the *Schiavo* case tested the efficacy of such entrenchment.

Schiavo's parents proceeded to file a suit under the Act but were ultimately unsuccessful in preventing the termination of life support.[207] Despite the extraordinary nature of the federal intervention, the issue of the constitutionality of the Act only arose in one of the proceedings in the Court of Appeals, and then only in the reasoning of one judge, Birch J, who agreed on the outcome that the parents ought not be granted rehearing.[208] The other judges, including the two dissenters, assumed the constitutionality of the Relief Act. This only brought the judgment of Birch J into sharper relief.

In his reasoning, the Act did not simply regulate federal jurisdiction, which was within congressional competence. Rather, section 2 'constituted legislative dictation of how a federal court should exercise its judicial functions (known as a "rule of decision"), and thus breached the

---

[207] *Schiavo ex rel Schindler v Schiavo* 403 F 3d 1223 (11th Cir 2005), application for stay of enforcement denied, 544 US 945 (2005); *Schiavo ex rel Schindler v Schiavo* 404 F 3d 1270 (11th Cir 2005), application for stay of enforcement denied, 544 US 957 (2005).
[208] *Schiavo ex rel Schindler v Schiavo* 404 F 3d 1270 (11th Cir 2005), application for stay of enforcement denied, 544 US 957 (2005).

separation doctrine' on the basis of the *Klein* principle.[209] This was because the section was 'setting a particular standard of review' by denying the federal courts 'the ability to exercise abstention or inquire as to exhaustion or waiver under State law' and thus 'the Act robs federal courts of judicial doctrines long-established for the conduct of prudential decisionmaking'.[210] Further, 'the establishment of a standard of review often dictates the rule of decision in a case, which is beyond Congress's constitutional power', citing *Klein* as authority.[211]

The doctrines which the Act prohibited the federal courts from applying were those which would normally be applied when considering matters previously determined by State courts. They required or encouraged the federal courts to exhibit some deferential restraint in this context.[212] Thus, the preclusion doctrine prevented the re-litigation of cases and issues which had been finally decided by the State courts. The abstention doctrine required federal court restraint when there were ongoing State proceedings relating to the same matter. The exhaustion doctrine did not permit federal court proceedings until all relevant matters had been dealt with in the State courts. Section 2 of the Relief Act could thus not be regarded as a change in the law, particularly as it was precisely targeted to these particular proceedings and in no other way did it seek to amend the law relating to the above-mentioned doctrines which were otherwise left unaffected. As Caminker observed,

> [t]here is no affirmative statement in these provisions that any law or legal standards have been changed, even narrowly or temporarily. Rather, the Act simply directs the District Court to apply these bodies of restraint law in a particular way, and that particular way is to ignore them as potential barriers to said suit … The District Court is told that, as it 'determines' the resolution of any claim of Terri's on the merits, the court must simply close its eyes to these defences and adjudicate the case as if these restraint doctrines did not exist and hence were unavailable for the defendants to invoke.[213]

He concluded that '[i]n sum, if the *Schiavo Relief Act* does not violate the principle established in *Klein*, then that case is essentially confined to its facts (and indeed probably wrongly decided on those facts)'.[214]

The present writer agrees with Caminker's observations in light of the prescriptive nature of the legislation and its targeting of particular litigation. Professor Steven Calabresi, however, did not think there was a

---

[209]   *Ibid*, at 1273–4.
[210]   *Ibid*, at 1274.
[211]   *Ibid*.
[212]   E Caminker, '*Schiavo* and *Klein*' (2005) 22 *Constitutional Commentary* 529 536–7 and see footnotes thereto for the details of these doctrines.
[213]   *Ibid*, at 540.
[214]   *Ibid*, at 541.

breach of the direction principle. His conclusion was based simply on the view that Congress, in any event, did have authority to amend the law with respect to jurisdiction by enacting a general statute amending the applicable law on the restraint doctrine. Accordingly, the particular intervention did not offend constitutionally because the result could have been achieved by constitutional means.[215] This reasoning, however, misses the point. In testing the constitutionality of any particular statute pursuant to the direction principle, it is simply not relevant that Congress had the competence to achieve the same result by non-directive means. If anything, this should be a factor indicative of direction because it begs the question why the legislature did not adopt the constitutionally innocuous means to achieve its ends. It tends to indicate that no general change in the law was desired, but rather a change which was targeted to a particular situation. Moreover, testing constitutionality pursuant to the direction principle, and indeed pursuant to any constitutional principle, requires the scrutiny of the particular method adopted, not the methods which were available. In the *Schiavo* case there were more than sufficient indicators of direction at least to engage the judges with the possibility of an unconstitutional direction.[216]

Professor Michael Allan also regarded the Relief Act as constitutional. He emphasised the fact that the statute was simply regulating jurisdiction by removing the prudential doctrinal impediments to the case being heard by the federal court, but did not interfere with the court's adjudication on the substantive merits of the case.[217] Relying on *Miller v French*, he adopted that case's soft approach to the *Klein* direction principle to suggest that a breach of *Klein* would only occur in circumstances where the court's adjudicatory role in the substantive issues would be affected by direction.[218] He did acknowledge, however, that 'there would unquestionably be a point at which Congress, under the guise of mandating a "procedure" could intrude on the core judicial function of adjudication'.[219] Unfortunately, he did not elaborate on this point. The argument that the Act was constitutionally innocuous because it dealt exclusively with procedural doctrines should be rejected. The doctrines which were denied to the federal court in this case were those very doctrines which would preclude the rehearing of the matter, which was the very outcome desired by the government and by the parents, and which would have constituted the central issue in the case. Procedure here was critical to

[215]   SG Calabresi, 'The Terri Schiavo Case: In Defence of the Special Law Enacted by Congress and President Bush' (2006) 100 *Northwestern University Law Review* 151 at 161–4.

[216]   See Caminker, '*Schiavo* and *Klein*', n 212 above, 542.

[217]   MP Allan, 'Congress and Terri Schiavo: A Primer on the American Constitutional Order?' (2005) 108 *West Virginia Law Review* 309 at 339 ff.

[218]   *Ibid*, at 348.

[219]   *Ibid*.

adjudication. The federal intervention must not be considered in isolation, but in the context of the pre-existing State litigation. As Caminker pointed out,

> Congress turned what under pre-existing law was a clear loser for Terri's parents (independent of the merits of their substantive claims) into a potential winner (depending on the merits of their claims). To be sure, perhaps a 'paradigmatic' *Klein* violation (if there is such a thing) turns a dispute for which either party might win (depending on the merits of the claims) into a clear winner for a particular party. But both moves involve telling the court how to articulate 'what the law is'—in the former case, how the laws of preclusion, abstention and exhaustion apply to the claims, and in the latter case, how the laws defining substantive rights apply to the claims. And more importantly to my mind, (since federal courts adjudicate cases rather than merely articulate 'what the law is'), both moves directly influence which party wins and loses without changing the content of the law being applied. It is not clear to me why it should matter whether the law whose application is being congressionally directed is deemed procedural rather than substantive, so long as it potentially disposes of the claims one way or the other.[220]

If this were not so, then it is difficult to imagine any continuing relevance for the *Klein* doctrine. Again, the contrary argument fails to address the very question that *Klein* was urging: does the impugned legislation in substance amend the law? If not, because it is purely directive, even under the guise of otherwise legitimate legislation, then it must be unconstitutional.

The further difficulty, of course, with the Calabresi/Allan view is that the federal intervention was clearly *ad hominem* and directed to these precise proceedings. Allan did not see any problem with this in the present context because, as he stated correctly, there is no constitutional bar to *ad hominem* legislation, and because in this context, the court is left free to make it own determination of the substantive issues. The problem, of course, is that he fails again to take into account the legal significance of the previous State litigation acting as a potential procedural bar, and thus having a considerable impact on the success or otherwise of the respective litigants. Moreover, Allan fails to treat the *ad hominem* nature of the legislation as an indicator of direction. This is the critical point.

The argument that the Relief Act breached the direction principle is compelling. The fact that only one judge was willing to consider it is indicative of the decline of the principle in the jurisprudence of the United States. If the *Klein* direction principle was not seen as being breached in the circumstances of this extraordinary case, it is difficult to

---

[220] Caminker, '*Schiavo* and *Klein*', n 212 above, 544.

envisage the continuing relevance of the principle in the United States except in the most extraordinary circumstances.

IX.   FURTHER CONFIRMATION OF THE DIRECTION PRINCIPLE

Preliminary to the evaluative analysis which follows in the next section, it is noted that the same form of the direction principle had also developed independently in Irish constitutional law, also founded upon an entrenched separation of powers. This reinforces the point that the principle does tend to emerge as a discrete constitutional principle when the separation doctrine is entrenched. In that jurisdiction it has been referred to as the 'doctrine of non-interference with the courts'[221] which limits that form of legislative interference which, in the words of Professor David Gwynn Morgan,

> was either a direct attempt to settle the result in a court case or, more indirectly, an attempt to change the law in a way which (because of its timing or its *ad hominem* nature) is considered to be illegitimate. This attempt may be either made or authorised by an act of the [legislature].[222]

In the leading case of *Buckley v Attorney-General*[223] (the *Sinn Fein Funds* case), the plaintiffs, claiming they were the beneficiaries, sought orders that they be paid funds held by the trustees of the *Sinn Fein* organisation. The Sinn Fein Funds Act 1947 was enacted while the matter was pending before the High Court. It provided that if an application was made ex parte on behalf of the Attorney-General, the High Court must make an order dismissing the claim to the funds and order that the funds be disposed in the manner prescribed by the Act. The Act was held unconstitutional on separation of powers grounds in both the High Court and by the Supreme Court on appeal, and a form of the direction principle was articulated similar to that in the United States and Australia.

O'Byrne J, writing the judgment of the Supreme Court, clearly based the constitutional limitation on the constitutional entrenchment of the separation of powers in the Irish Constitution, by which was 'vest[ed] in the Courts the exclusive right to determine justiciable controversies between citizens or between a citizen or citizens ... and the State'.[224] The Supreme Court proceeded to find that the Act was unconstitutional because the

---

[221] DG Morgan, *The Separation of Powers in the Irish Constitution* (Dublin, Roundhall, Sweet and Maxwell, 1997) at 133.
[222] *Ibid*, at 136.
[223] *Buckley v Attorney-General* [1950] IR 67.
[224] *Ibid*, at 84.

substantial effect of the Act is that the dispute is determined by the Oireachtas [the legislature] and the Court is required and directed by the Oireachtas to dismiss the plaintiff's claim without any hearing and without forming any opinion as to the rights of the respective parties to the dispute. In our opinion this is clearly repugnant to the provisions of the Constitution, as being an unwarrantable interference by the Oireachtas with the operations of the Courts in the purely judicial domain.[225]

Unfortunately, the Supreme Court did not engage in any deeper analysis beyond these comments. The Irish courts did not articulate a precise set of indicia of direction, although it was clear that they were sensitive to those aspects of the legislation which, taken as a whole, indicated that the Act was no more than a legislative direction, and therefore unconstitutional. The Act contained classic indicia of direction: retrospectivity, the *ad hominem* nature of the Act, the empowering of the Attorney-General to make the relevant application even though he was actually the defendant in the case, and the passing of the Act while the matter was pending. Although there was insufficient elaboration to expand upon the position achieved in Australia and the United States,[226] that the direction principle was regarded as a fundamental constitutional limitation was clearly accepted. Morgan noted the competing imperatives of the Changed Law Rule on the one hand, which emphasised the integrity of legislative power, and the 'the principle that there must be no undue interference with a court in the performance of its duties' on the other.[227] In addition, he noted that a change in the law after final hearing but before final judgment would not be applicable to the particular case as the matter would be res judicata by that stage, although presumably, such a law would be applicable if the matter went on appeal. Moreover, as will be noted in the next chapter, if the legislation specifically required the overruling of a final judgment, this would clearly be a breach of the separation of powers.

The direction principle and its application in the pending case scenario was confirmed in the more recent case of *Re Camillo*[228] in which the Supreme Court explicitly accepted the principle's fundamentals.[229] However, as Morgan noted, this brought the Irish authorities up to about the point of *Liyanage* in terms of the development of principle,[230] that is, there was little precise guidance as to how to determine the existence or otherwise of direction.

---

[225] *Ibid.*
[226] See, eg, JM Kelly, *The Irish Constitution*, 3rd edn (Dublin, Butterworths, 1994) 360 ff.
[227] Morgan, *The Separation of Powers in the Irish Constitution*, n 221 above, 139.
[228] *Re Camillo* [1988] IR 104.
[229] *Ibid*, at 108.
[230] Morgan, *The Separation of Powers in the Irish Constitution*, n 221 above, 141.

X.   GENERAL CONCLUSIONS ON THE SEPARATION OF POWERS AND THE PENDING CASE SCENARIO

Following this series of cases in the United States, and indeed the most recent cases in Australia and Ireland, it has become clear that the direction principle continues to suffer from a lack of certainty in application and indeed a more general lack of appreciation, with some notable exceptions. In this particular regard, the success of an entrenched separation of powers as a source of precise principles regulating the difficult interplay between legislative and judicial power has been mixed. This is particularly apparent following cases such as *Nicholas v The Queen* in Australia, and, more obviously apparent in the United States following the cases of *Robertson, Plaut, Miller* and indeed *Schiavo*. On the other hand, the persistence of a rigorous method in application of the direction principle in some Court of Appeals decisions, and those of the lower federal courts, with the general concurrence of the constitutional scholars, should not be overlooked, suggesting that the principle may ultimately survive the apparent set backs, especially in the United States.

It is for this reason that an attempt will be made in the remainder of this chapter to suggest a formulation of principle which provides greater clarity in definition and certainty in application. An attempt will be made to analyse more precisely the problems which currently pertain to the direction principle as formulated in order to suggest a way forward. To the extent that the judiciary is restraining its hand because of the uncertainties and unpredictability of principle, the points made in the remainder of this chapter may alleviate this concern.

It is not possible to ascertain precisely whether the primary difficulty lies in a lack of judicial appreciation of the underlying principles, or in the very imprecision which results from the definitional imperatives of legal entrenchment. It is probably occasioned by both, yet, both are capable of remedy. Given the emergence of an almost identical formulation of the direction principle and its indicia in those jurisdictions with an entrenched separation of powers—quite independently of each other it would seem—there remains a sufficient foundation for the establishment of a principle protecting the decisional independence of the judicial branch. The current uncertain status of the principle, therefore, is not a manifestation of the failure of the legal entrenchment of the separation doctrine and its transformation from a tenet of political philosophy into a legal rule. First, the imperative created by legal entrenchment to achieve at least a core definition of branch functions can be met. This is confirmed by the writings of the early constitutional scholars, judicial exegesis and modern constitutional scholarship, particularly in the United States. Secondly, given that the judicial functions which are critical to the decisional independence of the judicial branch can be considered as core, or 'typical'—to use the words of Zines[231]—branch functions, it is possible to overcome the tensions inherent in the formalism/functionalism divide to achieve a set of principles which can be applied rigorously in this context. It is significant, both in terms of its precise nature and of the precise function it is seeking to protect, that the direction principle has in many ways transcended this particular dichotomy and thus avoided many of the uncertainties resulting from the differences between the two schools. That is not to deny the difficulties which emerge in attempting to define in legal terms what is not always susceptible to precise legal definition.

The first problem encountered is a tendency not to give sufficient recognition to decisional independence as a discrete issue governed by discrete principles. In Australia, in particular, it has often been melded with those principles relating to the *exercise of*—as opposed to *interference with*—the judicial power, the maintenance of the integrity of the judicial process, and the due process concerns that were mentioned above.[232] That is, the emphasis has been to test whether the legislature is exercising or usurping any exclusive, core, or 'typical' element of the judicial power, or whether it is seeking to remove such a core element from the exercise of judicial functions by the judicial branch. It is true that while these general concerns are apparent within the direction principle, it seeks to address them exclusively in the context of the pending case. Where the principle does identify legislative direction, it can indeed also be said that the core element of independent adjudication on the relevant issue, or indeed ultimate outcome, is sought to be removed or undermined. Nevertheless, the determination of the existence of direction, and the precise nature of this direction, remains the pivotal issue, which can only be resolved in the context of the pending proceedings.

The subtlety of this difference in all likelihood constitutes a major cause for the significant lack of appreciation, and uncertain reception, of the direction principle. In Australia, there has not been a single case which has drawn together precisely the principles that exist in the various authorities in order that they be consistently understood or applied. There is no comprehensive, classic statement of principle to which reference may be made. The judgment of Kirby J in *Nicholas*, and those of Street CJ and Kirby P in *BLF (NSW)* are the only exceptions; but they remain isolated instances, and certainly have not been endorsed unconditionally by the High Court. In the United States, at least, the issue has a much higher profile with *Klein* being clearly identified as the seminal case in a particular line of authority. That this is an issue of

---

[231] L Zines, *The High Court and the Constitution*, 5th edn (Sydney, Federation Press, 2008) 220.

[232] See the discussion of the *Nicholas* case, ch 2, 90, above.

profound importance to the whole American constitutional settlement, and a critical catalyst for the very entrenchment of the separation doctrine, is similarly recognised. Furthermore, constitutional scholars in that jurisdiction have perceived the serious problems in the current 'soft' approach to the principle, and, together with the dissentient voices in the lower federal courts, there remains a persistent and persuasive advocacy to reverse the trend emerging in the Supreme Court decisions. However, the ambivalent and uncertain attitude which has been exhibited by the Supreme Court in *Robertson*, *Plaut* and *Miller* nevertheless remains. *Plaut* considered the issue only in passing in dicta. *Robertson* was more problematic, and in the opinion of the writer together with the consensus in the academic commentary, the method of its application of the direction principle was flawed, some judicial statements verging at times on the erroneous. It has already been suggested that the *Miller* decision, with its unfounded qualifications to the principle, should not be followed.

Secondly, there is a failure to appreciate the precise relationship and delicate balance between the direction principle and the Changed Law Rule, namely, that the direction principle acts as a threshold test for the operation of the Changed Law Rule. The *Robertson* opinion was the worst offender in this regard. Although the position adopted by the High Court of Australia is more consistent with the proper understanding, the tendency in the Australian cases—with the exception of *BLF (NSW)* and the dissent in *Nicholas*—has been to emphasise the imperatives of the Changed Law Rule over those of the direction principle.[233] Similarly, in the United States, there is often too great a readiness to assume that there has been a change in the law, as evidenced by *Robertson* and *Plaut* in particular. This undermines both rules.

Thirdly, there is lacking a precise articulation of the method that should be adopted in the application of the direction principle. In Australia, the position has not really moved much beyond the quandary expressed in *Liyanage* relating to the difficulty in 'tracing where the line is to be drawn between what will and what will not constitute such an interference'.[234] Similar comments were made by Kirby J in *Nicholas*, although he did proceed beyond these difficulties to articulate a workable set of principles. There needs to be an explicit recognition that the principal scrutiny must be reserved for the *legislative* nature of the impugned legislation. It is this recognition which will prevent the melding of this issue with the more dominant principles emerging from the separation of judicial power and, given the uncompromising nature of the Changed Law Rule, ensure that the threshold test of direction is used

---

[233]   The decision of the United States Supreme Court, *Robertson v Seattle Audubon Society* 503 US 429 (1992) is also illustrative of this.
[234]   *Liyanage v R* [1967] 1 AC 259 at 289–90.

to ameliorate its rigours. This was evident in *Robertson* and *Plaut*, which combined too great a readiness to apply the Changed Law Rule with an easy assumption that there was in fact a substantive change in the law. In *Miller*, with the introduction of novel qualifications, there appeared to be a pointed unwillingness to apply the direction principle.

Nevertheless, it must be recognised that the courts have had to come to terms with inherently unstable, complex, subtle and uncertain principles. It should be acknowledged that the imperative for precise definition of functions and constitutional limitations can be met only up to a point. Moreover, within the principle itself there is an uneasy combination of both formalist and functionalist tendencies. The formalist tendencies, broadly speaking, are evident in the central distinction upon which the rule is based. Functionalist tendencies are evident in the definition of the criteria by which impugned legislation is judged to be an unconstitutional direction. That is, no closed set of definitive criteria determinative of direction is recognised in all cases; reliance being placed rather on indicia as they might arise on a case-by-case basis. No one indicator, or indeed combination thereof, is necessarily decisive. Moreover, the existence of unconstitutional direction is determined by the interrelationship and cumulative effect of the various indicia in any particular case. It is therefore very difficult to predict the outcome, particularly in the hard case, although it should not be as difficult as these more recent cases have made it. Thus, for example, the facts of *BLF (NSW)*, *Nicholas*, and the four American cases—*Robertson*, *Plaut*, *Miller* and *Schiavo*—all furnish illustrations of circumstances where a breach of the direction principle could have been made out without too much controversy. Yet, apart from *Liyanage* and *Klein*, it was only in *BLF (NSW)* and in the Irish cases above-mentioned that a court has been willing to invalidate legislation based on the direction principle, not including the Court of Appeals decisions in the United States cases. Admittedly, in hard cases, the words of Kirby J in *Nicholas* that 'minds will reasonably differ'[235] certainly do resonate. Nevertheless, it is the easy dismissal of the direction principle which is the concern, not the fact per se that it is rarely that a breach of the principle is declared.

The uncertainties inherent in the indicia of direction may explain this phenomenon, especially the fact that their strength as indicators is very much dependant on the precise circumstances of each case. Given this inherent fluidity, the rigour with which the rule is applied is therefore dependent on the approach taken by individual judges, and the extent to

---

[235] *Nicholas v the Queen* (1998) 193 CLR 173 at 256 (Kirby J); although *Nicholas* cannot be regarded as a hard case.

which they defer to Parliament. Although manageable, these uncertainties are problematic in light of the fundamental importance of the limitations being considered, reflected in the overriding importance attached to them by those who originally advocated the legal entrenchment of the separation of powers, the United States Framers.[236]

XI.   TOWARDS A RESOLUTION

Consideration must be given to the reformulation of the principle to overcome the inherent weaknesses in its formulation, and to prevent its gradual slide to irrelevance in all but the most egregious situations. The formalist core of the principle—the dichotomy between a substantive change in the law and an unconstitutional direction—remains sound, thus meeting the definitional imperatives resulting from the legal entrenchment of the separation of powers. The major difficulties, however, reside in that aspect of the principle which relies on the identification of indicia of unconstitutional direction. It is submitted, therefore, that a greater formalisation of the status of certain indicia, or combinations thereof, is necessary. One way to achieve this may involve mandating a finding of unconstitutional legislative interference where certain precise indicia, or combinations thereof, are present. To the writer's knowledge, this has only been suggested by one commentator. This is a suggestion to which the writer does not subscribe because of the degree of artificial rigidity which would result. Rather, in order to achieve this greater formalisation, the writer advocates the setting up of rebuttable presumptions of unconstitutional direction where certain key indicia, or combinations thereof, are present.

The mandatory approach to the determination of the issues was advocated by the American scholar Professor Amy Ronner following her scathing evaluation of the reasoning of the Supreme Court in *Robertson*.[237] Where the following elements in the legislation are found to exist, according to Ronner's formulation, there must be a finding of unconstitutional direction[238]:

First, the legislation must purport to amend the law, or introduce new law, which affects the outcome of pending litigation and it must be 'so precisely tailored to address the issues in the pending matter that it can

---

[236]   See ch 1 at 10ff above.
[237]   Ronner, 'Judicial Self-Demise', n 3 above.
[238]   *Ibid*, at 1071.

be said to fit glove-like around a living case or controversy'.[239] Secondly, either one of the following factors is found to exist in the circumstances of any particular pending case:

(a)   the government is a party, and the impugned legislation has the effect of favouring it in the litigation; or,

(b)   the legislation infiltrates a domain that can be regarded as tradition-ally a judicial one (such as for example in *Lim* where it related to the issue of penal detention, or in *Nicholas*, where it related to the exercise of the critical judicial discretion whether to admit illegally obtained evidence.)

In relation to the first factor, it could be said without difficulty that the facts of, for example, *Liyanage*, *BLF (NSW)* and *Nicholas*, would meet this requirement. Further, as the government was a party in the pending proceedings in each of those cases, and the legislation favoured it in those proceedings, there would be a straightforward application of the Ronner test to mandate a finding that unconstitutional legislative direction existed in each of those cases. As the writer has maintained, to mandate a finding of unconstitutional direction in such a fluid scenario might lead to an artificial result, particularly if there were countervailing circum-stances. For this reason, the writer would find greater merit in the precise Ronner formulation if it went no further than establishing rebuttable presumptions. The application of such a test would certainly require that legislation such as that in *Nicholas* and *Robertson* be at least scrutinised far more rigorously. Applying this test, either in its mandatory form, or in the rebuttable presumption form, it is clear that the dissentient judgment of Kirby J in *Nicholas* would be vindicated. In the United States, the *Robertson* and *Miller* cases would clearly be decided differently and the view of the lower federal courts would prevail. Even in situations where the government was not a party, the existence of the two alternatives in the second compulsory element would ensure that the principle was nevertheless applicable.

While this formalisation of the test would enable a more straightfor-ward resolution of hard cases, that is not to say that all difficulties would be overcome. For example, the requirement that the legislation be tai-lored to fit 'glove-like' around the pending issues is not necessarily straightforward and is also a difficult requirement to meet. For Ronner it would appear to be sufficient that the legislation does affect the court's consideration of critical issues in the pending litigation, doing so in such a way that it is relatively specific to that litigation. However, this too would require a difficult balancing act in hard cases and uncertainties

---

[239]   *Ibid.*

would still result. It is in relation to this point that the *ad hominem* element becomes critical, as would the element of retrospectivity, to establish the requisite targeting of the litigation. It would not be necessary to establish that the legislature expressly dictated a particular *final* outcome, it being sufficient if the legislation addressed particular legal issues which nevertheless had significant consequences for the outcome. Thus, it would still be possible to hold as constitutional, for example, the legislation in the *BLF (Cth)* which completely by-passed the legal issues in the pending case. On the other hand, it would also be more difficult for legislation such as that in *Nicholas* or in *Roberston* to be considered a substantive legislative change in the law. Thus, the Ronner formula can accommodate the direction principle and the Changed Law Rule in a way that maintains an efficacious separation of powers doctrine, while also maintaining the balance between these two fundamental rules. In light of the uncertain reception of the direction principle, and its uncertain current status in both the United States and Australia, such a formalisation of the indicia of direction in the overall scheme of the direction principle would certainly remove many of the difficulties which lie in the way of establishing the rule as a discrete separation of powers limitation.

While the degree of formalisation advocated by Ronner is excessive, that some form of formalisation of the direction principle is both necessary and possible cannot be denied. It remains the case that where a matter of great political moment comes before the courts, legislatures are liable to significant temptation to intervene and the need for well-defined constitutional limitations remains an imperative. The spectre of the *Burmah Oil* case in the United Kingdom, in which the final decision of the House of Lords in the specific case was overruled by Parliament, still hovers.[240] In Australia, in particular, the recent jousting between court and parliament in relation to immigration and refugee matters throws up a situation where the temptations to which legislatures have been prone in the past, especially in the United States, comes to the fore. In *Lim*, it was with a pending refugee case in mind that Parliament directed that '[a] court is not to order the release from custody of a designated person'.[241] One need only refer, for a further example, to the high political drama arising from the *MV Tampa* Incident, in which the Australian government took action to remove from Australian waters the Norwegian ship which had taken on board some 400 persons seeking asylum in Australia after it had rescued them from their own sinking vessel. Litigation on behalf of the asylum seekers failed when it reached

---

[240]   *Burmah Oil Company (Burma Trading) Ltd v Lord Advocate* [1965] AC 75. This case and its impact is discussed in detail in the next chapter.
[241]   *Lim v Minister for Immigration, Local Government and Ethnic Affairs* (1992) 176 CLR 1.

the full Federal Court. Special legislation dealing with these circumstances was enacted while an application for special leave to appeal was pending in the High Court. Such appeal was refused, the matter did not proceed further, and the question whether such legislation may have constituted an unconstitutional interference in a pending case was not raised.[242] The *Schiavo* litigation is another case in point. The compelling demands on legislatures to deal with terrorism are also liable to throw up these issues and no doubt continue to create similar tensions.[243] It is precisely in these circumstances that a strong direction principle is needed to ensure that Parliament limits itself to its primary legislative functions without intervening in the judicial process.

Therefore, the question remains: what degree of formalisation of the direction principle is appropriate short of mandated results based on formulas such as Ronner's? If, instead, use is made of rebuttable presumptions a solution may be achieved which will be far more sympathetic to the symmetry which currently exists in the principle, combining a functionalist overlay to a formalist core.

XII.   A REFORMULATED DIRECTION PRINCIPLE

As a preliminary point, it must be accepted that once the separation of powers is entrenched in a written constitution, then the imperative toward some definition of functions must be met. It is not necessary that the present issue be mired irretrievably in the difficult formalism/functionalism debate, given that decisional independence relates to such a core area of legislative and judicial power. In both schools, it would certainly be accepted that a clear legislative direction to the judiciary, which does not constitute a substantive amendment to the law, breaches the separation of powers. The central distinction on which the direction principle is based remains uncontroversial, and, like the fundamental principle that the judicial power of the Commonwealth cannot be conferred on non-judicial bodies, is a principle which can be safely assumed to be established as a central separation of powers constitutional limitation. The other critical preliminary point is that there needs to be maintained a sufficient degree of flexibility with respect to the indicia of direction to enable their accurate application in the myriad of unpredictable circumstances in which they will be relied on. Avoiding excessive and artificial formalisation in these circumstances, but allowing that

---

[242] For detailed coverage of the various constitutional and legal issues to which this incident gave rise, see the special edition of the *Public Law Review* titled 'The Tampa Issue' (2002) 13 *Public Law Review*.

[243] See the discussion of the *Hamdam* case in the US in ch 6 at p 309, and see also *Lodhi v The Queen* (2006) 199 FLR 303.

some is necessary, the writer would therefore make the following suggestions with respect to the indicia of direction:

Because there have been a number of cases in which the issue has arisen, an attempt should be made to identify and catalogue those certain indicia whose nature and recurrence warrant their identification as principal indicia of direction. Where any one of these indicia is present—more so if more than one is present—then this should immediately put the court on notice that unconstitutional legislative direction is a serious possibility. If the three indicia listed below are present, this should give rise to a presumption of unconstitutional direction. These common indicia share the critical characteristic of removing the impugned legislation from the norm, or 'typical' nature, of an exercise of legislative function as a prospective change in the law that is of general applicability, altering rights and obligations into the future. These major indicia are as follows:

First, there is the specificity of the legislation either as clearly *ad hominem* legislation, or being of sufficient specificity to enable the easy identification of the persons, or class thereof, to whom it is applicable. As an indicator of direction it becomes more compelling to the extent that it extends no further than those involved in the pending litigation, or potential identifiable future litigation. The impugned enactments in the *Liyanage*, *Robertson*, *Nicholas* and *Schiavo* litigation are classic illustrations.

Secondly, there is the specificity of the legislation with respect to the pending litigation. The timing of the enactment and commencement of operation of the legislation would also be regarded as relevant in this context. The greater the extent to which it can be shown that the legislation is dealing exclusively with the issues which arise in pending litigation—and not beyond those in a more general way—then the greater the likelihood of direction. In other words, the more the legislation is 'tailored', to use the words of Ronner, to deal with the issues in the pending litigation, the more it removes itself from the typical legislative function of prospective amendment of the law that is of general application.

Thirdly, there is the status of the government as a party to the pending proceedings, or at least as an entity which has a significant interest therein, and where the legislation favours its interests in the pending litigation. This would be a particularly relevant indicator where the government had a pecuniary or proprietary interest in the outcome. However, this will also be a significant indicator in circumstances where the government has an interest with respect to the implementation of its policy agenda, or various other public policy reasons, meritorious or otherwise. Thus, in *Liyanage* and *Nicholas*, the government was keen to secure a conviction; in *BLF (NSW)* to ensure the deregistration of the union; in *Lim* to ensure the continued detention of asylum seekers; and in *Plaut*—where the government was not a party—to reinstate meritorious civil actions for securities fraud.

If either of the following two indicia are also present, the rebuttability of the presumption should be put at a higher threshold.

First, the object of the legislation is a traditional judicial discretion, such as, for example, in *Nicholas* where it interfered with the judicial discretion to admit evidence obtained as a result of illegal conduct, or in *Lim* where it purported to regulate the discretion of the court with respect to releasing persons from custody. Of course, it may be the case that the legislation is successfully declared invalid on the separate ground that it usurps a core judicial function or that it prevents a court from properly exercising such a function. Nevertheless, with respect to the issue of legislative interference, it still remains an indicator of direction.

Secondly, the wording of the legislation is clearly directive, such as where it uses the words 'directs' or 'orders' with reference to the judicial branch, or if it contains a deeming provision. Although the wording is not determinative of the issue, the existence of such words does constitute an important indicator. Moreover, if the legislation specifically mentions the persons to whom it is applicable, or if it refers to the litigation specifically by name (such as in *Robertson*) then this will reinforce the existence of direction. This particular element can be a very powerful indicator of direction, and can almost stand alone if the language used is sufficiently unequivocal. On the other hand, it must not be assumed that the use of these words automatically results in a finding of direction.

While the above-listed constitute the most obvious indicia of direction (in addition to being the most commonly found in the cases), the writer does not advocate that they should be regarded as a closed set, nor that any of the indicia, or combinations thereof, be regarded as determinative per se. That degree of formalisation would clearly not be warranted as discussed above. For one thing, there is always the danger that, even if the conditions of the relevant formula are made out, in all the circumstances there may be present other factors which might indicate that unconstitutional direction is not occurring. As it is not possible to predict what these may be, allowances must be made. Also, even if only one or two of the above indicia are present, it may be the case that particular indicia are found in a particular case which are not listed above, and yet clearly may warrant a finding of unconstitutional direction.

This, it is submitted, would be the most appropriate response to the problems facing the direction principle. The suggestions made above should help alleviate the weaknesses, and sometimes excessive subtleties within the formulation of the rule itself, and prevent the further erosion of the principle as a protector of the judiciary from those admittedly rare circumstances where a legislature may seek to ensure its will in the face of pending litigation. It is arguable, however, that this should be only of limited concern given that the separation of powers will prevent a legislature from itself exercising judicial power, and also prevent it from obvious and egregious directions to the judiciary in pending cases. One can hardly envisage a court not declaring *Liyanage*-style legislation as constituting a breach of the direction principle. However, as those who adopt a formalist approach to separation of powers analysis realise, the concern is that if the principle is not maintained in the less obvious cases, or those cases where the legislature is interfering with judicial functions for good public policy reasons—as in *Plaut* for example—the maintenance of the limitation on legislative interference with judicial functions will be eroded over time even in the more egregious cases. The consequences of *Robertson* in particular have borne this out.

XIII.   SPECULATIVE PROPOSITIONS

An appreciation of the principles governing the pending case scenario would be incomplete without mentioning certain more speculative propositions, which have arisen exclusively in the context of the United States jurisprudence. These are arguably to be found in the critical *Klein* judgment. They will be addressed for the sake of completeness, and also to reinforce the need for some degree of formalisation and explicit restatement of the direction principle according to its original formulations.

As stated, the one significant counterbalance to the direction principle, the Changed Law Rule, provides for legislative interference to occur lawfully if it is effected by a change in the law. Both rules clearly operate within the context of the separation of powers and operate in a logical juxtaposition. The imperatives of the Changed Law Rule have not seriously been challenged by any court decision. It was suggested above that a failure to appreciate the balance between the Changed Law Rule and the direction principle will significantly weaken the latter.[244] However, the effect on the former will also be quite adverse. It may result, as will be discussed below, in a weakening, instead of a reinforcement, of the hitherto unchallenged precepts of the Changed Law Rule. It will be seen that the maintenance of a more rigorous approach to the direction principle, particularly its 'formalist' core, is essential for the maintenance of a strong Changed Law Rule.

The vulnerability of the Changed Law Rule arises from speculation—it cannot at this stage be put any higher than this—that any principle

---

[244]   At p 172 above.

emanating from the separation doctrine protecting the decisional independence of the judiciary extends beyond the confines of the existing principles. It is based on the idea, traced back to *Klein*, that even where there is a substantive change in the law which affects a pending case, there may be circumstances where such a law will nevertheless be in breach of the separation of powers if made applicable to pending proceedings. Concerns are thus raised that the Changed Law Rule may be insufficient, at least in certain circumstances, to prevent the domination of the legislature over the judicial branch. In *Klein*, Chase CJ had pondered the consequences of giving effect to the '1870 proviso': 'Can we do so without allowing one party to the controversy to decide it in its own favor?'[245] He was clearly sensitive to the fact that the United States was a party in the case and that the government had a significant advantage in its ability to amend the law applicable on appeal. The issue is a difficult one because a direct conflict between separation of powers principles arises. Was it being postulated that there are circumstances which justify a court *not* applying a substantive change in the law in a pending case, contrary to the Changed Law Rule? Are there defined circumstances where the decisional independence of the courts is to take precedence even over the exercise of legislative power?

Such conjecture emanated from no less a source than GC Young, who postulated that 'Chase might well have extended preexisting constitutional principles in order to rule in *Klein* that the government cannot change the law to favor itself on appeal'.[246] If this is so, then the position to emerge from *Klein* is that the Changed Law Rule will not apply in such circumstances to require the court to apply the amended law. The difficulty of course is that such an outcome favourable to government is the usual result. Clearly the acceptance of such a proposition would seriously undermine the Changed Law Rule, for the mere existence of a pending case in which the government is a party would trump the legislature in its ability to amend the law applicable in that case if the government thereby secured an advantage. While Young was not able to take the position beyond mere—albeit serious—consideration, such a principle has never received authoritative acceptance, although the judicial disquiet evident in *Klein* cannot be denied.

Just such a submission was put to the Supreme Court in the *Robertson* case by the Public Citizen amicus, contending that 'even a change in law, prospectively applied, would be unconstitutional if the change swept no more broadly, or little more broadly, than the range of applications at

---

[245]   *United States v Klein* 80 US (13 Wall) 128 (1871) at 146.
[246]   Young, 'Congressional Regulation of Federal Courts Jurisdiction and Processes', n 22 above, 1244.

issue in the pending cases'.[247] This proposition was not addressed by the Supreme Court, although it is clear from the judgment that the submission was not accepted. Young, however, was of the view that there was considerable merit in the submission and that it should not be dismissed out of hand. That submission, if ever accepted, would make the direction principle as a constitutional limitation modest by comparison in its impact. The proposition is at least a respectable one, particularly given its obvious congruity with the values and purposes underlying the separation of powers. That is, a limited suspension of the Changed Law Rule in circumstances where the government is a party and where the changed law favours it on appeal is a very reasonable proposition, indeed arguably quite necessary, to establish a more substantial protection to the courts' decisional independence. One of the weaknesses of the direction principle, identified above, was its failure to prevent a determined legislature from circumventing it by deft legislative drafting, and yet still directing an outcome which, because of form, did not breach the principle. This is illustrated by the legislation in *BLF (Cth)* and *BLF (NSW)* where both sought to achieve the result of securing the de-registration of the BLF in the face of litigation seeking to prevent such an outcome. By the adoption of words which clearly indicated that the de-registration was achieved by force of the legislation, the Commonwealth legislation survived separation of powers scrutiny, whereas the State legislation was regarded as being in breach of the direction principle even though the result in both instances was the same. It should also be noted that this element—the government being a party and the legislation favouring it on appeal—was considered by Ronner as being a decisive factor against constitutionality if her first requirement—that the legislation was tailored to the pending proceedings—was made out.

It is unlikely, however, that this view will be accepted as an established principle. There is very little to suggest, even by those who support a rigorous approach to the direction principle, that there may be such an exception to the Changed Law Rule. Nevertheless, an exploration of the consequences of this novel proposition are quite significant and may be used, at least, to justify the type of formalisation of the direction principle which was advocated above. First, it extends the constitutional limitations beyond the direction principle and the limits which that principle sets upon itself. Secondly it suspends the operation of the Changed Law Rule in certain circumstances, but it is not clear what the extent of these precise circumstances might be. There appear to be two possibilities: The first is where the government is a party and the legislation favours it in the pending litigation, regardless of the sweep of the legislation beyond

---

[247] *Robertson v Seattle Audubon Society* 503 US 429 (1992) at 441.

the matters in issue in the pending case. This is probably too broad a proposition. The second, and the more likely to be favoured, is the situation where the government is a party, the legislation favours it in the pending litigation, but the effect of the legislation beyond the matters in issue is limited. A further issue is whether it makes any difference whether the government's interest in the proceedings is a pecuniary or proprietary one, on the one hand, or merely one which facilitates its role as regulator. Is the government's interest sufficient in both circumstances to warrant the suspension of the Changed Law Rule? An affirmative answer would be more likely in the former circumstance. Speculating further, the proposition might be put that if the legislation is precisely designed to address issues in the pending proceedings, and no others more generally, the Changed Law Rule should be suspended regardless of whether or not the government is a party. As this is the most broadly stated of the speculative propositions, its chances of ever receiving authoritative acceptance are slim. Nevertheless, from the perspective of the separation of powers, the issue remains a nagging one: does the dominant configuration of direction principle and Changed Law Rule create sufficient protection to decisional independence so as not to require at least some exceptions to the Changed Law Rule?

The above possibilities have been raised because of the concern that the Changed Law Rule permits, albeit indirectly, the revision of a judicial decision on appeal by non-judicial means. In a sense, this has the tendency to render the decision of a federal court merely an advisory opinion. In both the United States[248] and in Australia this would have constituted a breach of the separation doctrine.[249] However, even though parallels may be drawn with an advisory opinion, the circumstances of the pending case scenario are different. For one thing, these parallels only arise if a decision is appealed, as otherwise the decision retains the characteristic of final judgment. There is nothing to suggest that a decision of a court, from which an appeal is permissible, is in any way an advisory opinion, given that the decision is entirely valid and enforceable at the time it is handed down. To that extent, there can be no breach of the separation of powers in the mere existence of the Changed Law Rule. Nevertheless, where an appeal occurs, and given the imperatives of the

---

[248] *Hayburn's case* 2 US 408 (2 Dall 409) (1792).
[249] For a more complete discussion in the American context see Young, 'Congressional Regulation of Federal Courts Jurisdiction and Processes', n 22 above, 1247; and for the Australian position see Zines, *The High Court and the Constitution*, n 231 above, 212 and 215–16.

Changed Law Rule, the similarities with an advisory opinion are sufficient to raise serious separation of powers concerns. As Young pointed
out, '[t]hey are members of a common class—opinions which prove to
have been unnecessary'.[250]

While recognising that it is not feasible entirely to avoid unnecessary
opinions, whether advisory or not, Young argued that those which are
'dangerous'—one assumes to separation of powers values—and 'easily
avoidable' should be prohibited.[251] He was referring to that situation
where 'by means of a new law, the government changes a [judicial]
decision that is unfavorable to its interests'.[252] It is at this point that
Young expressly raised concerns with the Changed Law Rule in circumstances where the government is a party. Given that the separation of
powers was expressly entrenched to protect the judicial branch from
legislative encroachment and to subject the legislature to some degree of
judicial scrutiny, the existence of the Changed Law Rule does compromise the accountability of government to law, and thus, to a certain
extent, undermines the rule of law. Therefore, the proposition that some
qualification needs to be made to the Changed Law Rule to accommodate these concerns is a very respectable proposition, exemplified by
Young stating that it should be taken as a given that the government and
its actions be subject to some degree of judicial scrutiny in the pending
case scenario.[253] It is at this point that Young indicates that he favours the
distinction between the government as property owner and the government as regulator, suggesting that the suspensions to the Changed Law
Rule should be considered in the former instance.

> When Congress acts as a regulator of public rights, it may need to change the
> rules governing a pending case on a rationale similar to that relied on by the
> Court in the *Wheeling Bridge* case. On the other hand, when the contest involves
> claims to money or property, such justification may not be present. Particularly
> in cases like *Klein*, where, arguably, the government has a sovereign immunity
> privilege that allows it to avoid a constitutional attack, to permit the govern-
> ment to change the law because of some dissatisfaction with the result in
> pending cases would be to allow the government to hedge its bets from the
> start. Congress can open its courts to claims against the government hoping for
> a favourable resolution. If it wins, it wins twice; once with the favorable
> verdict, and second by the fact that the government appears to have subjected
> itself to the rule of law. If the government loses, it loses once; it can change the
> law on appeal. Indeed, it may not even lose an appearance of accountability if
> its refusals to abide by judgments are few. Perhaps a prohibition against

---

[250]   Young, 'Congressional Regulation of Federal Courts Jurisdiction and Processes', n 22
above, 1247.
[251]   *Ibid.*
[252]   *Ibid.*
[253]   *Ibid*, at 1248.

Congress' changing the law on appeal, to favor the government, rests on a judgment that the judicial branch ought not to participate in Congress' giving the false impression that it has opened the government to judicial scrutiny. If so, a prohibition against changing the law on appeal to favor the government is one which increases legislative accountability, by requiring that Congress either clearly open or clearly close the courts to certain claims.[254]

Thus, according to Young, a strong case can be made to suspend the operation of the Changed Law Rule in circumstances where the government's interest in the pending case do not exceed the purely proprietary or pecuniary—that is, its interest resembles that belonging to a private litigant—as opposed to situations where its interest is that of a regulator of public rights.[255] Young noted that 'we can see that Chase's apparent concern with the government's power to change the law to favor itself is an intelligible constitutional argument that does not call into question the general validity of the Changed Law Rule'.[256] Moreover, one could concede to the legislature the power to change the law governing an appeal in cases where the legislature acts as a regulator—ie, where it is seeking prospective relief—but deny the legislature that power where the case involves a contest over property. While this distinction between two government roles may collapse if put under pressure, Chase might well have entertained it.[257]

There is much to be said for this proposition, but Young cannot support it with any authority beyond the proposition that it may have been a point which emerged from *Klein*.[258] He noted the difficulty with identifying the source for such an exception to the Changed Law Rule except in the 'earliest separation of powers principle which prohibits or at least discourages non-judicial revision of federal courts' judgments'.[259] If such a proposition were to be accepted and established as a particular exception to the Changed Law Rule, many of the inherent instabilities in the application of the direction principle could be avoided, at least in situations where the government's interests were purely pecuniary or proprietary and where there was no issue of the government being involved in the case in a regulatory sense. The prohibition would be straightforward and indeed limited to the pending case. It is just such speculative explorations of principle, with some basis in seminal cases such as *Klein*, which may form the basis for future developments of principle to carve out exceptions to the currently dominant Changed Law

---

254 *Ibid*, at 1248–9.
255 *Ibid*, at 1249.
256 *Ibid*.
257 *Ibid*, at 1241.
258 *Ibid*.
259 *Ibid*, at 1244.

Rule, to prevent legislative interference in pending cases, even by a substantive amendment to the law. The protections then afforded by an entrenched separation of powers will be enhanced. However, before such a position is reached, the dilution of the direction principle, and indeed the misunderstanding thereof, which appear in the most recent cases in the United States and Australia must be reversed.

XIV.   CONCLUSION

Drawing together the threads that have emerged in the last two chapters, the conclusions which can be drawn in relation to the pending case scenario can be summarised thus.

The separation of powers, when entrenched in a written constitution and allowing for inter-branch checks on power and in particular judicial review of legislative action, creates an imperative for some degree of definition of branch functions. This remains the case, although to a lesser extent, even when the doctrine is not entrenched but is nevertheless influential as a convention or constitutional principle. This imperative must be met in order to enable the creation of a point of demarcation between branch powers, at least at some level, even though it is recognised that a comprehensive, mutually exclusive definition of branch functions is not possible.

While acknowledging this problem, it has been argued that this definitional imperative can be met at the level of indisputably core branch functions. This has meant that at this level a degree of formalism in conceptual analysis is both warranted and feasible. The point is that the separation of powers must be capable of defending core branch functions.

The limited formalism which the writer espouses is not without purposive content. The response to the definitional imperatives at the core level is not for the sake of some neat, pedantic categorisation. Rather, it is informed by the values which the separation of powers has sought to defend. The writer, in a qualified way, shares the fears of the formalists that unless core branch functions are so protected, the separation of powers and its values will themselves be eroded. Beyond this level, however, it is difficult to maintain formalist rigour consistently with the definitional problems discussed above,[260] and therefore the purposive functionalist approach must hold sway.

It has been suggested that even if a functionalist approach is taken with respect to core branch functions the same rigorous demarcation and protection thereof will almost always be achieved. Thus, it is possible to

---

[260]   Above ch 1.

overcome the formalist/functionalist divide at this level. Coming to terms with these questions is essential in order to achieve a platform for a definition of the relevant constitutional limitations in the pending case scenario. Because the decisional independence of the judicial branch is very much at the core of judicial power, and indisputably so, when attempting the definition of constitutional principles which apply to protect it, the differences between formalist and functionalist approaches tend to fade away. This has enabled a definition of the difficult direction principle to proceed uniformly given that, even under a functionalist approach, the protections it provides in virtually all situations are so fundamental that legislative directions must be seen as breaches of the separation of powers.

The direction principle has then been defined in light of the Changed Law Rule and is based on the fundamental distinction between a change in the law and direction to the courts in the pending case which is not substantively legislative. The principle has emerged independently, yet uniformly, in those common law jurisdictions which have been examined and which maintain an entrenched separation of powers.

It is a principle which is discrete even though it is often overshadowed by, sometimes confused with, other separation of powers principles relating to the protections of due process and the integrity of the exercise of judicial power. The significance of the principle is that if impugned legislation is not offensive in any other way except that it is prescriptive, then it is the direction principle alone which determines the existence of unconstitutional prescription. By testing the substantively legislative nature of the legislation—the discrete aspect of the direction principle which is so often overlooked—the decisional independence of the judicial branch is thus protected.

The rationale and justification for a strong direction principle emanates most forcefully from the purer form of the separation of powers adopted in the United States Constitution quite deliberately. It is an easier step to suggest in such a constitutional setting, which allows also for 'checks and balances', that it is the independent judicial branch whose task it is to keep in check the political branches of government. Where an entrenched separation of powers coincides with responsible government, as in Australia, a more liberal attitude to the separation of legislative and executive power gives way to a strict separation of judicial power identical in many respects to that of the United States. Accordingly, the same conclusions can be drawn as to the role it should play. The difficulty with the direction principle, however, is that it insists that the legislature engage only in substantive legislative acts. It is the failure to appreciate this particular point that has resulted in the overlooking of the direction principle. It must always be borne in mind that the direction principle is blind to the actual outcome of the litigation, that is, after it has determined that there will indeed be an affect on outcome to trigger its potential application. Its only concern is the method adopted by the legislature to effect the outcome because it seeks to prohibit only those legislative acts which are so directive as to impugn their substantively legislative nature. The real importance of the direction principle is that it uncovers those directions which are hidden beneath the guise of otherwise valid enactments. It is beside the point to suggest that such hidden directions should not cause concern if the legislature has the competence to enact relevant legislation which achieves the same outcome without resorting to direction. The point of the principle is to ensure that the legislature achieves its objectives using constitutional means in order that the substance of its actions is transparent. Redish has stated this point well:

> What we derive from *Klein* ... is a far more subtle precept of American political theory: that the judiciary has the constitutional power and obligation to assure that Congress has not deceived the electorate as to the manner in which its legislation actually alters the pre-existing legal, political, social or economic topography. The legislative deception that is of concern, we should emphasize, does not go to the legislator's private motivation in enacting the legislation, or what incidental or collateral effects the legislation may have, beyond its direct and immediate impact. Instead we are focussed exclusively on the much more fundamental concern about deception as to what the legislation actually does ... The deception about which we are concerned, however, comes not from within the text of the operative substantive provisions of the statute. The deception to be avoided, rather, may be accomplished by other means...When a legislature ... leaves the generalized substantive law intact, but legislatively directs that a particular litigation (or group of litigations) arising under that law be resolved in a manner inconsistent with the dictates of the pre-existing generalised law ... [it] has altered the reach of the substantive law in specific applications ... As a result, the essential elements of the democratic process will have been undermined, because the electorate may have been deceived as to the nature and extent of its chosen representative's political commitment in voting for or against that legislation. A legislator's vote for or against a proposed substantive law means little if the legislature has furtively altered the reach or impact of that law, by resorting to a form of legislative shell game ... the legislature accomplishes this sleight-of-hand without clearly informing the electorate how its procedural legislation has transformed the political, social or economic landscape ... The key theoretical insight that may be gleaned from *Klein* is that the judiciary—the one government branch insulated from the electorate—provides the only effective means of assuring that the democratic process operates in the manner necessary for the attainment of the normative goals that underlie the nation's chosen form of representative government.[261]

---

[261] Redish and Pudelski, 'Legislative Deception, Separation of Powers, and the Democratic Process', n 48 above, 439–40.

If the courts therefore, do not apply the direction rule rigorously, the perception may arise that they may be facilitating, or are otherwise complicit in, this legislative deception and thus undermining in part the integrity of representative government. The maintenance of a strong direction principle therefore ensures, in part, the continuing efficacy of the separation of powers as an entrenched constitutional rule, but also the other fundamental pillars of the liberal democratic polity, representative government. On the one hand, it insists that an amendment to the law be applied by the courts. The happenstance of pending litigation to which the amendment may be applicable, is no consideration to the efficacy of the law. On the other hand, the direction principle will not permit an interference with the decisional independence of the judicial branch if it is in fact a direction under the guise of legislation. Applied in this way, an entrenched separation of powers can provide a surer protection to branch integrity than it might if it remained as a convention, albeit one with significant normative influence.

4

The Separation of Powers and Final Judgments:

Defining the Principle Limiting Legislative Revision of Final Judgments

I do not forget the position assumed by some, that constitutional questions are to be decided by the Supreme Court; nor do I deny that such decisions must be binding in any case, upon the parties to a suit, as to the object of that suit . . . And while it is obviously possible that such decision may be erroneous in any given case, still the evil effect following it, being limited to that particular case, with the chance that it may be over-ruled, and never become a precedent for other cases, can better be borne than could the evils of a different practice.

Abraham Lincoln in his First Inaugural Address (1861)[1]

I. INTRODUCTION AND DEFINITION OF FINAL JUDGMENT

THIS CHAPTER IS concerned with the protection of a yet more fundamental aspect of the 'decisional independence' of the judicial branch than that which arises in the pending case scenario, viz, the protections afforded the integrity of *final* judgments by the separation of powers. It will attempt to define constitutional limitations protective of that very element of finality, or conclusiveness, which constitutes such a core, defining element of judicial power. In the oft-referred-to 'classic' Australian definition, Griffith CJ spoke of it as the power

which every sovereign must of necessity have to decide controversies between its subjects, or between itself and its subjects, whether the rights relate to life, liberty or property. The exercise of this power does not begin until some

---

[1] RP Basler, *The Collected Works of Abraham Lincoln*, vol IV (New Brunswick NJ, Rutgers University Press, 1953) 268.

tribunal which has power to give a binding and authoritative decision (whether subject to appeal or not) is called upon to take action.[2]

Kitto J also emphasised that quality of finality and conclusiveness when he stated that

a judicial power involves, as a general rule, a decision settling for the future, as between defined persons or classes of persons, a question as to the existence of a right or obligation, so that an exercise of the power creates a new charter by reference to which that question is in future to be decided as between those persons or classes of persons.[3]

At first sight, the protection which an entrenched separation of powers might afford finality seems obvious and uncontroversial; that is, an absolute protection against interference by the legislative and executive branches, intolerant of exception or qualification. This is not to deny the inherent jurisdiction in the courts themselves to reopen or revise final judgments in certain very limited circumstances—a jurisdiction, of course, which is perfectly consistent with the separation of powers because it is the judicial branch itself which is exercising this discretion, not the non-judicial branches.

In this context, given the fundamental aspect of branch power which finality represents, the recurring problem of the precise definition of judicial power tends to recede. As a result, any divide between formalist and functionalist approaches to the separation of powers tends also to recede as it did when consideration was given to the direction principle in the pending case scenario.[4] The term 'final judgment' will be referred to throughout as one from which there is no further avenue for appeal because a matter has been decided by the highest court in the judicial hierarchy or the time for an appeal has elapsed (or special leave to appeal has not been granted). As a fundamental and distinctive outcome of the exercise of judicial power, a final judgment is the judiciary's last word on the rights and obligations of the particular parties in a particular suit. The extent to which a legislature may second-guess this outcome is the issue to be considered here.

The separation of powers provides a more absolute protection to final judgments than it does to decisional independence in the pending case scenario. In that scenario, to establish a breach of the direction principle, the indicia of direction impugn the substantively legislative nature of the legislation in question. In the final judgment scenario however, it is questionable whether this same requirement needs to be met, or indeed

---

[2]   *Huddart, Parker & Co Pty Ltd v Moorhead* (1909) 8 CLR 330 at 357 (Griffith CJ).
[3]   *R v Trade Practices Tribunal; Ex Parte Tasmanian Breweries Pty Ltd* (1970) 123 CLR 361 at 374.
[4]   See ch 1 above.

whether it is at all relevant. It may be, even if the legislation affecting the final judgment can be regarded as a change in the law, that there are nevertheless limits to its applicability to finally decided cases. If so, then a more absolute protection is afforded decisional independence when it comes to final judgments. What this more absolute protection might be is the central consideration of this chapter, even though, at first sight, it appears to be a relatively straightforward issue. As will be seen in the following discussion, it deserves concentrated attention because of a number of unexpected subtleties which emerge.

Constitutional limitations on legislative competence over final judgments have clear civil liberties implications, in particular, the objective that legal disputes be resolved by adjudication according to law by independent judges 'free from potential domination by the legislative and executive branches of government',[5] and that the fruits of litigation are not denied a successful litigant. The Rule of Law implications are also obvious in these circumstances. Prima facie, the protection of final judgments must constitute a basic minimum protection afforded by the separation of powers, even if it were to protect nothing else.

Commencing with the most obvious limitation, it would clearly be a breach of the separation of powers if the legislature were to constitute itself a tribunal or to set up another non-court tribunal, to decide cases at first instance or to review, in the way of an appellate court, the final decisions of the courts, with power to substitute and enforce its own orders.[6] This was described by Kirby J in *Nicholas v The Queen* as the 'most obvious derogation' from the principle founded in the separation of judicial power that 'Parliament may not enter into the activities properly belonging to the judicial power in a way inconsistent with its exercise by the courts'.[7] Such egregious institutional breaches of the separation of powers are generally rare and unlikely to occur except in extreme situations. However, this was the experience of the United States in its colonial and pre-Constitution period where such interferences were common and which convinced the American Framers of the need for an entrenched separation of powers.[8] More likely, although also rare, would be an attempt by a legislature to revise a final judgment under the guise of otherwise properly enacted legislation; that is, as a purported exercise

---

[5] *Harris v Caladine* (1991) 172 CLR 84 at 159 (McHugh J).

[6] Cf the power of the lower house of Parliament to convict for contempt of Parliament upheld in *R v Richards; Ex parte Fitzpatrick and Browne* (1955) 92 CLR 157; affd 92 CLR 171. See A Mason, 'A New Perspective on Separation of Powers' (1996) 82 *Canberra Bulletin of Public Administration* 1 at 5. Professor Geoffrey Lindell has argued that this issue might now be decided differently: 'Parliamentary Inquiries and Government Witnesses' (1995) 20 *Melbourne University Law Review* 383 at 414–15.

[7] *Nicholas v The Queen* (1998) 193 CLR 173 at 255.

[8] See ch 1 at p 10 above.

of legislative power. This would also constitute a breach of the separation of powers. As Professor George Winterton has noted in the Australian context, '[t]he Commonwealth Parliament could not validly specifically set aside the decision of a court exercising federal jurisdiction; in Quick and Garran's aphorism, "the legislature may *overrule* a decision, though it may not *reverse* it"'.[9]

Alexander Hamilton wrote in *The Federalist*, by way of exegesis of Article III, section 1, of the United States Constitution, that a 'legislature without exceeding its province cannot reverse a determination once made, in a particular case; though it may prescribe a new rule for future cases'.[10] Thus, the separation of powers would not prohibit legislation amending the law as applied or declared by the court, so long as it did not act retrospectively to revise or annul the final judgment as between the parties.[11] In a further refinement, Winterton correctly observed that the legislature 'can effectively reverse the outcome of particular litigation by enacting retrospective general legislation which effectively renders the decision irrelevant by altering the legal rights and obligations upon which it is based'.[12] It must do this, however, without expressly overruling the actual decision it thereby renders redundant. This is illustrated by the decision of the High Court of Australia in *R v Humby; Ex parte Rooney*[13] which upheld legislation, operating retrospectively, providing that in the matrimonial cause jurisdiction vested in State courts, the decrees issued by Masters would have the same force and effect as if they had been issued by judges. The legislation sought to overcome the effect of two High Court decisions which required that only judges could issue binding decrees in such matters.[14]

These straightforward principles may, however, be subject to a number of qualifications based on a consideration of the following issues: To what extent can a legislature waive the benefits of a judgment in the government's favour without breaching the separation of powers? And, to what extent does the prohibition against the revision of a final

---

[9]   G Winterton, 'The Separation of Judicial Power as an Implied Bill of Rights' in G J Lindell (ed), *Future Directions in Australian Constitutional Law* (Sydney, Federation Press, 1994) 192 at 199 (citations omitted).

[10]   Alexander Hamilton, *The Federalist* No 81 J Cooke (ed), *The Federalist* (Middletown, CT, Wesleyan University Press, 1961) 545.

[11]   See Winterton, 'The Separation of Judicial Power as an Implied Bill of Rights', n 9 above, 198. Winterton cites *R v Tilley* (1991) 56 SASR 140 at 143 and 147, a State case relevant by analogy, and also, the very significant US decision, *Pennsylvania v Wheeling and Belmont Bridge Co* 59 US (18 How) 421 (1855), to which detailed reference will be made below.

[12]   Winterton, 'The Separation of Judicial Power as an Implied Bill of Rights', n 9 above, 199.

[13]   *R v Humby; Ex parte Rooney* (1973) 129 CLR 231.

[14]   *Kotsis v Kotsis* (1970) 122 CLR 69 and *Knight v Knight* (1971) 122 CLR 114.

judgment depend on the nature of the judgment itself? Thus, for example, will an award of damages, or an order for costs, receive greater absolute protection than an injunction, which is dependent on the maintenance of the state of the law pursuant to which it was granted? Should the nature of the relevant constitutional limitation differ accordingly? Thus, are some judgments less 'final' than others? The situation illustrated by the *Rooney* case above-mentioned bears further scrutiny in this regard and these refinements will be examined in more detail below. Though somewhat neglected, these concerns are of course not novel and arise whether the separation of judicial power is legally entrenched or exists as a matter of convention.

In the pending case scenario, the direction principle intervened prior to the point of finality and permitted only those interferences which were effected by a change in the law. However, if this were to be applied to final judgments, finality would not be adequately safeguarded, especially in light of the high threshold set for a breach of the direction principle. The countervailing requirement of the separation of powers that the courts must apply the law as enacted, even in a pending case, ceases to apply when the point of finality is reached; for at that point, the separation of powers would render any direct revision of a final judgment as between the parties an impermissible legislative intrusion. An absolute protection thus appears to be demanded, establishing a certain inviolability to finality. This is the case whether or not the interference is effected by an otherwise valid exercise of legislative power. While the severity of this principle is ameliorated by the limited qualifications abovementioned, these do not detract from the central proposition. However, while the principle of inviolability ('the inviolability principle') is amenable to qualifications, it is not open to exceptions. These qualifications are directed to the very concept of finality, exploring situations where a judgment may not be 'final' in the sense required to attract absolute protection.

As a counterpoint to this absolute position, the position which pertains in jurisdictions where the separation of powers is not entrenched will first be examined.

II.   REFLECTIONS ON FINALITY WHERE THE SEPARATION PRINCIPLE IS NOT ENTRENCHED

In the United States, the Supreme Court only once, in *Plaut v Spendthrift Farm Inc*,[15] had occasion to strike down legislation which purported to

---

[15] *Plaut v Spendthrift Farm Inc* 514 US 211 (1995). This case will be discussed in detail below.

require the revision of a final judgment. In Australia, the High Court has not yet been required to do so. The observations of Kirby J in *Nicholas v The Queen*[16]—that it would be a serious breach of the separation of powers for the Commonwealth Parliament to set itself up as a body with power to revise final judgments—are founded in that development of Chapter III jurisprudence which resulted in the very strict institutional and functional separation of judicial powers established in *Boilermakers*.[17] The principle that 'the judicial power of the Commonwealth' cannot be vested in any body except a Chapter III court clearly also prevents Parliament from vesting this power in itself. The revision of a final judgment by Parliament, as between the parties, would clearly and unambiguously amount to a usurpation of judicial power. This is also the position in Ireland.[18]

This dearth of cases reflects the fundamental nature of this principle and its appreciation by the legislative branch. This bespeaks of the efficacy of the legal entrenchment of the separation of powers, particularly in light of the fact that legislative revisions of final judgments have occurred, albeit rarely, in jurisdictions where the separation of powers is not so entrenched. In *BLF (NSW)* Kirby P catalogued a number of New South Wales statutes which had the effect of revising final judgments; although they were not the subject of legal challenge.[19] In Ontario, Canada[20] the KVP Company Ltd Act 1950 specifically dissolved a court injunction which restrained that company from polluting the waters of the Spanish River, which injunction had previously survived an appeal to the Supreme Court in *McKie v KVP Co Ltd*.[21] In the United Kingdom, the most famous example of legislative revision of a final judgment was the War Damage Act 1965 (UK), which reversed the decision of the House of Lords in *Burmah Oil Company (Burma Trading) Ltd v Lord Advocate*.[22] This case also afforded an interesting case study of the issues which come to the fore where there is no entrenched separation of powers to render the final judgment inviolable vis-à-vis the legislature.[23]

---

[16]   *Nicholas v The Queen* (1998) 193 CLR 173 at 255 (Kirby J).

[17]   See above ch 2.

[18]   See below at 215.

[19]   *BLF (NSW)* (1986) 7 NSWLR 372 at 391.

[20]   In relation to Canada, it should be noted that there is no general separation of powers in the British North America Act 1867, renamed the Constitution Act in 1982. See PW Hogg, *Constitutional Law of Canada*, 4th edn (Scarborough, Ontario, 1997) 190ff.

[21]   *McKie v KVP Co Ltd* [1948] SCR 698, [1948] 3 DLR 39 (Ontario High Court); and [1949] 1 DLR 39 (Ontario Court of Appeal). See S Shetreet, 'The Administration of Justice: Practical Problems, Value Conflicts and Changing Concepts' (1979) 13 *University of British Columbia Law Review* 52 at 59 and P Anisman 'Water Pollution Control in Ontario' (1972) 5 *Ottawa Law Review* 342 at 373.

[22]   *Burmah Oil Company (Burma Trading) Ltd v Lord Advocate* [1965] AC 75.

[23]   Although see now the consequences of the Human Rights Act 1998 (UK) and the European Convention on Human Rights discussed in ch 6 of this book.

In the well-rehearsed facts, the Burmah Oil Company sought compensation for damage to its installations in Burma during the World War of 1939–45 by the actions of British military forces seeking to deny resources to the enemy. The House of Lords held, by a majority,[24] that the company had a right to claim compensation, quantum to be determined subsequently. Even though the demolitions were carried out lawfully in exercise of the royal prerogative, this did not mean that the government could avoid paying compensation. The British government had taken a keen interest in the case well before it reached the House of Lords.[25] The Deputy Treasury Solicitor had written to the company advising it that, in the opinion of the government, it did not have a legal claim for compensation and that in the event that the courts held otherwise, legislation would be enacted to reverse the decision.[26] Following the decision, the government introduced into Parliament the War Damage Bill (No 2), section 1 of which provided that compensation was not payable for lawful acts performed by the Crown, or under its authority, during a war, or in contemplation of its outbreak,

> in respect of damage to, or destruction of, property … (whether before or after the passing of this Act, within or outside the United Kingdom).

Sub-section (2) provided that

> where any proceedings to recover at common law compensation in respect of such damage or destruction have been instituted before the passing of this Act, the court shall on the application of any party, forthwith set aside or dismiss the proceedings, subject only to the determination of any question arising as to costs or expenses.[27]

It was a highly controversial measure, not only in relation to the substantive issue of compensation for damages in these circumstances, but also because of its retrospectivity and its effect on the final judgment of the House of Lords which was not exempted from the retrospective effect of the proposed law.[28] Although the Lords originally returned the Bill to the Commons, removing the retrospective element,[29] the Lords eventually passed the Bill when the Commons refused to amend, expressing strong

---

[24] Lords Reid, Pearce and Upjohn; Viscount Radcliffe and Lord Hodson dissenting.

[25] See JW Bridge, 'Retrospective Legislation and the Rule of Law in Britain' (1967) 35 *University of Missouri at Kansas City Law Review* 132.

[26] *Ibid*, at 140–44.

[27] See also *Malloch v Aberdeen Corp* 1974 SLT 253 and the Education (Scotland) Act 1973 (UK); and *Lambeth BC v Secretary of State for Social Services* (1980) 79 LGR 61 and the National Health Service (Invalid Directions) Act 1980 (UK).

[28] See the record of the second reading of the bill: *Parliamentary Debates, House of Commons*, Vol 705 (No 49); *House of Lords*, Vol 264 (No 56). See also AL Goodhart, 'The Burmah Oil Case and the War Damage Act 1965' (1966) 82 *Law Quarterly Review* 97 at 98.

[29] For an account of the passage of the Act, see *ibid*, at 98 and 108 ff.

reservations. Those opposing the retrospective element saw it as repugnant to the rule of law precisely because its effect would be to revise the
final decision of a court affecting the parties thereto. Other voices in
Parliament argued that there were circumstances, albeit exceptional ones,
in which parliamentary revision of final judgments was warranted.[30]
Lord McNair responded by saying:

> When an important question of principle is involved, it is rash to listen to those
> who say 'This is quite exceptional; this can never happen again'. If this Bill in
> its present form becomes an Act, it will, sooner or later, be invoked as an
> argument for some further invasion of the rights of the subject against the
> Crown.[31]

Thus, in the United Kingdom, parliamentary supremacy was asserted
over the final determination of a legal dispute by an independent
judiciary, in exceptional circumstances at any rate. It would seem therefore that if Parliament was sufficiently determined about a particular
issue, final judgments were not secure from legislative interference in the
absence of a constitutionally-entrenched separation of powers. As Professor Goodhart noted, 'the basic principles against retroactive legislation
were reaffirmed in no uncertain terms, but, on the other hand, it was
recognised that, in certain circumstances, justice might require such
legislation'.[32] JW Bridge was blunt: '[t]hus Parliament demonstrated its
omnipotence'.[33] In relation to this particular development, Lord Devlin
referred to 'the fundamental principle that the Crown and its subjects are
equal before the law and that once issue is joined, they are both bound by
the decision of the judge'. He continued,

> [w]hat it [the Crown] is doing is to institute Parliament as a supra-final court of
> appeal (to which alone it has access) which will decide the case on the merits
> and not according to law and which will takes its views on the merits from the
> Crown itself.[34]

Academic criticism of the legislation resulted precisely from this affirmation of legislative power over a final judgment, albeit in exceptional
circumstances. The independent adjudication of legal disputes, and the
rule of law principles which sustained it, were compromised. Doubts
were expressed whether the caveats—exceptional circumstances, or
where 'justice might require' it—were sufficiently extraordinary so as not

---

[30] *Ibid.*
[31] Quoted in Goodhart, 'The Burmah Oil Case and the War Damage Act 1965', n 28
above, 111.
[32] See *ibid*, at 99 ff and Bridge, 'Retrospective Legislation and the Rule of Law in Britain',
n 25 above, 140.
[33] Bridge, 'Retrospective Legislation and the Rule of Law in Britain', n 25 above, 141.
[34] *The Observer*, 16 May 1965, quoted in P Jackson, 'War Damage Act, 1965' (1965) 28
Modern Law Review 574 at 576.

to undermine the general rule. Bridge for one was not convinced. In the absence of some more precise definition of the situations in which exceptions might be made, his concern was certainly warranted. He advocated the right of the litigant to have a legal dispute resolved by a court in accordance with the law as it existed at the time the action arose. And if that litigant had succeeded in achieving a favourable final judgment—especially if the suit had made its way up to the highest court in the jurisdiction—that litigant had 'the right to rest on the decision of that court'.[35] It would be quite a different matter if the law as declared by the court was subsequently amended by a statute of prospective nature. But,

> by not merely reversing a decision of the House of Lords but also reversing retrospectively Parliament is acting as a court of appeal from the House of Lords and is thus substituting its judgement for the judgement of the highest court in the land. This must necessarily undermine the independence of the judiciary and endanger the freedom of the individual. The argument that the case for retroactivity is strengthened when the effect of the legislation is to restore the law to what it was previously believed to be is a specious one. The fact is that this act constitutes a dangerous precedent which could be used to persuade Parliament to reverse retrospectively decisions of the courts which do not accord with the government's view of the law.[36]

Bridge emphasised that his concern was not with the particular substantive issues at stake in the case, but with the

> deprivation visited upon successful litigants, whether rich or poor, of the fruits of successful litigation which has been conducted, properly, before the courts culminating in a decision of the final court of appeal … It is surely contrary to elementary justice for a plaintiff to bring a successful action and then to find that his adversary has caused the decision to be reversed retrospectively. The fact that the plaintiff was warned in advance that this would happen if the action proved to be successful is certainly no justification. It was in the face of threats of this sort that judicial impartiality and independence were eventually established; recourse to them must be regarded as a retrograde step.[37]

For Shimon Shetreet, 'retrospective reversal, which renders ineffective a judicial ruling in a specific case, undermines the position of the judiciary and smacks of a bill of attainder'.[38] Professor TRS Allan wrote that 'the 1965 statute is hard to defend: where rights against the government have

---

[35] Bridge, 'Retrospective Legislation and the Rule of Law in Britain', n 25 above, 143.
[36] *Ibid*, at 143.
[37] *Ibid*, at 144.
[38] Shetreet, 'The Administration of Justice', n 21 above, 59.

been crystallized in the final judgment of a court, their deliberate negation by legislation seems to mock the independence of the judiciary'.[39]

These arguments were not predicated upon an entrenched separation of powers, written as they were in the context of the unwritten constitution of the United Kingdom. That is not to say that the values which they sought to uphold were not those sought to be upheld also by that doctrine. For Bridge, the Act 'must be regarded as being contrary to the principles of elementary justice and contrary to the spirit of our law and the constitution as evidenced by the practice of Parliament and the courts'.[40] But these principles—without discounting them—are not susceptible to precise definition, and hence the difficulties which arise when reliance is placed upon them alone to found the resistance to claims of parliamentary competence to revise final judgments. What was so obvious a breach of 'elementary justice' to Bridge did not appear so for the parliamentary majority which voted for the enactment, which majority also was not sufficiently sensitive to the fact that the Act might be 'contrary to the spirit of our law and the constitution'.

Of course, had there been an entrenched separation of powers such legislation would have been subject to judicial review and almost certainly held unconstitutional. Absent such entrenchment, there is no guarantee that the doctrine will remain relevant or influential over time, even as a convention. Indeed, the experience of the United Kingdom is that the influence of the separation of powers has tended to wax and wane as the nation's polity and constitution evolves. In that jurisdiction, the status, and indeed the precise nature, of the separation of powers remains both ever-evolving and highly problematic.[41] Nevertheless, as indicated by Bridge, the fundamental significance, and appreciation, of the settlement of legal disputes by independent judges with professional expertise has been a prominent feature of the British constitutional scene since at least the eighteenth century.[42] That being the case, the War Damage Act 1965, and especially its retrospectivity, is all the more

[39] TRS Allan, *Law Liberty and Justice* (Oxford, Clarendon Press, 1993) 78.
[40] Bridge, 'Retrospective Legislation and the Rule of Law in Britain', n 25 above, 145.
[41] For an interesting discussion on the United Kingdom situation, see E Barendt, 'Separation of Powers and Constitutional Government' [1995] *Public Law* 599. The classic work remains that of MJC Vile, *Constitutionalism and the Separation of Powers*, 2nd edn (Indianapolis, Liberty Fund, 1998) chs 5 and 8 in particular.
[42] Vile, *Constitutionalism and the Separation of Powers*, n 41 above. Vile noted: '[T]he independence of the judges had been a matter of concern to Englishmen for well over a century and a half before Blackstone, and that the idea of a separate "judicial power" had begun in mid-seventeenth-century England' (at 113). He referred also to the evolution of the importance of an independent and professional judiciary, and hence the elevation of 'judicial power' in the British scheme, through Montesquieu and Blackstone (at 114).

worthy of comment. MJC Vile used the Act to illustrate his concerns regarding the state of judicial power in Britain:

> In Britain … one of the most marked governmental trends has been the continued decline of judicial power—[manifested by, among other things] a readiness to acquiesce in governmental and administrative acts … There have been a number of instances since the Second World War where decisions of the courts which went against the administration have been quickly reversed by Parliament, sometimes with incredible rapidity.[43]

Of the War Damage Act, which he regarded as an 'extreme' example, he stated that it offended against 'the basic rule of constitutionalism, the predictability of action'.[44] This decline of judicial power, and the dominance of the non-judicial branches, led Vile to express a degree of pessimism with respect to the situation in Britain:

> Thus even if we accept 'the rule of law' in the sense of a hierarchy of rules which can ultimately be tested against the final statutory or constitutional authority, we have to face the fact that this may become merely a matter of form. The outward forms of legality are retained, but they may be manipulated by party leaders in a way which makes a mockery of them. The twentieth-century concern with the solution of practical problems can be taken to the point where the desire to deal with particular issues overrides all consideration of the way in which these issues are dealt with.[45]

It is in the context of these concerns that the issue of constitutional limitations on the revision of final judgments by legislatures becomes a critical test of the vitality and continuing integrity of judicial power, and the means for its preservation becomes a critical issue. Absent a constitutional entrenchment of the separation of judicial power, the survival of the power, and its independence, must depend on the restraint of the non-judicial branches; and the degree to which they may heed the exhortations of scholars such as Allan, Bridge, Goodhart and Vile.

It has nevertheless been posited that the overruling of a final judgment in the United Kingdom can be declared unconstitutional. Relying on the theories of Dworkin, Joseph Jaconelli stated:

---

[43] *Ibid*, at 352. Query whether Vile's observations relating to the decline of judicial power in the United Kingdom are reflective of the current position in that jurisdiction, especially in light of the Human Rights Act 1998 and the courts role in making declarations of incompatibility with the rights protected by that Act. It is interesting to observe that in Australia and in the United States, with an entrenched separation of judicial power, quite the opposite is the case. Indeed, in both jurisdictions, the issue is the whether the courts are exceeding the proper scope of the judicial power in the constitutional scheme. See, eg, F Wheeler, 'The Rise and Rise of Judicial Power under Chapter III of the Constitution: a Decade in Overview' (2001) 20 *Australian Bar Review* 283.

[44] Vile, *Constitutionalism and the Separation of Powers*, n 41 above, 353.

[45] *Ibid*.

Professor Dworkin's propounds a legal theory which includes not only strictly legal rights but also moral and political rights. In addition to deliberately enacted rights, the law, for Dworkin, also consists of the political and moral rights that are implicit in the political theory which best explains and justifies the existing complex of legislation, precedent, convention and custom. On this view, there are certain things which even a legislature which appears to be legally unfettered may not have the right to do. It is submitted that the retrospective provisions of the *War Damage Act 1965* fall into this category. Retrospectively to deprive a litigant of the fruits of his victory in the courts is to make a nonsense of the independence of the judiciary. It secures, by less unpalatable methods, the same result as would the browbeating of the judges who tried the case.[46]

Support for such a view can also be derived from the thesis of Professor T R S Allan, as will be discussed in chapter six below.

However, in light of prevailing views of Parliamentary sovereignty, the United Kingdom courts have not accepted that they can invalidate legislation, even such legislation as the War Damage Act 1965. Of course, the power of judicial review in the United Kingdom has been given considerable impetus by the Human Rights Act 1998 (UK), which enables the courts to declare legislation incompatible with the enumerated rights, although direct invalidation is not provided for.[47] The seminal case of *A v Secretary of State for the Home Department*,[48] in which the House of Lords made just such a declaration with respect to detention provisions in the Anti-Terrorism, Crime and Security Act 2001 (UK), manifests an increasing appreciation by the courts themselves of their own role as a check on legislative and executive power. Lord Bingham said in that case that '[c]onstitutional dangers exist no less in too little judicial activism as in too much. There are limits to the legitimacy of executive or legislative decision-making, just as there are to decision-making by the courts'.[49]

III.   A MIDDLE CASE: INDIA

India provides an instructive middle case in that it has a written constitution, but not one which unequivocally establishes a separation of judicial power. The leading scholar of the Indian Constitution, HM Seervai, pointed out that

---

[46]   J Jaconelli, 'Constitutional Review in an Unwritten Constitution' (1985) 34 *International and Comparative Law Quarterly* 627 at 628. Jaconelli refers in particular to ch 4 of Dworkin's *Taking Rights Seriously*.

[47]   This is discussed in detail in ch 6 below.

[48]   *A v Secretary of State for the Home Department* [2005] 2 AC 68.

[49]   *Ibid*, at 110.

it ought to be stated that the machinery of Govt. set up by our Constitution follows in essentials the British and not the American model. The doctrine of the separation of powers ... do[es] not form part of the Constitution of Great Britain or the Constitution of India.[50]

There thus appears to be no entrenched constitutional protection of the decisional independence of the courts, although provision is made for the protection of judicial independence by securing tenure and remuneration in Articles 124–125. Although provision is made for the establishment of a Supreme Court, with its powers and jurisdictions defined in Chapter IV, there is no provision which vests the judicial power of the Union in the Supreme Court, as there is in the Australian and United States Constitutions. Accordingly, legislation cannot be invalidated on the grounds that it constitutes an invalid interference with, or usurpation of, the judicial power in breach of a legally-entrenched separation of powers.[51] However, the Supreme Court does have the power, in the manner of the United States Supreme Court and the High Court of Australia, to invalidate legislation where it is otherwise beyond the competence of the legislature as defined by the Constitution. As Malik pointed out,

[o]ur Constitution, unlike the English Constitution, recognises the Court's supremacy over the legislative authority, but such supremacy is a very limited one, for it is confined to the field where the legislative power is circumscribed by limitations put upon it by the Constitution itself. Within this restricted field the Court may, on a scrutiny of the law made by the Legislature, declare it void if it is found to have transgressed the constitutional limitations. But our Constitution, unlike the American Constitution, does not recognise the absolute supremacy of the Court over the legislative authority in all respects, for outside the restricted field of constitutional limitations our Parliament and the State Legislatures are supreme in their respective legislative fields and in that wider field there is no scope for the Court in India to play the role of the Supreme Court of the United States.[52]

Nevertheless, as in the United Kingdom, the separation of powers has a normative influence. The Indian authorities do express concern to maintain the inviolability of final judgments. The bulk of Indian case law arises where there has been retrospective legislative validation of executive action previously declared invalid by a court. The position adopted in these cases is that the validation is constitutional only if the prior final judgment is not altered as between the relevant parties. However, it is permissible for the party adversely affected by that final judgment to

[50] HM Seervai, *Constitutional Law of India, A Critical Commentary*, vol 1 (Bombay, NM Tripathi, 1991) 159.
[51] See *Gopalan v State of Madras* [1950] AIR SC 27, [1950] SCR 88.
[52] S Malik, *The Supreme Court on Constitutional Law* (Luknow, Eastern Book Co, 1974) Vol II at 990–91.

take advantage of the new legislation which amends the law upon which that judgment was based. Thus, while not actually revised by the legislature, the final decision is made redundant. Seervai quoted with approval[53] the following passage from the judgment of Mitter J in *Mahal Chand Sethia v WB* as a succinct statement of the constitutional position in India:

> A court of law can pronounce upon the validity of any law and declare the same to be null and void if it was beyond the legislative competence of the legislature or it infringed the rights enshrined in Part III of the Constitution … The position of a Legislature is however different. *It cannot declare any decision of a court of law to be void or of no effect.* It can however pass an Amending Act to remedy the defects pointed out by a court of law or on coming to know of it *aliunde.* An Amending Act simpliciter will cure the defect in the statute only prospectively. *But as a legislature has the competence to pass a measure with retrospective effect it can pass an Amending Act to have effect from the date which is past* … [T]here is nothing in our Constitution which restricts such jurisdiction of the legislature to cases where courts of law have not pronounced upon the invalidity or infirmity of any legislative measure. Instances of the legislature's use of such power, upheld by our courts, are copious.[54]

Why the legislature cannot declare any decision of a court to be void or of no effect is not made clear. This is a telling omission given the absence of an entrenched separation of powers. Is it simply a reflection of the deep normative influence of the separation of powers, the values of judicial independence and the rule of law? Or is it the more prosaic reason that the Constitution simply does not expressly grant the legislature that power whereas it does expressly grant the Supreme Court of India jurisdiction over certain matters?

This issue was considered in *Bakhtar Trust and ors v MD Narayan and ors.*[55] The High Court of Karnataka had previously held that a licence granted for a particular development was repugnant to state zoning regulations under the relevant legislation. A failure by the builders to comply with these orders resulted in contempt proceedings being brought against them in the High Court. While the contempt proceedings were pending, the State enacted new legislation modifying the relevant zoning regulations so that the proposed development was rendered consistent with the regulations. These amendments were made retrospective to the period when the licence in issue had been declared ultra vires by the court, and purported to declare valid and 'regularise' those

---

[53]   Seervai, *Constitutional Law of India, A Critical Commentary*, n 50 above, 223.
[54]   *Ibid*. This was an unreported judgment of the Supreme Court. The emphasis was added by Seervai.
[55]   [2003] AIR 2236.

developments which had been previously held invalid by the court.[56] Thus, pursuant to section 2, '[n]otwithstanding anything contained in any judgment, decree, or order of any Court, Tribunal or any other authority' the zoning regulations 'shall be deemed to have been modified' as from 1972 pursuant to the present amendments. The express reference to previous judgments approximated a legislative revision of final judgments. However, the Supreme Court held that this was a retrospective legislative validation of prior acts without actually revising final judicial decisions. The legislation merely cured

> the defects that led to their invalidation and thus makes ineffective judgments of competent Courts declaring their invalidity. It is also settled that a validating Act may even make ineffective judgments and orders of competent Courts provided it, by retrospective legislation, removes the cause of invalidity or the basis that had led to those decisions.[57] (Emphasis added.)

The Supreme Court was very careful to delineate the limits of constitutional activity in this regard. While previous judgments could validly be made redundant by retrospective legislation, the legislation had to be such as to render it impossible for the court to arrive at the same conclusion. 'In other words, the very premise of the earlier judgment should be uprooted, thereby resulting in a fundamental change of the circumstances upon which it was founded'.[58] However, it was impermissible for the legislature 'to declare that a judicial pronouncement given by a Court of law *would not be binding, as the legislature does not possess that power*'[59] (emphasis added). Thus, even though the proposed development could now proceed pursuant to the new law, the previous judicial decision was not revised, it still being a final and conclusive statement of the rights and obligations of the parties pursuant to the then existing law.

Given the absence of a legally-entrenched separation of powers in the Indian Constitution, it is difficult to understand why the legislature does not possess that power, as the United Kingdom Parliament did in the *Burmah Oil* case. It is perhaps because the Indian courts are simply limiting legislative competence to those subject-matters expressly provided for in the written Constitution and legislating to revise final judgments is simply not provided for, even if the subject-matter of the legislation is otherwise within power. That this is the rationale is not made entirely clear. However, if the subject-matter of the legislation is otherwise within a constitutional head of power, in the absence of an entrenched separation of powers, it is difficult to appreciate why it could

---

[56] *Ibid*, at 2240.
[57] *Ibid*.
[58] *Ibid*, at 2244.
[59] *Ibid*.

not retroact to revise final judgements. In any event, the Indian solution to this question does appear to emphasise form over substance. If the effect of the final judgment is rendered redundant by the retrospective change in the law, even though the decision itself is left intact, the outcome for the parties is the same. The consequence of this reasoning is that a written constitution which vests legislative power in a legislature, and judicial power in the judicial branch—and without necessarily entrenching a separation of powers—does afford a protection, ipso facto, to the final judgments of the judicial branch. Accordingly, an entrenched separation of powers will merely augment the protection which already exists. However, this position is somewhat strained, as it cannot be stated with any certainty that because the constitution omits expressly to grant a power to a particular branch, that branch does not have that power. This is to be contrasted with the position pertaining in Australia where the High Court inferred an entrenchment of the separation of powers in the separate vesting of branch powers in the executive, legislature and judiciary, even though there is no express reference made to the exclusive vesting of those powers.

These uncertainties are resolved in those jurisdictions which do have an entrenched separation of powers. Reference will now be made to the United States and Australia where reliance is placed on an entrenched separation of powers to protect the finality of judicial decisions, especially from legislative revision.

IV.   EARLY AUSTRALIAN COMMENTARY ON THE CONSTITUTIONAL PROTECTION OF FINAL JUDGMENTS

As indicated in chapter two, little guidance can be derived from the Australian Constitutional Convention Debates with respect to the position on legislative interference in either the pending case or final judgment scenario, unlike the position which pertains in the United States. However, the early Australian scholars appreciated the significance of this precise issue and the protections afforded by the entrenchment of the separation of powers. Harrison Moore stated:

> The power to adjudicate possessed by a court imports the observance of principles of legal administration essential to judicial office. The full extent of these principles cannot be easily determined; but whatever they are, they may not be interfered with by the Legislature. The Constitution empowers the Legislature to regulate the *incidents* of judicature—this power is expressly

conferred in sec 51 (xxxix)—but any interference with the essentials of judicial administration is a deprivation of the judicial power and an attempt to require the court to act in a non-judicial way.[60]

This meant that the Commonwealth Parliament could not act institutionally as a court, whether as a court of review, or a tribunal at first instance: '[T]he Legislature may not constitute itself or any other body unauthorised by the Constitution, a Court of justice with functions which might be validly performed by a Court regularly constituted, i.e. the determination, after hearing, of rights according to law'.[61] He also recognised that the separation of powers did not 'merely'[62] import an institutional guarantee to protect the integrity of judicial functions in the hands of the Chapter III courts. He was concerned to note that Parliament was prohibited from achieving the same ends under the guise of properly enacted legislation:

> The temptation to which Legislatures are liable, to which American Legislatures have succumbed, and which American Courts have met by the allegation of an invasion of judicial power, is to apply a new rule to past acts or events, or to deal with a specific matter of injury or wrong independently of all rule. However mischievous and dangerous may be *ex post facto* laws and *privilegia*, their very mischief lies in the fact that *they are something other than judicial acts; that what should have been done in a judicial way and according to law has been done by the assumption of arbitrary power*. The grant of judicial power to a special organ means that if the matter be one which from its nature is proper for judicial determination alone, the Legislature cannot deal with it otherwise, or authorise anyone, even a Court properly constituted, to deal with it except in the way of adjudication.[63] (Emphasis added.)

Moore, however, did not take the matter further in relation to the precise concerns of this chapter.

Quick and Garran did:'[I]t cannot be doubted that any attempt by Parliament, under cover of a declaratory law *or otherwise*, to set aside or reverse the judgement of a court of federal jurisdiction, would be void as an invasion of the judicial power'[64] (emphasis added). They explained further by referring to the instance of a legislature, by declaratory enactment, stating its intention as to how a particular statute should be interpreted, which interpretation differed from that previously given to it by a court. 'In such a case the Court, in the exercise of its function as

---

[60] W Harrison Moore, *The Constitution of the Commonwealth of Australia*, 2nd edn (Melbourne, Maxwell, 1910) 323.

[61] *Ibid*, at 322.

[62] *Ibid*.

[63] *Ibid*, at 322–3.

[64] J Quick and RR Garran, *The Annotated Constitution of the Australian Commonwealth* (1901, reprinted Sydney, Legal Books, 1976) 722.

interpreter, has declared what it believes to be the law; and the legislature has in effect declared the judicial interpretation to be unfounded and unwarrantable'.[65]

To determine whether this was a breach of the separation of powers, they referred to contemporary American learning on the point for assistance, and in particular to Cooley's *Constitutional Limitations*.[66] Thomas Cooley indicated that the answer would depend on the 'purpose which was in the mind of the legislature in passing the declaratory statute', that is, whether the statute was intended to 'have retrospective operation on a finally decided case' or whether the legislature wished merely 'to establish a construction of the doubtful law for the determination of cases that may arise in the future'.[67] If the former, it would be constitutionally objectionable and invalid, for, according to Cooley,

> this would not only be an exercise of the judicial power, but it would be its exercise in the most objectionable and offensive form, since the legislature would in effect sit as a court of review to which parties might appeal when dissatisfied with the rulings of the courts.[68]

Quick and Garran upheld Cooley's general principle but discounted the reference to 'purpose' and 'design' as apt to confuse the issue.[69] 'The simple rule', they said, 'would seem to be that, just as the legislature cannot directly reverse the judgement of the court, so it cannot, by a declaratory law, affect the rights of the parties in whose case the judgement was given'.[70] The position they adopted (correctly) was clear and unambiguous, indicating an adoption of strict approach in relation to final judgments, even if the attempt to revise them was cloaked in the form of legislation:

> [a] declaratory law must always be in a sense retrospective, and will not be unconstitutional because it alters existing rights; but it will be unconstitutional, and therefore inoperative, so far as it purports to apply to the parties or the subject-matter of particular suits in which judgement has been given. That is to say, the legislature may *overrule* a decision, though it may not *reverse* it; it may declare the rule of law to be different from what the courts have adjudged it to be, and may give a retrospective operation to its declaration, except so far as the rights of parties to a judicial decision are concerned. In other words, the

---

[65]   *Ibid.*

[66]   *Ibid.* See TM Cooley, *A Treatise on the Constitutional Limitations Which Rest Upon the States of the American Union.* Unfortunately, the authors did not state from which edition of Cooley they were quoting.

[67]   TM Cooley, *A Treatise on the Constitutional Limitations Which Rest Upon the States of the American Union*, 7th edn (Boston, Little, Brown & Co, 1903) 135.

[68]   Quick and Garran, *The Annotated Constitution of the Australian Commonwealth*, n 64 above, 722.

[69]   *Ibid*, at 722.

[70]   *Ibid*, at 722.

sound rule of legislation, that the fruits of victory ought not to be snatched from a successful litigant, is elevated into a constitutional requirement; but the general question of retrospective legislation is left to the discretion of the legislature.[71]

This absolute prohibition is to be contrasted with the position which pertains in the absence of a constitutional separation and where reliance is placed simply on 'rule of law' and 'judicial independence' conventions and standards, as in the United Kingdom.

Although not referred to by Quick and Garran, it is worth noting Cooley's expanded comments on this point:

> As the legislature cannot set aside the construction of the law already applied by the courts to actual cases, neither can it compel the courts for the future to adopt a particular construction of a law which the legislature permits to remain in force. 'To declare what the law *is, or has been* is a judicial power; to declare what the law *shall be*, is legislative. One of the fundamental principles of all our governments is that the legislative power shall be separate from the judicial'. If the legislature would prescribe a different rule for the future from that which the courts enforce, it must be done by statute, and cannot be done by a mandate to the courts, which leaves the law unchanged, but seeks to compel the courts to construe and apply it, not according to the legislative judgement.[72]

Cooley concluded with the following pertinent remark:

> But in any case *the substance of the legislative action should be regarded rather than the form*; and if it appears to be the intention to establish by declaratory statute a rule of conduct for the future, the courts should accept and act upon it, without too nicely inquiring whether the mode by which the new rule is established is or is not the best, most decorous, and suitable that could have been adopted.[73]

Acknowledging that properly enacted legislation can itself be invalidated on this ground, he noted, *a fortiori*, the prohibition on the legislature otherwise acting institutionally as a court:

> If the legislature cannot thus indirectly control the action of the courts, by requiring of them a construction of the law according to its own views, it is very plain it cannot do so directly, by setting aside their judgements, compelling them to grant new trials, ordering the discharge of offenders, or directing what particular steps shall be taken in the progress of a judicial inquiry.[74]

---

[71] *Ibid*, at 722.
[72] Cooley, *A Treatise on the Constitutional Limitations Which Rest Upon the States of the American Union*, n 67 above, 137 (footnotes omitted).
[73] *Ibid*.
[74] *Ibid*, at 137–8.

Inglis Clark did not explore all the various scenarios, but, noting that the Constitution did not prohibit retroactive laws,[75] stated that the legislature was not permitted by the separation of powers (quoting Cooley),

> [t]o retroact upon past controversies and to reverse decisions which the courts, in the exercise of their undoubted authority, have made; for this would not only be the exercise of it in the most objectionable and offensive form, since the legislature would in effect sit as a court of review to which parties might appeal when dissatisfied with the rulings of the courts.[76]

It is clear, therefore, that the early commentators envisaged a very strict constitutional limitation on the power of the legislature to revise final judgments resulting from the constitutional entrenchment of the separation of powers. It is immediately apparent that they regarded the constitutional limitation as being more fundamental and absolute than that envisaged by the direction principle. That the legislature was amending the law did not constitute an exception to the prohibition. However, beyond this, there was lacking an awareness of the considerable subtleties which may arise, even though these had already begun to emerge in the United States in the nineteenth century, as will be examined below.

V.   THE CURRENT AUSTRALIAN POSITION

The Australian position has not been substantially expanded upon since the writings of the early commentators. The fundamental principle remains that Parliament may not validly specifically set aside or revise the final decision of a court exercising federal jurisdiction.[77] The High Court has not had occasion to decide a case on this basis. Nevertheless, given the relative strictness by which the High Court has enforced the separation of judicial power,[78] and the fact that it has recognised that a core element of judicial power is the conclusive, and enforceable declaration of the rights and obligations of parties according to existing law, it can with confidence be stated that this reflects the Australian position. McHugh J in *Harris v Caladine* referred to the fact that the framers were conscious of the need

> to insulate the federal judiciary from the pressures of the Executive Government…and the Parliament … so that litigants in federal courts could

---

[75]   A Inglis Clark, *Studies in Australian Constitutional Law* (1901, reprinted Sydney, Legal Books, 1997) 41.

[76]   *Ibid*, at 41, quoting from Cooley's *Constitutional Limitations*, 6th edn (Boston, Little, Brown & Co, 1890) 112. In the 7th edn, (1903), n 67 above, it is at 136.

[77]   Winterton, 'The Separation of Judicial Power as an Implied Bill of Rights', n 9 above, 199.

[78]   See ch 1 at 7 above.

have their cases decided by judges who were free from potential domination by the legislative and executive branches of government.[79]

Referring approvingly to that statement, Kirby J in *Nicholas* stated it would be 'a danger to this principle' if attempts were made 'by the legislature, pursuing policies recommending themselves to it, to enact what the Supreme Court of the United States has described as laws which have the effect of "nullifying prior authoritative judicial action"'.[80] Kirby J cited the leading United States Supreme Court decision, *Plaut v Spendthrift Farm Inc*,[81] to which extensive reference will be made below, in support. The case—and hence its citation in Australia—is significant in that it is the only Supreme Court decision which held legislation to be invalid on the ground that it revised the final judgment of a federal court in breach of the separation of powers.[82]

Kirby J indicated his appreciation of the subtleties involved by asking whether the limitation was an absolute one in all cases or '[w]hether a law [which] has the effect of nullifying prior authoritative judicial action is but one factor, albeit an important one, to be taken into account when determining invalidity'.[83] This final point is a perceptive one, given that there are situations where the legislature amends the law rendering a final decision redundant without actually revising that decision. One example is a legislative amendment of the law upon which an injunction was granted with the result that the injunction, and the prior judicial decision upon which it was based, is rendered otiose. However, on a more fundamental level, it would be a breach of the separation of powers if Parliament were to constitute itself a tribunal, or to set up another non-court tribunal, to review, in the way of an appellate court, the final decisions of the Chapter III courts with power to substitute and enforce its own orders in the particular case.[84] Such egregious institutional breaches of the separation of powers, however, have not been evident either under the Commonwealth or the United States Constitutions, and it would be most unlikely for the position to return to that of the pre-Constitution period in the United States where such practices certainly did occur.

[79] *Harris v Caladine* (1991) 172 CLR 84 at 159.
[80] *Nicholas v The Queen* (1998) 193 CLR 173 at 255.
[81] *Plaut v Spendthrift Farm Inc* 514 US 211 (1995).
[82] *Ibid*, at 239.
[83] *Nicholas v The Queen* (1998) 193 CLR 173 at 255–6.
[84] Cf the power of the House of Representatives to convict for contempt of Parliament upheld in *R v Richards; Ex parte Fitzpatrick and Browne* (1955) 92 CLR 157; affirmed 92 CLR 171. See Mason, 'A New Perspective on Separation of Powers', n 6 above, 5. Lindell has argued that this issue might now be decided differently; 'Parliamentary Inquiries and Government Witnesses', n 6 above, 414–15.

VI. QUALIFICATIONS

Having established the inviolability of final judgments from legislative revision, the main issue to be considered is whether this strict separation of powers principle can accommodate qualification. The first and most obvious one has been stated by Winterton thus:

> [the legislature] can reverse the effect of a judicial decision by prospective alteration of the law. If such prospective legislation were directed solely at a successful litigant, it might contravene s 71 of the Constitution, not because it would be interfering with the exercise of judicial power in the concluded litigation, but because it might constitute a Bill of Pains and Penalties.[85]

In *R v Tilley*[86] at issue were the conflicting interpretations of the new section 302 of the Criminal Law Consolidation Act 1935 (SA),[87] a sentencing provision, by the South Australian Court of Criminal Appeal in *R v Dube and Knowles*[88] and the High Court in *Hoare and Easton v The Queen*.[89] To clarify the legal position in the State, the South Australian Parliament enacted section 12(2) of the Criminal Law (Sentencing) Act 1988 (SA) which provided:

> It is the intention of Parliament that subsection (1) should be interpreted in accordance with the judgment of the Full Court in *The Queen v Dube* and *The Queen v Knowles* ... and in so far as the principles of sentencing purportedly inferred by the Full Court from section 302 of the *Criminal Law Consolidation Act 1936* (the precursor of subsection (1)) were not properly so inferred, those principles must be taken to be founded on this subsection.

The defendant argued that this provision was a breach of the separation of powers in that it purported to revise the final decision of the High Court. Although finding that the separation powers was not entrenched in the South Australian Constitution, and could therefore not be a limitation on the plenary legislative powers of the Parliament of the State, nevertheless, the section was held not to be a breach of that doctrine. The legislation simply declared the meaning the legislation must bear in the future, and did not revise the effect of the final decision as between the parties. While the decision is relevant only by analogy, it is nevertheless a good illustration of the point.

---

[85] Winterton, 'The Separation of Judicial Power as an Implied Bill of Rights', n 9 above, 198–9 (citation omitted).

[86] *R v Tilley* (1991) 56 SASR 140. This case was cited by Winterton in support of this proposition, although only relevant by analogy given that there is no legally entrenched separation of judicial power in that jurisdiction: Winterton, 'The Separation of Judicial Power as an Implied Bill of Rights', n 9 above, 198, fn 63.

[87] Becoming operative on 8 December 1986.

[88] *R v Dube and Knowles* (1987) 46 SASR 118.

[89] *Hoare and Easton v The Queen* (1989) 167 CLR 348.

The second qualification which emerges from Australian authority is that Parliament can 'reverse the outcome of particular litigation by enacting retrospective general legislation which effectively renders the decision irrelevant by altering the legal rights and obligations upon which it is based'.[90] Winterton cited Quick and Garran in support of the proposition:

> The simple rule would seem to be that, just as the legislature cannot directly reverse the judgment of the court, so it cannot, by a declaratory law, affect the rights of the parties in whose case the judgment was given … [I]t may declare the rule of law to be different from what the courts have adjudged it to be, and may give a retrospective operation to its declaration, except so far as the rights of the parties to a judicial decision are concerned.[91]

This is well illustrated in the decision of the High Court in *R v Humby; ex parte Rooney*,[92] which was also discussed in the context of the pending case scenario.[93] The impugned legislation sought to overcome the effect of a prior High Court decision which effectively required the federal matrimonial causes jurisdiction vested in State courts to be exercised by judges thereof, not by Masters or Registrars. The legislation operated both prospectively and retrospectively, providing that decrees issued by Masters in matrimonial causes should have the same force and effect as if they had been issued by judges. This would have rendered unenforceable any decision which held that a matrimonial decree had been issued by a Master and was therefore invalid. Note, this was not achieved by a direct revision of a prior decision, but rather by indirectly rendering such a decision otiose.

Also illustrative is the New South Wales case of *Clyne v East*,[94] again relevant by analogy only.[95] The Court of Appeal held that even though the separation of powers was not applicable in the State,[96] the legislation in question did not, in any event, violate that doctrine. The Land and Tenant (Amendment) Act 1966 (NSW) set out the criteria by which Fair Rent Boards were to determine the rent levels at relevant premises. Section 5(3) reversed the effect of a previous decision of the New South

[90] Winterton, 'The Separation of Judicial Power as an Implied Bill of Rights', n 9 above, 199. This proposition was established in the United States in *Pennsylvania v Wheeling and Belmont Bridge Co* 59 US (18 How) 421 (1855).
[91] Quick and Garran, *The Annotated Constitution of the Australian Commonwealth*, n 64 above, 722.
[92] *R v Humby; ex parte Rooney* (1973) 129 CLR 231.
[93] See ch 2 at p 74.
[94] *Clyne v East* (1967) 68 SR (NSW) 385.
[95] See *Building Construction Employees and Builders Labourers' Federation of New South Wales v Minister for Industrial Relations* (1986) 7 NSWLR 372. See now the consequences of *Kable v Director of Public Prosecutions* (NSW) (1996) 189 CLR 51, ch 2 at 76, n 77.
[96] *Clyne v East* (1967) 68 SR (NSW) 385 at 397.

Wales Court of Appeal,[97] which allowed the Boards to take into account economic conditions as a criterion for adjusting rent levels. The legislation was retrospective, although it was to commence after the date of that previous decision. Significantly, it did not have an effect upon finally decided matters but it did have consequences for almost 600 applications for review of rent which were now to be decided solely according to the new criteria, and which also required that rents be reduced if in any case the rent had been increased by this criterion. It should be noted that the legislation did not direct that the rent be reduced in any particular case. Given that there was no effect on a previous decision as between the parties thereto, there was held to be no breach of the separation doctrine.[98]

An illustration of the ability of the legislature to reverse the effect of a judicial decision by prospective alteration of the law is the case of *Pennsylvania v Wheeling and Belmont Bridge Co*,[99] referred to extensively in chapter three.[100] In that case, the effect on the prior decision was not by way of direct reversal or revision thereof but by removing the legal basis for the continuing efficacy of the previously granted equitable relief. This type of legislation does not breach the separation of powers because it leaves intact the actual decision as between the parties, even though the decision is rendered redundant. This would remain the position even if the legislation were directed specifically at a successful litigant, so long as it did not amount to an Act of Attainder or Pairs and Penalties.

Thus, the Australian constitutional position is that the separation of powers establishes the inviolability of final judgments from legislative or executive revision. Given the dearth of authority, it is a position which has been reached almost entirely from first principles. However, beyond confirming the position adopted by the early scholars, the Australian authorities do not take the issue much further, nor do they explore further the critical issue of possible qualifications to the principle. Moreover, they do not address the question posited at the outset as to whether there are qualities in certain judgments, prima facie final ones, which render them less than 'final' such that the principle of inviolability is not applicable. It is at this point that the Australian cases begin to exhaust their usefulness, the dialogue being taken up by the authorities and academic commentary in the United States to which attention will now

---

[97]   *Rathborne v Hamill* (1966) 84 WN (Pt 1) (NSW) 504.

[98]   See R Anderson, 'Legislative Overruling of Judicial Decisions: The Concept of "Legislative Judgment": *Clyne v East*' (1969) 6 *Sydney Law Review* 283.

[99]   *Pennsylvania v Wheeling and Belmont Bridge Co* 59 US (18 How) 421 (1855); see nn 11 and 90 above.

[100]   See ch 3, at 129 above.

be given. Before examining the United States material, reference will be made to Irish cases to reinforce the position which has been developed to this point.

VII.   A REINFORCEMENT OF AUSTRALIAN JURISPRUDENCE: THE
IRISH POSITION ON FINAL JUDGMENTS

As discussed in detail in the previous chapter, the separation of powers is entrenched in the Irish Constitution,[101] resulting in the same constitutional limitation protecting the finality and conclusiveness of final judgments. In the words of Professor David Gwynn Morgan, 'the argument that the judgment should not be disturbed by legislation becomes irrefutable'.[102] In *Costello v DPP*[103] the District Court had ruled that in this criminal prosecution there was no case to answer. Relying on a power granted to the Director of Public Prosecutions ('DPP') by section 62 of the Courts of Justice Act 1936, the DPP proceeded to send the accused forward for trial on the same charges. The constitutional validity of this power was successfully challenged, the Supreme Court finding that it unconstitutionally revised the final decision of a court:

> When in the exercise of such judicial power, there is a determination of these justiciable issues, that determination cannot be set aside or reversed by any other authority. Such action would constitute an invasion of the judicial domain and an attempt to exercise a judicial power of government otherwise than by the organ of State established for this purpose by the Constitution.[104]

Had the DPP sent the accused forward to trial on different charges, as occurred in *O'Shea v DPP*,[105] then of course there would not have been a breach of the separation of powers. As Morgan pointed out, 'in assessing whether there has been an interference, a great deal depends on the precise shape and scope of the court's decision in relation to the act which is alleged to constitute the interference'.[106] An opportunity for the judicial consideration of the greater subtleties which may arise was presented in *Howard v Commissioners of Public Works (No 3)*,[107] where the High Court had made orders preventing a property development from proceeding on the basis that the permission for the development was

---

[101]   See above ch 3 at 168.
[102]   DW Morgan, *The Separation of Powers in the Irish Constitution* (Dublin, Roundhall, Sweet and Maxwell, 1997) 141.
[103]   *Costello v DPP* [1984] IR 436.
[104]   *Ibid*, at 454.
[105]   *O'Shea v DPP* [1989] ILRM 309.
[106]   Morgan, *The Separation of Powers in the Irish Constitution* (n 102 above) 142. See also *O'Connel v DPP* [1994] 2 ILRM 21.
[107]   *Howard v Commissioners of Public Works (No 3)* [1994] 3 IR 394.

ultra vires the statutory powers of the defendant. These orders were upheld on appeal to the Supreme Court. Subsequently, the State Authorities (Development and Management) Act 1993 was enacted, the relevant section providing:

> A State authority shall have, and be deemed always to have had, power ... to carry out ... development.

In the present case, it was argued that the legislation could not apply to this development, as the Supreme Court had already previously declared the development to be ultra vires under the existing law at the time. The Supreme Court accepted the argument, holding that that part of the provision which purported, in substance, to reverse a previous final judgment, was unconstitutional. The offending aspect of the provision in this regard was in the words 'and be deemed always to have had, power', as the effect was clearly and unambiguously to override the previous decision of the court. However, the Supreme Court pointed out that while the present legislation did offend constitutionally, the legislature nevertheless could remedy the situation by amending the law to validate the development. Its present judgment '[did] not decide that the matter which constituted the contravention cannot be corrected by legislation so as to allow appropriate steps to be taken *thereafter*'.[108] In other words, if legislation granted power to the defendant to proceed with the development after the original decision had been made, and without disturbing the final judgment that the development was ultra vires pursuant to the then relevant law, then there was no constitutional offence. There would be no contradiction, as Morgan pointed out, between the new legislation and the final judgment.[109] This case illustrates well the point made by Winterton above that retrospective general legislation may effectively render a decision irrelevant, without actually revising it, by altering the legal rights and obligations upon which it is based.[110]

In *State (Pine Valley Developments Ltd) v Dublin Corporation*[111] it was held by the Supreme Court that the Minister for Local Government had no power to grant planning permission for a development which otherwise would have been in breach of a development plan. This was contrary to the belief of the relevant parties prior to the case who had sought to rely on permission so granted. Legislation was enacted to validate retrospectively such permissions which had been previously granted.[112] However, the legislation was very careful not to breach the inviolability principle

---

[108]   *Ibid*, at 406.
[109]   Morgan, *The Separation of Powers in the Irish Constitution*, n 102 above, 143.
[110]   See Winterton, 'The Separation of Judicial Power as an Implied Bill of Rights', n 12 above, and accompanying text.
[111]   *State (Pine Valley Developments Ltd) v Dublin Corporation* [1984] IR 407.
[112]   Section 6(1) of the Local Government (Planning and Development) Act 1982 (Eire).

by preventing any person whose permission had already been declared invalid by a court from taking advantage of this retrospective validation. In short, while the legal position was amended with retrospective effect, final judgments were preserved. The court held that this was achieved by section 6(2) which provided that if section 6(1), which provided for the retrospective validation,

> would, but for this subsection, conflict with a constitutional right of any person, the provisions of that subsection shall be subject to such limitation as is necessary to secure that they do not so conflict but shall be otherwise of full force and effect.

In this case, Pine Valley had obtained planning permission only to have this declared invalid by the Supreme Court in the resulting litigation. The validating Act, however, prevented Pine Valley, and others subject to similar orders, from enjoying the benefits of the validation, causing one leading commentator to opine that '[i]t is not easy to see why Pine Valley should thus have been effectively penalised in this manner simply by reason of the happenstance of litigation'.[113] On the other hand, it was not denied that Pine Valley could resubmit its development application pursuant to the guidelines of the new legislation, at the same time leaving the final judgment intact. Apart from the added inconvenience and probable delay, Pine Valley could thus take advantage of the legislation.

The Irish cases thus provide reinforcement to the constitutional position developing in Australia but they also do not examine in more detail the issues which may result in qualifications to the inviolability principle. Accordingly, it is necessary to turn to the United States where this matter has been considered in more detail.

VIII.   THE UNITED STATES SUPREME COURT AND FINAL JUDGMENTS

The Framers of the United States Constitution were urgently concerned with the practice of legislative revision of final judgments, concluding (and advocating) that this practice could most surely be defeated by the entrenchment of the separation of powers.[114] It is therefore unremarkable that the issue received almost immediate judicial attention in the fledgling United States in *Hayburn's Case* in 1792.[115] The statute in issue

---

[113]   G Hogan and G Whyte, *JM Kelly The Irish Constitution* (Dublin, Butterworths, 1994) 363.

[114]   See ch 1 at 10ff above.

[115]   *Hayburn's Case* 2 US (2 Dall) 408 (1792).

purported to give jurisdiction to the federal courts to make determinations of eligibility for war pensions, and the quantum thereof, in individual cases. This, however, was made subject to review by the Secretary of War. Congress also reserved to itself a right of review. The (federal) Circuit Court for the New York District held it to be unconstitutional. It breached the separation of powers because an administrative, and therefore non-judicial, function was being imposed on the federal courts. The court was required to make a determination on the basis of uncontested applications and not by way of the hearing of disputed claims in an adjudicative judicial setting.[116] The offending aspects of the statute were repealed before the Supreme Court could rule finally on the constitutional issue. However, the Supreme Court noted the decision of the New York court on these particular issues in the margins of its own judgment, together with a letter from the justices of the (federal) Circuit Court of Pennsylvania to the President of the United States concerning the constitutional issues. In particular, that letter set out the reasons why they regarded the statute to be a breach of the separation of powers. The Supreme Court recently noted in *Morrison v Olson* that the first instance judgment and the letter to the President 'have since been taken to reflect a proper understanding of the role of the Judiciary under the Constitution'.[117]

What concerned the Pennsylvanian federal judges, in addition to the fact that the court was being required to exercise a non-judicial power, was that its judgment was rendered subject to legislative and executive revision:

> Because, if … the court had proceeded, its *judgments* (for its *opinions* are its judgments) might, under the same act, have been revised and controuled by the legislature, and by an officer of the executive department. Such revision and controul we deemed radically inconsistent with the independence of that judicial power which is vested in the courts; and consequently, with that important principle which is briefly observed by the Constitution of the United States.[118]

The constitutional prohibition on which they were relying was absolute: the review or amendment of the judgment of the court by the non-judicial branches was not permissible under any circumstances. There was a clear constitutional limitation on Congress from rendering final judgments mere advisory opinions—the consequence of making them subject to legislative or executive review. Thus, while it is clear that the principle which emerged cannot be said to be exclusively concerned with

---

[116] See the report of the Circuit Court decision, *ibid*, at 411.
[117] *Morrison v Olson* 487 US 654 (1988) at 678, fn 15.
[118] *Hayburn's Case* 2 US (2 Dall) 408 (1792) at 411–12.

the inviolability of final judgments, this early case was indicative that the Supreme Court from the outset had set its face against the revision of final judgments. This decision may also be regarded as manifesting the view of federal judges, and indeed what appears to be an assumption of the Framers, that the federal courts may refuse to give effect to legislation if it is inconsistent with their interpretation of the Constitution, even though this was not authoritatively stated until the landmark *Marbury v Madison* decision in 1803.[119]

This position was reinforced in *Calder v Bull*,[120] where the Supreme Court considered a statute passed by the Legislature of Connecticut setting aside the judgment of a State court in a civil case. Although the case was decided on other issues, viz, the interpretation of the express constitutional prohibition on retrospective legislation by federal and State legislatures,[121] Justice Iredell noted that

> the Legislature of [Connecticut] has been in the uniform, uninterrupted, habit of exercising a general superintending power over its courts of law, by granting new trials. It may, indeed, appear strange to some of us, that in any form, there should exist a power to grant, with respect to suits pending or adjudged, new rights of trial, new privileges of proceeding, not previously recognised and regulated by positive institutions . . . The power . . . is judicial in its nature; and whenever it is exercised, as in the present instance, it is an exercise of judicial, not of legislative authority.[122]

Accordingly, under the separation of powers, it must be unconstitutional.

In the other important early case, *United States v Schooner Peggy*,[123] at issue was the seizure of a French trading vessel by the United States, which vessel had been condemned and forfeited to the United States pursuant to an order by a federal court. While an appeal was pending, the United States entered into a treaty with France by which all vessels which were not yet 'definitively' condemned were to be returned to their respective nations and could not be made the subject of condemnation orders.[124] In considering what constituted 'definitive' condemnation, significant judicial comments were made in relation to final judgments. Marshall CJ, delivering the opinion of the court, first considered the

---

[119]   *Marbury v Madison* 5 US (1 Cranch) 137 (1803). See LH Tribe, *American Constitutional Law* (New York, Foundation Press, 2000) 207 ff and RH Fallon, DJ Meltzer and DL Shapiro, *Hart and Wechsler's The Federal Courts and the Federal System*, 4th edn (Westbury NY, Foundation Press, 1996) 11. For a detailed examination of the early federal decisions see J Goebel, *History of the Supreme Court of the United States, Antecedents and Beginnings to 1801* (New York, Macmillan, 1971) 554–68, 580–84.

[120]   *Calder v Bull* 3 Dall 386 (1798).

[121]   Art 1, ss 9 and 10 of the United States Constitution. The court held that the prohibition on ex post facto laws was confined to criminal laws.

[122]   *Calder v Bull* 3 Dall 386 at 398 (1798).

[123]   *United States v Schooner Peggy* 5 US (1 Cranch) 103 (1801).

[124]   *Ibid*, at 107.

argument that, as the ship had been condemned by the lower federal court, that judgment was final and therefore unassailable by reliance on the new law as between the parties. 'Definitive' condemnation[125] he held to refer to orders which had been finally made within the judicial branch, and not to condemnation orders made by a court from which an appeal was pending, as in this case.

> Every condemnation is final as to the court which pronounces it, and no other difference is perceived between a condemnation and a final condemnation, than that the one *terminates definitively the controversy between the parties*, and the other leaves that controversy still pending.[126] (Emphasis added.)

The implication was that had the condemnation been final, and not subject to appeal, it would not have been possible to reverse that decision. In the absence of a definitive condemnation in this case, the court held that the change in the law must be applied by the federal court on appeal, an early expression of the Changed Law Rule.[127] Significantly, the court also gave expression to the principle of the inviolability of final judgments in that the implication was that the law may only affect the case if it is pending, and not finally decided. However, this limitation on the legislature was not expressly stated to be based on the separation of powers, unlike the dicta in *Hayburn's case* and *Calder v Bull* above, although it certainly can reasonably be implied. The court, nevertheless, did express some disquiet about the consequences of a retroactive application of new law to pending cases which had been commenced under an old law, commenting that a court will 'struggle against a construction' which will by retroactive operation, affect the rights of the parties.[128] But such legitimate concerns did not translate into an invocation or identification of more precise constitutional limitations emanating from the separation of powers.

Judicial sensitivities relating to the protection of final judgments extended to the State courts of the immediate post-Constitution era. One example amongst many is *Bates v Kimball*,[129] where a special Act of the Vermont Legislature authorised a party to appeal from the judgment of a court, even though, under the general law, the time for appeal had expired. The court, noting that the unappealed judgment had become final, addressed the question: 'Have the Legislature power to vacate or annul an existing judgment between party and party?'[130] The reply was

---

[125] *Ibid*, at 109.
[126] *Ibid*.
[127] *Ibid*, at 110.
[128] *Ibid*.
[129] *Bates v Kimball* 2 Chipman 77 (Vt 1824).
[130] *Ibid*, at 83.

unequivocal. To annul the final judgment of a court was 'an assumption of judicial power' and therefore forbidden.[131]

> The necessity of a distinct and separate existence of the three great departments of government . . . had been proclaimed and enforced by . . . Blackstone, Jefferson and Madison [and] sanctioned by the people of the United States, by being adopted in terms more or less explicit, into all their written constitutions.[132]

This position on final judgments was certainly well understood and appreciated by the time Thomas Cooley wrote his influential *Constitutional Limitations* in the second half of the nineteenth century. Cooley found a wealth of authority, both federal and State, to support this proposition.[133] Unlike the pending case scenario, where the prerequisite element of legislative direction had to be established, here the very finality of the judgment was sufficient to render it unreviewable by the legislature. No allowances could be made—as there were in the *apologia* for the War Damage Act 1965 in the United Kingdom—for exceptional circumstances or the overriding interests of justice in the particular case. Finality itself represented the overriding interest of justice.[134] Cooley thus wrote:

> It must frequently happen, therefore, that a question of constitutional law will be decided in a private litigation, and the parties to the controversy, and all others subsequently acquiring rights under them, in the subject-matter of the suit, will thereby become absolutely and forever precluded from renewing the question in the matter then involved. *The rule of conclusiveness to this extent is one of the most inflexible principles of the law*; insomuch that even if it were subsequently held by the courts that the decision in the particular case was erroneous, such holding would not authorize the reopening of the old controversy in order that the final conclusion might be applied thereto.[135]

---

[131] *Ibid*, at 90. See also *Merrill v Sherburne* 1 NH 199 (1818)—a legislature may not vacate a final judgment and grant a new trial. And to the same effect: *Lewis v Webb* 3 Greenleaf 299 (1825); 3 Me 326 (1825).

[132] *Bates v Kimball* 2 Chipman 77 (Vt 1824) at 84.

[133] TM Cooley, *Constitutional Limitations*, 6th edn (Boston, Little, Brown & Co, 1890). See also J Sutherland, *Statutory Construction*, 2nd edn, J Lewis (ed), (Chicago, Callaghan & Co, 1904) 18–19.

[134] As far as this issue was concerned, the nineteenth century courts and commentators took a highly formalistic approach to the separation of powers. However, as will be discussed below, the inviolability of final judgments must also survive a purposive functionalist approach given that the finality of judgments is such an essential feature of the judicial power. To undermine it would be too great a usurpation of the core function of the judiciary, and therefore the inviolability principle with respect to final judgments must survive even a functionalist approach.

[135] Cooley, *A Treatise on the Constitutional Limitations Which Rest Upon the States of the American Union*, n 67 above. Cooley again cited many authorities in support of this proposition.

It was therefore clearly settled by the United States authorities, with the concurrence of its constitutional scholars, that final judgments were inviolable even from legislative revision where there was an entrenched separation of powers. This was in addition to the strictures and limitations imposed by the doctrine of res judicata. Significantly, however, it was also in the nineteenth century that the first qualifications and refinements to this absolute position were first considered. The first of these is commonly referred to as 'the *Wheeling Bridge* qualification'.

IX.   THE *WHEELING BRIDGE* QUALIFICATION

Because inviolability was attached to finality, it became an issue of fundamental importance to ascertain whether a particular judgment had the requisite quality of finality to attract absolute protection from legislative interference. Not an immediately obvious issue, it was not addressed until the mid-nineteenth century in a case where the relevant judgment provided for injunctive relief. The case arose from a dispute concerning navigation on the Ohio River and was decided by the Supreme Court in *Pennsylvania v Wheeling and Belmont Bridge Co* in 1856.[136] As mentioned briefly in the last chapter,[137] in an earlier decision involving the same parties and the same dispute—*Pennsylvania v Wheeling and Belmont Bridge Co* in 1852[138]—the Supreme Court held the defendant's bridge to be an unlawful structure to the extent that it obstructed navigation on the Ohio River in breach of federal statutes and thus rendering the structure an obstruction to the public right of free navigation. Injunctive relief was granted to the State of Pennsylvania, together with costs. The defendant was ordered to remove the bridge, or to elevate it to the levels prescribed by statute. Subsequently, Congress enacted legislation by which the bridge was rendered a lawful structure, no longer an obstruction, and mandated that ships be modified so as not to interfere with the bridge. The bridge company had lobbied Congress to amend the law in its favour,[139] raising the spectre of those earlier colonial and post-revolutionary abuses whereby final judgments were reviewed and amended by legislatures at the behest of private interests.

In the event, however, the bridge was destroyed by high winds and the State of Pennsylvania obtained a further injunction from a single judge of

---

[136]   *Pennsylvania v Wheeling and Belmont Bridge Co* 59 US (18 How) 421 (1856).
[137]   See ch 3, n 54 above.
[138]   *Pennsylvania v Wheeling and Belmont Bridge Co* 54 US (13 How) 518 (1852).
[139]   See JR Doigt, 'Is Purely Retroactive Legislation Limited By the Separation of Powers?: Rethinking United States v Klein' (1994) 79 *Cornell Law Review* 910 at 957.

the Supreme Court to prevent reconstruction except in a manner consistent with the order of the court in the previous proceedings.[140] The bridge company ignored this latter ruling and proceeded to construct the bridge lower than that required by the original court order. Pennsylvania brought the matter again before the court. The bridge company, as a defence, invoked the federal statute which declared the original bridge lawful, arguing that the requirements for a lawful structure were set out therein, rendering the requirements on which the original judgment was based redundant. At issue was the constitutionality of this statute to the extent that it overturned a final judgment of the Supreme Court in the form of the injunction in the 1852 proceedings.

The Supreme Court held the statute to be valid despite the fact that it had the effect, in substance, of overriding an earlier Supreme Court decision as between the parties. Nelson J, delivering the opinion of the court, reasoned that although the bridge 'still may be an obstruction in fact, [it] is not so in the contemplation of the law'.[141] The court vacated its injunction, but, significantly, not the original costs order against the bridge company. In so doing, the court maintained the general principle of the inviolability of final judgments pursuant to the separation of powers:

> [I]t is urged, that the act of congress cannot have the effect and operation to annul the judgement of the court already rendered, or the rights thereby determined in favor of the plaintiff. This, as a general proposition, is certainly not to be denied, especially as it respects adjudication upon the private rights of parties. When they have passed into judgement the right becomes absolute, and it is the duty of the court to enforce it.[142]

To distinguish the facts from such a situation, Nelson J distinguished different types of judicial remedy. Prior to the impugned statute, the right of navigation on the river was a public right, which the bridge obstructed. If a private party sustained special damage as a result of the obstruction, it could bring an action for damages, or, 'to prevent irreparable injury' seek an injunction to remove the obstruction. To Nelson J it was constitutionally significant that the remedy obtained was by way of equitable relief and not an award of damages:

> If the remedy in this case had been an action at law, and a judgement rendered in favor of the plaintiff for damages, the right to these would have reached

---

[140] Details of this injunction granted by Grier J can be found at 59 US (18 How) 421 (1856) at 424–7.
[141] *Pennsylvania v Wheeling and Belmont Bridge Co* 59 US (18 How) 421 (1856) at 430.
[142] *Ibid*, at 431.

beyond the reach of the power of congress . . .The decree before us, so far as it respects the costs adjudged, stands upon the same principles, and is unaffected by the subsequent law.[143]

While the costs order could not be altered by any subsequent legislation because it attracted the absolute protection afforded final judgments, different considerations applied with respect to the injunction because it lacked the requisite quality of finality which resided in an award of damages or costs. Granted pursuant to a law which made the bridge an unlawful obstruction, the continuing force of the injunction was itself subject to the maintenance of the unlawful status of the bridge. Accordingly, this was necessarily factored into the judgment such that its finality, being a conditional finality, could not attract the absolute protection of the separation of powers:

> [T]hat part of the decree, directing the abatement of the obstruction, is executory, a continuing decree, which requires not only the removal of the bridge, but enjoins the defendants against any reconstruction or continuance. Now, whether it is a future existing or continuing obstruction depends upon the question whether or not it interferes with the right to navigation. If, in the meantime, since the decree, this right has been modified by the competent authority, so that the bridge is no longer an unlawful obstruction, it is quite plain the decree of the court cannot be enforced. There is no longer any interference with the enjoyment of the public right inconsistent with law, no more than there would be where the plaintiff himself had consented to it, after the rendition of the decree.[144]

Thus, although Congress cannot revise the judgment, it can render it otiose by amending the law and thus remove the legal basis for its continuing operation, opening the way for a motion to have it stayed, or to be safely ignored, by the subject party. To this extent, this scenario resembles the pending case scenario where the legislature is permitted to 'interfere' in a pending case by substantive amendment to the law applicable in that case. However, any revision of such final judgments must remain exclusively within the discretion of the court.

X.   THE DEVELOPMENT AND CONSOLIDATION OF PRINCIPLE BY THE UNITED STATES SUPREME COURT

The *Wheeling Bridge* qualification was confirmed and accepted in the *Klein* case.[145] However, as with the direction principle, the Supreme Court did not deal with the issue of final judgments again in any detailed

---

[143]   *Ibid*, at 431.
[144]   *Ibid*, at 431–2.
[145]   *United States v Klein* 80 US (13 Wall) 128 (1871) at 146.

way until the later part of the twentieth century. The most recent decisions of that court have affirmed the inviolability principle subject to the *Wheeling Bridge* qualification. In *Plaut v Spendthrift Farm Inc*[146] the Supreme Court invalidated legislation on the precise ground that it purported to revise the final judgment of a federal court, doing so unequivocally on the basis of a breach of the separation of powers. The case is also significant in relation to the proper interpretive methodology applicable to separation of powers cases. In the introductory chapter, the position was taken that in relation to final judgments the judicial functions involved are of such a fundamental nature that it would be highly likely that both formalists and functionalists would agree as to their inviolability.[147] Even adopting a functionalist position, any breach of this principle must surely be regarded as so serious a breach of the separation of powers that it would seriously undermine the integrity of the decisional independence of the courts. Even the apparent hardship or injustice which may result in any particular case could not outweigh the serious consequences which would result in allowing for legislative revision of final judgments. The facts of *Plaut* set up a scenario which tested the limits of this proposition, tempting even those who might favour a formalist approach to make an exception.

The opinion of the court was delivered by Scalia J[148] who, adopting classically formalist reasoning, strongly endorsed the position as developed in the earlier cases above-mentioned that it was the element of finality per se which was to be afforded absolute protection. It was noted in the reasoning that it was the perceived need to remedy the abuses of legislative revision which constituted a major catalyst for the entrenchment of the separation of powers.[149] It was therefore unnecessary to identify any other feature of the legislation—such as, for example, direction—in order to invalidate it. In other words, the rule protecting final judgments went beyond the limitations of the direction principle, in particular the requirement that the substantively legislative nature of the legislation be successfully impugned. The impact of the case was heightened by the fact that the impugned legislation was unambiguously attempting to implement good public policy and was a legitimate legislative response to a matter of significant public concern. Congress had sought to come to the aid of victims of securities fraud by removing certain technical procedural bars to suits seeking remedies. This was not

---

[146]   *Plaut v Spendthrift Farm Inc* 514 US 211 (1995)('*Plaut*').
[147]   See ch 1 above.
[148]   The majority consisted of Rehnquist CJ and Scalia, O'Connor, Kennedy, Souter, and Thomas JJ. Breyer J filed an opinion concurring in the judgment (514 US 211 (1995) at 240) and Stevens J filed a dissenting opinion (514 US 211 (1995) at 246) in which Ginsburg J joined.
[149]   *Plaut v Spendthrift Farm Inc* 514 US 211 (1995) at 219.

a case of a legislature seeking to overturn a final judgment in the interests of the government or those to whom it wished to extend its patronage. That Congress was acting disinterestedly for the public good was not in question, although it was undoubtedly good politics.

As detailed in chapter three,[150] the impugned legislation was section 27A of the Securities Exchange Act 1934, coming into force on 19 December 1991.[151] Without reiterating the facts in detail here, it will be recalled that the legislation was the congressional response to two earlier Supreme Court decisions,[152] which had rendered statute-barred a significant number of meritorious civil actions for securities fraud which had been filed outside the now solely applicable federal limitation period; whereas previously plaintiffs could rely on the more generous State limitations period. This proved a considerable boon to defendants in pending suits, who wasted little time in successfully moving to dismiss claims that had been filed in reliance on the more generous State limitation periods.[153] Section 27A was enacted to overcome this result. The subsection dealing with pending cases was dealt with above in chapter three.[154] The case, however, was decided on the constitutional validity of section 27A(b) which provided for the reinstatement of proceedings which had been finally stayed by federal courts. Section 27A(b) provided:

> *Effect on Dismissed Causes of Action.* Any civil private action implied under section 10(b) of this Act that was commenced on or before June 19, 1991
>
> (1) which was dismissed as time-barred subsequent to June 19,1991, and
>
> (2) which would have been timely filed under the limitations period provided by the laws applicable in the jurisdiction, including principles of retroactivity, as such laws existed on June 19, 1991, shall be reinstated on motion by the plaintiff not later than 60 days after the date of enactment of this section.

---

[150]   See ch 3 at 145 above.

[151]   Now codified at 15 USC s 78aa-1.

[152]   *Lampf et al v Gilbertson* 501 US 350 (1991) and *James B Beam Distilling Co v Georgia* 501 US 529 (1990).

[153]   See Doidgt, 'Is Purely Retroactive Legislation Limited By the Separation of Powers?', n 139 above, 914–15; CH Sturdy, 'Section 27A Confronts *Lampf* and the Constitution' (1994) 74 *Boston University Law Review* 645. The many federal court decisions which examined s 27A are catalogued (at 648) in this article. See also MA Lazarus, 'Life After *Lampf*: The Constitutionality of New Section 27A of the Securities and Exchange Act of 1934' (1994) 68 *Tulane Law Review* 975 at 981 with the extensive catalogue of cases in fn 36; JO Himstreet, 'Section 27A and the Statute of Limitations in 10b-5 Claims: Section 27A is Necessary, It's Proper, but it's Probably Unconstitutional' (1994) 30 *Williametter Law Review* 151; CW Palm, 'The Constitutionality of Section 27A of the Securities Exchange Act: Is Congress Rubbing *Lampf* the Wrong Way?' (1992) 37 *Villanova Law Review* 1213; HJ Goldstein, 'When the Supreme Court Shuts its Doors, May Congress Re-Open Them?: Separation of Powers Challenges to S 27 A of the Securities Exchange Act' (1994) 34 *Boston College Law Review* 853 at 875–9.

[154]   See ch 3 at p 145 above.

The sub-section exhibited Congress's sensitivities to the question of final judgments. By expressly making the legislation operative subsequent to 19 June 1991, it avoided making it applicable to the previous decisions to which it was a response. Defendants who had now lost the protection afforded by those decisions proceeded to challenge the constitutional validity of s27A on grounds that, *inter alia*, Congress was in breach of the separation of powers by requiring federal courts to reopen finally decided cases.[155]

As an indication of the subtleties involved in what otherwise appears to be a straightforward final judgments issue, the decisions of the various federal courts did not produce consistent results.[156] The Court of Appeals for the Fifth Circuit in *Pacific Mutual Life Insurance Co v First Republicbank Corp*[157] upheld the constitutionality of section 27A with respect to final judgments based on that court's reading of the authorities which were held 'to support the constitutional proposition that Congress and the judiciary share authority to decide when the judiciary's word on a controversy is its last'.[158] This was a controversial outcome, with the potential to undermine any absolute principle protective of decisional independence. The Court of Appeals for the Sixth Circuit reached the opposite conclusion in *Plaut v Spendthrift Farm Inc.*[159] The court regarded as telling the fact that the statute mandated the re-opening of finally dismissed suits, albeit on the plaintiff's motion, ousting the discretion of the courts in this regard.[160] And in *Johnston v Cigna Corp*[161] the Court of Appeals for the Tenth Circuit agreed with the Sixth Circuit's finding that the section was unconstitutional as applied to final judgments, but later upheld its constitutionality in pending actions in *Anixter v Home-Stake Production Co.*[162]

The matter came before the Supreme Court on two occasions. In its consideration of the appeal in *Pacific Mutual*, namely *Morgan Stanley & Co v Pacific Mutual Life Insurance Company*,[163] the Supreme Court affirmed a decision of the Fifth Circuit and upheld the constitutional validity of section 27A in its application to final judgments. The court was equally divided on this issue, O'Connor J recusing herself, resulting in the

---

[155] The legislation was also challenged on the basis that it contravened the constitutional guarantee of due process but the case was decided on the separation of powers issue with respect to final judgments.

[156] For a detailed statement of the various federal court decisions dealing with the issue, see Sturdy, 'Section 27A Confronts *Lampf* and the Constitution', n 153 above, 648.

[157] *Pacific Mutual Life Insurance Co v First Republicbank Corp* 997 F 2d 39 (5th Cir 1993).

[158] *Ibid*, at 55.

[159] *Plaut v Spendthrift Farm Inc* 1 F 3d 1487 (6th Cir 1993).

[160] *Ibid*, at 1490.

[161] *Johnston v Cigna Corp* 14 F 3d 486 (10th Cir 1993).

[162] *Anixter v Home-Stake Production Co* 977 F 2d 1533 (10th Cir 1992).

[163] *Morgan Stanley & Co v Pacific Mutual Life Insurance Company* 511 US 658 (1994).

affirmation of the decision of the Fifth Circuit. As the court does not publish its reasons for decision in these situations, and as affirmation by an equally divided court settles no principles, the decision did not advance the resolution of the issue. This was remedied subsequently when the Supreme Court ruled on the appeal from the Sixth Circuit decision in the *Plaut* case.[164] By a majority of seven to two,[165] the Supreme Court held that the section contravened the separation of powers[166]: 'In s 27A(b) Congress has exceeded its authority by requiring the federal courts to exercise "[t]he judicial Power of the United States". U.S. Const., Art. III, s 1, in a manner repugnant to the text, structure, and traditions of Article III'.[167] The federal courts were left with no discretion as to whether suits should be re-opened, even though the legislation did require a plaintiff's motion before the reinstatement could be effected. The reinstatement was nevertheless automatic upon the motion being made and thus it was Congress who provided for the revision of finally decided cases. The decision appeared to resolve many of the uncertainties which were evident in the federal courts, particularly as a result of its formalist approach.

Scalia J, delivering the opinion of the court, first examined the various possible constructions of section 27A(b) to conclude that the section could only apply to suits which had been finally dismissed, and not merely to those pending on appeal.[168] Significantly, as indicative that he envisaged a principle which went beyond the limitations of the direction principle, he proceeded to distinguish the effect of this section from other forms of unconstitutional legislative interference. *Klein*[169] was not applicable because section 27A(b) 'indisputably does set out substantive legal standards for the Judiciary to apply, and in that sense changes the law (even if solely retroactively)', and because 'its prohibition does not take hold when Congress "amend[s] applicable law"'.[170] They referred to it as 'the new statute of limitations'.[171] *Hayburn's case* was distinguished on the basis that Congress there provided for legislative or executive review

---

[164]   *Plaut v Spendthrift Farm Inc* 514 US 211 (1995).

[165]   Scalia J delivered the opinion of the Court, with whom Rehnquist, CJ, O'Connor, Kennedy, Souter and Thomas JJ joined, Souter J filed a concurring opinion; Stevens and Ginsburg JJ dissenting.

[166]   The case was decided on separation of powers grounds and the absolute protection afforded final judgments by the principle. The majority rejected that argument that the section violated due process protections under the Fifth Amendment. (514 US 211 (1995) at 248 fn 2.

[167]   *Plaut v Spendthrift Farm Inc* 514 US 211 (1995) at 217–18.

[168]   *Plaut v Spendthrift Farm Inc* 514 US 211 (1995) at 217.

[169]   *United States v Klein* 80 US (13 Wall) 128 (1871).

[170]   *Plaut v Spendthrift Farm Inc* 514 US 211 (1995) at 218, citing a key pending scenario case, *Robertson v Seattle Audubon Society* 503 US 429 (1992) at 441.

[171]   *Ibid*, at 217.

of judicial decisions, whereas in the present circumstances the legislature was directly mandating that courts void stay orders.[172] The majority explained that 's 27A(b) offended [another] postulate of Article III just as deeply rooted in our law as those we mentioned'[173]:

> The record of history shows that the Framers crafted this charter of the judicial department with an expressed understanding that it gives the Federal Judiciary the power, not merely to rule on cases, but to *decide* them, subject to review only by superior courts in the Article III hierarchy—with an understanding, in short, that 'a judgment conclusively resolves the case' because 'a "judicial Power" is one to render dispositive judgments'. By retroactively commanding the federal courts to reopen final judgments, Congress has violated this fundamental principle.[174]

Express reference was made to the Framers' experience with colonial and post-revolutionary legislatures revising final decisions of the courts to reinforce this absolute position:

> This sense of sharp necessity to separate the legislative from the judicial power, prompted by the crescendo of legislative interference with private judgments of the courts, triumphed among the Framers of the new Federal Constitution … Before and during the debates on ratification, Madison, Jefferson, and Hamilton each wrote of the factional disorders and disarray that the system of legislative equity had produced in the years before the framing; and each thought that the separation of the legislative from the judicial power in the new Constitution would cure them.[175]

The majority further noted that '[j]udicial decisions in the period immediately after ratification of the Constitution confirm the understanding that it forbade interference with the final judgments of courts … The state courts of the era showed a similar understanding of the separation of powers'.[176] Thus, section 27A(b) was unconstitutional because it required 'its own application in a case already finally adjudicated' and therefore, by requiring a case which the courts had finally dismissed to be re-opened, it reversed 'a determination once made in a particular case'.[177]

The majority drew a very clear line between retrospective legislation which affected pending litigation—and in so doing clearly endorsed the Changed Law Rule[178]—and that which purported to revise final judgments:

---

[172] *Hayburn's case* 2 Dall 409 (1792), cited in 514 US 211 (1995) at 218.
[173] *Plaut v Spendthrift Farm Inc* 514 US 211 (1995) at 218.
[174] *Ibid*, at 218–19 (citations omitted).
[175] *Ibid*, at 221.
[176] *Ibid*, at 223.
[177] *Ibid*, at 225.
[178] *Ibid*, at 226: 'Congress can always revise the judgments of Article III courts in one sense: When a new law makes clear that it is retroactive, an appellate court must apply that

> It is the obligation of the last court in the hierarchy that rules on the case to give effect to Congress's latest enactment, even when that has the effect of overturning the judgment of an inferior court, since each court, at every level, must decide according to existing laws. Having achieved finality, however, a judicial decision becomes the last word of the judicial department with regard to a particular case or controversy, and Congress may not declare by retroactive legislation that the law applicable *to that very case* was something other that what the courts said it was.[179]

Extraneous considerations were not to be taken into account; for example, the fact that the legislation was motivated by a genuine concern to implement good public policy, even the laudable one of saving meritorious claims for securities fraud from a legal technicality.

> To be sure, a general statute such as this one may reduce the perception that legislative interference with judicial judgments was prompted by individual favoritism; but it is legislative interference with judicial judgments nonetheless. Not favoritism, nor even corruption, but *power* is the object of the separation-of-powers prohibition. The prohibition is violated when an individual final judgment is legislatively rescinded *for even the very best of reasons*, such as the legislature's genuine conviction (supported by all the law professors in the land) that the judgment was wrong; and it is violated 40 times over when 40 final judgments are legislatively dissolved.[180]

Also irrelevant was the fact that the legislation was concerned merely with mundane procedural issues such as statutes of limitations.

> The rules of finality, both statutory and judge made, treat a dismissal on statute-of-limitations grounds the same way they treat a dismissal for failure to state a claim, for failure to prove substantive liability, or for failure to prosecute: as a judgment on the merits.[181]

And, further: 'The issue here is not the validity or even the source of the legal rule that produced the Article III judgments, but *rather the immunity from legislative abrogation of those judgments themselves*'[182] (emphasis added). Stevens J, in dissent, was critical of this high formalism. He argued that if this approach were taken it would not, for example, be possible to set aside a civil judgment that had become final during a period when a natural disaster prevented the timely filing of an appeal.[183] The majority responded by laying the blame for such a result at the feet of the legislature whose responsibility it was to make provision

---

law in reviewing judgments still on appeal that were rendered before the law was enacted, and must alter the outcome accordingly' (citations omitted).

  [179]   *Ibid*, at 227.
  [180]   *Ibid*, at 228.
  [181]   *Ibid*, at 229.
  [182]   *Ibid*, at 230
  [183]   *Ibid*, at 262.

for such contingencies. The court could not remedy a lack of legislative foresight by overlooking clear breaches of the separation of powers.

> [T]he underlying statute *itself* enacts a 'rigid' jurisdictional bar to entertaining untimely civil petitions. Congress could undoubtedly enact *prospective* legislation permitting, or indeed requiring, this Court to make equitable exceptions to an otherwise applicable rule of finality, just as district courts do pursuant to Rule 60(b). It is no indication whatever of the invalidity of the constitutional rule which we announce, that it produces unhappy consequences when a legislature lacks foresight, and acts belatedly to remedy a deficiency in the law. That is a routine result of constitutional rules.[184]

In any event, as the majority noted, in such cases the courts themselves might exercise their own discretion to reopen cases.

Stevens J addressed a number of other significant issues which deserve attention but will be dealt with separately in the next chapter when detailed consideration is being given to the qualifications to the inviolability principle. One example suffices for present purposes. In commencing his *apologia* for the constitutional validity of section 27A(b), Stevens J stated: 'Throughout our history, Congress has passed laws that allow courts to reopen final judgments. Such laws characteristically apply to judgments entered before as well as after their enactment'.[185] But the point of concern is not that the legislation allows *the courts* to re-open final judgments. In the present case judicial discretion was entirely removed. The point may be a nice one, but surely an obvious one.

Functionalist tendencies were evident in the judgment of Breyer J, who, although concurring with the majority in the outcome, adopted a different line of reasoning. Breyer J, it would seem, was not enamoured of the idea of the inviolability of final judgments:

> [I]f Congress enacted legislation that reopened an otherwise closed judgment but in a way that mitigated some of the here relevant 'separation-of-powers' concerns, by also providing some of the assurances against 'singling out' that ordinary legislative activity normally provides—say, prospectivity and general applicability—we might have a different case. Because such legislation, in light of those mitigating circumstances, might well present a different constitutional question, I do not subscribe to the Court's more absolute statement.[186]

Such functionalist concerns did not receive a sympathetic reception in the more formalist majority reasoning, revealing the tensions that can still arise between these two schools even in situations where fundamental, core judicial functions are being considered. Breyer J's judgment echoes the sentiments of those who approved the War Damage Act in the United

---

[184]   *Ibid*, at 237.
[185]   *Ibid*, at 247.
[186]   *Ibid*, at 243.

Kingdom.[187] However, the constitutional climate in which that legislation was enacted was not encumbered by an entrenched separation of powers. The *Plaut* majority thus strongly rejected the notion that such mitigating factors might have any relevance in these circumstances:

> [I]t escapes us how this could in any way cause the statute to be any less an infringement upon the judicial power. The nub of that infringement consists *not* of the Legislature's acting in a particularized and hence (according to the concurrence) nonlegislative fashion; but rather of the Legislature's nullifying prior, authoritative judicial action. It makes no difference whatever to the separation-of-powers violation that it is in gross rather than particularized, or that it is not accompanied by an 'almost' violation of any other constitutional provision.[188]

This was not simply a rejection of functionalist considerations. The second sentence above is indicative that the majority were rejecting any suggestion that the relevant test here was the direction principle. The relevant test was whether the very finality of a final judgment was being compromised by the legislature, regardless of whether it was acting in a legislative or non-legislative fashion.

It is unclear whether Breyer J was advocating a functionalist approach to such questions or whether he was making a case that the direction principle be the sole applicable rule in the final judgment scenario. If the latter, then he was positing the rather incongruous position that the legislature may revise a final judgment as between the parties thereto so long as it changed the law in doing so. This would render the protection of finality less than absolute, contrary to developments in the case law and constitutional scholarship to this point. It is clearly contrary to the authority of *Hayburn's case*, which prohibited the legislative revision of particular judicial decisions, however effected. Nevertheless, aspects of his judgment would appear to follow the line of the direction principle because, as with pending cases, he argued that the court must look to relevant indicia of direction:

> In my view, the separation of powers inherent in our Constitution means that at least *sometimes* Congress lacks the power under Article I to reopen an otherwise closed court judgment. And … s 27A(b) … violates a basic 'separation of powers' principle—one intended to protect individual liberty. Three features of this law—its exclusively retroactive effect, its application to a limited number of individuals, and its reopening of closed judgments—taken together, show that Congress here impermissibly tried to *apply*, as well as *make*, the law.[189]

---

[187] See above, at 96.
[188] *Ibid*, at 239.
[189] *Ibid*, at 240–41.

If he was suggesting in the last sentence that Congress *required* the application of a law to a finally decided case, and it was this mandatory quality that made it unconstitutional, then this is entirely consistent with a principle of inviolability. However, the above passage would indicate that this factor was not enough to render the legislative act unconstitutional in the absence of other indicia of direction. In other words, it would appear as if it is the direction principle alone, and its methodology, which is relevant. Breyer J, however, did not seek to explain his position more precisely:

> But, it is far less clear, and unnecessary for the purposes of this case to decide, that separation of powers [and here he quoted from the majority judgment] 'is violated' *whenever* an 'individual final judgment is legislatively rescinded' or that it is 'violated 40 times over when 40 final judgments are legislatively dissolved'.[190]

His position might have been explained by reference to the different nature of final judgments along the lines indicated in the *Wheeling Bridge* qualification, but this was not what he was suggesting. On balance, his position is best explained by reference to the adoption of a functionalist approach, as the following passage would suggest:

> Because the law before us embodies risks of the very sort that our Constitution's 'separation-of-powers' prohibition seeks to avoid, and because I can find no offsetting legislative safeguards that normally offer assurances that minimize those risks, I agree with the Court's conclusion.[191]

Even though a great deal of common ground can be achieved between functionalists and formalists, this may nevertheless still lead to disagreements over relevant constitutional limitations in specific cases, even in relation to core judicial functions. Because Breyer J ultimately agreed that the impugned legislation was unconstitutional, this may be seen as a vindication of the view that the formalist and functionalist approaches will concur in the application of relevant constitutional limitations when core elements of branch power are being considered. On the other hand, differences are yet apparent. Breyer J did not acknowledge that finality constituted just such a core element of judicial power that even under a functionalist approach its protection was absolute. This resulted in the uncategorical rejection of this position by the majority in the following, classically formalist, passage:

> But the doctrine of the separation of powers is a *structural safeguard* rather than a remedy to be applied only when specific harm, or risk of specific harm, can be identified. In its major features (of which the conclusiveness of judicial

---

[190]   *Ibid*, at 240, quoting from 228 of the opinion of the court.
[191]   *Ibid*, at 246.

judgments is assuredly one) it is a prophylactic device, establishing high walls and clear distinctions because low walls and vague distinctions will not be judicially defensible in the heat of interbranch conflict.[192] … [T]he delphic alternative suggested by the concurrence (the setting aside of judgments is all right so long as Congress does not 'impermissibly tr[y] to *apply*, as well as *make*, the law') simply prolongs doubt and multiplies confrontation. Separation of powers, a distinctively American political doctrine, profits from the advice authored by a distinctively American poet: Good fences make good neighbors.[193]

Thus, in summary, the decision in *Plaut* clearly established in United States jurisprudence the inviolable quality of final judgments. The separation of powers prohibited the retrospective application of new law to finally decided judgments which had the effect of revising those judgments. The rationale differed from that pertaining to the direction principle. The offence here did not reside in that quality of the legislation which was mandating, or directing, the court under the guise of a properly enacted statute, to exercise its jurisdiction in a particular way. This was an irrelevant consideration. Rather, it lay in the violation of the finality of a judgment decided within the judicial hierarchy, rendering judgments of the courts other than 'dispositive'. Thus, all statutes which breach the direction principle will be unconstitutional in as much as they apply to final judgments; but not all statutes which breach the inviolability principle, will breach the direction principle. It is into this latter category that section 27A(b) belonged.

It is of course perfectly valid—although usually undesirable—for the legislature to enact retrospective law. A disadvantaged party in a concluded suit might seek to have the matter re-litigated on the basis of the new law. That party might claim that it is merely relying on a valid act of the legislature, which has priority over the finally declared judgment and upon which other parties, who were fortunate enough not to have litigated to final judgment, may rely. The successful party might object to this course on the basis that the court has finally and conclusively disposed of the matter as between the parties and that that must take priority over any legitimate act of the legislature altering the underlying law. In short, it is a priorities battle between a legitimate legislative act and the finally concluded judgment in the context of the declaration of the legal rights *of the parties*. The inviolability principle grants the victory to the latter, subject of course to the *Wheeling Bridge* qualification. But, of course, this does not prevent the judicial branch itself allowing for the matter to be reheard pursuant to its own discretion on application by the disadvantaged party. Scalia J's opinion in *Plaut* is a classic statement of a

---

[192]   *Ibid*, at 239.
[193]   *Ibid*, at 240.

formalist approach to separation of powers jurisprudence, epitomising the purposive nature of his approach: a 'structural safeguard', not a 'remedy to be applied only when specific harm', or 'risk of specific harm' can be identified. When a core aspect of branch power was at stake, 'of which the conclusiveness of judicial judgments is assuredly one', the high walls of inter-branch separation were not to be scaled. Any resulting inconvenience or hardship in the particular case was for the legislature, not the courts, to remedy, even if, as in *Plaut*, otherwise meritorious suits were allowed to fail on a technicality. The apparent rigour and inflexibility of formalism is not insisted upon for the sake of some neat, though otherwise meaningless, categorisation and ordering of the main branches of government. The clear purpose is to maintain the values which the separation of powers protects. Indeed, at the level of core branch functions, it could even be said that the purposes of the functionalist school may well be best served by this purposive formalism.

However, as with the pending case scenario, this settlement of principle was seriously compromised in *Miller v French*.[194] Before considering this case, however, it is noted that one particular interpretation of *Klein* suggests that the principle of inviolability is not limited to final judgments. Even if the legislature were to amend a law in such a way as to affect the consideration of the issues *on appeal*—which amended law the appellate court must apply pursuant to the Changed Law Rule—an inviolability principle would apply to protect the decision from which an appeal is made in these circumstances. The suggestion is that *Klein* enables the inviolability principle to override the Changed Law Rule in the pending case scenario. As noted by Gordon Young, 'if one takes this view, the Chase Court recognised a constitutional right of a successful litigant to retain the judgment of a federal … court as long as that judgment was not erroneous when entered'.[195] This possible interpretation of *Klein* was initially raised by the authors of *Hart and Wechsler's The Federal Courts and the Federal System*,[196] based on those aspects of Chase CJ's reasoning in *Klein* where he expressed concern that ruling in favour of the government might allow the legislature to prescribe rules of decision to the judiciary in pending cases. The consequence of allowing the application of amended law in the pending appeal was to allow for the *legislative* revision of decisions.[197] This particular view of *Klein*, however, ought to be rejected. By 1871 the Changed Law Rule was a

[194] *Miller, Superintendent, Pendleton Correctional Facility, et al v French, et al* 530 US 327 (2000).
[195] GG Young, 'Congressional Regulation of Federal Court's Jurisdiction and Processes: *United States v Klein* Revisited' (1981) *Wisconsin Law Review* 1189 at 1239.
[196] PM Bator , DJ Meltzer, PJ Mishkin and DL Shapiro, *Hart and Wechsler's The Federal Courts and the Federal System*, 2nd edn (Mineola NY, Foundation Press, 1973) 316, fn 4.
[197] *United States v Klein* 80 US (13 Wall) 128 (1872) at 146.

principle well established in the authorities[198] and it is most unlikely that Chase CJ intended to override it by any extension of the inviolability principle. Young, who also considered this proposition in detail, concurred with this conclusion for the same reasons, even though there was 'language in *Klein* which suggests a general repudiation of the Changed Law Rule'.[199] To argue that it is applicable to all judgments whether or not an appeal is possible is to draw too long a bow from *Klein*.

XI.   THE INVIOLABILITY PRINCIPLE TESTED: *MILLER V FRENCH*

Unlike the uncertainty surrounding the direction principle following *Roberstson*, the inviolability principle appeared settled following *Plaut*. This was short-lived, however. The novel qualifications which *Miller v French* applied to the direction principle were also applied to the principle of inviolability of final judgments.[200] It is remarkable that, while the opinion of the court was delivered by O'Connor J, Scalia J—who wrote the *Plaut* opinion—joined in this judgment, as did the other advocates of a formalist approach to these matters, Rehnquist CJ and Thomas J.[201] *Miller v French* was a hard case for reasons similar to *Plaut*. The legislative interference with judicial functions was certainly not egregious. Nevertheless, the legislation considered in this case was in certain respects more offensive to separation of powers sensibilities and, accordingly, it was quite open for the Supreme Court simply and uncontroversially to follow *Plaut* and declare the legislation unconstitutional. As mentioned in the previous chapter, at issue was the constitutionality of particular provisions of the Prison Litigation Reform Act 1995 ('PLRA'),[202] which provided for an automatic stay of previous injunctions regulating prison conditions upon the expiration of 30 days from a motion challenging any such injunction and lasting until the court makes its final decision. The effect of the automatic stay on prior judgments was, unlike the *Plaut*

---

[198]   Bator, Meltzer, Mishkin and Shapiro, *Hart and Weschsler's The Federal Courts and the Federal System*, n 196 above.

[199]   Young, 'Congressional Regulation of Federal Court's Jurisdiction and Processes', n 195 above, 1240.

[200]   See above, at 152.

[201]   The opinion of the court was delivered by O'Connor J with whom Rehnquist CJ, Scalia, Kennedy and Thomas JJ concurred. Souter J, with whom Ginsburg J joined, filed an opinion concurring with the view that the impugned provision was not held to be unconstitutional; although see below where this judgment is examined in more detail. Breyer J filed a dissenting opinion in which Stevens J joined. Because of their construction of the automatic stay provision, they did not find that there was an issue here to be decided relating to the legislative revision of final judgments. This judgment will also be examined in more detail below.

[202]   See above, at 153.

legislation, a temporary measure. Nevertheless, it did involve a legislative revision of a final judgment, particularly as it made no provision for the maintenance of relevant judicial discretion, and thus the constitutional validity of the provision was impugned on this basis by the respondents. The District Court agreed it was a breach of the inviolability principle, and the Court of Appeals for the Seventh Circuit affirmed this.[203] The Supreme Court majority, on the other hand, upheld the constitutional validity of the automatic stay despite its clear and unequivocal effect on final judgments, that they acknowledged that federal courts were precluded from exercising any equitable jurisdiction to maintain any existing injunction,[204] and the fact that they confirmed *Plaut*.[205] *Hayburn* was dealt with on the basis that the present case did not involve a review of a judicial decision by the legislature or the executive in the relevant sense.[206] *Plaut*, however, was regarded as both relevant and good law, the following passage indicating the extent of the majority's approval:

> But once a judicial decision achieves finality, it 'becomes the last word of the judicial department'. And because Article III 'gives the Federal Judiciary the power, not merely to rule on cases, but to *decide* them, subject to review only by superior courts in the Article III hierarchy', the 'judicial Power is one to render dispositive judgments', and Congress cannot retroactively command Article III courts to reopen final judgments.[207]

However, the majority proceeded to distinguish *Plaut* by relying on the *Wheeling Bridge* qualification,[208] even though there was a critical difference between the impugned provisions. That qualification, the majority noted correctly, provided that there would be no breach of the inviolability principle if the legislature amended the law, which removed the legal basis for previously-granted injunctions such that an affected party could safely ignore the imperatives of such an injunction.[209] This qualification, they reasoned, was applicable in the present circumstances. However, the majority failed to note that the *Wheeling Bridge* qualification did not apply to allow the actual *legislative* revision of the final judgment, which is exactly what the automatic stay provision was attempting, as indeed the majority had acknowledged. In *Wheeling Bridge*, the legislation was silent as to how the courts were to treat applications for the removal of prior

---

[203] *French v Duckworth* 178 F.3d 437 (7th Cir 1999).
[204] *Miller v French* 530 US 327 (2000) at 337–41.
[205] *Ibid*, at 342.
[206] *Ibid*.
[207] *Ibid*, quoting directly from *Plaut*.
[208] *Ibid*, at 346.
[209] *Miller v French* 530 US 327 (2000) at 344–5. The relevant passages in *Plaut* are at 514 US 211 (1995) at 232.

injunctions, leaving judicial discretion in this regard intact. Thus, the present case is to be *distinguished* from *Wheeling Bridge*, not *Plaut*.

The majority commenced its salvaging of the automatic stay provision by attempting a construction of the automatic stay provision by reference to the PLRA read as a whole. After making (erroneous) reference to *Wheeling Bridge*, the majority proceeded to state that the impugned provision

> does not by itself 'tell judges when, how or what to do'. Instead *[it] merely reflects the change implemented by s 3626(b)*, which does the 'heavy lifting' in the statutory scheme by establishing new standards for prospective relief … The PLRA's automatic stay provision *assists in the enforcement of ss 3626(b)(2) and (3)* by requiring the court to stay any prospective relief that, due to the change in the underlying standard, is no longer enforceable, i.e., prospective relief that is not supported by the findings specified in ss 3626(b)(2) and (3).[210] (Emphasis added.)

The central point underlying the writer's critical attitude to the reasoning is that the majority did not deny that the automatic stay provision legislatively revised or annulled the final judgments of federal courts. Rather—or so they would appear to reason—because the provision facilitated, or 'merely reflected the change' wrought by the PLRA, or 'assisted in the enforcement' thereof, it was not thereby in breach of the inviolability principle. The majority were in fact establishing a *new*, albeit highly questionable, qualification to that principle. This qualification is inconsistent with the line of reasoning in *Plaut* by which a less innocuous provision was found to be unconstitutional. Indeed in *Plaut* the majority focused exclusively on the impugned provision and its effect on final judgments, regardless of its overall effect with respect to statutory limitation periods in securities fraud cases and indeed the remainder of the Act. The fact that it mandated re-opening of final judgments was not excused by the fact that it merely reflected the (commendable) purpose of the amendments taken as a whole, or that it assisted, or indeed was essential to, their implementation. The whole focus remained the precise effect of this single subsection on final judgments.

The majority opinion in *Miller* did not seek to reconcile its novel approach with that in *Plaut*, nor did it deign to make clear precisely the basis for the adoption of these qualifications, or exceptions, to the inviolability principle. Indeed, if the very same qualifications had been applied to section 27A(b) of the Securities Exchange Act in *Plaut*, that provision should have been declared constitutional because, if read in the context of the statute as a whole, it too facilitated or assisted in the enforcement of the main relevant provisions of the Act. Also, the majority

---

[210]   *Ibid*, at 346 (citations omitted).

opinion did not attempt to address the fact that these qualifications or exceptions represented a clear departure from *Plaut's* purposive formalist line—the 'structural safeguard', 'prophylactic' view of the separation of powers—instead adopting what appears to be a more functionalist approach. Of itself, this is not necessarily problematic. However, the justification for finding no breach of the separation of powers was not of the type usually relied on by functionalists. A closer examination reveals that novel *exceptions* were being carved out from a hitherto settled legal position based on formalist reasoning. The majority departed from *Plaut* for the sole reason that the automatic stay provision was consistent with and facilitated, albeit merely procedurally, the amendments made by the Act as a whole. Yet, such a reason is surely insufficient of itself to excuse what was, in the majority's own admission, a legislative revision of a final judgment, albeit a temporary one. Such a factor has certainly never been the basis for a functionalist approach to a particular separation of powers issue. Other factors may have been taken into account to excuse the prima facie breach, such as the temporary nature of the suspension of final judgments, and the fact that the legal status of the previous injunctions was ultimately left in the hands of the federal courts. While it cannot be denied that such considerations may have played a role in the court's decision, these were not themselves expressly stated to be factors in the setting up of exceptions to inviolability. It was not, therefore, functionalist reasoning which lay behind the decision but, it would appear, a rather a misguided attempt by formalists to ameliorate the rigours of their own position.

There were other curious aspects of the opinion. For example, there was the assertion that '[t]he entry of the [automatic] stay does not reopen or "suspend" the previous judgment'.[211] Leaving aside the inconsistency with the majority's own previously stated position, why this did not constitute a legislatively mandated suspension of a previous judgment the opinion did not deign to explain, although its temporary nature may have been one explanation. The reasoning simply continued by stating that the legislation did not 'divest the court of authority to decide the merits of the termination motion', that is the ultimate outcome of the motion.[212] Of course this was so, but was this really the point? The majority opinion also stated that the automatic stay did not by itself 'tell judges when, how or what to do'.[213] That is true to the extent that it allowed the judges to make their own determinations as to the ultimate outcome. It was true also to the extent that it did not expressly identify by

---

[211] *Ibid*, at 348.
[212] *Ibid*.
[213] *Ibid*, at 346.

name, or enumerate, any particular injunction and particular proceedings to which the automatic stay might apply. However, it was mandating the stay of previously obtained judgments of federal courts, albeit pending a final decision of the court on the substantive issues. Is this not 'telling' the relevant judges that these injunctions must now be stayed? If this reasoning were to be followed, it would appear that unless there is an even more direct and specific 'telling' of the judges what to do, the legislation will stand. It seems that the absolute nature of the inviolability principle, as established in *Plaut*, was transformed into a form of the direction principle to be applied in the final case scenario.

As an aside, it should be noted that even if one were to accept that the direction principle alone could invalidate the legislation, then, for reasons which were indicated in the previous chapter, the mandatory nature of the automatic stay provision must also surely lead to the conclusion that that principle was breached. The legislature ordered, in the way of an appellate court, that a previous injunction was to be stayed, albeit temporarily, regardless of the court's own view.

It may, however, be possible to interpret *Miller* narrowly, to minimise its impact on the inviolability principle, so that it was authority for no more than the following: In addition to the *Wheeling Bridge* qualification, which the majority clearly endorsed (although incorrectly applied to the facts of this case), there will arise an exception to the inviolability principle only if all the following conditions are met:

(a)   the judgment is in the nature of a continuing prospective remedy of an equitable nature, such as an injunction, and its continuing operation is susceptible to a change in the law upon which it is based;

(b)   the legislation prescribes the mere *temporary* suspension of the judgment in circumstances where the underlying law on which the judgment was based has been amended, the court is being moved to reconsider its previous orders and the temporary nature of the suspension applies only until the court makes its final decision as to whether or not to maintain its original order; and

(c)   the purpose of the temporary suspension is to facilitate the changes to the underlying law sought to be achieved by the legislation.

If, however, the rule emerging from *Miller v French* is that final judgments can be revised whenever such revision facilitates the implementation of the new statutory regime, then the inviolability principle will be seriously undermined, particularly as a case for such facilitation would not be difficult to make out. Lloyd Anderson, for one, recognised enormous dangers in this decision:

It is crucial to understand that the automatic stay provision suspends injunctions for prospective relief against official conduct that courts have found violate the Constitution solely upon the passage of a specified time period after the filing of a motion. The Court's assertion, that the stay operates only if such injunctions are no longer enforceable because they do not meet the new standards for injunctive relief, is simply not true. The unambiguous words of the statute state that it is the motion to terminate prospective relief that operates as a stay, not any ruling by a court that the new standards are not satisfied.[214]

In Anderson's view, the majority

conferred upon Congress a new power to control the way in which the judicial branch exercises existing jurisdiction: a power to suspend prospective injunctive relief whether or not such relief satisfies new legal standards, so long as the suspension can be said to 'merely reflect,' or 'assist in the enforcement' of, or 'help to implement' the new legal standards.[215]

Anderson, queried

whether this apparently unprecedented power … properly [strikes] the balance achieved by the Madisonian Compromise between the need for an independent judiciary to enforce the supremacy of federal law and the need for a political check against abuse of authority by an unelected federal judiciary.[216]

Moreover, Anderson's concerns are not alleviated by attempting to limit the impact of the decision along the lines suggested above. He appreciated the high significance of the *Plaut* case and accordingly deprecated the dilution of its impact in *Miller v French*:

Once the judiciary has made its final decision in a case so that it is no longer pending, *Plaut v Spendthrift Farm* established that a congressional effort to reopen the case *by amending the relevant law* violates separation of powers.[217] Had the Court held otherwise, it would have posed a serious threat to judicial independence. It would have conferred power upon Congress, not merely to change the law applicable to a case, as in *Robertson*, but to direct the judicial branch not to apply the law in existence at the time it rendered its final decision and to apply new law that was not in existence at the time of final decision. The power to declare and apply the law in existence at the time of decision is a core function of the exercise of judicial power, hence the *Plaut* Court's rejection of congressional authority to take over that power preserves

---

[214]   LC Anderson, 'Congressional Control Over the Jurisdiction of the Federal Courts: A New Threat to James Madison's Compromise' (2000) 39 *Brandeis Law Journal* 417 at 442.

[215]   *Ibid*, at 443.

[216]   *Ibid*, at 444.

[217]   This sentence indicates agreement with the position taken in this monograph that the inviolability rule is applicable in the final judgment scenario, as opposed to the more limited direction principle. In other words, Anderson agrees that the inviolability principle applies to protect final judgments as between the parties even where Congress does amend the applicable law.

judicial independence. Conversely, the rule against congressional reopening of final judgments does not undermine the need for political control of the judiciary because Congress remains free to amend the relevant law for all pending and future cases … If the principle of *Miller* expands to include congressional power to dictate final judgments without amending the relevant law, however, James Madison's Compromise will have been broken.[218] (Emphasis added.)

The reasoning in *Miller v French* may create doubts about the suggested convergence of formalism and functionalism at the level of core branch functions. This occurs, however, not because of the failure of functionalists to appreciate the absolute inviolability of final judgments vis-à-vis the legislature, but rather because of the unnecessary and novel qualifications being adopted within the formalist position. However, that functionalists will always maintain the inviolability of final judgments was undermined by the position adopted by those functionalist minority judges who agreed with the majority on the outcome. This was most evident in the judgment of Souter J, in which Ginsburg J joined. They agreed that the automatic stay was mandatory in nature; that it removed judicial discretion. They recognised a separation of powers issue, but not one based solely on the fact that the legislation mandated a stay of a final judgment. Rather, such an issue would arise only 'if the time [the automatic stay] allows turns out to be inadequate for a court to determine whether the new prerequisite to relief is satisfied in a particular case'.[219] They agreed that Congress, without breaching the separation doctrine, may impose 'new conditions precedent for the continuing enforcement of existing, prospective remedial orders and require courts to apply the new rules to these orders'.[220] However, whether the automatic legislative stay of an existing order was unconstitutional depended on the provision of 'adequate time to determine the applicability of a new rule to an old order and to take the action necessary to apply it or vacate the order'.[221] It was not the inviolability principle which was being applied here by Souter and Ginsburg JJ. If 'adequate time' was provided, 'there seems little basis for claiming that Congress has crossed the constitutional line to interfere with the performance of any judicial function'.[222] Because the question of the sufficiency of time could only be determined by the relevant federal court considering a motion, then the separation of powers issue could not be decided. They would have remanded the matter to the District Court for a determination on this

[218] *Ibid*, at 447–8.
[219] *Miller v French*, 530 US 327 (2000) at 351.
[220] *Ibid*.
[221] *Ibid*.
[222] *Ibid*, at 352.

issue. In contrast to the confused formalism of the majority, this minority position clearly manifested a functionalist methodology and a marked departure from *Plaut.* Souter and Ginsburg JJ stated:

> But if determining whether a new rule applies requires time (say, for new factfinding) and if the statute provides insufficient time for a court to make that determination before the statute invalidates an extant remedial order, the application of the statute raises a serious question whether Congress has in practical terms assumed the judicial function. In such a case, the prospective order suddenly turns unenforceable not because a court has made a judgment to terminate it due to changed law or fact, but because no one can tell in the time allowed whether the new rule requires modification of the old order. One way to view this result is to see the Congress as mandating modification of an order that may turn out to be perfectly enforceable under the new rule, depending on judicial fact finding. If the facts are taken this way, the new statute might well be treated as usurping the judicial function of determining the applicability of a general rule in particular factual circumstances.[223]

It is thus not possible to state uncategorically that all functionalists will agree that finality is such a core element of judicial functions that in all circumstances it will be given absolute protection. To the extent therefore that this becomes a dominant position in Supreme Court jurisprudence, the whole question of defining the constitutional limitations on legislative interference will become very much a factor of whether a formalist or functionalist approach is taken. What can be acknowledged—hardly a radical acknowledgment—is that the convergence between formalism and functionalism is sorely tested in a hard case such as *Miller v French.* In the more obvious case, the proposition remains intact that finality remains such a core element of judicial power that both formalists and functionalists will agree that it does deserve absolute protection. Would there have been this divergence of views between formalists and functionalists if the automatic stay provision had required a permanent stay of the previous orders and the court was required to reconsider its order entirely. The writer thinks not.

Finally, the dissent of Breyer and Stevens JJ was not significant for present purposes because they held that the statute in fact said nothing as to whether the federal courts could modify or suspend the operation of the automatic stay after the period in which it was to be operative. In that silence, the majority found sufficient authority for the court to create an exception to the 90-day time limit where circumstances make it necessary to do so. As so read, the statute would neither displace the court's

---

[223] *Ibid.*

traditional equitable authority nor raise significant constitutional difficulties.[224] However, they did state that if the majority construction were correct, they would concur that there was a serious constitutional question to be considered:

> So read, the statute directly interferes with a court's exercise of its traditional equitable authority, rendering temporarily ineffective pre-existing remedies aimed at correcting past, and perhaps ongoing, violations of the Constitution. That interpretation … might give rise to serious constitutional problems.[225]

As they said no more about this, it would be speculating to attempt to gauge whether they would have followed the majority reasoning and the qualifications adopted therein.

In contrast to the Supreme Court, the Court of Appeals for the Seventh Circuit adopted a more formalist line, without any of the qualifications invented by the Supreme Court majority. In a judgment reminiscent of *Plaut*, it held that the automatic stay provision precluded courts from exercising their equitable powers to enjoin operation of the automatic stay, and so construed, was unconstitutional on separation of powers grounds.[226] Like the Supreme Court majority, it regarded the provision as unequivocal in its terms, clearly providing that a motion to terminate *'shall* operate' as a stay during a specified time period[227]; although acknowledging that courts should not lightly assume that Congress meant to restrict the equitable powers of the federal courts. But the Seventh Circuit found it 'impossible to read this language as doing anything less than that'.[228] Thus, it was 'a self-executing legislative determination that a specific decree of a federal court . . . must be set aside at least for a period of time'.[229] Accordingly, the provision directly suspended a court order 'in violation of the separation of powers doctrine' under *Plaut*. The Seventh Circuit also quoted from the decision of the Court of Appeals in *Hadix v Johnson*,[230] which made a similar ruling with respect to the automatic stay provision:

> There is no principle under which the legislative branch should enjoy a privilege of reviewing particular decisions of Article III courts that the executive branch does not have … Yet (e)(2) [the automatic stay] places the power to review judicial decisions outside of the judiciary: it is self-executing legislative determination that a specific decree of a federal court—here the decree of

---

[224] *Ibid*, at 354. This was the submission of the Solicitor General, which Breyer and Stevens JJ accepted.
[225] *Ibid*, at 357.
[226] *French v Duckworth* 178 F 3d 437 (7th Cir 1999).
[227] *Ibid*, at 443.
[228] *Ibid*.
[229] *Ibid*, at 446.
[230] *Hadix v Johnson* 144 F 3d 925 (6th Cir 1998).

addressing conditions at Pendleton—must be set aside at least for a period of time, no matter what the equities, no matter what the urgency of keeping them it in place. This amounts to an unconstitutional intrusion on the power of courts to adjudicate cases.[231] (Emphasis added.)

The Seventh Circuit also applied *Wheeling Bridge* correctly, and noted that the automatic stay was very different to the legislation considered there, as was pointed out above:

[W]e think there is an important difference between legislation that affects prospective relief, and legislation that prevents the court from preserving the status quo in whole or in part during the pendency of a suit. The former is permissible, as *Plaut* observed, but the latter touches upon the heart of the adjudicative process and as such is reserved for the Judicial Branch of government.[232]

This is no mere pedantic formalism. The Seventh Circuit looked beyond the temporary effect of the automatic stay provision to recognise that the power to review final judgments was placed 'outside the judiciary'. This placement was at the very centre of the abuses which were occurring at the time of the framing of the United States Constitution and it was this precise concern to prevent such placement that acted as a very significant catalyst for the legal entrenchment of the separation doctrine as a bulwark against such abuses. Given these sensitivities, the position taken by the Seventh Circuit, and indeed that of the Supreme Court in *Plaut*, is a more accurate reflection of the Framers' intention in this regard. The purpose of such formalism is to prevent any exceptions to this core element of judicial power, any derogation from which, even if justifiable for the best of reasons, may form the basis for others and hence the slow erosion of these critical protections. As with the pending case scenario, it was the Court of Appeals' decisions which stuck steadfastly to the developed line of authority.

XII. CONCLUSION

It is of course clear that under both formalist and functionalist approaches, the principle of the inviolability of final judgments should not be lightly departed from. The purposive formalism advocated by the writer where core functions are concerned does provide a surer protection, however. Thus, it is maintained that the correct position is reflected accurately in the majority decision in *Plaut* and that of the Seventh Circuit in *Miller v French*. The final position adopted by the Supreme

---

[231] *French v Duckworth* 178 F 3d 437 (7th Cir 1999) at 446.
[232] *Ibid*, at 445.

Court in the latter case should not be followed, or should be limited strictly to its facts. If the revision of the final judgment does not exceed these very limited parameters, and the court is left with the final word as to the future status of the injunction, then it is a proposition which may be accepted. However, the position does remain, as noted by the Seventh Circuit in *Miller v French*, that, even if the above conditions are met, a legislative revision of a final judgment has still occurred given that judicial discretion has been removed. Thus, even such a limited development should not be adopted in jurisdictions where the separation of powers is constitutionally entrenched. Should this not occur, the writer shares the formalists' concern that to make allowances at this level has the potential to result in a piecemeal erosion of separation of powers protections and will undermine the values that doctrine seeks to uphold.

Despite the difficulties outlined above, it can be concluded that the dominant rule applicable in the final judgment scenario remains the inviolability principle and not the direction principle. The question remains whether the *Miller v French* or the stricter approach will prevail. Before proceeding to draw any further conclusions, the very important and difficult issue of qualifications to the inviolability principle will be examined in detail in the following chapter.

5

Qualifications to the Inviolability of Final Judgments and Final Summation

I. INTRODUCTION

DOES THE ABSOLUTE protection of final judgments allow for any qualifications? This is an important question not least because it tests the consistency of the approach of formalists and functionalists to core separation of powers issues. In light of the writer's view that *Miller v French* should not be followed, or its reasoning should be avoided or limited strictly to its facts, the qualifications which will be examined are not those which were postulated in that case. Before examining the various individual qualifications, consideration will first be given to a number of miscellaneous preliminary issues.

It is noted that retrospectivity does not per se result in a breach of the inviolability principle[1] unless the legislation retroacts to reopen or revise a finally decided case. As stated succinctly in *Plaut*,

> [h]aving achieved finality … a judicial decision becomes the last word of the judicial department with regard to a particular case or controversy, and Congress may not declare by retroactive legislation that the law applicable *to that very case* was something other than what the courts said it was.[2]

Merely because the legislation deals with procedural issues or minor technical legal issues, such as those relating to limitation statutes, or costs, does not excuse it from the rigours of inviolability.[3] Neither is any allowance made for legislation which reopens final judgments in a whole class of cases as opposed to a particular case:

> To be sure, a general statute … may reduce the perception that legislative interference with judicial judgments was prompted by individual favoritism;

---

[1] As to the constitutional validity of retrospective laws, see *Polyukhovich v Commonwealth* (1991) 172 CLR 501, where a minority only were willing to regard retrospective criminal laws as unconstitutional as a breach of the separation of powers.

[2] *Plaut v Spendthrift Farm Inc* 514 US 211 (1995) at 227.

[3] *Ibid*, at 228.

but it is legislative interference with judicial judgments nonetheless. Not favoritism, nor even corruption, but power is the object of the separation-of-powers prohibition.[4]

Equally irrelevant in this precise context are the merits of the legislation in terms of public policy, even in circumstances where the purported revision is adverse to the interests of government. Again, as noted in *Plaut*,

> [t]he prohibition is violated when an individual final judgment is legislatively rescinded for even the *very best* of reasons, such as the legislature's genuine conviction (supported by all the law professors in the land) that the judgment was wrong; and it is violated 40 times over when 40 final judgments are legislatively dissolved.[5]

This is a proposition which was not countered by the Supreme Court majority in *Miller v French*.

The inviolability principle should not be confused with the jurisdiction invested *in courts*, whether by statute or inherent jurisdiction, to revise final judgments, or re-open previously decided suits. In *Plaut* the majority dealt with an argument that such jurisdiction, when conferred by relevant procedural rules of court, was indicative that legislatures can provide for the revision of final judgments. Federal Rule of Civil Procedure 60(b), expressly referred to in *Plaut* in this context, authorised federal courts to relieve parties from a final judgment on grounds such as fraud, new evidence, excusable neglect or 'any other reason justifying relief'. Stevens J in dissent had stated that such a provision was an example of legislation retroactively requiring final judgments to be re-opened.[6] The majority correctly dismissed this argument because the discretionary *judicial* revision of judgments

> does not impose any legislative mandate to reopen upon the courts, but merely reflects and confirms the courts' own inherent and discretionary power, 'firmly established in English practice long before the foundation of our Republic,' to set aside a judgment whose enforcement would work inequity. Thus Rule 60(b) and the tradition that it embodies ... are irrelevant to the claim that legislative instruction to reopen impinges upon the independent constitutional authority of the courts.[7]

Moreover, the majority did not doubt the constitutional validity of a statute which provided, for example, that all default judgments rendered in the future may be reopened within ninety days after their entry.[8] The

[4] *Ibid.*
[5] *Ibid.*
[6] *Ibid*, at 256.
[7] *Ibid*, at 234.
[8] *Ibid.*

majority reasoned that if 'the law then applicable says that the judgment may be reopened for certain reasons, that limitation is built into the judgment itself, and its finality is so conditioned'.[9] In other words, such judgments are not sufficiently 'final' so as to secure the absolute protection of the inviolability principle.

Similarly, the inherent jurisdiction of superior courts to revise their own judgments in particular circumstances is not inimical to the inviolability principle. This jurisdiction stems from those residual powers which a court may draw upon 'as necessary whenever it is just or equitable to do so, and in particular to ensure the observance of due process of law, to prevent improper vexation or oppression, to do justice between the parties and to ensure a fair trial between them'.[10] The relevant circumstances in which the court may exercise this inherent jurisdiction are virtually identical in common law systems. Thus, while a final judgment determines finally the dispute between the parties,[11] the courts maintain a limited equitable power to set aside a judgment which was procured by fraud or where relevant new evidence is discovered after the trial.[12] However one defines the jurisdiction, it is a jurisdiction residing in the *judicial* branch, and accordingly, there is no breach of the inviolability principle if legislation reinforces it.

The above propositions are straightforward and uncontroversial. More problematic, and therefore deserving greater consideration, are those issues which arise from the *Wheeling Bridge* qualification, introduced in the previous chapter, and the issue of the waiver by the government of its rights secured by a final judgment in its favour. It is these issues that will be the main concern of the remainder of this chapter.

II.   THE *WHEELING BRIDGE* QUALIFICATION, THE REGULATION OF PUBLIC RIGHTS AND 'CONDITIONAL' FINAL JUDGMENTS

The *Wheeling Bridge* qualification was established in circumstances where the legislature amended the law so as to render an injunction ordered by the court otiose and thus unenforceable. It will be recalled that in

---

[9]   *Ibid.*

[10]   P de Jersey, 'The Inherent Jurisdiction of the Supreme Court' (1985) 15 *Queensland Law Society Journal* 325 at 351. See also K Mason, 'The Inherent Jurisdiction of the Court' (1983) 57 *Australian Law Journal* 449; W Lacey, 'Inherent Jurisdiction, Judicial Power and Implied Guarantees Under Chapter III of the Constitution' (2003) 31 *Federal Law Review* 57, esp 63ff.

[11]   JD Heydon, *Cross on Evidence*, 6th edn (Sydney, Butterworths, 2000) 153. See also KR Handley, G Spencer Bower and AK Turner, *The Doctrine of Res Judicata*, 3rd edn (London, Butterworths, 1996) ch 5.

[12]   B Cairns, *Australian Civil Procedure*, 5th edn (Sydney, Law Book Co, 2002) 494. The relevant principles were summarised in *Wentworth v Rogers (No 5)* (1986) 6 NSWLR 534 at 538. The public interest in the finality of final judgments was referred to at 538.

Wheeling Bridge, as noted in the previous chapter, Congress had legislated to regulate the public right to navigation on rivers. The Supreme Court upheld legislation which altered the legal specifications for bridges over the Mississippi River despite the fact that previously—pursuant to the then applicable legislation—the court had found a bridge to be an unlawful structure and ordered by way of injunction that the relevant party comply with those legislative requirements. This injunction was rendered susceptible to being vacated on the basis of the new law, which the court proceeded to do, refusing nevertheless to vacate the costs order.

It has been suggested that the rationale underlying the court's decision was the fact that the impugned legislation was regulating a public right; thus setting up a possible 'public rights' exception to the inviolability principle. In the words of CH Sturdy,

> [w]hile the Court refused to upset private rights settled by final judgment, it recognized the power of Congress subsequently to affect public rights, such as the right to free navigation involved in this case ... This ... narrow exception to the separation of powers doctrine permitted Congress to disturb a final judgment only to the extent that it affected a public right.[13]

In support of this proposition, Sturdy referred to *Hodges v Snyder*,[14] a case where the Supreme Court dissolved an injunction against the formation of a consolidated school district following legislation which authorised such a consolidation, and yet upheld the judgment in the previous decision relating to an award of damages. Also cited in support was *Johnston v Cigna Corp* where the Court of Appeals for the Tenth Circuit attributed to *Wheeling Bridge* the proposition that 'a judgment declaring a public right may be annulled by subsequent legislation'.[15]

So to define this 'exception' is to put too fine a point on the reasoning from these cases. The better view is that this is but a particular instance of a broader proposition that where the judgment is itself conditional on the continuation of a particular state of the law then the legislation will not breach the inviolability principle when it purports to amend the relevant law, even if this would render previous injunctive relief otiose and no longer enforceable. This is on condition, of course, that the actual final judgment is not itself revised by the legislation. If the proposition was based purely on the fact that the legislature was regulating a public right, this would constitute a rather arbitrary exception to the inviolability principle and one which could not be logically sustained as arising from the separation of powers. Merely because a legislature may be seeking to

---

[13]   CH Sturdy, 'Section 27A Confronts Lampf and the Constitution' (1994) 74 *Boston University Law Review* 645 at 656.
[14]   *Hodges v Snyder* 261 US 600 (1923) at 604.
[15]   *Johnston v Cigna Corp* 14 F 3d 486 (10th Cir 1993) at 492.

achieve a legitimate regulatory end does not grant constitutional immunity from the inviolability principle to the resulting legislation. Thus, given that the rationale rather lies in the nature of the judgment which is being amended, the role of the court in supervising its own judgments is maintained.

Although in both *Wheeling Bridge* and *Hodges* the court did allow the legislation to undermine the effectiveness of a previously granted injunction, it did not allow the change in the law to interfere with the costs order. The implication is that that would similarly be the position with an award of damages, or any orders which were not clearly subject to any future amendment of the law. While the court retained its inherent discretion to revise its judgments, it did not allow this to be the automatic consequence of legislative action. Thus, for example, in *System Federation No 91 v Wright*,[16] the Supreme Court—noting its continuing supervisory role in relation to equitable relief[17]—recognised the continuing power of the judicial branch to modify or indeed deny 'the enforcement of rights the statute no longer gives'.[18] The judgment added that the 'court must be free to continue to further the objectives of [a statute] when its provisions are amended'.[19] That, in the view of the writer, is the ultimate basis for the *Wheeling Bridge* qualification, and not an independently standing 'public rights' qualification.

III.   THE WAIVER QUALIFICATION

In his examination of the Australian constitutional position, Winterton noted that the 'Commonwealth Parliament could not validly specifically set aside the decision of a court exercising federal jurisdiction', adding that 'it presumably could waive the benefits of a decision given in its favour'.[20] He is undoubtedly correct. There is nothing in the separation of powers to suggest that the government, like any other litigant, could not waive the benefits of a judgment in its favour.

However, this apparently straightforward proposition may still give rise to critical separation of powers issues relating to the method adopted to effect the waiver. It is one thing for the government, for whatever policy reason, simply not to seek to enforce a particular judgment in its favour. It is a more complicated issue when the government might seek

---

[16]   *System Federation No 91 v Wright* 364 US 642 (1961).
[17]   *Ibid*, at 647.
[18]   *Ibid*, at 652.
[19]   *Ibid*, at 651–2.
[20]   G Winterton, 'The Separation of Judicial Power as an Implied Bill of Rights' in GJ Lindell (ed), *Future Directions in Australian Constitutional Law* (Sydney, Federation Press, 1994) 189 at 199.

to effect the waiver by way of legislation to that effect. No offence to the inviolability principle would occur were the legislation simply to provide that the government would not enforce the judgment. Merely waiving a benefit in no way interferes with a final decision. This proposition was clearly accepted by the United States Supreme Court in the series of cases which will be examined in more detail below.[21] In any event, it is a proposition which can be sustained from first principles.

   This seemingly straightforward position is rendered complex when the aim of the legislation is to waive not the benefits of the judgment, but rather the particular benefit accruing from the legal status of the finally decided proceedings as res judicata, thus enabling the other party to seek to have the matter re-litigated. Such legislation, which has been enacted in the United States, usually expressly purports to empower a federal court to rehear a particular matter previously decided in the government's favour. Prima facie, it would not cause offence to the inviolability principle if the legislation merely facilitated re-litigation by preventing the government itself from relying on a res judicata plea. As defined by Spencer Bower, Turner and Handley, a res judicata

> is a decision pronounced by a judicial tribunal having jurisdiction over the cause and the parties which disposes once and for all of the matters decided, so that except on appeal they cannot afterwards be relitigated between the same parties or their privies.[22]

As a result, the final decision 'estops ... any party to the litigation or his privies from disputing the correctness of the decision in later litigation against any other party'.[23] This is applicable to both matters of fact and law. Also, and very significantly for present purposes, '[n]o further claim may be made upon the same causes of action in subsequent proceedings between the parties or their privies ... Every *res judicata* operates as an estoppel'.[24] The principle is not simply for the benefit of litigants. '[I]t is against public policy, and oppressive to the individual, to re-agitate disputes which have been litigated to a conclusion'.[25]

   A separation of powers problem arises, however, if the legislation goes one step further and provides that *the court* is not to entertain a res judicata plea and must proceed to rehear a matter finally decided. Although very rare, such legislation has emerged in the United States where matters of some political sensitivity are involved and the government is anxious to allow for a particular matter to be reconsidered by the

---

[21]   *Cherokee Nation v United States* 270 US 476 (1926); *Pope v United States* 323 US 1 (1944); *United States v Sioux Nation of Indians* 448 US 371 (1980).
[22]   Handley, Spencer Bower and Turner, *The Doctrine of Res Judicata*, n 11 above, 1.
[23]   *Ibid.*
[24]   *Ibid.*
[25]   *Ibid.*

courts. This has occurred with compensation awards by federal courts to indigenous people for the acquisition of land by the federal government and with which the indigenous litigants were dissatisfied. Rather than legislating to address this dissatisfaction, that is, by simply legislating a settlement, Congress deflected the matter back to the courts. The motivations may be similar to those, identified by Professor Geoffrey Lindell,[26] which influence governments in the setting up of tribunals of enquiry, made up of judges, to investigate and report on matters of considerable political moment. The removal of the resolution of such controversies from the political arena at once depoliticises them, sends a message that the government shares the concerns of the public, buys time and allows interest in the matter to wane.[27] It may well be the case that the government is able to avoid a lot of the 'political fall-out' from making a direct decision itself. However, it comes at the significant cost of exposing the courts to political controversy and the serious possibility of 'political abuse and adverse criticism'.[28]

In the context of such legislation, the inviolability principle takes on critical significance. Here, the central distinction must be maintained between legislation which facilitates the rehearing of a previously decided matter by merely waiving the *government's* right to plead res judicata, and legislation which goes further to interfere with the *court's* own discretion in this regard. Although this would most likely fall foul of the direction principle, it would breach the inviolability principle in that it would in substance be legislating for the re-opening of a finally decided case. It would also breach that rule because, absent any formal plea in this regard, the res judicata could otherwise come to the attention of the court and the court is prevented from raising the res judicata issue on its own motion. In Australia, the position is that it is no longer strictly necessary for one of the parties to plead res judicata before the court may consider the issue.[29] As in the United States, as will be seen below, the court may itself raise the matter on its own motion. The difficulty in maintaining this distinction is well illustrated by the United States cases.

The United States Supreme Court regards as constitutionally valid any legislative waiver of the plea of res judicata, while also declaring unconstitutional legislation which either prevents a non-government party from relying on the plea, or prevents the court itself from considering it on its own motion. This is unobjectionable and is a position which can

---

[26] G Lindell, *Tribunals of Inquiry and Royal Commissions* (Sydney, The Federation Press, 2002).

[27] *Ibid*, at 8.

[28] *Ibid*.

[29] *Laws Holdings Pty Ltd v Short* (1972) 46 ALJR 563; Heydon, *Cross on Evidence*, n 11 above, 172; Handley, *Spencer Bower and Turner, The Doctrine of Res Judicata*, n 11 above, 218–19.

clearly be followed in all jurisdictions with an entrenched separation of powers. The difficulties which have emerged in the United States relate rather to the maintenance of the distinction between a mere waiver and a requirement that the court not consider the plea. The Supreme Court has tended to read down liberally legislation so as to characterise it as effecting a mere waiver, even in circumstances where the legislation is clearly effecting a prohibition on the plea even on the court's own motion. This is clearly illustrated in the leading case, *United States v Sioux Nation of Indians*,[30] which will be examined in detail below.

From a functionalist perspective, such liberality may be unobjectionable given that the government, acting in the public interest, is waiving a benefit in favour of the non-government party. Be that as it may, one need not adopt a formalist position to reject this proposition on the basis that the government has nevertheless chosen to effect its waiver by means of a legislative re-opening of a finally decided case, albeit indirectly by precluding the consideration of res judicata by the court. By deflecting the matter to the courts through the adoption of such a method, the inviolability principle has thereby clearly been breached. Even from a functionalist perspective, this must give rise to countervailing policy considerations because such methods constitute an umambiguous threat to the separation of powers given the core element of branch function represented by finality.

The waiver qualification was first mentioned in uncontroversial circumstances in *Nock v United States*,[31] where the Court of Claims held that Congress may legislate to prevent the government from relying on a final judgment in its favour to prevent the other party from re-litigating the matter. In this case, at issue was whether a particular government supply contract was in fact binding on the government, the Court of Claims deciding in an earlier decision that it was not.[32] Congress, however, subsequently came to the view that 'there were equities existing between the government and said Nock, arising out of this contract',[33] and that it was therefore appropriate that Nock be compensated. Congress resolved that the matter 'be, and it is hereby, referred to the Court of Claims for its decision, in accordance with the principles of equity and justice'.[34]

When the Court of Claims did reconsider the matter, it did not regard the resolution of Congress as breaching any particular constitutional separation of powers principle. The Court stated that 'it cannot be

---

[30] *US v Sioux Nation of Indians* 448 US 371 (1980) ('*Sioux Nation*').
[31] *Nock v US* 2 Ct Cl 451 (1867).
[32] *Ibid*, at 455.
[33] *Ibid*, at 457.
[34] *Ibid*.

doubted that a legislative direction to a court to find a judgement in a certain way would be little less than a judgement rendered directly by Congress'.[35] However, in the present instance, by its resolution Congress did not attempt to 'grant a new trial *judicially*', nor had it '*reversed* a decree of this court; nor attempted in any way to interfere with the administration of justice' as all it was doing was coming 'into court through this resolution and *say*[ing] that it will not plead the former trial in bar, nor interpose the legal objection which defeated a recovery before'.[36] Moreover, the legislation did not prevent the court itself from dealing with the question of res judicata on its own motion. Thus, it was clearly permissible for Congress to have a finally decided matter revisited by the court in such circumstances. The significant point was that it was left to the Court of Claims to decide whether it would rehear the matter.

This position was affirmed by the Supreme Court in *Cherokee Nation v United States*.[37] In a prior decision between the parties, the Supreme Court had affirmed a judgment of the Court of Claims for the payment of principal and interest by the United States to the Cherokee Nation, which amount was paid in full.[38] The Cherokee presented a further claim arguing that the Court of Claim's calculation of interest was erroneous. Congress, not being unsympathetic but also not willing to deal with it by exclusively legislative means, enacted a Special Act of Congress in 1919,[39] which 'conferred' upon the Court of Claims 'jurisdiction' to 'hear, consider, and determine' the claim for interest, expressly referring to the prior judicial calculation.[40] The court was

> authorised, empowered, and directed to carefully examine all laws, treaties, or agreements … in any manner affecting or relating to the question of interest on said funds.[41]

The court did reconsider the interest payable but did not alter the amount, a decision which the Supreme Court unanimously affirmed on appeal.[42] The latter court, when it examined the legislation but for which 'the question here mooted would have been foreclosed as res judicata',[43] and despite the use of the word 'directed' in the statute, read down the

---

[35] *Ibid*.
[36] *Ibid*, at 457–8.
[37] *Cherokee Nation v United States* 270 US 476 (1926).
[38] *Cherokee Nation v United States* 202 US 101 (1906).
[39] 40 Stat 1316.
[40] *Cherokee Nation v United States* 202 US 476 (1926) at 478.
[41] *Ibid*.
[42] The opinion of the court was delivered by Taft CJ.
[43] *Ibid*, at 486.

provision as a mere waiver by the United States of its right to plead res judicata.[44] 'The power of Congress to waive such an adjudication of course is clear'.[45]

It also emerged that the court exhibited an easy willingness to identify a new right or obligation which was being created by the legislation, so as to characterise the legislation as merely facilitating the judicial determination of a matter pursuant to this new right. This became first apparent, again in uncontroversial circumstances, in *Pope v United States*.[46] The Supreme Court unanimously affirmed the general waiver proposition outlined above, but here articulated an additional qualification. The legislation in issue provided that 'notwithstanding any prior determination' or 'any statute of limitations', jurisdiction was conferred on the Court of Claims to 'hear, determine and render judgment' upon certain claims with respect to a building contract between Pope and the United States.[47] It continued in section 2 to provide that the Court of Claims

> is hereby directed to determine and render judgment at contract rates upon the claims of the said Allen Pope for certain work performed for which he has not been paid, but of which the Government has received the use and benefit; namely, for the excavation and concrete work found by the court to have been performed by the said Pope in complying with certain orders of the contracting officer.[48]

As there had already been litigation between Pope and the government on this very issue, section 3 provided that

> the court shall consider as evidence in such suit any or all evidence heretofore taken by either party in the previous case which was expressly mentioned.[49]

The Act proceeded to go into some detail as to how the amount to be paid to Pope under the contract was to be calculated.

At first instance, the Court of Claims held the legislation to be unconstitutional as a direction to the Court, thus breaching the *Klein* principle.[50] This was in addition to the fact that it had already conferred on the plaintiff 'the unusual privilege of litigating the same case a second time in a court which once had finally decided it'.[51] The Supreme Court on the other hand, held that the legislation merely effected a waiver of

---

[44] *Ibid.*
[45] *Ibid.*
[46] *Pope v United States* 323 US 1 (1944). The opinion of the court was delivered by Stone CJ.
[47] Section 1 Special Act of 27 February 1942.
[48] *Pope v United States* 323 US 1 (1944) at 3.
[49] *Ibid.*
[50] *Pope v United States* 100 Ct Cl 375 (1944).
[51] *Ibid*, at 379.

the right to plead res judicata. The judgment against Pope in the earlier litigation remained 'undisturbed by any subsequent legislative or judicial action'.[52] Moreover, the legislation created

> a new obligation … of the Government to pay petitioner's claims where no obligation existed before. And such being its effect, the Act's impact upon the performance by the Court of Claims of its judicial duties seems not to be any different than it would have been if petitioner's claims had not been previously adjudicated there.[53]

Congress merely created a new legal right as a 'recognition of a moral … obligation' to pay the petitioner's claims.[54] Thus, the *Wheeling Bridge* qualification became relevant because the further litigation between the parties was based on an amendment to the law, and not a legislatively mandated revision of a final judgment.

In these circumstances, there remains the concern that the government is seeking to avoid an earlier judgment of the court under the guise of the legislative creation of a new legal obligation. The facts of this case bear scrutiny, however, because the legislation was not creating a new legal right generally, but rather one which was directed very specifically to the matters in issue between the government and Pope, and which had generally been decided upon previously. The concern is that, in substance, the legislation was effecting a revision of a final decision under the guise of establishing a new right. This may be ameliorated by the fact that the benefit accrued to the non-government party. Nevertheless, if excessive liberality is applied so as to interpret the statute as one creating a new legal right in highly specific and individualised circumstances, then the protections afforded by the inviolability principle may be eroded.

This problem became apparent in the leading case, *United States v Sioux Nation of Indians*.[55] The particular difficulties to which it gave rise were highlighted by the compelling lone dissent of Rehnquist J.[56] While confirming the principle that Congress may waive the benefit of a judgment in its favour, and indeed waive its plea of res judicata to facilitate relitigation, it was only Rehnquist J who, correctly in the view of the writer, held that the legislation in question did breach the inviolability principle in unambiguously directing the re-opening and revision of a final judgment.

---

[52]   *Pope v United States* 323 US 1 (1944) at 9.
[53]   *Ibid.*
[54]   *Ibid*, at 10.
[55]   *United States v Sioux Nation* 448 US 371 (1980).
[56]   The opinion of the Court was delivered by Blackmun J, in which Burger CJ, Brennan, Stewart, Marshall, Powell and Stevens JJ joined. White J filed a separate opinion concurring in part and concurring in the judgment. Rehnquist J was the sole dissentient.

At the heart of the case was the claim by the Sioux Nation for compensation with interest for the taking of reservation land by the United States in breach of an 1868 treaty between the parties. That taking was effected by an 1877 statute in purported compliance with an agreement between the parties subsequent to the original treaty. The Sioux maintained that the 1877 statute breached the original treaty, a position from which they did not resile. Eventually, in 1920, Congress enacted a special jurisdictional Act to enable the Sioux to litigate their claim in the Court of Claims, before which the matter came in 1942. The Sioux argued, inter alia, that the 1877 statute effected a taking of the land in breach of the Just Compensation Clause in the Fifth Amendment to the Constitution.[57] Although finding that the Sioux did have a moral claim, the court found that there was no unconstitutional taking, as did the Supreme Court on appeal. The court's precise finding on the Fifth Amendment point was the subject of some confusion when the Supreme Court came to consider the matter again in 1980, where the majority maintained that the Court of Claims had not decided the Fifth Amendment point, but rather had declined to rule on it because of lack of jurisdiction. Rehnquist J, on the other hand, found that the constitutional point had in fact been finally decided upon against the Sioux, a finding which appears to be the only one open on the reading of the 1942 decision. As will be seen, this difference of views was significant in defining the different attitude to the impugned legislation in that case.

Subsequent to the 1942 decision, Congress enacted the Indian Claims Commission Act 1946, which empowered the Sioux to resubmit their claim to the Indian Claims Commission. After protracted litigation, the Indian Claims Commission decided in 1968 that:

- the 1877 Act effected a taking for which the Sioux were entitled to just compensation under the Fifth Amendment;
- the Court of Claims, in its 1942 decision, had dismissed the Fifth Amendment claim for want of jurisdiction and had not determined the merits of the taking claim;
- the 1942 decision did not bar further action as res judicata with respect to the specific issue of the Fifth Amendment just compensation claim;
- Congress in 1877 had made no effort to give the Sioux the full value for the ceded reservation lands but allowed instead merely subsistence rations; and that, therefore, the consideration given the Sioux in the 1877 Act bore no relationship to the property acquired; and
- Congress did not act as trustee for the Sioux when taking the land,

---

[57]   *Sioux Tribe v United States* 97 Ct Cl 613 (1942); cert denied: 318 US 789 (1943).

but acted pursuant to its power of eminent domain when it passed the 1877 Act, and must pay the Sioux just compensation.

The United States appealed to the Court of Claims[58] where it was held, without reaching the merits, that the claim relating to the taking of the relevant land was barred by the res judicata effect of its 1942 decision; the constitutional claim having been determined and, whether resolved 'rightly or wrongly',[59] such claim was now barred as res judicata. However, because the United States did not raise objection to the finding of the Commission that it had acquired the land through a course of unfair and dishonourable dealing, it was held that the Sioux were entitled to damages in this regard (US$17.5 million), although interest could not be awarded because they had not succeeded on the constitutional point.[60] The Sioux, nevertheless, continued to maintain that they were entitled to such interest. Congress, although competent to legislate so that such payment could be made, nevertheless legislated to deflect the matter back to the courts. It was aspects of this legislation which were challenged in the 1980 *Sioux* case.

Thus, in 1978, Congress purported to amend section 20(b) of the Indian Claims Commission Act 1946[61] to provide expressly for de novo review by the Court of Claims of the merits of this particular constitutional compensation claim based on a violation of the Fifth Amendment, without having regard to the doctrines of res judicata and collateral estoppel.[62] This was no mere waiver of the right to plead res judicata. The provision was unambiguously prescribing the re-litigation of the very issue which had been dealt with earlier, directing the court that there should be no 'regard to the defence of res judicata or collateral estoppel' and that it should reconsider the matter de novo on motion by the claimants. This is despite the fact that the matter had been already twice considered by the Court of Claims and in relation to which certiorari had been denied by the Supreme Court on both occasions, thus rendering the Fifth Amendment issue final. In the event, the Court of Claims proceeded to reconsider the matter,[63] this time affirming the Indian Commission's earlier holding that the 1877 Act effected a taking of the land which was not a non-compensable act of congressional guardianship over tribal property. It characterised the Act as an unconstitutional taking, an exercise of Congress's power of eminent domain over Indian property,

[58] *United States v Sioux Nation* 207 Ct Cl 234, 518 F.2d 1298 (1975).
[59] *Ibid* at 249; 1306.
[60] *Ibid* at 214; 1302.
[61] United States Code s 70s(b) (1976 edn, Supp II).
[62] *United States v Sioux Nation* 448 US 371 (1980). Statute set out in full at 391.
[63] *United States v Sioux Nation* 220 Ct Cl 442 (1979); 601 F. 2d 1157 (1979).

and held that the Sioux were in fact entitled to just compensation, together with an award of interest calculated as from the time of the taking.

The United States appealed to the Supreme Court against that aspect of the decision that held the original Act was an unconstitutional taking in breach of the Fifth Amendment, and for which the federal government had to pay interest on the amount of compensation. The Supreme Court, by a majority, upheld the constitutional validity of the legislation.[64] The opinion, delivered by Blackmun J, was unexceptionable in terms of legal principle, confirming the existence of the inviolability principle, the waiver qualification, and indeed the *Wheeling Bridge* qualification.[65] However, it dismissed the res judicata point on the basis that the Court of Claims, in its 1942 consideration of the matter, had declined for want of jurisdiction to decide the Fifth Amendment point and therefore did not find that the Sioux were not entitled to compensation under the Fifth Amendment. Accordingly, it was held that the 1975 decision of the same court erroneously found that the constitutional issue was res judicata.[66]

Thus, despite the clear purport of the 1978 statute, the majority were able to hold that it did not impermissibly disturb the finality of a judicial decree by the Court of Claims, nor did it render the earlier judgments of the Court of Claims merely advisory opinions which were now being reviewed by legislative fiat, albeit by the courts themselves.[67] Moreover, although not relevant for present purposes, the majority held that the statute did not breach the *Klein* direction principle. Congress, rather, merely exercised its broad constitutional power to define and 'to pay the Debts … of the United States', recognising its obligation to pay a moral debt not only by direct appropriation, but also by waiving any valid defence to a legal claim against the United States which might be available. Thus, when the Sioux returned to the Court of Claims following the passage of the 1978 Act, the court held that they were seeking the 'judicial enforcement of a new legal right'.[68] This was, in other words, a similar situation to that found to exist in *Pope.* The way was thus open for the Sioux to raise the Fifth Amendment point for consideration in current proceedings:

> Congress had not 'reversed' the Court of Claims' holding that the claim was barred by res judicata, nor, for that matter, had it reviewed the 1942 decision rejecting the Sioux' claims on the merits. As Congress explicitly recognised, it only was providing a forum so that a new judicial review of the Black Hills

---

[64]   *United States v Sioux Nation* 448 US 371 (1980).
[65]   *Ibid*, at 390 ff.
[66]   *Ibid*, at 384.
[67]   *Ibid*, at 392.
[68]   *Ibid*, at 406.

claim could take place. This review was to be based on the facts found by the Court of Claims after reviewing the merits of the Court of Claims' decisions, and did not interfere with the finality of its judgments. Moreover, Congress in no way attempted to prescribe the outcome of the Court of Claims new review of the merits. The court was left completely free to reaffirm its 1942 judgment that the Black Hills claim was not cognizable under the Fifth Amendment, if upon its review of the facts and the law, such a decision was warranted.[69]

This reasoning raises some concern, particularly in relation to that aspect which led to the conclusion that the legislation did more than merely waive res judicata, but in fact facilitated the enforcement of a 'new legal right'. However, in its very acknowledgement that the court was at liberty 'to reaffirm its 1942 judgment that the Black Hills claim was not cognizable under the Fifth Amendment', was not the majority accepting that the statute's requirement that the Court of Claims reconsider the merits of the claim—the Sioux' 'new legal right'—was indeed requiring the revision of a final judgment? Surely, it is not relevant with respect to this particular point that the court was at liberty to reaffirm. The point is that Congress was directing the federal courts to reconsider a suit on which it had twice ruled previously, the latter judgment finding that its reconsideration of the matter was barred by res judicata. Indeed, the Court of Claims was being required, at the very least, to revise its 1975 decision that the matter was res judicata. Be that as it may, this did not excuse the statute from prohibiting the consideration of the defence of res judicata, whether formally pleaded or on the court's own motion. The legislation purported positively to prohibit the court, by legislative fiat, from considering the issue at all. This conclusion was not reached by the adoption of functionalist reasoning. Rather, it appears to be the result of a failure of judicial will to adhere strictly to its own reasoning in its adoption of a very liberal interpretation of the statute.

By contrast, the judgment of Rehnquist J adhered to the inviolability principle and exhibited the particular merits of the purposive formalist position in circumstances where the core elements of the judicial power were at issue. For Rehnquist J the problematic aspect of the legislation was not that it was an expression of congressional concern to ensure the appropriate compensation to the Sioux, the merits of which he did not dispute. Rather it was that it sought to address this problem by other than strictly legislative means and by deflecting the matter to the courts. Because the very legal issue on which the question of interest depended had been already judicially decided, it could not ensure that this strategy would succeed unless it also removed any obstacle to the re-opening of a finally decided case; in effect mandating the re-opening. Merely waiving

---

[69]   *Ibid*, at 406–7.

the right of the United States as a party to plead res judicata would not have guaranteed success; Congress had to ensure that res judicata would not be considered in any way by the court. It was precisely to guard against such legislative actions, in the quite reasonable and accurate assessment of Rehnquist J, that the separation of powers was constitutionally entrenched.

Critical to his finding was his conclusion that the Court of Claims in 1942 had ruled upon the Fifth Amendment point, where it had held that Congress had not taken the land unconstitutionally but had exchanged the relevant land for rations and other grazing lands. When the Supreme Court declined to review that judgment[70] it thus rendered the decision final. This finality was reinforced when, after the Sioux again resubmitted their claim on the unconstitutional taking of their land in 1975, the United States successfully pleaded res judicata in the Court of Claims. The court held in the 1975 case that the original Court of Claims decision had clearly decided that the appropriation of the relevant land was not an unconstitutional taking because Congress in 'exercising its plenary power over Indian tribes, took their land without their consent and substituted for it something conceived by Congress to be an equivalent'.[71] As stated by Rehnquist J,

> the court found no basis for relieving the Sioux from the bar of *res judicata* finding that the disability 'is not lifted if a later court disagrees with a prior one'. The court thus considered the equities entailed by the application of *res judicata* in this case and held that relitigation was unwarranted. Again, this Court denied certiorari.[72]

There was thus no basis for the majority view that the constitutional point was being litigated as if it had not been judicially decided previously. The fact that the 1978 legislation left the court at liberty to affirm its previous decision did not detract from the fact that it was a legislative re-opening of a final judgement, there being no judicial principle justifying the decision to afford the respondents an additional opportunity to litigate the same claim.[73] Indeed, the mere fact that Congress did not dictate to the court the particular result to be reached did not negate the fact that a breach of the inviolability principle had occurred. He equated the legislation with the action of an appellate court when it reversed 'a

[70] *Sioux Tribe v United States* 318 US 789 (1943).
[71] *United States v Sioux Nation* 207 Ct Cl 234 at 243; 518 F 2d 1298 at 1303 (1975).
[72] *United States v Sioux Nation* 448 US 371 (1980) at 426–7.
[73] *Ibid*, at 425–6.

trial court for error, without indicating what the result should be when the claim is heard again'.[74] The text itself was unambiguously prescriptive in this regard.[75]

Rehnquist J expressly stated his concern that the protection afforded the judicial power would be seriously eroded if this legislation were allowed to stand. He noted that, in this latest rehearing of the matter, neither party submitted additional evidence. The Court of Claims had recourse merely to the record generated in 1942 before the Commission. On this very same record, the Court of Claims now decided that Congress had not acted in the best interests of the Sioux, contrary to its own prior finding, and held instead that the United States had in fact appropriated the land in question without affording just compensation. 'This Court now embraces this second, latter-day interpretation of the facts in 1877'.[76] In effect, Congress had thus

> reviewed the decisions of the Court of Claims, set aside the judgment that no taking of the Black Hills occurred, set aside the judgment that there is no cognizable reason for relitigating this claim, and ordered a new trial. I am convinced that this is nothing other than an exercise of judicial power reserved to Art. III courts that may not be performed by the Legislative Branch under its Art. I authority.[77]

He impliedly likened the concerns and actions of Congress with the legislative revision of judicial decisions prevalent in colonial times and at the time of the drafting of the United States Constitution:

> It is also apparent that Congress must have 'reviewed' the merits of the litigation and concluded that for some reason, the Sioux should have a second opportunity to air their claims. The order of a new trial inevitably reflects some measure of dissatisfaction with at least the manner in which the original claim was heard. It certainly seems doubtful that Congress would grant a litigant a new trial if convinced that the litigant had been fairly heard in the first instance. Unless Congress is assuming that there were deficiencies in the prior judicial proceeding, why would it see fit to appropriate public money to have the claim heard once again? It would seem that Congress did not find the opinions of the Court of Claims fully persuasive. But it is not the province of Congress to judge the persuasiveness of the opinions of federal courts—that is the judiciary's province alone. It is equally apparent that Congress has set aside the judgments of the Court of Claims. Previously those judgments were dispositive of the issues litigated in them; Congress now says that they are not. The action of Congress cannot be justified as the regulation of the jurisdiction

---

[74]   *Ibid*, at 430.
[75]   *Ibid*, at 426.
[76]   *Ibid*, at 427.
[77]   *Ibid*.

of the federal courts because it seeks to provide a forum for the purposes of reviewing a previously final judgment in a pending case.[78]

Indicating that his formalism did not blind him to the relevant subtleties and qualifications which attach to the separation of powers in this context, Rehnquist J acknowledged that the mere fact that the judicial process was being affected by an Act of Congress did not thereby, ipso facto, result in a breach the separation of powers. Such would be the case, for example, where it regulated jurisdiction, or changed the import of a final judgment by subsequently amending the law, creating new legal rights or obligations, or by waiving available defences. 'But, as the Court apparently concedes, Congress may not, in the name of those legitimate actions, review and set aside a final judgment of an Art. III court, and order the courts to rehear an issue previously decided in a particular case'.[79] The majority did not disagree with these particular constitutional propositions, only with their application to the present legislation. Thus, in response to the position taken by the majority that Congress was merely providing 'a forum so that a new judicial review of the Black Hills claim could take place', Rehnquist J responded that this was 'the essence of an appellate or trial court decision ordering a new trial'.[80] This was no mere regulation of jurisdiction by Congress, but the ordering of a retrial of a previously decided case.

Rehnquist J then proceeded to explore in more detail the critically important qualifications to the rule of inviolability. He accepted that it is certainly valid for a litigant to alter the consequences of a judgment by agreeing to obligations beyond those required by that judgment.[81] He also accepted the *Wheeling Bridge* qualification. Thus, it was open to Congress simply to enact a law providing that the Sioux should recover all the interest on the value of the Black Hills since 1877. But, there was no attempt to enact such a law here.

> Counsel for respondents in fact stated at oral argument that he could not persuade Congress 'to go that far'. Congress has not changed the rule of law, it simply directed the judiciary to try again. Congress may not attempt to shift its legislative responsibilities and satisfy its constituents by discarding final judgments and ordering new trials.[82]

The present legislation, by not limiting itself to a mere waiver, purported to prevent the court from exercising its inherent jurisdiction to maintain the finality of a prior judgment by raising the issue of res judicata on its

---

[78]   *Ibid*, at 430–31.
[79]   *Ibid*, at 429.
[80]   *Ibid*.
[81]   *Ibid*, at 431.
[82]   *Ibid*, at 431–2.

own motion.[83] Rehnquist J pointed out that the policy factors underlying the doctrine were not limited to protecting the individual litigant from vexatious multiplication of suits, but also related to the broader public interest in the administration of justice, and, in particular, the termination of disputes, the firm establishment of the finality of judicial decisions (beyond separation of powers concerns) and 'the avoidance of unnecessary judicial waste'.[84] It made no difference whether one party consented to re-litigation, given the judiciary's independent concern to prevent the misallocation of judicial resources and 'second-guessing prior panels of Art III judges when the issue has been fully and fairly litigated in a prior proceeding'.[85] He continued:

> Since the Court of Claims found in this case that there was no adequate reason for denying res judicata effect after the issue was raised and the respondents were given an opportunity to demonstrate why res judicata should not apply, it is clear that the issue has been heard again only because Congress used its legislative authority to mandate a rehearing. The Court of Claims apparently acknowledged that this in fact was the effect of the legislation, for it did not state that readjudication was the product of a waiver, but rather that through its decision the court 'carried out the *obligation imposed upon us* in the 1978 jurisdictional statute … It is quite clear from a comparison of the 1942 decision of the Court of Claims and the opinion of the Court today that the only thing that has changed is an interpretation of the events which occurred in 1877. The Court today concludes that the facts in this case 'would not lead one to conclude that the Act effected "a mere change in the form of investment of Indian tribal property."' But that is precisely what the Court of Claims found in 1942. There has not even been a change in the law, for the Court today relies on decisions rendered long before the Court of Claims decision in 1942. It is the view of history, and not the law, which has evolved. The decision is thus clearly nothing more than a second interpretation of the precise factual question decided in 1942. As the dissenting judges in the Court of Claims aptly stated: 'The facts have not changed. We have been offered no new evidence'. It is therefore apparent that Congress has accomplished more than a private litigant's attempted waiver, more than legislative control over the general jurisdiction of the federal courts, and more than the establishment of a new rule of law for a previously decided case. What Congress has done is uniquely judicial. It has reviewed a prior decision of an Art. III court, eviscerated the finality of that judgment, and ordered a new trial.[86]

Although the view of Rehnquist J did not prevail, *Sioux Nation* did remain authority for the proposition that the government's right to plead res judicata may be waived by legislation. His difference with the

---

[83] *Ibid.*
[84] *Ibid.*
[85] *United States v Sioux Nation* 448 US 371 (1980) at 433.
[86] *Ibid*, at 433–4.

majority related more to the rigour with which the inviolability principle should be applied. Irrespective of the merits of the legislation, it is very difficult to refute Rehnquist J on the point that the legislation went further than a mere waiver to effect a re-opening of a finally decided case. The inviolability principle was clearly breached. His concern to protect the courts' inherent jurisdiction to raise res judicata was favourably received in the *Plaut* case.[87] The Solicitor General, in his amicus curiae role in that case, argued that even if *Sioux* was read in accord with its holding, it nevertheless established that Congress may require Article III courts to re-open their final judgments, since 'if res judicata were compelled by Article III to safeguard the structural independence of the courts, the doctrine would not be subject to waiver by any party litigant'.[88] The Supreme Court majority in *Plaut* thought that this was putting too fine a point on the proposition:

> What may follow from our holding that the judicial power unalterably includes the power to render final judgments, is not that waivers of res judicata are always impermissible, but rather that, as many federal Courts of Appeals have held, waivers of res judicata need not always be accepted—that trial courts may in appropriate cases raise the res judicata bar on their own motion. See, *e.g.*, *Coleman* v. *Ramada Hotel Operating Co.*, 933 F. 2d 470, 475 (CA7 1991); *In re Medomak Canning*, 922 F. 2d 895, 904 (CA1 1990); *Holloway Constr. Co.* v. *United States Dept. of Labor*, 891 F. 2d 1211, 1212 (CA6 1989).[89]

Thus, if the government's legislative waiver of res judicata left intact the court's discretion to consider the res judicata effects of a prior decision, there would be no constitutional problem.[90] There is no reason to suggest why this position should not also be the position which pertains in all jurisdictions maintaining a constitutional separation of judicial power.

However, the tendency of the courts in the United States to read down impugned enactments so that they do not offend the above principle is notable. Is this part of the same trend which has seen the erosion of the direction principle in that jurisdiction? Is it reflective of such deference to Congress that constitutional limitations arising from the separation of powers protecting decisional independence are not applied as rigorously as they might be? This is epitomised in *Sioux Nation* where the legislation unambiguously directed the court to disregard the plea of res judicata, in all circumstances. It is for this reason that Rehnquist J's dissent is compelling, and in the view of the writer, to be preferred. If the inviolability principle is to mean anything, if its absolute nature is to be respected (in light of the fact that it is protecting such a fundamental

---

[87]   *Plaut v Spendthrift Farm Inc* 514 US 211 (1995).
[88]   *Ibid*, at 231.
[89]   *Ibid*.
[90]   *Ibid*.

element of judicial power), then it is submitted that such a liberal reading of legislation should not become the norm. Nor should the establishment of new rights, in highly particularised circumstances, be too easily read into the impugned legislation, which rights are then regarded as being the basis for new litigation, as opposed to the re-opening of a final decision. The constitutional limitations which are derived from the separation of powers are endangered by what appears to be a failure of will to apply them rigorously. Unlike the direction principle, the inviolability principle is relatively straightforward to apply and any justification for departure from its consequences is therefore lessened. The present writer is of course not unsympathetic to the unfortunate results which may result in the individual case. The concern to maintain a strong inviolability principle is rather a reflection of the broader harm which will ensue to the polity and to public confidence in the independent exercise of judicial power if its tenets are not observed steadfastly.

IV. CONCLUSIONS ON THE FINAL CASE SCENARIO

In summing up, it is possible to identify the following constitutional limitations based on the separation of powers which govern the relationship between legislatures and the courts in the final judgment scenario:

The general rule is that final judgments cannot be legislatively revised or amended as between the parties thereto: the inviolability principle. A fortiori, the legislature cannot constitute itself a tribunal, or set up another non-court tribunal, to review, in the way of an appellate court, the final decisions of courts with power to substitute and enforce its own orders in the instant case, or indeed to order a rehearing of the matter. The following considerations do not allow for exceptions to be made to the principle:

(a) that the legislation retroacts upon final judgments where purely procedural or technical legal issues have been decided in the final case, such as those arising for example from limitations statutes, orders for costs, or orders staying proceedings;

(b) that the legislation purports to re-open a class of case as opposed to a particular case; and

(c) that the legislation self-evidently implements good public policy or is otherwise meritorious, even in circumstances where the legislation is adverse to the immediate interest of the government.

The inviolability principle does not prevent the enactment of procedural rules which expressly preserve or define the jurisdiction of the courts to amend their own decisions pursuant to their own discretion on specified grounds. The legislature may, however, overrule (as opposed to revise) a final decision in the sense that it amends the law applied or declared by a court as long as the legislation does not retroact to revise the final judgment as between the parties. The legislature may also nullify the effect of a final judgment by enacting retrospective general legislation which effectively renders the decision irrelevant by altering the legal rights and obligations on which it is based but without expressly revising the actual decision. The classic example is the circumstance which pertains in the scenario covered by the *Wheeling Bridge* qualification; that is, the law on which injunctive relief is based is amended—for example, where the law now permits what it previously prohibited—such that the injunction is rendered unenforceable if the party against whom the order was made now acts in ways permitted by the new law. The new law cannot directly reverse the final decision, which remains intact albeit rendered otiose. This qualification only applies to those final judgments and resulting orders whose continuing efficacy is conditional upon the maintenance of the particular state of the law. Thus, for example, an award of damages, or an order for costs, cannot be nullified in this way.

The legislature may waive the benefits of a final judgment in favour of the government by requiring that the government shall not seek to have the decision enforced. The legislature may also waive the right of the government to plead res judicata in circumstances where such a plea would otherwise be open to it in its status as litigant. However, a legislature cannot require the court to refuse to entertain such a plea, even on its own motion, as the substantial effect of such a requirement would be to re-open for revision the final judgment of the court. The tendency apparent in the United States cases, *Sioux Nation* in particular, to read down legislation which clearly and unambiguously prevents a court from considering res judicata at all, should be avoided. Similarly, the tendency, also apparent in the majority judgment in *Sioux Nation*, to characterise too easily the legislation as establishing a 'new right', and then to facilitate the hearing of matter on the basis of this new right, should also be avoided. This is not to suggest that where the law is amended in such circumstances as covered by *Wheeling Bridge* that the qualification emerging from that case should not be followed. Rather, in highly particularised circumstances such as in *Pope* and *Sioux Nation*, the courts should not too easily seek to find a new right being created by the amendment as a means of saving it from offence to the inviolability principle. The more rigorous approach to such matters, as manifested in the judgment of Rehnquist J in *Sioux Nation*, is to be preferred.

Finally, in relation to the *Miller v French* qualifications as they pertain in the United States, there is no basis on which to suggest that these should be followed. That is, no allowance should be made for a specific provision of an Act which, although the provision itself breaches the inviolability principle, when read in the context of the Act as a whole can be characterised as facilitating the implementation of the Act, assists in its enforcement, or merely reflects the change wrought by the Act. These grounds cannot justify an exception being made to the inviolability principle.

6

Protections Afforded Decisional Independence in Jurisdictions without an Entrenched Separation of Powers

I.   INTRODUCTION

THE DIFFICULTIES WITH the constitutional principles emanating from the separation of powers protecting decisional independence were made evident in the previous chapters. These difficulties, it was argued—while partly inherent in the separation of powers doctrine, and acknowledged by constitutional scholars—became evident in the more recent cases, resulting in considerable uncertainty as to the precise scope of the principles and their rather tentative application. Remedies were suggested.

It was also observed that the constitutional entrenchment of the separation of powers made imperative the definition of branch functions, at least at some basic level, and that the direction and inviolability principles, applied pursuant to a purposive formalist methodology, would provide the surest protection for the decisional independence of the courts. Prima facie, the corollary is that in the absence of such entrenchment, and in the absence of other relevant constitutional principles, it may not be possible to declare invalid offending legislation in this regard, even where the separation of powers is respected as an important constitutional convention or otherwise informs a jurisdiction's constitutional ethos. An examination of the constitutional position in the United Kingdom thus becomes particularly germane as a counterpoint to those jurisdictions with an entrenched separation of powers. Excluding for the moment considerations arising from its European Union involvement, the position which appears presently to pertain in the United Kingdom is that the separation of powers does not provide judicially-enforceable constitutional limitations on the legislative competence of Parliament. This general proposition is subject to certain important qualifications which will be discussed below, but, as foreshadowed when the *Burmah*

Oil case was discussed in this context,[1] the extent to which decisional independence is protected is largely dependant on the degree of self-restraint exhibited by Parliament in deference to judicial independence and to the rule of law. Even when breaching decisional independence, Parliament may nevertheless seek justification by invoking the existence of 'exceptional' circumstances which trump the maintenance of the constitutional niceties in the instant case. In the context of this chapter, the extent to which the protections afforded decisional independence can emanate from other sources, particularly rule of law principles, canons of statutory interpretation, and extra-legislative sources such as rights conventions, becomes particularly important.

II.   THE UNITED KINGDOM AND THE SEPARATION OF POWERS

Britain's unwritten constitution and the influence of Diceyan orthodoxy, emphasising parliamentary sovereignty and a fusion of powers which did not countenance judicial invalidation of legislative action, has meant that the separation of powers has not become a source of judicially-enforceable constitutional limitations.[2] The precise status of the doctrine has varied from time to time and the extent to which the doctrine nevertheless provides some restraint on legislative interference with judicial process cannot be determined with precision. It can be said, however, that constitutional entrenchment of the separation doctrine has not been part of the Westminster constitutional tradition; a tradition which has not, in any event, placed much store by written constitutions with their accompanying legalism and rigidities.[3] The prevailing influence from that quarter has been the maintenance of judicial independence in terms of *institutional* independence through the protection of tenure and remuneration, and afforded statutory protection in the Act of Settlement in 1701,[4] as opposed to the protection of judicial power in a functional sense. While separate 'judicial' and 'executive' functions had received recognition by this time in English constitutional theory, MJC Vile significantly noted that

> it is the irony of this period [that this recognition] was not associated very closely with the establishment of the independence of the judges, formally

---

[1]   *Burmah Oil Company (Burma Trading) Ltd v Lord Advocate* [1965] AC 75.
[2]   See above, ch 4 at 196.
[3]   See above, ch2 at 57ff.
[4]   MJC Vile, *Constitutionalism and The Separation of Powers*, 2nd edn (Indianapolis, Liberty Fund, 1998) 60.

achieved ... with the *Act of Settlement*, but rather the judicial function came to be associated with the House of Lords as a final court of appeal.[5]

It is significant that Locke, who did emphasise the importance of an independent and impartial judiciary, did not give recognition to a strictly separate 'judicial' power.[6] Even after there emerged a more explicit recognition of a distinct judicial power in the writings of Montesquieu and Blackstone,[7] a legal separation of that power was not adopted. Speaking of the influence of the separation of powers in British constitutionalism, Professor Eric Barendt made the following salient observation:

> [C]ommentators on United Kingdom constitutional law have paid relatively little attention to the principle. Dicey set in this ... a very bad example. Virtually the only mention made of it in the *Introduction to the Study of the Law of the Constitution* occurs in his treatment of the *droit administratif* in France, when he explains the doctrine's influence on the administration's independence from judicial review by the ordinary courts. In contrast Sir Ivor Jennings did discuss the separation of powers at some length. He devoted much of the opening chapter of *The Law and the Constitution*, as well as an entire appendix, to the doctrine, only to dismiss its coherence and significance for the protection of civil liberties ... Other treatments tend to be either brief or dismissive ... One important collection of essays even ignores the principle altogether.[8]

The doctrine has thus come to be overshadowed by the more dominant constitutional principles of parliamentary sovereignty and the rule of law and, despite the statutory protection afforded institutional independence,[9] there has not been the same imperative as in those jurisdictions already examined to define precise constitutional limitations deriving from it. Those scholars who relegate the doctrine to minor influence point to the fact, correctly, that the British constitutional scene is to be characterised more by an empirical, pragmatic approach than adherence to theoretically 'pure' or 'checks and balances' approaches. This is manifested in a certain fusion of powers at both an institutional and functional level.[10] Examples abound. Ministers of the Crown are both part of the Executive and also members of Parliament; the Lord Chancellor was a

---

[5] *Ibid.*

[6] *Ibid*, at 65.

[7] *Ibid*, at 83–105, 111–16, 173.

[8] E Barendt, 'Separation of Powers and Constitutional Government' [1995] *Public Law* 599 at 599–60.

[9] In addition to the relevant provisions of the Act of Settlement, see also s 11(3) of the Supreme Courts Act 1981, and ss 33 and 133 of the Constitutional Reform Act 2005 (UK).

[10] See C Munro, *Studies in Constitutional Law*, 2nd edn (London, Butterworths, 1999) at 304, who cites a number of constitutional scholars in this regard, including O Hood Phillips, de Smith, Holdsworth, Emden, Robson and Griffith. See also E Barendt, 'Fundamental Principles' in D Feldman (ed), *English Public Law* (Oxford, Oxford University Press, 2004) 38; A Tomkins, *Public Law* (Oxford, Oxford University Press, 2003) 37) See the numerous examples now cited in Tomkins (*ibid*) 37–8 and Feldman, *English Public Law* (*ibid*) 37–9.

member of Cabinet (prior to the Constitutional Reform Act 2005 (UK)) and at the same time eligible to sit as a judge in the Appellate Committee of the House of Lords; the judicial committee of the House of Lords was the highest court even though the House was also the upper house of the legislature; in its enforcement of parliamentary privilege Parliament exercises judicial functions; delegated legislation enables the executive to exercise legislative functions; and the chairing by judges of public enquiries indicates that judicial office is no bar to exercising executive roles. As Professor Adam Tomkins has pointed out,

> [w]hile we can as a matter of practice identify a distinct legislature, executive, and judiciary, that is to say, we can say descriptively that there exists in England a Parliament, a government, and a court structure, we cannot argue that the constitution prescribes that such a division should exist. To the limited extent that there is some separation along these lines, it is merely descriptive and not normative.[11]

On the other hand, scholars such as Professors Colin Munro,[12] Eric Barendt[13] and TRS Allan[14] regard the doctrine as a fundamental underlying constitutional principle which informs the whole British constitutional structure. Munro states that the doctrine has shaped, and continues to shape, the constitutional arrangements and thinking in the United Kingdom in a number of important ways.[15] Barendt structures his analysis of British constitutional law around the separation of powers but has conceded that 'the constitution in England does not strictly observe the separation of powers in either version [pure or modified] of the theory'.[16] Moreover, even though in Barendt's view the doctrine plays a much greater role than allowed for by others, the point remains, as he concedes, that '[t]he courts may not control the constitutionality of legislation in England, with the single exception of incompatibility with EC law'.[17] Allan does take the argument a step further to suggest that the orthodox conception of parliamentary sovereignty, and the positivist assumptions upon which it is based, ought not be followed in all respects. He has argued that the separation of powers doctrine, and other underlying fundamental constitutional principles (especially the rule of

---

[11]   Tomkins, *Public Law*, n 10 above, 38.

[12]   Munro, *Studies in Constitutional Law*, n 10 above, 328–32.

[13]   *An Introduction to Constitutional Law* (Oxford, Oxford University Press, 1998). See also 'Separation of Powers and Constitutional Government' [1995] *Public Law* 599.

[14]   TRS Allan, *Law Liberty and Justice, The Legal Foundations of British Constitutionalism* (Oxford, Clarendon Press, 1993) chs 3 and 8, and TRS Allan, *Constitutional Justice, A Liberal Theory of the Rule of Law* (Oxford, Oxford University Press, 2001).

[15]   Munro, *Studies in Constitutional Law*, n 10 above, 328–32.

[16]   Barendt, 'Constitutional Fundamentals, Fundamental Principles', n 10 above, 39.

[17]   *Ibid*, at 40.

law and equal justice[18]), should be relied on in the appropriate case to invalidate Acts of Parliament, particularly when the independence of the judiciary is threatened. Allan's thesis will be explored in more detail below, but it is noted here that should his thesis ever be accepted more fully by the courts in Britain, it is arguable that the constitutional limitations represented by the direction principle and the inviolability principle may establish themselves in the context of an unwritten constitution. Taking together all the various scholarly views of the present position, and subject to compatibility requirements with European law, the most that can be said is that the separation of powers does play an influential role as a constitutional principle, but as a non-binding one. Professor Robert Stevens has summarised the position well:

> In modern Britain the concept of the separation of powers is cloudy and the notion of the independence of the judiciary remains primarily a term of constitutional rhetoric. Certainly its penumbra, and perhaps even its core, are vague. No general theory exists, although practically the English have developed surprisingly effective informal systems for the separation of powers; although it should never be forgotten that the system of responsible government is based on a co-mingling of the executive with the legislature. The political culture of the United Kingdom, however, provides protections for the independence of the judiciary, which are missing in law.[19]

Despite this fluid situation, the independence of the judiciary has enjoyed a particular respect as a principle of fundamental importance. The ancient protections in the Act of Settlement 1701 have been reinforced in the reforms established by the Constitutional Reform Act 2005 which manifest a continuing, and heightened, influence of the separation of powers as a significant constitutional principle. The protections of tenure and salary of course remain,[20] and while the office of the Lord Chancellor is retained, that office is no longer at the head of the judiciary in England and Wales and is replaced by the Lord Chief Justice, who is also President of the Courts of England and Wales.[21] The Lord Chief Justice has been given enhanced powers to influence decisions relating to the administration of the court system, including its resourcing. Section 3(1) of the Constitutional Reform Act places a general obligation on the Lord Chancellor and other Ministers of the Crown and 'all with the responsibility for matters relating to the judiciary or otherwise to the

---

[18]   See Allan, *Constitutional Justice*, n 14 above, chs 1 and 2.
[19]   R Stevens, 'A Loss of Innocence?: Judicial Independence and the Separation of Powers' (1999) 19 *Oxford Journal of Legal Studies* 365 at 365.
[20]   See also s 11(3) of the Senior Courts Act 1981, and ss 33 and 133 of the Constitutional Reform Act 2005.
[21]   See C Turpin and A Tomkins, *British Government and the Constitution*, 6th edn (Cambridge, Cambridge University Press, 2007) 118.

administration of justice' to 'uphold the continued independence of the judiciary'. Sub-section 3(5) requires the Lord Chancellor, and other Ministers of the Crown, not to seek to influence particular judicial decisions through any special access to the judiciary; and sub-section (6) requires that the Lord Chancellor must have regard to:

(a) the need for judicial independence;
(b) the need for the judiciary to have the support necessary to enable them to exercise their functions'.[22]

The Act also provides for the Lords of Appeal in Ordinary to be removed from the Upper House of Parliament and for the creation of a new Supreme Court as a final court of appeal for the United Kingdom,[23] a reform which will come into place in 2009. The Supreme Court will assume the jurisdiction of the former Appellate Committee of the House of Lords and also the jurisdiction of the Judicial Committee of the Privy Council. By adding to the protections of institutional independence of the judicial branch, the Constitutional Reform Act has augmented more generally the independence of that branch and manifests a heightened appreciation and influence of the separation of judicial power as a significant constitutional principle. While this may stay the hand of Parliament from breaching judicial decisional independence, subject to what is said below, it is not possible to say unequivocally that the direction and inviolability principles thereby achieve the same status as in constitutions with an entrenched separation of powers. In other words, this solicitude toward the judicial power still falls short of enforceable constitutional limitations. Even scholars like Barendt who highlight the role of the separation of powers concede that in a *Liyanage*-type situation, '[i]t is unlikely that an English court would take the same approach, which would entail a departure from the fundamental principle of parliamentary supremacy'.[24]

It is at this point that the thesis of Professor TRS Allan becomes especially relevant. Allan has written:

If there were ultimately no limits to legislative supremacy, as a matter of constitutional theory, it would be difficult to speak of the British polity as a constitutional state grounded in law. Although the form of the separation of powers may vary between constitutions, the independence of the superior courts from government and legislature seems fundamental to the rule of law.

---

[22] *Ibid*, at 119–20 for more details.
[23] *Ibid*, at 125.
[24] See Feldman (ed), *English Public Law*, n 10 above, 41.

It follows that if we deny all restrictions on legislative competence—even in respect of the adjudication of particular cases—we thereby reject constitutionalism.[25]

Allan's thesis deserves far more attention than the scope of the present monograph allows but, in its essentials, it adopts the position that in any polity which claims allegiance to the rule of law and basic tenets of constitutionalism, there are fundamental principles which inhere in the nature of that polity and which can be enforced by the judiciary, even against Parliament, in the absence of a written constitution. As succinctly stated by Professor Jeffrey Goldsworthy,

> [a]ccording to Allan, Parliament's authority ultimately derives from deeper principles, which turn out to be indistinguishable from the deepest principles of the common law. The law is a matter of reason rather than arbitrary will because it is grounded in these principles. It is the responsibility of the judges to ascertain and apply the law, and therefore, its deepest principles. They must reject as mistaken any rule that is inconsistent with those principles, and the doctrine of parliamentary sovereignty is such a rule.[26]

Allan's position manifests a certain scepticism toward the positivist assumptions upon which much of the support for the doctrine of parliamentary sovereignty is based. It relies rather on the position taken by Lon Fuller that there exists an 'internal morality' to law based on certain fundamental tenets of procedural due process. As Allan himself explains,

> [i]nvoking Lon Fuller's explanation of the nature of law, which reflects assumptions about individual dignity and autonomy intrinsic to our conception of constitutional democracy, I have argued that there are modest, but significant, moral constraints on the nature and content of law. An enactment that makes no pretence to generality, identifying specific persons for adverse treatment, cannot constitute a source of legal obligation, properly understood. An assertion of obligation or authority entails an implicit appeal to the citizen's moral assent; but a measure whose discrimination between persons is essentially arbitrary, lacking in any plausible basis in justice or the common good, can make no such appeal: it contradicts on its face its purported claim to obedience.[27]

Accordingly, 'the principles of procedural due process and equality imposed constitutional limits on the kinds of enactment that can qualify

---

[25] Allan, *Law, Liberty and Justice*, n 14 above, 69.
[26] J Goldsworthy, *The Sovereignty of Parliament, History and Philosophy* (Oxford, Clarendon Press, 1999) 249.
[27] Allan, *Constitutional Justice*, n 14 above, 202 (footnotes omitted).

as "law"'.[28] Moreover, these principles 'assume the existence of a separation of powers between the principal organs of government, each responsible for distinctive functions'.[29] The separation of powers thus may achieve, in Allan's thesis, the same position as it assumes in constitutions which entrench it as a legal and constitutional rule.

> [T]he superior courts must be clearly independent of the legislature, acting as servants of the constitutional order as a whole rather than merely as instruments of a majority of elected members of the legislative assembly. It is ultimately for the courts to determine the validity of statutes in accordance with the principle of equality and with due regard for the other essential constituents of the rule of law. There must be an appropriate reconciliation between the legislative sovereignty of Parliament, as the supreme law-maker, and the legal sovereignty of the courts, as the final arbiters of the law in particular cases.[30]

Thus, the judicial branch may enforce these fundamental principles even to the point of declaring invalid the enactments of an otherwise sovereign parliament. Allan in fact regards these principles to be so fundamental as to take priority over constitutional amendments to a written constitution. Writing with particular reference to the Constitution of the Commonwealth of Australia, he has argued that certain 'freedoms', one of which he stated to be the independence of the judiciary, are 'so elementary' as to 'arise by implication from the concept of the Commonwealth itself' and are therefore 'not subject to amendment, even by the process provided for by the constitutional instrument itself'.[31] This would appear to apply by extrapolation at least to all Westminster-style polities whether or not they maintain a written constitution, as well as to the United States.

Acknowledging the difficulty in identifying the precise ambit and scope of these restrictions, Allan's arguments achieve particular clarity in the context of legislation dealing with specific individuals or particularised circumstances and legal disputes. I will attempt to summarise his position with respect to the issues which are the main concern of this monograph[32]:

---

[28] *Ibid.*

[29] *Ibid*, at 2.

[30] *Ibid*, at 3.

[31] TRS Allan, 'The Common Law as Constitution: Fundamental Rights and First Principles' in C Saunders (ed), *Courts of Final Jurisdiction: The Mason Court in Australia* (Sydney, Federation Press, 1996) 158.

[32] Allan, *Law, Liberty and Justice*, n 14 above, 69 ff. See also Allan, *Constitutional Justice*, n 14 above, ch 7, esp 238 ff.

First, he acknowledged the existence of a form of the Changed Law Rule which allows for the extension of parliamentary competence to the alteration of existing rights, 'even where such rights are simultaneously the subject of judicial decision'.[33]

> The legislative process could not be impeded by the fortuitous circumstance of current litigation. A distinction must therefore be drawn between legislation which affects rights in issue before the courts, and enactments which invade the judicial process by interfering directly with the exercise of judicial power. Legislation of the latter kind strikes unacceptably at the kernel of the rule of law, which depends on the distinction between the formulation of general rules and their application, by an independent judiciary, to particular cases.[34]

Secondly, Allan acknowledged the potential for legislatures to enact a legislative judgment or other prescriptive interference in judicial process—*ad hominem* legislation and legislation targeted at specific proceedings—under the guise of otherwise properly enacted legislation.

> In one sense, of course, if the judicial function involves the application of law in the ascertainment of pre-existing rights, the 'legislative judgment', providing *ex post facto* for the outcome of a particular case, is not itself an exercise of judicial power. In substance, however, it invades the judicial function in precisely the manner that the separation of powers forbids. It permits a 'political' arm of government to act directly against an individual or private organisation without any of the intermediate safeguards of legal process, based on general rules. It is an exercise of legislative power which circumvents, and thereby frustrates, the judicial function.[35]

Thirdly, Allan argues that the separation of powers 'must entail a principle against *ad hominem* legislation'.[36] This, as a general proposition, as discussed in previous chapters, has not been adopted by courts in jurisdictions maintaining a separation of powers, absent other indicia of legislative direction or unless the enactment is an Act of Attainder. Nevertheless, the critical underlying thesis of the direction principle— that it is possible to test the substantively legislative nature of parliamentary action—is reinforced even though Allan takes the point a step further. Directive legislation, especially if it is *ad hominem* and with respect to pending proceedings, becomes adjudicative as opposed to 'legislative',[37] and thus an unconstitutional interference with the judicial process. Allan, however, acknowledged the 'inconclusive' nature of this

---

[33] Allan, *Law, Liberty and Justice*, n 14 above, 69.
[34] *Ibid.*
[35] *Ibid*, at 69–70.
[36] *Ibid*, at 69.
[37] *Ibid*, at 71.

distinction in jurisdictions which do not maintain an entrenched separation of powers.[38] In this context he referred to the *BLF (NSW)* case[39] in
which the New South Wales Court of Appeal sharply criticised legislation which provided that the de-registration of a particular industrial
union should 'for all purposes'—thus not excluding the pending judicial
proceedings in which this very issue was being tested—be taken to be
validly made. The legislation was indisputably *ad hominem* and targeted a
pending appeal in which this very issue was to be tested. Yet, as Allan
noted,

> [i]n the absence … of a well-established separation of powers doctrine such as
> applied under the Federal Constitution [of Australia], or special entrenchment
> of the judicial power in the existing courts, the validity of the statute was
> upheld.[40]

Allan also noted the distinction drawn in that case by Kirby P between
'legal restrictions' on parliamentary competence and those based on
'politics and convention, grounded in history',[41] which could not be
judicially enforced against Parliament.

Fourthly, Allan proceeded to challenge the distinction between law and
convention, which prevented the New South Wales Court of Appeal, and
by implication all courts of similar jurisdiction, from invalidating the
legislation, arguing that the court should not have been so reticent. The
common law, Allan argued,

> [a]s a body of principle, whose content is largely dependent on reasoning from
> fundamental (including constitutional) axioms, … must take account of (legiti-
> mate) expectations. Expectations, based on accepted practice, form part of the
> material from which political principle is derived—necessarily so if we are
> talking of a particular legal system rather than abstract, ideal theory. And no
> distinction can be made between legal and political principle: these are
> ultimately different labels for the same phenomenon—legitimate constitutional
> behaviour. Dicey's dichotomy cannot finally be sustained; and invasion of the
> judicial sphere—if unconstitutional—must, it follows, be equally illegal.[42]

Accordingly,

> [a]s a primary modern convention, the separation of powers must, as a matter
> of *(legal)* principle, impose limits on the legislative sovereignty of Parliament.
> Acts of attainder would today be universally condemned as contrary to
> fundamental principle. As the 'archetypal violation of the generality of the law'
> the Act of attainder is a law only in form: 'In substance it is a *measure* bearing

---

38   *Ibid.*
39   *BLF (NSW)* (1986) 7 NSWLR 372, discussed in detail ch 2 at 79, above.
40   *Ibid*, at 72.
41   *BLF (NSW)* (1986) 7 NSWLR 372 at 401.
42   Allan, *Law, Liberty and Justice*, n 14 above, 72.

all the earmarks of an arbitrary executive act'. Is it not grotesque today that constitutional theory permits any and every legislative invasion of the judicial function because Parliament once decided that the Bishop of Rochester's cook should be boiled to death?[43]

It is at this point that Allan's examination of *Liyanage*[44] becomes particularly pertinent. He conceded that the Privy Council did hold that lack of generality in legislation and *ad hominem* enactments would not necessarily involve a breach of the separation of powers.[45] However

> [i]t is reasonable to suppose that there are some constraints on the exercise of legislative sovereignty, implicit in the constitutional scheme of the separation of powers as settled by modern convention, even in the absence of entrenched provisions.[46]

Thus, *Liyanage*-style *ad hominem* legislation, together with bills of attainder, should be invalidated as unconstitutional by the English courts as breaching the separation of powers and the rule of law.[47]

> Although it is the hallmark of an act of attainder that it imposes punishment without the safeguard of judicial trial, an equivalent injustice may be inflicted whenever the elements of legal protection that a court characteristically provides are removed or curtailed. When a person is punished pursuant to provisions framed with his specific case in view, or unfairly tailored to fit an unpopular group he belongs to, the principle of equality is violated even when the elements of fair judicial process are preserved. When, moreover, a measure provides for special procedures to facilitate the conviction or punishment of identifiable persons, the principles of equality and due process are both infringed.[48]

He also impugned the distinction which the New South Wales Court of Appeal in *BLF (NSW)* set up between constitutional arrangements in New South Wales, which did not entrench the separation of powers, and therefore could not declare the legislation invalid on that ground, and those in Ceylon which did. 'Would the court have found the distinction as persuasive if the facts of the two cases had been truly analogous—involving a similar usurpation of the judicial function in respect of the criminal law?'[49] He contrasted the reluctance of Kirby P in that case to substitute 'judicial opinion about entrenched rights for the lawful powers of Parliament, unless anchored in a Bill of Rights duly enacted'[50] with the

43 *Ibid*, at 73 (footnotes omitted).
44 Discussed in detail at p 67 above.
45 Allan, *Law, Liberty and Justice*, n 14 above, 74.
46 *Ibid*, at 74. See also Allan, *Constitutional Justice*, n 14 above, 232 ff.
47 *Ibid*, at 148–57.
48 *Ibid*, at 233.
49 Allan, *Law, Liberty and Justice*, n 14 above, 74.
50 *Ibid*, at 76.

position taken by Street CJ and Priestly JA, of which he approved, who were open to the notion that the words in the New South Wales Constitution—that Parliament had power to make laws for 'the peace, welfare and good government' of New South Wales—were words of limitation and that similar considerations applied in the United Kingdom:

> Can it be supposed that Parliament has authority to legislate for purposes inimical to the peace, welfare and good government of the United Kingdom? Or that any presumption that its enactments satisfy such implicit conditions is irrebuttable—whatever the circumstances?[51]

Allan concluded thus:

> It seems to follow that the independence of the judiciary and of the judicial process may be regarded as ineradicable features of the 'Westminster model' of constitutions—including, therefore, the constitution of the United Kingdom. In the absence of a single, venerated document, legal reasoning must depend on 'what, though not expressed, is none the less a necessary implication from the subject-matter and structure of the constitution'.[52]

It would appear to follow therefore that the separation of judicial power, and thus the institutional and decisional independence of the judiciary, can be treated as the source of constitutional limitations in the manner of a constitutionally-entrenched separation of powers in a written constitution. That being the case, it would be possible to argue that the direction principle and the inviolability principle, in addition to the prohibition on acts of attainder and *ad hominem* legislation pursuant to Allan's argument, applied equally in the United Kingdom. In the context of *BLF (NSW)* he stated:

> The most persuasive interpretation of the New South Wales constitution, sensitive to the deeper structure of Australian constitutionalism, would none the less deny the legislature the power to remove basic protections that the principles of due process and equality provide. No formal entrenchment of the judicial power is needed because, contrary to orthodox wisdom, the State Parliament has no legal authority to pass legislation inconsistent with these fundamental common law rights[due process and equality]: the legislature cannot, in other words, act in violation of the rule of law.[53]

Accordingly, he expressly endorsed the view of Street CJ in a passage that deserves to be set out in full:

> Street CJ's view that the court could properly reject oppressive laws, as inimical to the 'peace, welfare, and good government of New South Wales',

[51] *Ibid*, at 76–7.
[52] *Ibid*, at 75.
[53] Allan, *Constitutional Justice*, n 14 above, 239.

was persuasive, being grounded in the nature of the polity to which the Constitution Act refers. The reference to 'New South Wales' had a 'conceptual character', indicating the body politic or 'political organism' rather than the geographical area of the people within it. The sovereign powers of the State legislature were therefore circumscribed by its role as law-maker for a 'parliamentary democracy—an entity rule by a democratically elected Parliament whose citizens enjoy the great inherited privileges of freedom and justice under the protection of an independent judiciary'. The ultimate constitutional constraints entailed by the general conditions of 'peace, welfare, and good government', as the Act expresses the basic requirements of the common good, enabled the courts to protect the parliamentary democracy, 'not only against tyrannous excesses on the part of a legislature that may have fallen under extremist control', but against other breaches of Parliament's constitutional trust ... The limitations on parliamentary sovereignty that respect for the common good entails do not depend on formally entrenched constitutional provisions. While according ample scope for democratic decision-making by elected representatives, legislative supremacy must none the less be made harmonious with its judicial (interpretative) counterpart. In preserving inviolate the principles of equality and due process, the rule of law secures the values of individual autonomy and dignity intrinsic to the common good. The constraints on parliamentary sovereignty derive from the general recognition—or established 'convention', as Street CJ termed it—that 'the judiciary is the arm of government charged with the responsibility of interpreting and applying the law as between litigants in individual cases'.[54] (Emphasis added.)

Allan applied his argument to the facts of the Australian case *Kable v Director of Public Prosecutions (New South Wales)),*[55] a constitutional challenge in the High Court to *ad hominem* legislation of the New South Wales Parliament directed expressly at one Gregory Wayne Kable. Kable was serving a prison sentence for the murder of his wife. While in prison, he had made threats to outside persons. The Act vested jurisdiction in the Supreme Court of New South Wales to order the further penal detention of Kable for a period of six months if, on application by the Director of Public Prosecutions, the court was satisfied on reasonable grounds that Kable 'was more likely than not to commit a serious act of violence; and that it is appropriate, for the protection of a particular person or persons or the community generally, that [he] be kept in custody'.[56] The Act did not prevent the DPP from making further such applications.

Kable argued, inter alia, that the impugned statute was not in substance a 'law' within the meaning of section 5 of the Constitute Act 1902 (NSW)—which provided that the parliament of the State could make

[54] *Ibid*, at 241 (footnotes omitted).
[55] *Kable v Director of Public Prosecutions (NSW)* (1996) 189 CLR 51.
[56] S 5 Community Protection Act 1994 (NSW).

laws for the 'peace, welfare and good government of the State in all cases whatsoever '—because of its *ad hominem* nature.[57] Allan's thesis in this regard was thus judicially tested. Only Brennan CJ, Dawson and McHugh JJ paid any attention to this argument, although rejecting it out of hand. Brennan CJ stated that a 'purported law has never been held to lack the character of a law simply because it affects the liberty or property of only a single individual'.[58] Dawson J remarked that 'nothing is to be gained for present purposes by a jurisprudential analysis of what constitutes a law'.[59] McHugh J simply remarked that the State parliament 'has the constitutional power to pass legislation providing for the imprisonment of a particular individual' whether by the 'order of a Minister, public servant or tribunal'.[60]

In the event, the legislation was held invalid on other grounds. Although it is difficult to discern a precise ratio decidendi, the following remarks by McHugh J are most indicative:

> Because the State courts are an integral and equal part of the judicial system set up by Ch III [of the Commonwealth Constitution], it also follows that no State or federal parliament can legislate in a way that might undermine the role of those courts as repositories of federal judicial power. Thus, neither the Parliament of New South Wales nor the Parliament of the Commonwealth can invest functions in the Supreme Court of New South Wales that are incompatible with the exercise of federal judicial power.[61]

The constitutional offence in the Act was primarily the fact that it compromised the institutional independence of the State court, by, in the words of McHugh J, making it 'the instrument of a legislative plan, initiated by the executive government, to imprison the appellant by a process that is far removed from the judicial process that is ordinarily invoked when a court is asked to imprison a person'.[62]

Allan took issue with the reasoning upon which the decision was based, particularly the rejection of the submission that this *ad hominem* act was not 'law' and McHugh J's view that there was no bar to the enactment of a law providing for the imprisonment of a single individual.

---

[57]   For an excellent examination of this case and the surrounding political circumstances, see HP Lee, 'The *Kable* Case: A Guard-Dog that Barked But Once?' in G Winterton (ed), *State Constitutional Landmarks* (Sydney, Federation Press, 2006) 391. See also GJ Lindell, 'The Australian Constitution: Growth, Adaptation and Conflict—Reflections About Some Major Cases and Events' (1999) 25 *Monash University Law Review* 257.

[58]   *Kable v Director of Public Prosecutions (NSW)* (1996) 189 CLR 51 at 64.

[59]   *Ibid*, at 76.

[60]   *Ibid*, at 121.

[61]   *Ibid*, at 116.

[62]   *Ibid*, at 122.

Is it not paradoxical that Kable's detention was held unlawful solely on the ground that it required the intervention of the court, even if its discretion were truly as limited as was assumed? ... An *ad hominem* statute of the kind considered in *Kable* must be regarded as falling outside the concept of 'law' envisaged by, or implicit in, the ideal of the rule of law. Brennan CJ denied that a purported law had even been held to the lack the character of a law merely because it concerned the liberty or property of a single individual: acts of attainder were traditionally treated as laws; private Acts of Parliament were a familiar form of law in the nineteenth-century English Parliament. Historical precedent, however, may lose its persuasive power when found, on analysis, to be incompatible with constitutional theory, as it has developed in the light of experience and reflection on the basic principles of the legal order. The High Court's present commitment to the integrity of the judicial process, as a concomitant to the separation of judicial power, makes sense only in the context of a constitution that protects the principal interests of the citizen from arbitrary legislative or executive interference. The constitutional scheme is undermined when the safeguards inherent in judicial procedure are side-stepped by allowing the executive to discriminate unfairly against specific individuals. The primary purpose of the court's intervention in *Kable*, and its principal justification, must surely have been to uphold the dignity and independence of the citizen rather than the honour and integrity of the State courts.[63]

Allan did not object to the making of detention orders by courts 'outside their ordinary function of sentencing convicted offenders ... [in] response to a grave and probable threat to violence'.[64] However, the requirements of the rule of law dictate that such laws be in general terms and must not embody a judgment concerning the appropriate treatment of a specific individual.

The demands of the rule of law are met when the court is satisfied that detention is justified by the terms of a general statute, whose purpose corresponds to an intelligible requirement of the public good, consistent with other generally accepted requirements, and whose consequences for the individual concerned are reasonably proportionate to the public need. Whether the court acts on review of a minister's order or issues the order itself, it must therefore defend or adapt its procedure to allow the rigorous scrutiny that a proposal to imprison any citizen demands. By ensuring natural justice, permitting full consideration of the justice of the citizen's treatment under an appropriately general statute, it precludes any arbitrary abrogation of rights. The invalidity of the *Community Protection Act* was a product of its lack of generality, on one hand, and its failure to secure due process, on the other.[65]

---

[63]   Allan, *Constitutional Justice*, n 14 above, 236–7 (footnotes omitted).
[64]   *Ibid*, at 237.
[65]   *Ibid*, at 238.

While the view that fundamental principles or rights—whether based on notions of a higher law which inhere in a polity based on constitutional-ism and the rule of law, or whether sourced in rights embedded 'deep' in the common law—has both academic and judicial support (in obiter dicta),[66] it is a view which has yet to translate into an unambiguous statement by the courts in the United Kingdom that they can be solely relied on to invalidate Acts of Parliament. Moreover, it is a view which has been subject to rigorous, and often compelling, criticism from both historical and jurisiprudential perspectives. Goldsworthy, after his exten-sive historical examination of the issues in *The Sovereignty of Parliament*,[67] remarked:

> Judges in Britain, Australia and New Zealand are sometimes invited to repudiate the doctrine of parliamentary sovereignty. It is said that '[t]his would not be at all revolutionary. What is revolutionary is talk of the omnicompetence of Parliament'. This is false. There can be no doubt that for many centuries there has been a sufficient consensus among all three branches of government in Britain to make the sovereignty of Parliament a rule of recognition in H.L.A Hart's sense, which the judges by themselves did not create and cannot unilaterally change. That is what is meant by saying that the rule is a 'political fact'. At the fundamental level of a rule of recognition there is no difference between legal and political facts'.

Professor George Winterton has compellingly argued that the 'funda-mental norm' of parliamentary sovereignty is not a rule of the common law subject, like other common law rules, to judicial amendment and qualification:

> That characterisation is inappropriate since, unlike other common law rules, it may not in all respects be subject to amendment or repeal by parliament. It is in fact, *sui generis*, a unique hybrid of law and political fact deriving its authority from acceptance by the people and by the principal institutions of the state, especially parliament and the judiciary.[68]

---

[66] In addition to the judicial support of Street CJ and Priestley JA in *BLF (NSW)* referred to above, Winterton has set this out in 'Constitutionally Entrenched Common Law Rights: Sacrificing Means to Ends?' in C Sampford and K Preston (eds), *Interpreting Constitutions: Theories, Principles and Institutions* (Sydney, Federation Press, 1996) 121, 138–9, referring to the views of former justices of the High Court of Australia Murphy, Deane and Toohey JJ, those of several New Zealand judges, particularly Sir Robin Cooke (now Lord Cooke), as well as English judges. See also Sir R Cooke, 'Fundamentals' [1988] *New Zealand Law Journal* 158; Lord Woolf, 'Droit Public-English Style' [1995] *Public Law* 57; Sir John Laws, 'Law and Democracy' [1995] *Public Law* 72. See also M Detmold, 'The New Constitutional Law' (1994) 16 *Sydney Law Review* 228 and Allan, *Constitutional Justice*, n 14 above, 201 and 260.

[67] Goldsworthy, *The Sovereignty of Parliament* (Oxford, Clarendon Press, 1999) 234 (footnotes omitted).

[68] Winterton, 'Constitutionally Entrenched Common Law Rights', n 66 above, 136.

Concurring with Goldsworthy on the weakness of the historical basis for the doctrine of fundamental law providing constitutional principles overriding the supremacy of parliament,[69] he concluded also that it

> faces serious difficulties of principle, the most fundamental objection being the doctrine's unavoidable selectivity. The common law is inherently subject to legislation yet, pursuant to the doctrine of fundamental rights, some common law rules, principles or doctrines would be considered 'fundamental' and capable of overriding statutes ... It is difficult to avoid the conclusion that the individual judge's preference will largely determine into which category the relevant common law principle falls. Moreover, the content of the supposed 'fundamental' principle and the degree to which it is limited by considerations of reasonableness and proportionality will differ according to the views of the judges ... As Leslie Zines has aptly remarked, such notions 'invite a judge to discover in the Constitution his or her own broad political philosophy'.[70]

In similar vein, Goldsworthy concluded his evaluation of Allan's position thus:

> [T]he orthodox understanding [is] that the doctrine of parliamentary sover-eignty is currently part of the constitutional law of all three countries [United Kingdom, Australia and New Zealand] albeit in heavily modified form in Australia. If it were not, there would be no need to debate about the merits of a Bill of Rights: judges would already have authority to invalidate legislation that they regard as inconsistent with fundamental rights. Since they do not already have that authority, proponents of judicial review must persuade us that they ought to. To give judges that authority would require a fundamental constitutional change in all three countries, which should be brought about by consensus, rather than judicial fiat. That is surely a requirement of democracy itself. I have argued ... that it is also a requirement of law.[71]

Unfortunately this is a debate the resolution of which the scope of the present work does not permit, although the views of Allan, and his critics, certainly deserve greater exposition than given above. The conclu-sion which can be drawn for present purposes is that in the absence of further development in this regard, and in the absence of a written constitution which entrenches a separation of powers, it remains an uncertain proposition, at best, that reliance can be placed on such a view to protect the decisional independence of the judicial branch. That the matter might come to a head is becoming increasingly less likely because a lot of the work in this regard is being performed by the Human Rights

---

[69]   *Ibid*, at 141.
[70]   *Ibid* at 143, quoting from L Zines, *Constitutional Change in the Commonwealth* (Cam-bridge, Cambridge University Press, 1991) 52. See L Zines, 'Courts Unmaking the Laws' in Australian Institute of Judicial Administration, *Courts in a Representative Democracy*, (Aus-tralian Institute of Judicial Administration, 1995) and L Zines 'A Judicially Created Bill of Rights?'(1994) 12 *Sydney Law Review* 166.
[71]   Goldsworthy, *The Sovereignty of Parliament*, n 67 above, 279.

Act 1998 (UK) and the European Convention on Human Rights and also because of the slim chance—although one can never be certain—of abhorrent or iniquitous legislation creating the extreme case which makes the issue unavoidable. Even in Australia, with its written constitution, the issue has not quite disappeared and the spectre of fundamental law does still make its presence felt, especially when considered in the context of 'extreme' cases. The matter was left open by the High Court in *Union Steamship Co of Australia Pty Ltd v King*,[72] although it had rejected an argument that the words 'peace, welfare and good government' in the Constitution Act of New South Wales provided for anything less than plenary legislative power; and in *Durham Holdings Pty Ltd v New South Wales* Kirby J appeared to have recognised that limitations to plenary legislative power may apply in circumstances of extreme laws.[73] Be that as it may, it remains a far too uncertain proposition upon which presently to recognise enforceable constitutional principles protecting judicial decisional independence.

III.   THE EUROPEAN CONVENTION ON HUMAN RIGHTS

As things presently stand, therefore, the protections afforded the decisional independence of courts in the United Kingdom would appear to remain a matter of political morality and convention, the observance of which is dependent on the degree of self-restraint exhibited by Parliament. The United Kingdom's European involvement does, however, provide some further protection independently of the separation of powers doctrine. This is a consequence of the particular provisions of the European Convention for the Protection of Human Rights and Fundamental Freedoms ('ECHR'), which will be considered below.

Absent these Convention provisions, and despite the rights-consciousness in European law, there is no express protection of decisional independence and indeed none which can be sourced from an entrenched separation of powers in the manner of the United States.[74] Indeed, while the separation of powers is respected as a doctrine, it is not ultimately the source of constitutional principles enforceable by the European Court of Justice ('ECJ'). This is illustrated well by the circumstances of the *Barber* case and the response to it of the Member States of

---

[72]   *Union Steamship Co of Australia Pty Ltd v King* (1988) 166 CLR 1 at 10.
[73]   *Durham Holdings Pty Ltd v New South Wales* (2001) 205 CLR 399 at 424–5.
[74]   See Feldman, *English Public Law*, n 10 above, 379. See also MLF Estaban, *The Rule of Law in the European Constitution* (London, Kluwer Law International Law, 1999) 46–7 and 156–9 and K Lenaerts, 'Some Reflections on the Separation of Powers in the European Community' [1991] 28 *Common Market Law Review* 11.

the European Community.[75] In that case the ECJ held that Article 119 of the Treaty of Rome, which stipulated that there be equal pay for equal work irrespective of sex, was applicable to benefits paid under private pension schemes because such benefits were to be regarded as 'pay'. In light of past practices, where men and women were treated differently in this regard, this ruling had quite severe and adverse consequences for pension funds of all Member States. To stem the confusion, the Court stated that

> the direct effect of Article 119 … may not be relied upon in order to claim entitlement to a pension with effect from a date prior to that of this judgment [17 May 1990] except in the case of workers or those claiming under them who have before that date initiated legal proceedings or raised an equivalent claim under the applicable national law.[76]

This ruling was, however, capable of a number of interpretations. Tamara Hervey noted that it was unclear whether Article 119 was thus made applicable only to

(a)   pensions schemes set up after the judgment; or
(b)   employees who became members of pension schemes after the judgment; or
(c)   benefits received after the judgment; or
(d)   all pension payments after the judgment.[77]

As a consequence, requests were made by national courts for clarification, thus rendering the final interpretation of *Barber* by the ECJ a pending case.[78] Before the ECJ could clarify its ruling, the Member States themselves sought to clarify the position by adopting Protocol No 2 of Article 119, 'the *Barber* Protocol', which was annexed to the Treaty of European Union, and which made the principle of equal pay applicable only to benefits attributable to periods of employment commencing after the date of the judgment. This may or may not have been the interpretation of its judgment in *Barber* intended by the ECJ. The result was that, as noted by Hervey,

> a non-judicial organ of government of the European Community, that is, the Member States acting in an intergovernmental conference … gave an authoritative interpretation of a provision of Community law. Moreover, the Member

---

[75] Case C-262/88 *Barber v Guardian Royal Exchange* [1990] ECR 1889.
[76] *Ibid*, at [45].
[77] TK Hervey, 'Annotation of Case 152/91, *Neath v Hugh Steeper Ltd*' (1994) 31 *Common Market Law Review* 1387 at 1392; and TK Hervey 'Legal Issues Concerning the Barber Protocol' in D O'Keeffe and PM Twomey, *Legal Issues of the Maastricht Treaty* (London, Wiley Chancery Law, 1994) ch 21, at 330.
[78] See D O'Keefe, 'The Uneasy Progress of European Social Policy' (1996) 2 *Columbia Journal of European Law* 241 at 256.

States determined the precise temporal effect of the *Barber* ruling. In other words, the Member States usurped the judicial function, which, in accordance with the doctrine of separation of powers, ought properly to be exercised by the judicial organ of the European Community, the Court of Justice.

The Community is a legal entity *sui generis*, not an intergovernmental organization. As Lenaerts points out … one of the principal functions of the rule of law in general, and the separation of powers in particular, in the context of the European Community, is to protect the Community interest from the influence of intergovernmentalism. Similarly, in the context of the Court's monopoly of interpretative competence, the preservation of separation of powers can effectively protect Community law from intergovernmentalism. The *Barber* Protocol, therefore, is particularly disturbing, since it is evidence of the breakdown of the separation of powers in the European Community, and, by extension, evidence of the mistrust of the Member States of the roles of the Community institutions in a Community governed by the rule of law.[79]

Hervey has thus concluded that

[t]he grounds on which the *Barber* Protocol may be held to be unconstitutional (breach of the separation of powers, destabilization of the institutional balance, promotion of intergovernmentalism), although undoubtedly part of the *acquis communautaire*, are, in my opinion, insufficiently fundamental to the Community as a whole to justify a ruling from the Court of Justice that the Protocol is invalid. After all, the separation of powers in the Community is not complete, the institutional balance is constantly developing, and intergovernmentalism has always been a part of Community practice, end even provided for in the Community treaties.[80]

Judge Federico Mancini also noted the limited role which could be played by the separation of powers. Referring to the *Barber* Protocol he remarked:

Some might go so far as to regard it as an outright assault on the separation of powers. But even there we must concede that, if the governments of the Member States, which are after all endowed with greater domestic legitimacy than the Court of Justice, are firmly persuaded that a particular view as to the correct interpretation of a Treaty article must prevail, on grounds of economic and social necessity, that are entitled to incorporate that view in a proposed amendment of the Treaty, notwithstanding the pendency of litigation concerning the point in issue … The painful lesson for the Court is that nothing that it does cannot be undone and that no aspect of the *acquis communautaire* is safe from abrogation if it proves unpalatable to the Court's political masters.[81]

---

[79]   Hervey, 'Legal Issues Concerning the Barber Protocol', n 77 above, 334.
[80]   *Ibid*, at 336–7.
[81]   GF Mancini and DT Keeling, 'Language, Culture and Politics in the Life of the European Court of Justice' (1995) 1 *Columbia Journal of European Law* 397 at 410.

In the event, the interpretation contained in the Protocol was endorsed by the court.[82] Professor David O'Keefe thus noted that

[t]he Court's approach in its interpretation of the *Barber* decision has thus been to recognize the political decision of the Member States, as expressed in the Protocol. However, whatever the merits of its decision … a most dangerous precedent has been set whereby the Member States can interfere with the judicial process. It seems unduly cautious to interpret the Protocol as a declaratory interpretation. If the Member States had wished to express their views on the Protocol, they were given the opportunity to do so at hearings in the cases pending before the Court. Alternatively, they could have issued a political declaration to be annexed to the TEU.

By inserting the Protocol on Article 119, which cannot be subject to judicial review as such, the Member States demonstrated a severe distrust of the Court and placed the Court in the position of being practically forced to follow their interpretation in pending cases. In this author's view, the Protocol is an attack on the separation of powers and thus on the acquis communautaire.[83]

This history clearly indicates that the separation of powers stands on uncertain ground in European law, that it appears not to offer any protection to interference with decisional independence in pending cases, or indeed with respect to finally decided cases. It is for this reason that the focus of attention must turn to the ECHR. The position in the United Kingdom prior to the Human Rights Act 1998 (UK), which incorporated into English law the provisions of the ECHR, was that the United Kingdom government was bound only by international law to honour its obligations under the ECHR, as were the other European nation signatories. The United Kingdom Parliament usually honoured the decisions of the European Court of Human Rights ('ECtHR'), which hears disputes arising under the Convention, by introducing amending legislation to remove incompatibility of existing legislation with the ECHR and thus honouring its obligations under international law. European human rights law, stemming from the ECHR and not European Union law, thus did play a critical role in shaping British statutes.[84]

In relation to decisional independence, the key provisions of the ECHR are Article 6, providing for a right to a fair trial, and Article 7, prohibiting

---

[82] Case 109/91, *Ten Oever v Stichting Bedrijfspensioenfonds voor het Glazenwassers-en Schoonmaakbedrijf* [1993] ECR I-4879.

[83] D O'Keeffe, 'The Uneasy Progress of European Social Policy' (1996) 2 *Columbia Journal of European Law* 241 at 256–7.

[84] See Feldman (ed), *English Public Law*, n 10 above, 378. For detail on the origins and respective status of these two distinct bodies of law see Turpin and Tomkins, *British Government and the Constitution*, n 21 above, 68 ff and 265 ff.

retrospective criminal laws. These provisions are more a manifestation of rule of law principles than principles based on the separation of powers. Article 6(1) provides:

> In the determination of his civil rights and obligations or of any criminal charge against him, everyone is entitled to a fair and public hearing within a reasonable time by an independent and impartial tribunal established by law.

The requirement for an independent and impartial tribunal is particularly pertinent, as it has not been interpreted to be limited to concerns about judicial independence in the purely institutional concerns of tenure, terms of office, or guarantees against external influences and pressure.[85] Prima facie, legislative direction affecting pending cases, or permitting the overruling of final judgments, compromises the right to adjudication by an independent and impartial tribunal. The protections afforded by Article 6 are reinforced by Article 1 of Protocol 1, which provides:

> Every natural or legal person is entitled to the peaceful enjoyment of his possessions. No one shall be deprived of his possessions except in the public interest and subject to the conditions provided by law and by the general principles of international law.

Thus, where a legal claim can be regarded as a 'possession', such claim may not be extinguished by legislation.

Article 7 prohibits retroactive criminal laws, a prohibition which of course applies irrespective of any targeting of particular prosecutions. However, the prohibition does not apply to 'the trial and punishment of any person for any act or omission which, at the time when it was committed, was criminal according to the general principles of law recognised by civilised nations'.[86] Nevertheless, the protections afforded by such express prohibitions on retrospective laws may be more effective than those sourced exclusively from an entrenched separation of powers. The High Court of Australia, for example, upheld the constitutional validity of the retrospectively applicable War Crimes Amendment Act 1988 (Cth) which provided for the prosecution in Australia of war crimes committed during the Second World War. The majority[87] did so because, in the absence of any express constitutional prohibition to that effect, there was no constitutional prohibition against such laws which could be derived from the separation of powers. If, however, the retrospective law could be characterised as in substance an Act of Attainder, or if it were

---

[85] Feldman (ed), *English Public Law*, n 10 above, 378 and see cases referred to at nn 90 and 91.
[86] European Convention on Human Rights Art 7(2).
[87] *Polyukhovich v Commonwealth* (1991) 172 CLR 501; Mason CJ, Dawson, Toohey and McHugh JJ.

otherwise directed at specific individuals and declared their guilt, only then would it be invalid as a breach of the separation of powers.[88] Although such legislation, dealing as it did with heinous war crimes, would most likely not fall foul of the European prohibition on retrospective criminal laws because of the Article 7(2) exception, the point remains that absent an express constitutional prohibition, an entrenched separation doctrine without more could not prevent retrospective criminal laws. In the ECHR, the importance of such a provision is underscored by the fact that it is expressly exempted from the derogation provision.[89] In relation to the more precise concerns of this monograph, this prohibition would prevent the retrospective effect of an amendment to the criminal law in any pending or finally decided prosecution without the need to resort to the application of the direction principle or the inviolability principle.

Article 6 and Article 1, Protocol No 1 are not limited to criminal statutes and are therefore of assistance to litigants in all proceedings. Unlike Article 7, however, they are not exempted from the derogation provisions of the ECHR. Nevertheless, in its jurisprudence on Article 6, the ECtHR has defended the principle that persons should be able to conduct their affairs on the basis of existing law without the fear that that law will be retrospectively invalidated or amended to their detriment, especially where this occurs to hinder the execution of a final judgment.[90] It has also relied on Article 6 to condemn legislative intervention aimed at influencing cases that are pending or not yet initiated.[91] The court appears to be concerned less with the maintenance of separation of powers values than with the more specific concern of protecting the legitimate expectations of litigants. In *National & Provincial Building Society, Leeds Permanent Building Society and Yorkshire Building Society v United Kingdom*,[92] the applicant building societies challenged a retroactive tax law which worked to their detriment and which had been enacted while proceedings were pending. The law attempted to remedy certain defects in the taxation laws, which the applicants were seeking to exploit to their advantage by seeking restitution of taxes paid. The

---

[88]   Of course, in the United States, because of the ex post facto clause (Art 1 s 9 of the United States Constitution), there is no equivalent legislation of retrospective effect, the War Crimes Act 1996 being prospective only.

[89]   European Convention on Human Rights Art 15(2).

[90]   See P Popelier, 'Legitimate Expectations and the Law Maker in the Case Law of the European Court of Human Rights' (2006) 1 *European Human Rights Law Review* 10 at 16, and *Ogis-Institut Stanislas, Ogec St Pie X and Blanche de Castilles v France* (App Nos 42219/98 and 54563/00, judgment of 27 May 2004) at [71].

[91]   See, eg, *Anagnostopoulos v Greece* (App No 39374/98, judgment of 7 November 2000); *Scordino v Italy* (App No 36813/97, judgment of 29 July 2004).

[92]   *National & Provincial Building Society, Leeds Permanent Building Society and Yorkshire Building Society v United Kingdom* (1998) 25 EHRR 127.

ECtHR noted the applicants' legitimate expectation with respect to their tax position, and that that expectation was clearly thwarted by the retrospective law. However, it found no breach of Article 6 or Article 1 of Protocol 1 in this instance despite the fact that the law clearly affected the outcome of the pending proceedings, was enacted while the proceedings were pending and was clearly targeted at the particular legal issue to be determined. The court reasoned that Article 6 did not constitute an absolute prohibition against retrospective laws which breach the legitimate expectations of those relying on them, even in the context of pending litigation, and that the prohibition was subject to compelling public interest requirements. Because in the present case the defect in the relevant tax provisions had caused significant uncertainty over a period of years, affecting substantial amounts of revenue, there was significant public interest in having this remedied. This, it was held, was the purpose of the legislation, with the effect on the pending proceedings being merely incidental. The ultimate aim was

> restoring Parliament's original intention with respect to all building societies whose accounting periods ended in advance of the start of the fiscal year. That the extinction of the restitution proceedings was a significant consequence of the implementation of that aim cannot be denied. Nevertheless, it cannot be maintained that the Leeds and National & Provincial were the particular targets of the authorities' decision.[93]

The court emphasised that the public interest must be compelling in order to override the requirements of Article 6, although retrospective legislation which affects pending proceedings would be subject to particular scrutiny.

> The Court is especially mindful of the dangers inherent in the use of retrospective legislation which has the effect of influencing the judicial determination of a dispute to which the State is a party, including where the effect is to make pending litigation unwinnable. Respect for the rule of law and the notion of a fair trial require that any reasons adduced to justify such measures be treated with the greatest possible degree of circumspection.[94]

The court distinguished those cases in which the targeting of litigants and proceedings had occurred without any compelling public interest rationale, such as the *Stran Greek Refineries and Stratis Andreadis* case, discussed below.[95] Moreover, the court noted that

> the applicant societies in their efforts to frustrate the intention of Parliament were at all times aware of the probability that Parliament would equally

---

[93]   *Ibid*, at 180 [110].

[94]   *Ibid*, at 180 [112]. See also *Stran Greek Refineries and Stratis Andreadis v Greece* (1995) 19 EHRR 293 at [49].

[95]   See below n 99 and accompanying text.

attempt to frustrate those efforts…They had engaged the will of the authorities in the tax sector, an area where recourse to retrospective legislation is not confined to the United Kingdom, and must have appreciated the public interest considerations in placing the 1986 Regulations on a secure legal footing would not be abandoned easily.[96]

The qualification to the application of Article 6 based on compelling grounds of the general interest was confirmed in *Agoudimos and Ceffalonian Sky Shipping Co v Greece*[97] and in *Zielinski, Pradal, Gonzalez and others v France*.[98] The ECtHR thus maintained the prohibition on legislative intervention in pending proceedings absent such grounds.

These cases confirmed the strong stance the court had taken in *Stran Greek Refineries and Stratis Andreadis v Greece*[99] The applicant had sued the Greek government for moneys it claimed were owed to it under a contract it had entered into under the former military regime. The government took the matter to arbitration, as provided for in the contract, where a substantial award of damages was made in favour of the applicants. The government's appeals in the municipal courts were rejected. While a further appeal by the government to the Court of Cassation was pending, the Parliament enacted legislation declaring all terms of all contracts entered into under the military regime to be repealed, that arbitration awards were not valid or enforceable, that any claims against the State were time-barred, and that any pending proceedings were void. The ECtHR held that the enactment of this law while the appeal was pending, in the circumstances of the case, were indicative that the legislative intervention targeted the applicants and their proceedings. The court noted that

> the principle of the rule of law and the notion of a fair trial [note, not the separation of powers] enshrined in Art 6 preclude any interference by the legislature with the administration of justice designed to influence the judicial determination of the dispute[100]

and that the State had 'infringed the applicants' rights under Article 6(1) by intervening in a manner which was decisive to ensure that the (imminent) outcome of the proceeding in which it was a party was favourable to it'.[101] The court was of the view that this legislation was not

[96] *National & Provincial Building Society, Leeds Permanent Building Society and Yorkshire Building Society v United Kingdom* (1998) 25 EHRR 127 at 180 [112].

[97] *Agoudimos and Ceffalonian Sky Shipping Co v Greece* (2003) 36 EHRR 60.

[98] *Zielinski, Pradal, Gonzalez and others v France* [2001] EHRR 19.

[99] *Stran Greek Refineries and Stratis Andreadis v Greece* (1995) 19 EHRR 293. See also *Holy Monasteries v Greece* (1995) 20 EHRR 1.

[100] *Ibid*, at [48].

[101] *Ibid*, at [50].

serving any compelling public interest apart from the government's own interest in defeating the suit against it.[102]

While Article 6 does constitute a significant protection, its application can prove difficult in the hard case, as in *Zielenski, Pradal, Gonzales and others v France*.[103] The applicants were employees of social security bodies in the Alsace-Moselle region of France, who, because of the particular circumstances of that region, were entitled to be paid a 'special difficulties allowance' in addition to salary, pursuant to an agreement dating from 1953. Because this allowance had been allowed to decrease in real terms, the applicants had applied to five regional industrial tribunals to have it restored to its 1953 value. These tribunals could not agree on a single method of calculation and thus the matter reached the regional court of appeal. While the matter was pending, the government amended a bill on its passage through the legislature, on an unrelated matter, setting a fixed amount for the special allowance. Upon passage of the amended bill, the appeals by the applicants and other social-security staff were dismissed because the legislation now prescribed the relevant amount.

Before the ECtHR, the applicants alleged that there had been a breach of Article 6(1) because the introduction of legislation during pending court proceedings had been designed to influence the judicial determination of a dispute, and consequently, there had not been a fair trial. The court stated that Article 6 did not preclude 'retrospective provisions to regulate rights under existing law' even when these affected pending proceedings, but only 'where there had been compelling grounds of serving the general interest'.[104] In the instant case, however, the legislation had simply endorsed the position taken up by the government in the pending proceedings, despite the fact that a majority of the earlier decisions of the tribunals of fact had been favourable to the applicants. Without more, the mere fact that there had been conflicting decisions in the tribunals as to method of calculation did not constitute compelling public interest grounds for legislative intervention and consequently the legislation breached the right to a fair trial by an independent tribunal enshrined in Article 6.

This case reveals the differences which are beginning to emerge between the protections afforded by Article 6 and those afforded by the direction principle. First, in finding that there had been a breach of Article 6, the ECtHR did not enquire as to whether the legislation was in fact substantively legislative, that is, a genuine amendment of the law.

---

[102]   See S Phillips, 'The Court v. the Executive: Old Battles on New Battlegrounds' (1996) 1 *European Human Rights Law Review* 45.
[103]   *Zielinski, Pradal, Gonzalez and others v France* [2001] EHRR 19.
[104]   *Ibid*, at [59].

Indeed, in the present case, it is difficult to deny that the legislature made law within its competence by setting the level of the relevant allowance. This is to be contrasted with the position adopted by the High Court of Australia in *BLF (Cth)*, which applied separation of powers principles, in particular the direction principle.[105] It will be recalled that the BLF, a builders' industrial union, had challenged in the courts the legality of the administrative procedures by which it had been de-registered. The government intervened by enacting *ad hominem* legislation which simply de-registered the union, thus rendering the pending proceedings redundant. The legislation was held valid and not a breach of the direction principle despite the fact that the union was being targeted and that the legislation addressed the very issue which was to be decided by the court. It was held that the legislation was nevertheless substantively legislative and was not prescriptive vis-à-vis the pending proceedings. Despite the rather unedifying prior conduct of the BLF, which enjoyed little public support in any event, the issue of public interest did not come into consideration. Had Article 6 been applied to these facts, and especially in light of the decision in *Zielenski,* it is more likely that the legislation would have been held invalid, leaving aside the public interest issue. Thus, in certain circumstances, Article 6 may provide surer protection to decisional independence. Indeed, it avoids the difficult exercise of determining the substantively legislative nature of an enactment. As a consequence of the legitimate expectations rationale underlying Article 6, it is sufficient if the law targets the proceedings and affects the rights of the parties thereto.

On the other hand, in situations at least where the direction principle would be breached, the qualification based on compelling public interest grounds may save the legislation, although admittedly the threshold for the application of the public interest exception appears to have been set at a high level. Therefore, although considerable flexibility is given to the operation of Article 6, in those circumstances of a clear legislative direction, the direction principle provides a surer protection to the courts' decisional independence.

In *Agoudimos and Cefallonian Sky Shipping Co v Greece*[106] the court expressly followed *Stran Greek Refineries* and the *Zielinski* case to establish that interference with rights in pending proceedings will constitute a breach of Article 6 in the absence of compelling public interest grounds. At issue was whether the purchaser of a ship in a compulsory sale by auction was liable for debts owed to social security and tax authorities by the previous owners. The applicants, who were such purchasers, had

[105] See ch 2 at p 76 above.
[106] *Agoudimos and Cefallonian Sky Shipping Co v Greece* (2003) 36 EHRR 60.

challenged their liability in this regard through the Greek courts in protracted litigation. The matter was pending determination in the superior Greek courts when legislation was enacted which purported to interpret in an authoritative manner the relevant law in question. The new law provided that the law relating to the payment of unpaid social security and tax debts did apply to owners who had acquired a ship through compulsory auction sale. Pursuing the pending litigation was thus rendered futile.

Before the ECtHR the Greek government argued that the impugned law was a general law which sought to clarify the previous uncertainty and thus served the compelling public interest in maintaining certainty in the law.[107] It was merely coincidental that legislation was passed when the hearing of the appeal was imminent. The law, it was argued, was not targeting the pending proceedings in order to favour the government and prejudice the applicants. It was rather a law of general application designed to remove uncertainty as to the precise meaning of the earlier law. The court stated that, in principle, the legislature is not precluded in civil matters from enacting retrospective laws to regulate rights arising under existing law.[108]

> However, the principle of the rule of law and the notion of a fair trial enshrined in Art. 6 preclude any interference by the legislature—other than on compelling grounds of the general interest—with the administration of justice designed to influence the judicial determination of the dispute.[109]

In the present case, the court stated that it could not ignore the fact that, in addition to the timing of the legislation, it had a very precise consequence for the pending proceedings, dealing specifically with the critical legal issues therein.

> To begin with, while [the law] expressly excluded from its scope court decisions that had become final, it settled once and for all the terms of the dispute before the ordinary courts and did so retrospectively. Therefore, the adoption of [the law] while the proceedings were pending in reality determined the substance of the dispute. The application of it by the Court of Cassation in its judgment … made it pointless to carry on the litigation.[110]

Thus the court concluded that 'the State infringed the applicants' rights under Article 6 by intervening in a manner which was decisive to ensure the outcome of proceedings in which it was a party and was favourable to it'.[111] There were no compelling public interest grounds to justify a

---

[107]   *Ibid*, at [28].
[108]   *Ibid*, at [30].
[109]   *Ibid*.
[110]   *Ibid*, at [32].
[111]   *Ibid*, at [35].

different conclusion. Even though the law did not expressly direct the outcome of the pending litigation, it nevertheless revealed that the ECtHR was willing to take into account such factors as the timing of the legislation and the fact that it addressed the very issues to be addressed in the pending proceedings. In other words, the court was looking at factors which in substance amounted to a legislative direction so that the decision was taken away from the court as to the interpretation of the relevant law, leaving it merely to declare and apply the law in the way that the legislature had interpreted it. Thus a fair trial by an independent tribunal was denied the applicants.

Again, this decision reveals that Article 6 may constitute a stronger protection than the direction principle because the Greek law could be regarded as substantively legislative and thus not liable to invalidation by the latter rule. Thus, pursuant to Article 6, a law can nevertheless be successfully impugned on the basis of the timing of the legislative intervention, its immediate relevance to pending proceedings, its retrospectivity, and its settling of the critical points in issue in favour of the government. This does not involve, to the same extent, the need to identify indicia of direction in order to impugn the substantively legislative nature of the enactment.

The difficulty of course remains the definition of 'compelling public interest'. Given that targeted legislative intervention tends to occur in cases of high public importance, as the previous chapters have borne out, this may not be such a difficult requirement to meet. At the very least, it does provide the government with a strong foundation upon which to base a justification for its intervention. If the separation of powers were the solely applicable attack on the legislation, pursuant to the direction principle, such an exception would not be available to the government.

A further, though less direct, limitation on legislative intervention affecting rights in issue in pending cases can be located in Article 1 of Protocol No 1, relating to property rights. In *Pressos Compania Naviera SA and Others v Belgium*,[112] following collisions in which its ships were involved, the applicant commenced legal proceedings for compensation against the Belgian State and a private company which had provided pilot services. While these matters were pending in the Belgian courts, legislation was enacted which provided that no claim in negligence could be brought against ships' pilots for damage caused by or sustained by a ship under pilotage. The potential damages involved in such cases were very large. The legislation was given a 30-year retrospective effect and consequently deprived the applicants of their right to compensation. The ECtHR held that Article 1 of Protocol 1 reflected three basic principles:

---

[112] *Pressos Compania Naviera SA and Others v Belgium* (1996) 21 EHRR 301.

the protection of the peaceful enjoyment of property; the subjection of deprivations of certain possessions to certain conditions; and the principle that '[c]ontracting States are entitled, amongst other things, to control the use of property in accordance with the general interest'.[113] Because the impugned statute exempted the State, and other providers of piloting services, from liability for negligent acts for which they would otherwise have been answerable, this resulted in

> an interference with the exercise of rights deriving from claims for damages which could have been asserted in domestic law up to that point and, accordingly, with the right that everyone, including each of the applicants, has to the peaceful enjoyment of his or her possessions.[114]

Thus, because the claims could be classified as possessions, it was held that in so far as the statute affected claims which had arisen prior to its enactment, 'the interference amounted to a deprivation of property' for the purposes of Article 1 of Protocol 1.[115] The State's argument of compelling public interest—protecting the State from large financial liability, establishing legal certainty in tort law and bringing Belgian law into line with neighbouring countries—was held not to be sufficient to override the prohibition in Article 1. Acknowledging the margin of appreciation allowed legislatures in the determination of what is in the public interest, the court found that the public interest claim was held in this case not to be reasonably based; and even if it were, the response of extinguishing all past claims was disproportionate.[116] Accordingly, the court did not find it necessary to proceed to examine any issues relevant to Article 6.

In more recent cases, the ECtHR has affirmed the position that the right to property enshrined in Article 1 of Protocol 1 may be violated by legislation barring claims and made applicable to pending cases.[117] In *Draon v France* and *Maurice v France*,[118] the court considered the validity of legislative curtailment of claims for 'wrongful birth' and 'wrongful life'. The French courts had recognised both claims. In 2002, legislation was enacted which excluded any claim by a person born with congenital or other disabilities (not caused directly by medical negligence) for the negligent non-prevention of birth. Similarly, any claim by a parent for the negligent failure to detect actual or possible disabilities in a foetus was

---

[113]   *Ibid*, at [35].
[114]   *Ibid*, at [34].
[115]   *Ibid*.
[116]   *Ibid*, at [36] ff.
[117]   See A Du Bois-Pedain, 'On Being Dispossessed of a Head of Claim in a Pending Case' (2006) 65 *Cambridge Law Journal* 257.
[118]   *Draon v France* (2006) 42 EHRR 40; and *Maurice v France* (2006) 42 EHRR 42.

curtailed so that 'the special burdens arising from the disability through-out the life of the child' would no longer form a part of the parent's claim. The law was made applicable to pending cases except where 'an irrevocable decision on the principle of compensation' had already been taken. The applicants were affected by the birth of seriously disabled children requiring permanent care and attendance and claimed that they had been negligently misinformed about the results of amniocentesis. They had commenced legal proceedings in 1999 and 2000 respectively and would have been entitled to compensation for the cost of raising their disabled children but for the 2002 law.

The court held in each of these cases that the 2002 law breached Article 1 of Protocol 1 because legal claims were to be treated as 'possessions' in the relevant sense. To be so regarded, the claim must have a firm basis in the settled law of the particular nation.[119] The claimant thus had a legitimate expectation that the established case law of the national courts will continue to be applied in respect of damage that has already occurred. On the present facts, it was held that the applicants had a claim which, prior to the enactment of the impugned law, they could legitimately have expected to be determined according to the ordinary law of liability for negligence, and therefore had a 'possession' protected by Article 1 of Protocol 1. Apart from the lawfulness requirement confirmed in this case and *Pressos*, as with Article 6, the application of Article 1 of Protocol 1 was subject to the overriding requirements of the general interest.

The court, however, did recognise that

> the applicability of legislation to pending proceedings does not necessarily in itself upset the requisite fair balance [between the demands of the general interests of the community and affected individuals' fundamental rights], since the legislature is not in principle precluded in civil matters from intervening to alter the current legal position through a statute which is immediately applicable.[120]

But in the present case, the new legislation 'abolished purely and simply, with retrospective effect, one of the essential heads of damage, relating to very large sums of money'.[121] This step could not be taken without providing the applicants with compensation 'reasonably related to the value of their lost asset'.[122] Thus, indirectly, decisional independence is protected because established pending claims are protected from inter-vening legislation and are therefore protected.

---

[119] See *Kopecky v Slovakia* (2005) 41 EHRR 43.
[120] *Maurice v France* (2006) 42 EHRR 42 at [89].
[121] *Ibid*, at [90].
[122] *Ibid*, at [91].

The assistance which can be provided by Article 1 of Protocol 1 was summarised as follows by Patricia Popelier[123]: 'Possession' does include claims in respect of which there is a legitimate expectation that the claim will be heard in a court.[124] To constitute a requisite 'possession' the claim must be sufficiently established in law to be enforceable.[125] To be sufficiently established, and if reliance is being based on precedents, these must be finally-decided cases, and not those which have been overturned by a higher court. However, reliance can be placed on decisions which are not final:

> A judgment overturned by a superior court can still legitimise expectations if it was overturned only on procedural grounds but was not isolated as for its content. A judgment obtained at first instance which has, due to appeal, not become final, can still legitimise expectations if that judgment conformed to other judgments delivered by domestic courts in similar cases. Applicants can thus expect that, without legislative interference, established case law would continue to be applied and the appeal court would have given judgment in their favour.[126]

However, the ECtHR has held that it does not suffice to have a 'genuine dispute' or an 'arguable claim' to establish the legitimate expectation necessary for the protections of Article 1 of Protocol 1.[127] Similarly, a belief that a law will be invalidated or amended to the applicants' advantage on the ground of unconstitutionality does not constitute a relevant form of legitimate expectation.[128] It is clear, as Popelier notes, that the central requirement is the need for some legal certainty for the requisite legitimate expectation to be set up.[129]

IV.   THE UNITED KINGDOM, THE ECHR AND THE HUMAN RIGHTS ACT 1998.

Like other contracting States to the ECHR, the United Kingdom is bound by Articles 6 and 7. With the passage of the Human Rights Act 1998 (UK) ('HRA'), which incorporated the rights protected in the Convention into

---

[123]   P Popelier, 'Legitimate Expectations and the Law Maker in the Case Law of the European Court of Human Rights' (2006) 1 *European Human Rights Law Review* 10 and the cases cited at 12.

[124]   *Ibid*, at 14.

[125]   See *Stran Greek Refineries and Stratis Andreadis v Greece* (1995) 19 EHRR 293 at [59].

[126]   Popelier, 'Legitimate Expectations and the Law Maker', n 123 above, and the cases cited at 14. See also *Stran Greek* (n 125 above) [59] and *Pressos*, n 112 above, [31].

[127]   *Kopecky v Slovakia* (2005) 41 EHRR 43 at [52].

[128]   *Gratzinger and Gratzingerova v Czech Republic* (App No39794/98) decision of 10 July 2002 at [73].

[129]   Popelier, 'Legitimate Expectations and the Law Maker', n 123 above, 16.

domestic law, including Articles 6 and 7,[130] remedies became available in the domestic courts of the United Kingdom, although they fall short of a declaration of invalidity of any impugned statute. The HRA does not seek to override the sovereignty of Parliament but rather to provide a mechanism whereby conflicts between United Kingdom legislation and the ECHR can be resolved. In brief, the HRA renders it unlawful for any public authority to act in a way which is incompatible with Convention rights (section 6), requiring the courts and tribunals which deal with Convention rights to take into account the relevant decisions of the ECtHR, the European Commission and the Committee of Ministers (section 2). They are directed to read and give effect to both primary and secondary legislation in a way which is compatible with Convention rights so far as is possible (section 3(1)). Subordinate legislation which remains incompatible with Convention rights may be invalidated, but this power does not extend to primary legislation or to subordinate legislation that is rendered immune to invalidation by the primary legislation which authorised it (section 3(2)). The court is authorised to make a 'declaration of incompatibility' with respect to primary legisla- tion which is found to be incompatible with Convention rights (section 4). This declaration, however,

> does not affect the validity, continuing operation or enforcement of the provision in respect of which it is given; and … is not binding on the parties to the proceedings to which it is made [section 4(6)].

As a result of such a declaration, a minister of the Crown is empowered by order to make such amendments as he considers necessary to remove the incompatibility (section 10).[131] Although this procedure therefore does provide some remedy in the domestic courts against infringements of sections 6 and 7 of the ECHR, these are not as immediate as an invalidation of the relevant Act. In effect, given the significant role of the Minister in determining precisely how the situation is to be played out, one can only query how effective this will be in cases of supreme importance and in which the government is highly desirous of a particu- lar result. In any event, the process is fraught with uncertainty and it is not precisely clear how these mechanisms will operate. As Professor Evelyn Ellis has concluded,

> [t]he full practical consequence of these provisions will take some years to become plain. If the invariable reaction to a declaration of incompatibility proves to be an immediate remedial order, it might be concluded that the

---

[130]   See Human Rights Act 1998 s 1 and Schedule 1.
[131]   The procedure for this is set out in Sch 2 para 2(b) which requires that a draft remedial order must have been laid before Parliament for 60 days and approved by resolution of each House of Parliament unless the matter is an urgent one.

authority of Parliament has in fact been considerably diminished and its supremacy relinquished to the Convention and the courts. The effect of such a position would, in practice, be only slightly different from a power of judicial review over primary legislation. Furthermore, although the HRA itself is ordinary legislation enacted in the usual way by Parliament and thus theoretically capable of both express and implied repeal, it is of course highly improbable, and would be politically well-nigh unthinkable, that it would ever be removed from the statute book.[132]

Nevertheless, the protections which Articles 6 and 7 ECHR provide are thus reinforced and provide in the United Kingdom a protection for decisional independence which is otherwise not available due to the absence of an entrenched separation of powers. These protections to judicial independence based on the ECHR and HRA are generally reinforced by Britain's membership of the European Union, subject to the observations made above in relation to the uncertain status of the separation of powers in the European Union. The decisions of the European Court of Justice, which interprets and applies Community law, have been prominent in this regard. As Professor Feldman has pointed out,

> [a]fter some hesitation, the Court of Justice of the European Communities accepted that it, and national courts interpreting Community law, would have regard to the fundamental rights forming general principles of Community law when they became relevant to a question of Community law, either as grounds for judicial review of the action of the Community institutions or as guides to the interpretation of Community law. The 'general principles' are derived from the common constitutional traditions of the member states (where they can be identified), and from international treaties to which member states have contributed. They therefore include the rights under the ECHR. Although the Court of Justice has rarely struck down a legislative or executive act by a Community institution on the ground of an incompatibility with a Convention right, the ECHR has increasingly influenced the thinking of member states about the structures of the European Communities and the European Union.[133]

The recognition of these standards was given more concrete expression in European instruments. Feldman notes that '[t]he human rights standards recognised by the Court of Justice were finally given expression in the Treaties, in what is now article 6(2) of the Amsterdam Treaty 1997'.[134] Furthermore,

> [t]he protection for human rights in EU law was then extended by the EU Charter of Fundamental Rights … The Charter covers a wide range of social

---

[132]   In Feldman (ed), *English Public Law*, n 10 above, 150.
[133]   *Ibid*, at 378 (footnotes omitted).
[134]   *Ibid*.

and economic rights alongside the core (mainly civil and political) rights derived from the ECHR, and is expressed to apply to EU institutions and to institutions in member states when implementing Community law. In the view of the UK government, the Charter has no binding legal force, but it is being used by the Court of Justice as an aid to interpreting EU law, including the human rights obligations recognized in Article 6(2) of the Amsterdam Treaty.[135]

These developments would appear to exert an increasingly normative influence protective of judicial decisional independence, but it cannot be put higher than that. Feldman points out that

> [f]or the moment, gaps remain in the protection offered to rights through the Court of Justice. There is a lack of clarity as to the rights which can be protected. There is no clear statement of the acceptable grounds for interfering with rights. Finally, there is no guarantee that the Court of Justice will interpret rights as generously as the European Court of Human Rights would. This creates a risk that inconsistent decisions will emerge from the two courts. The European Union is not a party to the ECHR, and the European Court of Human Rights has no powder to hold the European Union or its institutions (as distinct from the member states, which are all parties to the ECHR) to account for violations of rights under ECHR.[136]

In conclusion, therefore, the above discussion would indicate that the type of protections afforded by express provisions in fundamental instruments such as the ECHR can offer some protection to the decisional independence of the judiciary. It emerges from an examination of the above cases that the protections afforded by Article 6 ECHR can apply even if the impugned statute is regarded as indeed a substantively legislative amendment to law. All that is required is that there is a clear, targeted effect on pending proceedings and there is no compelling public interest ground to justify such an intervention. The difficulty with this position, as intimated above, is that such interventions do tend to occur in cases involving matters of high public importance and therefore the opportunity to rely on the compelling public interest exception may present itself in many of these cases. While this does offer a degree of flexibility to the application of Article 6, it nevertheless erodes the protection to decisional independence which is particularly necessary in such cases where a determined legislature may seek to enforce its policy interest by legislative intervention. The direction principle based on the separation of powers does not provide such an opportunity and to that extent its protection is more certain. However, the direction principle can only apply if the substantively legislative nature of the relevant statute is

---

[135] *Ibid*, at 379.
[136] *Ibid*, at 379.

successfully impugned, and, as outlined in chapters two and three above, this can cause considerable difficulties and uncertainties.

V.   CANONS OF STATUTORY INTEPRETATION

Before concluding this monograph, mention must be made of the limited, although not insubstantial, protection to decisional independence provided by the canons of statutory interpretation. Of particular relevance is that canon which requires legislation not be interpreted in such a way that its retrospective consequences are regarded as intending to apply to pending cases in the absence of a clear and express words to that effect. It is a narrower application of the broader principle that laws with retrospective effect will not be intended by the legislature to remove vested rights in the absence of clear words to that effect. This is a universal canon of statutory interpretation recognised in the United Kingdom and other Westminster-style jurisdictions irrespective of the entrenchment of the separation of powers, as well as in the United States. Its rationale is the maintenance of the rule of law, in particular those aspects thereof relating to the maintenance of certainty, reasonable reliance, fair notice and settled expectations for the citizenry in the conduct of their affairs.[137] In *R v Secretary of State for the Home Department, ex parte Pierson* Lord Steyne stated that the rule 'enforces minimum standards of fairness, both substantive and procedural'.[138] More recently, in this context, reference is being made to the principle of 'legality' of which this particular canon is an application.[139]

The rigour with which this canon of statutory interpretation is applied in particular instances depends largely on a number of considerations such as, for example, whether the legislation deals with substantial or procedural matters or with criminal or civil matters, whether it has an effect on pending proceedings and whether it is of benefit or detriment to those affected.[140] The classic statement of principle remains that of Willes J in *Phillips v Eyre*:

> Retrospective laws are, no doubt, prima facie of questionable policy, and contrary to the general principle that legislation by which the conduct of mankind is to be regulated ought, when introduced for the first time, to deal with future acts, and ought not to change the character of past transactions

---

[137]   See generally JW Bridge, 'Retrospective Legislation and the Rule of Law in Britan' (1967) 35 *University of Missouri Kansas City Law Review* 132 and C Sampford, *Retrospectivity and the Rule of Law* (Oxford, Oxford University Press, 2006).

[138]   *R v Secretary of State for the Home Department, ex parte Pierson* [1998] AC 539 at 575.

[139]   See J Spigelman, 'The Principle of Legality and the Clear Statement Principle' (2005) 79 *Australian Law Journal* 769 at 774–6.

[140]   See Sampford, *Retrospectivity and the Rule of Law*, n 137 above, ch 4.

carried on upon the faith of the then existing law … Accordingly, the Court will not ascribe retrospective force to new laws affecting rights, unless by express words or necessary implication it appears that such was the intention of the legislature.[141]

While affording therefore some protection to decisional independence against retrospective laws, not all retrospective laws were to be thus automatically treated. Willes J continued: 'But to affirm that it is naturally or necessarily unjust to take away a vested right of action by act subsequent is inconsistent both with the common law of England and the constant practice of legislation'.[142] Although a well-settled principle, it nevertheless remains an interpretative principle which itself allows the legislature to override its presumption by clear and unambiguous terms. Accordingly, absent an entrenched separation of powers or other express constitutional principles to the contrary, it is a principle whose protections are not absolute, and, as noted by Lord Ashburner in *Smith v Callendar*, where it appears 'very clearly in the terms of the act, or arise by necessary and distinct implication … [i]t is obviously competent for the Legislature in its wisdom to make the provisions of an act of Parliament retrospective'.[143] However, as stated by Lindley LJ in *Lauri v Renaud*, it is 'not to be construed so as to have a greater retrospective operation than its language renders necessary'.[144]

The presumption against the retrospective effect of legislation is applied with particular rigour in the context of pending cases, and the case law in various jurisdictions generally treats this as a special case.[145] As stated by Lord Roger of Earlsferry in *Wilson v First County Trust*, '[s]ince the potential injustice of interfering with the rights of parties to actual proceedings is particularly obvious, this…presumption will be that much harder to displace'.[146] However, if the change in the law relates merely to procedural matters, a less stringent view is taken and procedural provisions will generally be assumed to be applicable to pending cases unless a party to the pending proceedings may suffer detriment as

---

[141]   *Phillips v Eyre* (1870) LR 6 QB 1 at 23.
[142]   *Ibid.*
[143]   *Smith v Callendar* [1901] AC 297 at 305.
[144]   *Lauri v Renaud* (1892) 3 Ch 402 at 421.
[145]   See eg, *Lodhi v The Queen* (2006) 199 FLR 303 (Spigelman CJ and the cases therein cited): *Re Joseph Suche & Co Ltd* (1875) 1 Ch D 48 at 50; *Hutchinson v Jauncey* [1950] 1 KB 574 at 579; *Continental Liquers Pty Ltd v GF Heublein and Bros Inc* (1960) 103 CLR 422 at 427; *Zainal bin Hashim v Government of Malaysia* [1966] AC 734 at 742; *L'Office Cherifien des Phosphates v Yamashita-Shinnihon Steamship Co Ltd* [1994] 1 AC 486 at 495–96 and 524–5; *Wilson v First County Trust Ltd (No 2)* [2004] 1 AC 816 at [19], [153], [186], [193]–[198], [200]–[201] and [219]; *Victoria v Robertson* (2000) 1 VR 465 esp at [21]–[22], [25]; *Attorney-General (NSW) v World Best Holdings Ltd* (2005) 63 NSWLR 557 at [49]–[63].
[146]   *Wilson v First County Trust* [2004] 1 AC 816 at [198].

a result.[147] Thus, even if it is clear that Parliament intended the application of the law to pending cases, the extent to which the statute applies in this way does still require the statute to be interpreted. As stated by Spigelman CJ, in *Lodhi v The Queen*, citing English and Australian authority,

> [a] statute will only be given retrospective operation to the extent intended by the Parliament and to no greater extent. This is to be determined by the words of the statute, construed in their full context, and in accordance with the scope and purpose of the legislation.[148]

This presumption against retrospectivity does not emanate from the doctrine of the separation of powers, although it is certainly consistent with it, but rather from general rule of law principles, and as indicated above, it has been regarded as falling within the unifying higher principle of legality. In *R v Secretary of State for the Home Department; ex parte Simms*, Lord Hoffman stated:

> [T]he principle of legality means that Parliament must squarely confront what it is doing and accept the political costs. Fundamental rights cannot be overridden by general or ambiguous words. This is because there is too great a risk that the full implications of their unqualified meaning may have passed unnoticed in the democratic process. In the absence of express language or necessary implication to the contrary, the courts therefore presume that even the most general words were intended to be subject to the basic rights of the individual. In this way the courts of the United Kingdom, though acknowledging the sovereignty of Parliament, apply principles of constitutionality little different from those which exist in countries where the power of the legislature is expressly limited by a constitutional document.[149]

This statement does certainly indicate that this principle of statutory interpretation provides a very strong protection to judicial decisional independence and certainly reinforces the position taken by TRS Allan. Of course, this is qualified by the recognition that clear and express words in a statute may nevertheless override the presumption and hence it needs to be reinforced by the added protections which arise from an entrenched separation of powers.

However, the rigour with which the courts are willing to scrutinise such legislation should not be underestimated, especially in criminal cases. In *Lodhi*, at issue were whether amendments to the anti-terrorist

---

[147] See *Carson v Carson* [1964] 1 WLR 511; *Plewa v Chief Adjudication Officer* [1994] 3 WLR 317.

[148] *Lodhi v The Queen* (2006) 199 FLR 303 at 310 [23]; *Reid v Reid* (1886) 31 Ch D 402 at 408–9; *Lauri v Renad* [1892] 3 Ch 402 at 420–21, *Moss v Donohoe* (1915) 20 CLR 615 at 621.

[149] *R v Secretary of State for the Home Department; ex parte Simms* [2000] 2 AC 115 at 131.

provisions of the Criminal Code Act 1995 (Cth),[150] which had an adverse affect on the defendant, were retrospectively applicable to his pending prosecution. The New South Wales Court of Criminal Appeal[151] held that because the statute did not use express words to this effect, the presumption was applied that the statute was not to be understood as being applicable to criminal proceedings that had already been instituted. The presumption was applied with particular rigour because retrospective effect was sought to be given to a provision creating a criminal offence.[152]

In the United States, the issue emerged in dramatic circumstances in *Hamdam v Rumsfeld*, in which the Supreme Court held that the military commissions set up by the United States government for the trial of terrorist suspects detained at Guatanamo Bay, Cuba, were in violation of both United States municipal law and international law.[153] The issue relevant for present purposes was whether the provisions of the Detainee Treatment Act 2005,[154] which removed the jurisdiction of federal courts over habeas corpus petitions filed by Guantanamo Bay detainees applied to cases pending when the law became operative. The majority opinion, written by Stevens J, held that the statute could not apply retroactively to pending cases in the absence of express words to that effect, based on settled principles of statutory interpretation.[155] The court regarded this as a particular application of settled principle, citing *Landgraf v USI Film Products*[156] and *Bruner v United States*.[157] In the *Landgraf* case, the court considered those sections of the Civil Rights Act 1991 (US) which provided for compensatory and punitive damages to be awarded to victims of discrimination. The Supreme Court held that these provisions did not apply retrospectively to legal suits which had commenced prior to the enactment. The statute did not express its intention in this regard sufficiently clearly and the court was therefore reluctant to allow for the provisions' retrospective operation given that they conferred a new right to damages which increased the liability of those in breach of anti-discrimination legislation.[158] It is significant to note, however, that the court did acknowledge that the change in the law, even if retrospective,

[150] Introduced by the Anti-Terrorism Act 2005 (Cth) and the Anti-Terrorism Act (No 2) 2005 (Cth).
[151] *Lodhi v The Queen* (2006) 199 FLR 303 (Spigelman CJ, Mclellan CJ and Sully J).
[152] *Attorney General of NSW v World Best Holdings* (2005) 63 NSWLR 557.
[153] *Hamdam v Rumsfeld* 126 S Ct 2749 (2006).
[154] Pub L 109–148, 119 Stat 2739 (30 December 2005).
[155] *Hamdam v Rumsfeld* 126 S Ct 2749 (2006) at 2763 (Kennedy, Souter, Ginsburg and Breyer JJ concurring).
[156] *Landgraf v USI Film Products* 511 US 244 (1994).
[157] *Bruner v United States* 343 US 112 (1952).
[158] See Sampford, *Retrospectivity and the Rule of Law*, n 137 above, 128 and more generally ch 4. See also SM Pearson, 'Canons, Presumptions and Manifest Injustice: Retroactivity of the Civil Rights Act of 1991' (1993) 3 *Southern California Interdisciplinary Law Journal* 461.

must be applied by the courts to pending cases if the intention is expressed clearly, citing *Schooner Peggy* and thus affirming the Changed Law Rule. In so doing, the majority also acknowledged the inability of the presumption ultimately to overcome the power of the legislature in this regard, absent of course the application of the direction principle derived from an entrenched separation doctrine. They also noted that there were circumstances when retroactivity could be allowed to operate without necessarily offending rule of law principles, that is, 'when the intervening statute authorizes prospective [ie injunctive] relief', in particular where the affected party has no 'vested right' in previous decrees entered by the courts; when the jurisdiction of the relevant court was removed by a jurisdictional statute, so long as the rule does not remove any substantive rights; and when procedural rules are being changed.[159] The court was not indicating that the presumption against retrospective application was being ousted in these circumstances, merely that the presumption was to be applied less stringently in these circumstances given that the rule of law concerns were considerably diminished.[160]

The conclusion to be drawn from all these cases, however, is that while the above principles do afford a high degree of protection to judicial decisional independence in pending and finally-decided suits, the situations remains that, absent other express constitutional limitations, a clear and unequivocal expression of intent of the legislature will prevail. The higher protections afforded by the direction rule and inviolability principles emanating from the separation of powers doctrine will only be applicable in jurisdictions where that doctrine is entrenched, or indeed in jurisdictions which proscribe retroactive statutes in their constitutions.

---

[159] See n 156, at 273–5 above. See JE Fisch, 'Retroactivity and Legal Change: An Equilibrium Approach' (1997) 110 *Harvard Law Review* 1055 at 1063–6 and 1091–4.
[160] See *Ins v St Cyr* 533 US 289 (2001).

7

Conclusion

T HIS MONOGRAPH HAS sought to address critical issues which
arise from the interpretation and application of the doctrine of the
separation of powers as an entrenched legal and constitutional
principle, with particular focus on the regulation of the relationship
between the legislative and judicial branches, the more precise aim being
to appreciate the protections afforded to judicial *decisional* independence.

The analysis has been conducted at essentially two levels. At one level,
it is accepted that the legal separation of judicial power constitutes a
source of enforceable constitutional limitations on the legislature, and the
analysis then proceeds to define those limitations which protect judicial
decisional independence. This precise issue has not received the attention
that it warrants, and accordingly an attempt has been made to fill a
significant lacuna in separation of powers scholarship relevant to
Westminster-based systems and the United States. At this level, the
emphasis has been on the definition and evaluation of the relevant
constitutional limitations, as opposed to an evaluation of the separation
of powers doctrine per se, its place in the relevant constitutions considered, and the way it has been interpreted and applied. This emphasis is
justified for two main reasons. First, the fact that such constitutional
limitations exist is indicative that the *legal* entrenchment of the separation
of powers contributes an added layer of protection to the independence
of the judicial branch beyond its 'institutional independence', that is, the
non case-specific protections of tenure and salary. Secondly, the decisional independence of the courts constitutes an issue of the highest
constitutional significance, and yet the jurisprudence on this issue has
not developed as fully as it might. As discussed in chapters one and two
in particular, the desire to protect the judicial branch from legislative
interference in relation to both pending cases and final judgments was a
primary rationale for the original *legal* entrenchment of the separation of
powers in the United States Constitution. In Australia, even though this
issue did not figure prominently, if at all, in the deliberations of the
Framers of the Commonwealth Constitution, nevertheless, the fundamental importance of the decisional independence of the judicial branch

was appreciated by the early commentators and is self-evidently significant in any polity which attempts to maintain liberal government and the
rule of law. Its importance has not been lessened by the passage of time
or the fact that egregious legislative interferences with judicial functions
are rare. The extent to which the separation of powers is the source of
constitutional limitations in this regard is an important measure of its
efficacy as an entrenched legal rule.

At another level, this monograph has addressed the difficult question
of the most appropriate interpretative methodology to be applied to the
separation of powers doctrine. This has been centred on an examination
of the tensions which arise between a formalist approach and a more
purposive functionalist approach. This level of the enquiry has not of
course progressed in isolation from the first. It is simply not possible to
attempt a definition of the precise constitutional limitations emanating
from the separation of powers—either in the precise context of the issue
of decisional independence or indeed any other aspect of inter-branch
relationships—without addressing the questions which arise at this level
of interpretive methodology. Furthermore, a resolution of this issue is
essential in order to make some assessment of the efficacy of the
separation of powers as an entrenched legal rule.

A stumbling block to the adoption of a uniform formalist position, as
acknowledged by leading constitutional scholars both in Australia and in
the United States, is the impossibility of providing a completely
mutually-exclusive definition of the elements of branch power. Yet, an
entrenchment of the doctrine results in a persistent imperative to provide
some definition thereof, at least at a fundamental level. The immediate
temptation is to resort to purely conceptual definition, pursuant to a
formalist approach, in order to meet the law's more rigid requirements
for definition to ensure legal enforcement. However, such an approach
simply cannot accommodate the subtleties which arise in the various
overlapping inter-branch relationships. How to resolve this tension is
probably the greatest and most persistent theme in separation of powers
jurisprudence. To come to terms with this tension, it has been conceded
that some degree of formalism is unavoidable, indeed desirable and
possible, at a certain fundamental level, at which level the definitional
imperative also can be met. However, a formalism based on an exclusively conceptual analysis of the constituent elements of branch power
has been eschewed. Rather, a moderate, purposive formalism has been
advocated where appropriate, with reliance being placed on custom,
usage, history and tradition, and the institutional parameters in which
branch power is exercised. Even so, the limits of this approach have been
acknowledged. It has not been suggested that the adoption of a uniform
formalist approach in all separation of powers issues will resolve this
tension. The weakness inherent in formalism—that it is simply not

possible to provide mutually-exclusive definitions of branch power—is compelling and acknowledged. A purposive functionalism, therefore, certainly has its place, especially with regard to those elements of branch power which cannot be regarded as core and predominantly non-transferable.

While it has it not been the purpose of this monograph to explore the most appropriate approach which should be adopted in relation to all the various aspects of inter-branch relationships, the position was adopted that a purposive functionalism was appropriate in separation of powers jurisprudence, except at the level of core, fundamental, 'typical', 'non-transferable' elements of branch power. Indeed, as indicated, at this level of core functions, a certain formalist rigidity may be warranted. To take one instance, such would be the case to ensure the maintenance of that critical constitutional limitation that the judicial power can only be vested in the judicial branch. So fundamental is this principle to the integrity of branch power that to allow any exceptions on functionalist grounds—except perhaps very limited ones already based on long-established usage and custom, such as in the case of military tribunals—would certainly warrant those formalist concerns about the piecemeal erosion of fundamental protections afforded by the separation of powers doctrine. It is therefore at this level of core elements of branch power (those elements of branch power which are indisputably non-transferable, even pursuant to a functionalist analysis), that formalism comes into its own. Indeed, at this level, a reconciliation between formalism and functionalism is achievable because even though functionalism will take into account policy and efficiency considerations, there is a certain point at which even a functionalist will not be able to make an allowance for a breach of the separation doctrine; although, as witnessed, for example, in the United States Supreme Court decisions *Miller v French*[1] and *Plaut v Spendthrift Farm Inc*,[2] differences may still emerge when an uncompromising functionalist line is taken. This point is reached where the allowance would so undermine the integrity of branch power that it would not justify, on public policy grounds, any allowances to be made.

Without attempting to identify all the elements of branch power which fall into this category of fundamental or core elements, the position was taken in chapter one that those elements of judicial power, and the judicial functions related thereto, which are essential to the decisional independence of the judicial branch, can be so identified. These elements are contained in the classic definition of judicial power, which is the

---

[1] *Miller v French* 530 US 327 (2000).
[2] *Plaut v Spendthrift Farm Inc* 514 US 211 (1995).

conclusive adjudication of controversies between parties in litigation
resulting in an authoritative and binding declaration of their respective
rights and obligations according to existing law. To ensure that judicial
decisional independence is maintained, the separation of powers can be
applied strictly to these elements pursuant to a purposive formalism,
which, it has been argued, will produce an outcome which would
coincide with that produced by a functionalist approach. Thus, it has
been possible to conclude that the legal separation of judicial power does
result in the establishment of a discrete set of constitutional limitations
which protect the decisional independence of those courts from legislative interference.

In the pending case scenario, examined in detail in chapters two and
three, it was submitted that these principles are centred on what has been
termed the 'direction principle'. This rule is based on the critical distinction between a valid legislative amendment to the law which the courts
must apply in the pending case and a mere legislative direction to the
court as to how it is to exercise its jurisdiction; the latter being unconstitutional. The existence of an unconstitutional direction is determined by
reference to various indicia of direction such as the *ad hominem* nature of
the legislation, its retrospectivity, and the extent to which it is tailored to
address the precise issues in the pending case, either in relation to the
final outcome of the case, or indeed a particular aspect thereof. There is
no closed set of indicia. In order to protect the legitimate exercise of
legislative power, the direction principle must operate together with the
'Changed Law Rule', that is, the rule which requires the application of a
new law or an amendment to the law in the pending case. The precise
relationship between the two rules is that the former operates as a
threshold test before the latter rule can apply. Determining whether the
direction principle is breached requires the rather subtle evaluation of the
existence of the various indicia of direction, whose interplay and cumulative effect in the context of the pending proceedings must be balanced
to determine whether the substantively legislative nature of the legislation should be impugned. This interplay between the Changed Law Rule
and the direction principle is critical to ensure the appropriate balance of
protection of both the judicial power, exclusively vested in the judicial
branch, and legislative power, vested in the legislative branch. Given the
subtleties, and attendant difficulties, involved in establishing a breach of
the direction principle, it is important that the rule be applied rigorously
and substance not be sacrificed to form. The notion that otherwise
properly enacted legislation might not be substantively legislative, that it
may not be 'law', was reinforced in the thesis of Professor Allan (as
discussed in chapter six), who argued that such was the case with Acts of
Attainder and *ad hominem* legislation. This view of course applied regardless of the entrenchment of a separation of powers and, although it has

yet to achieve unambiguous acceptance by the courts, it does reinforce the argument that an entrenched separation of powers does require some content to be given to the concept of 'legislative' power, that its enactments be in substance 'law', and that the legislature be prevented from intruding in a non-legislative way with judicial power.

In the final judgment scenario, considered in detail in chapters four and five, the more absolute principle, referred to as the 'inviolability principle', applies. Final judgments cannot be *legislatively* revised, amended or re-opened by the legislature as between the parties thereto. This also applies to prohibit the legislature constituting itself a tribunal, or setting up another non-court tribunal, to review the final decisions of these courts. Detailed consideration was given to the qualifications to the rule which ameliorate its rigour somewhat, as detailed in chapter five.[3] These qualifications were articulated more precisely in the United States authorities. They were centred either on the nature of 'finality', that is, whether particular judgments could be considered sufficiently final as to attract absolute protection, or on the extent to which the revision of a final judgment was left within the discretion of the court. Thus, the *'Wheeling Bridge* qualification' established that there are certain judgments which are only *conditionally* final in their prospective and continuing effect because they are subject to the continuance of the state of law as at the time the judgment was handed down. Should the law be changed, the judgment is rendered otiose in that it will no longer be enforced by the court should the party in whose favour it was granted seeks to enforce it. However, although this qualification allows the final judgment to be rendered redundant in this way, it does not permit its explicit legislative revision as between the parties; although it is of course subject to *judicial* revision. This qualification will not apply to the more absolute final judgments, such as those resulting in an order awarding damages or costs, or indeed orders permanently staying proceedings, subject of course to any *judicial* discretion which may be available to revise such judgments. Also, there will be no breach of the inviolability principle should a legislature provide that the government will waive the benefit of a judgment in its favour by not seeking to have it enforced, or should it waive its right to plead res judicata where the other side seeks to have a matter re-litigated—as long as it does not prohibit the courts from considering whether the matter is res judicata. While these waiver qualifications can be derived from first principles, it is again the United States authorities which have given them precise articulation to confirm the position which should also pertain in other jurisdictions maintaining a separation of judicial power. None of these qualifications prevent the

---

[3] See above, ch5 at 247ff.

legislature from overruling the statement of the law made by a court by legislating to change the law, even retrospectively, absent, of course, any direct legislative interference with a previous final judgment as between the parties.

This monograph has evaluated the judicial exegesis on the relevant constitutional limitations so defined in each scenario by detailed reference to first principles and the assistance to be gained from constitutional scholarship. While the discrete set of principles centred on the Changed Law Rule, the direction and inviolability principles have certainly been formulated as above-stated in the seminal cases such as *Liyanage*, the *BLF* cases, *Klein* and *Plaut*, the reluctance in subsequent decisions to provide a more explicit and precise recognition of, and definition to, the discrete principles governing legislative interference with judicial functions has been noted as the most significant hurdle for the continued efficacy of these rules as constitutional limitations. This is particularly so in relation to the pending case scenario. In Australia, this was most evident in *Nicholas*, and mirrored in the United States in *Robertson* and *Miller v French.* This monograph has attempted to explain why these clear rules have not been applied with sufficient rigour by the courts in these more recent cases. It has been suggested that the reason is not the failure of the separation of powers as an entrenched legal rule to produce efficacious principles regulating branch power. Rather the rules which are emerging have yet to be sufficiently formalised so as to enable a surer recognition and application thereof.

The judicial tendency not to apply the direction principle rigorously, or at least with a minimum rigour so as to ensure its efficacious operation in all relevant cases, was noted as a particular problem. In the Australian context, detailed reference was made to *Nicholas* in chapter three where it was submitted that only Kirby J correctly applied the direction principle consistently with *Liyanage* and previous Australian authority. The other judges either did not see the relevance of the rule on the facts, or circumscribed the operation of the rule to such an extent that its successful implementation would only be assured in the most egregious cases. Moreover, there was a tendency in some of the judgments unnecessarily to circumscribe the principles which emanated from *Liyanage*. In the United States, an almost identical tendency was evident in the wake of *Robertson* in the Supreme Court, despite the rigorous application of the direction principle by the Courts of Appeal. However, in both jurisdictions, despite being weakened, the direction principle was never overruled and the fundamental distinctions on which it was based survived, even though there is the significant risk that the principle will continue to be misunderstood in application and indeed be relevant only in the most egregious of circumstances.

This has resulted in the curious situation whereby there exists a clearly articulated constitutional limitation, yet one whose continuing efficacy is uncertain. The monograph has attempted to locate the possible causes for such an outcome in the nature of the direction principle itself, and in particular the subtle and case-specific operation of the indicia of direction. Following detailed analysis of the Australian and United States cases, reinforced by an examination of Irish cases, and the extensive scholarship on this issue in the United States in chapter three, it was submitted that the solution to this problem has two limbs. First, at the most basic level, it is imperative that more explicit recognition be given to the direction principle as a precise constitutional limitation in the pending case scenario. It is disconcerting that in obvious situations, such as arose in *Nicholas*, its pertinence was not obviously appreciated. Secondly, the writer has advocated a greater formalisation of the indicia of direction, at the core of the successful application of the principle, to enable a more straightforward application and avoid some of the confusions which have become apparent. While the notion of a greater formalisation has only been suggested by one other commentator to the writer's knowledge—Amy Ronner in the United States—the degree of formalisation advocated was regarded as being excessive.[4] Such a reaction was understandable in light of the Supreme Court's extraordinary reasoning in *Robertson*. This monograph adopted the approach whereby the existence of certain specific indicia in particular combination should give rise to a rebuttable presumption that an unconstitutional legislative direction has occurred. Ronner did not rely on such presumptions but rather argued for an actual finding of unconstitutional direction if certain defined indicia were present, and in particular combination. The writer, however, favours the use of presumptions because allowance must be made in each case for the existence of unpredictable factors which on balance may negate the existence of unconstitutional direction. While there has been no other advocate of such an approach, the writer believes it is the only one which confronts most appropriately the challenges facing the direction principle following *Nicholas* and *Miller v French*. The bulk of the academic criticism of the 'soft' approach to the application of the direction principle manifested in these cases has merely exhorted the courts to return to a 'substance over form' approach and a rigorous application of the direction principle in the *Klein* and *Liyanage* tradition. While it is hoped that such an exhortation will be heeded, it does not address the inherent problems in the principle itself. It is submitted that the approach advocated here based on the formalisation of the indicia of direction and the use of rebuttable presumptions will not only refine the

---

[4] See above, at 176ff.

definition of the principle, but also significantly increase its efficacy without upsetting the delicate balance between this principle and the Changed Law Rule.

The need for a more precise articulation of the direction principle, and indeed its greater formalisation and refinement, is underlined by developments in the United States following *Miller v French*, a decision which introduced quite novel and, with respect, inappropriate qualifications to both direction and inviolability principles, which cannot be sustained either on first principles or on even a very liberal interpretation of the separation of powers doctrine.[5] While it has been argued that this case should not be followed and, if not overruled, restricted very strictly to its facts, it nevertheless reveals the unfortunate tendencies which can result if the direction principle is not put on a surer footing. Unless this occurs, this constitutional limitation will become relevant only in the most extreme, and therefore, highly unlikely circumstances. Moreover, this will result in a rather anomalous situation in Australia, for example, in that the High Court will have adopted a very strict approach to the separation of judicial power in almost every other respect, and yet, on this highly significant issue of protecting the decisional independence of federal courts—without a doubt a separation of powers issue of the highest order—it will have failed to apply with sufficient rigour a fundamental constitutional limitation.

In relation to the final judgment scenario, as discussed in detail in chapters four and five, the inviolability principle stands on surer ground. There is nothing to suggest that it will not be applied rigorously to protect the final judgments of courts from interference by the legislature. The reference to the United States jurisprudence, and also that of Ireland and India, has been of assistance in articulating the possible qualifications to the principle and in providing concrete examples of their application. Its more advanced and subtle exploration of the concept of 'finality', of the distinction between *judicial* and *legislative* revision of final judgments, and the complex issue of legislative waiver by government of the benefits of a final judgment, has enabled a refinement of principle. The only real concern arising from the United States authorities again relates to *Miller v French* and the application of its extraordinary qualifications to the inviolability principle.[6] They cannot be sustained on first principles, nor can they be justified on any functionalist grounds. Indeed, the curious aspect of these qualifications is that they were articulated as formalist exceptions to the inviolability principle, not as functionalist allowances to what otherwise would constitute a breach of the separation

---

[5] See above at 152.
[6] See above at 236.

of powers. The other, lesser concern, relates to the waiver qualification, discussed in chapter five, and the tendency apparent in the Supreme Court jurisprudence, evident in cases such as *Sioux Indians*, to read down legislation as merely effecting a waiver of the plea of res judicata by the government, when in fact the legislation clearly goes further to prohibit the Article III courts from considering the plea, even on their own motion. However, to hold as valid legislation which clearly and unambiguously purports to prohibit federal courts from disregarding an otherwise res judicata within their own discretion will enable a *legislative* re-opening of final cases, otherwise clearly prohibited by the inviolability principle. This tendency, it has been suggested, should not be followed.

It must be conceded that the separation of powers does not, overall, suffer well the transition from principle of political philosophy, albeit pragmatically based, into a legal rule entrenched in a written constitution. Most obviously, it has difficulty in coming to terms with the greater definitional rigidities which attach to legal rules, whereas in the realm of convention and political philosophy the principle itself is allowed to evolve and develop in the way of political structures, institutions and theory. Here, a purposive functionalist approach will ease this transition somewhat. But, as indicated, functionalism has its limitations and may not be the most appropriate approach when dealing with fundamental elements of branch power. Nevertheless, the considerable overlap of branch functions, the existence of numerous crossroads of branch power, will create continuing difficulties and tensions for the separation of powers, and which will continue to pose considerable challenges to the courts which must apply the doctrine.

On the other hand, it is not just the separation doctrine itself which tends to become fossilised when constitutionally entrenched. It will itself also tend to restrain novel developments in inter-branch relationships which may be otherwise quite desirable on public policy grounds, especially if it is applied with excessive formalism. To take an obvious example of the point, unless the *Boilermakers* decision in Australia is overruled, there will be little continuing experience of the Chapter III courts exercising non-judicial functions, including those which may not be incompatible with the judicial process. Be that as it may, is it not the case that when such a critical principle of political theory is entrenched in a written constitution by design, a certain rigidity and constancy in the application and maintenance of the principle, and the institutional arrangements which thereby result, is impliedly intended and desired? Indeed, the enforceability of the constitutional limitations on branch power which result, the fact that it becomes far more difficult to alter, amend or remove these, is the very raison d'être of its entrenchment in the first place. In short, the Framers of that particular constitution desired, intended and planned for a certain rigidity. They planned for the separation doctrine to form an integral part of the constitutional foundation, and despite the vicissitudes of the political process—or indeed because of them—to remain a secure foundation for liberal and representative government and the rule of law. This is clearly the position which pertains in the United States. Indeed, as was also pointed out, one of the major catalysts for this was the specific concern of the United States Framers to protect the decisional independence of the courts from legislative interference in pending cases and with final judgments. Where such clear intention is expressed, the case for purposive formalism is strengthened, and indeed is warranted when defining the constitutional limitations to which entrenchment gives rise. In Australia, purposive formalism stands on less certain ground because of the uncertain intentions of the Framers in relation to the separation of powers and the fact that the acceptance of a legal separation of powers has been reached less by reference to the express intention of the Framers than by reference to the writings of the early constitutional scholars and the interpretation of the principle by the courts. Moreover, the situation is complicated by the fact that the Australian constitutional arrangements contain British elements (notably responsible government), which tend against a strict adoption of separation of powers. For this reason, the proper interpretative methodology applicable to separation of powers jurisprudence will remain a vexed one in Australia and, at the very least, one which will not accommodate a universal formalist approach.

Nevertheless, it can be said finally that the separation doctrine as entrenched constitutional principle remains efficacious as the source of constitutional limitations regulating branch power. The protections afforded decisional independence as a result remain on surer footing than if its status remained one of constitutional convention, no matter how influential or fundamental. In the latter case, as discussed in chapter six, its efficacy remains very much in the hands of a dominant legislature. While the canons of statutory interpretation may assist, for example, in requiring clear and unambiguous words before a retrospective law can be applied to pending proceedings, the legislature nevertheless will have the final word. This is not to suggest, of course, that breaches of decisional independence will occur as a matter of course, but that rather, in a case of sufficient import and where the stakes are highest, the legislature may override separation of powers conventions. In the United Kingdom, therefore, recourse must be had to the provisions of European Convention on Human Rights, Articles 6 and 7, and the Human Rights Act 1998, rather than the separation of powers, to remedy interferences with judicial decisional independence. Absent therefore such protections, or other express constitutional prohibitions, the surer protection afforded by entrenchment is particularly evident at the level of core branch functions which are capable of being identified on the basis of conceptual analysis combined with experience, usage, custom, history, public policy considerations and the institutional setting in which they are most commonly exercised. In relation to the precise concerns of this mono-graph, this has been borne out by the ability to identify a discreet set of constitutional limitations—centred on the Changed Law Rule, direction principle and the inviolability principle—which can effectively regulate legislative interference with the decisional independence of the judicial branch.

Index